TALKING TAP

Terry Dill

Dedicated to

Hazel Bergh
who brought theater dance to northwest Iowa.

PALMETTO
PUBLISHING
Charleston, SC
www.PalmettoPublishing.com

A Studio Globe Publication

Copyright © 2023 by Terry Dill
Previous Copyright © 2012 by Terry Dill

All rights reserved

No portion of this book may be reproduced, stored in a retrieval system, or transmitted in any form by any means–electronic, mechanical, photocopy, recording, or other–except for brief quotations in printed reviews, without prior permission of the author.

Paperback ISBN: 979-8-8229-5205-8

Tapping Globie back cover art created by Nancy McGuire

INTRODUCTION

It's time we had a talk, about tap, and we need to understand each other; so, I have provided this manual for our mutual benefit. This discussion is about the language of tap – what it is, why it is, and how to use it. **TALKING TAP** has several sections, intended to achieve several objectives.

First, it is a foundation technique reference and communication guide for tap dancing students, instructors, choreographers, and tapphiles. Learning to tap dance requires the rapid acquisition of a wide variety of deceptively similar movement and rhythm sequences. Accurate vocabulary and documentation can significantly ease presentation, understanding, and memorization.

WHAT IS TAP DANCING provides a technical introduction, preparing you to apply the footwork described under **TAP TERMINOLOGY**.

TAP TERMINOLOGY provides categorical definitions of common tap terms and techniques while noting useful interassociations. Included are important rhythm, music, movement, style, and staging concepts essential to moving with music. This listing tends to be progressive and comparative, naturally developing a spoken, notational, and relational familiarity with tap steps and related body movement. Ongoing use leads, not only to easily conveyed combinations of steps, but also, with practice, their spoken rhythmic accuracy when explaining or demonstrating (see **TALKING RHYTHMS**).

The **TERMINOLOGY INDEX** provides an alphabetical cross reference by item number and page to listed terms. If a term is unfamiliar, look it up.

The **ABBREVIATIONS INDEX** similarly lists abbreviation definition locations, either where first used in the manual or where explained. With moderate experience, abbreviations facilitate tap notation writing and reading (see **APPLICATION EXAMPLE**).

Following the indexes is a brief listing of suggestions for **DEVELOPING PERSONAL TECHNIQUE.**

Second, the application sections introduce the breadth of tap and tapping as a study subject and movement art. A tap routine Step **APPLICATION EXAMPLE** includes an approach to effective routine notes analysis. **A DISCUSSION** explores the sources and range of tap associated vocabulary including suggested motion picture dance examples. Whether or not a tapper, you may find the vignettes and quizzes interesting, enjoyable, and even spur curiosity about tap while further clarifying and expanding appreciation of the dance form. **ALTERNATE TERMINOLOGY** lists terms, definitions, and formats not herein used, which may be elsewhere encountered. **TALKING RHYTHMS** offers an approach for verbally unifying danced steps with rhythm. The **ROUTINES** introduce different tap styles and choreographic motivations while implementing much of the earlier content and providing applied tap notation experience.

The third purpose of this book is to improve communication among all associated with tap dance. Unlike the long established organized structure of ballet, the origins, development, and instruction of tap have been widely scattered, frequently personalized, and from largely unrecorded sources. The result is a wealth of dance steps and styles, but also a confusion of personal, regional, and even historically specific terminology. Not only are there terms common to some users which are completely unfamiliar to others, but identical terms may have several different regional or dated definitions (see **ALTERNATE TERMINOLOGY**). These same problems, as well as frequent unnecessary complexity (resulting from the use of no to little terminology), may be true of various notational systems. The following introduces an attempt to compile an ever-expanding list of tapping knowledge in a format allowing clearly recognizable and easily remembered and interpreted verbal and written communication.

It is understood that many in the field will disagree with various specifics of these contents, layout, or even the underlying philosophy. However, perusal may yield some new insights and, of course, the user may choose to apply only the concepts with which he is comfortable. I invite anyone to offer their corrections, additions, references, or opinions. Through an ongoing pooling of information and ideas this reference may expand to prove of increasing value to anyone actively interested in tap dancing.

Terry Dill
talkingtap@wiatel.net

NOTE: All offerings of information, especially copies of early dance notes and other terminology documentation, will be gratefully accepted and, if not otherwise noted, will be assumed non-copyrighted and may be freely used in future **TALKING TAP** and associated revisions. Your interest in tap dancing is appreciated.

TABLE OF CONTENTS

WHAT IS TAP DANCING	1
TAP TERMINOLOGY	2
THE BASICS	2
BASIC SOUNDS AND MOVEMENTS	2
BASIC STEPS	3
BUFFALOS and BOMBERSHAYS	4
WALKS	5
RIFF WALKS	6
ADVANCED RIFFS	6
KICKS	6
TURNS	7
ADVANCED TURNS	8
TWISTS	8
ROLLS	9
CLIPS	9
PICKUPS	10
WINGS	10
ADVANCED WINGS	11
GLIDES and TOE STANDS	11
RHYTHM PATTERNS	12
MAXIE FORDS	12
TAP DANCE STYLES	13
TIME-STEP STYLES	13
WALTZ CLOG TIME-STEPS	13
BUCK TIME-STEPS	13
VARIOUS BEGINNINGS	14
VARIOUS ENDINGS	14
BUCK TIME-STEP BREAKS	14
Time-step Break Notation	15
MORE BUCK TIME-STEPS	15
OTHER COMMON STYLES	15
BUCK and WING	16
RHYTHM	16
SOFT SHOE	16
SHIM SHAM	16
SHIM SHAM COMBINATIONS	16
MILITARY	17
NOVELTY STYLES	17
ECCENTRIC	17
RAILROAD	18
BODY POSITIONS	18
FEET and LEGS	19
ARMS and HANDS	20
GENERAL TAP TERMS	21
ARRANGEMENT TERMS	21
DANCE STRUCTURE	21
MUSIC STRUCTURE	22
SIMPLE RHYTHM NOTATION	23
TYPES of RHYTHM	23
RHYTHM SYMBOLS	24
RHYTHM NOTATION	24
FORMATTING	24
STAGING TERMS	25
STAGE AREAS	25
BODY DIRECTIONS	25
STAGING ARRANGEMENTS	26
INTRODUCTION TO PARTNERING	26
CLARIFICATIONS	27
TERMINOLOGY INDEX	28
ABBREVIATIONS INDEX	34
DEVELOPING PERSONAL TECHNIQUE	37
APPLICATION EXAMPLE	38
NOTATION FORMAT	38
THE PARTS	38
READING NOTES	39
VIDEO vs. NOTES	39
WRITING NOTES	39
A PERSONAL ASIDE	39
A DISCUSSION	40
DISCUSSION ASSISTANCE	84
ALTERNATE TERMINOLOGY	95
FORMATTING SYMBOLS	95
NUMERICAL	95
ALPHABETICAL	96
TALKING RHYTHMS	110
INTRODUCTION	110
TIMING	110
STUDENT INTERPRETATION	110
CUEING	111
ROUTINES	112
WALTZ CLOG	112
GOING DUTCH	112
PREPARING A ROUTINE	113
TECH-TAP	114
TOTS' TAP	114
SUE'S BUCK AND WING	115
SOFT SHOE	116
STILL IN LOVE WITH AMY	116
NEW SOFT SHOE	118
SHIM SHAM	120
SHIM IT UP	120
RHYTHM	122
SHOWOFF	122
RHYTHM FILL	124
IRISH CLOG	126
WILD-n-IRISH	126
IT'S AN ORIGINAL	128
SCALAN SYNCOPATIONS	128
AFTERTHOUGHTS	131

WHAT IS TAP DANCING

Tap dancing is one of the five foundation training theater dance forms. The other four are, historically: acrobatic, ballet, modern, and jazz. Each of these training forms has been developed to achieve specific distinct physical, mental, and aesthetic capabilities. The training objectives of tap are buoyancy in relevé (on the balls of the feet), nimbleness (especially the ankles), and complex audio rhythmics, all while easily moving and freely traveling. Simply stated, tap dancing should be simultaneously enjoyable to observe and interesting to hear. Because technique progress and class presentation tends to be more rapid and ankle actions more subtle than with other dance forms, the need to quickly interpret the combined visual and audio patterns encourages keen observation and rapid memorization.

The historical predecessors of tap are an amalgamation of various European folk and character dance styles with African ethnic dance movement and rhythms. This blend matured parallel with jazz music during the early 20th century, reaching its developmental peak and popularization through 1930s-1950s vaudeville then Broadway and motion picture musicals. There are three traditional classifications of *tap dancing* footwear reflected in current dance styles. Historically, **clog** styles are derived from wooden soled folk dance, more relaxed **soft shoe** styling brought the movement freedom permitted by leather soled shoes, with rhythmically complex **tapping** becoming possible by attaching metal (now, aluminum alloy) taps to leather bottom shoes. Many traditional and character styles, such as soft shoe and country-western clog, are now commonly represented by dancers using taps.

There are two standard dance **taps**, the toe or ball tap and the heel tap. The toe tap is attached to the shoe sole from the front edge (tip) extending toward the ball of the foot. The heel tap is attached to the bottom of the heel from the back edge, covering as much as possible of the heel. While coverage area (tap size) and placement centering may vary, it is desireable that the toe tap tip be capable of vertical floor contact behind the supporting leg (see photo), the back edge of the heel tap can strike the floor when the ankle is flexed (toe lifted), and the centers of both taps may easily be struck against the floor or may be comfortably stood on together (flat foot) or ball of either foot alone. Young beginners' shoes frequently are fitted with toe-lip taps which include a perpendicular tap-lip which covers the tip edge of the sole, making toe-taps easier. Generally, youngsters' taps should be attached with crimped nails, requiring no maintenance. Better sound quality and tonal adjustability are achieved with screw-on hollowed taps attached over pre-nailed audio reflective *sounding boards*. Screws should be attached using synthetic rubber shoe cement and do require user inspection and possible adjustment before each use.

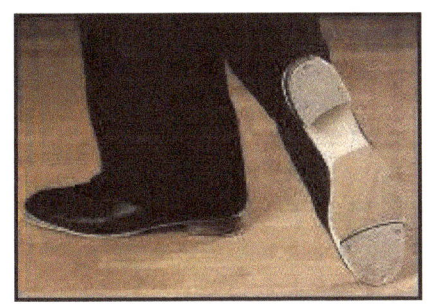

Nearly all tap dancing is done from a stance of a *supporting* leg and a nonsupporting *working* leg. Generally, if the working leg becomes supporting, the other foot simultaneously raises, assuring that a *free* working foot/leg is always available for continuing movement. Although young beginning level students commonly train *flat footed*, the quickness of tap technique requires that the supporting leg functions from a position of plié-relevé (knee bent and heel lifted) hopping and bouncing from foot to foot as though running on the balls of the feet. The resulting nearly continuous bouncing is the buoyancy required for rapid tapping.

The *starting position*, for most training, is with the working foot lifted beside and slightly rear of the supporting leg ankle, ready to move downward, forward, sideward, or across behind the supporting leg. For a few tap movements other starting positions may be advisable, especially for youngsters. The *lead* foot is that required for the first tap sound or movement of a pattern, usually the working foot. However, if the first movement requires using the supporting foot (such as a heeldrop), usually it is considered the lead foot. Nearly all the movement definitions in this manual are lead right foot/leg.

The simplest position for most tap movements is feet parallel with toes directed forward, not turned-out to the sides. However, most crossing and many sideward movements are more efficiently done with a natural turn-out; i.e., the toes directed comfortably somewhat sideward, not forced 90° sideward.

The other unique physical requirement for tap dancing is the development of quick, flexible, accurate ankle control. As technique progresses, the initial forward then backward lower leg (from the knee) movements become less leg swing and more subtle ankle coordination. Keeping the feet closer to the floor permits more rapid tap sequencing, but requires greater ankle flexibility allowing diagonal, sideward, and circular foot actions with differing tap edges producing tap sounds. Such minimal movement is called *sophistication* and presents the impression of tapping without sufficient leg movement. Another result of well developed buoyancy and nimbleness is the execution of taps while airborne, without support. Because all theater dance should appear effortless, the more complex sophisticated and airborne tap techniques are generally considered advanced and are herein so listed.

Unless otherwise specified, the body and head remain comfortably upright with the focus (direction of the face) toward the general direction of action. The arms naturally counterbalance the body by ranging from shoulder to hip height and front to sides. The overall appearance should be an effortless flow of movement with accompanying rhythm.

Tap dance training requires minimal physical conditioning, permitting relatively rapid understanding and skill development through the basic tap steps and their combining into actual dance combinations (performable step sequences). As with any area of study, progress is accelerated by concise, consistent verbal and written communication. Toward that end this manual has been prepared.

Enjoy your tapping!

Above graphic of shoes with Tele Tone taps is reprinted with permission from Capezio/Ballet Makers Inc.

TAP TERMINOLOGY

This is a listing of well established terms used in tap classes, during rehearsals, and in written dance descriptions. Some less common items are included as technique extensions or for comparison with other presented dance concepts. The abbreviations are term reductions, intended to speed writing and reading dance notes.

Indexed terms are introduced in **bold** type. The first appearance of an abbreviation will be [square bracketed]. Nearly all combinations of sounds and movements are notated for a lead (first action) right foot [R] and downstage [D-S] presentation unless otherwise indicated. To avoid format confusion, terms which may be proper nouns do not begin [bgn] in upper case unless starting a 'sentence'. The most common rhythms are included.

This description format is commonly used for choreographic notation. Each musical phrase (or less) is a sentence, dance steps separated by commas. Each routine Step is a numbered paragraph. The first three pages are foundation techniques, a good place to start. The TERMINOLOGY format is:

###. term [abbreviation] {specific example notated:} (Preparation) description (clarifying and body notes).
may include rhythm notation {even rhythm}(Appended notes.)
NOTE: Associated information. Most *italic* terms are dance/movement/music associated and, hopefully, self explanatory.

THE BASICS

BASIC SOUNDS AND MOVEMENTS

Following are the foundation coordinations with sounds from which all tapping is built. All are single or joined sounds.

1. **step** — Striking single [sgl] tap, weight [wt] is deposited on ball of indicated foot [Ft].
2. **tap** — Striking sgl tap with [w/] ball of Ft, wt is not deposited on Ft.
3. **toe-tap** [tt] — Sgl tap no weight [n/w] w/ **tip** (front edge) of toe tap, usually across [x] back [bk] or x front [frt].
4. **stamp** — Accenting (loud) sgl sound, wt is deposited on indicated flat Ft (simultaneous ball and heel taps).
5. **stomp** — Accent, wt is not deposited on indicated flat Ft; that is, stamp n/w.
6. **brush** [br] — Swing leg (usually lower leg) in indicated direction [dir], striking sgl tap w/ ball of Ft.
7. **scuff** — Swing leg in indicated dir, striking sgl tap w/ bottom bk edge of heel.
8. **heel** — A heeldrop. (From a position [pos] of ball of Ft on floor [flr] with heel raised) drop heel to flr striking sgl tap. May be briefly with weight [w/w] before lifting heel.
9. **dig** — Striking sgl sharp tap, bk edge of heel strikes ('digs into') flr, usually n/w.
10. **snap** — (From a pos of heel on flr with toe raised) drop toe striking sgl sharp tap. (Also, fingers snap.)
11. **hop** — An elevation (become airborne or unsupported) w/ takeoff and landing on (ball of) same Ft.
12. **leap** — An elevation w/ takeoff from one Ft and landing on ball of the other Ft.
13. **jump** — Hop or leap landing on balls of both Ft (feet) at the same time [a-s-t] (or flat Ft if specified). Or, if both Ft are on flr, an elevation from both Ft into various actions and/or landings. Depending on starting pos, a both Ft either elevation or landing.
14. **hamp** — An accented hop onto the flat Ft; that is, hop into a stamp.
15. **lamp** — An accented leap onto the flat Ft; i.e., leap into a stamp.
16. **catch** — (With little or no leap) supporting Ft is replaced by the other Ft (*catch* the body wt), usually in place [i-p]. (Also, grasp a moving object; for example, partner's [ptnr's] hand [Hn] or airborne cane.)
17. **fall** — Wt drops onto ball of Ft, usually w/ no elevation.
18. **sluff** — A sliding movement [mvmt] of the free Ft, making a scraping/swishing sound, usually w/ ball tap.
19. **chug** — (From a pos of Ft on flr) ball of Ft is sluffed then stopped by dropping heel striking sgl sharp tap, usually taking wt; that is, a short sluff-heel, usually forward [fwd].   a1
(A sgl hyphen [-] without [w/o] spaces indicates connected actions; e.g., b/c L-R or compound step.)
20. **slide** — An elevated traveling [trav'g] sluff dragging one Ft while making a scraping/swishing tap sound. Usually during a hop or leap but may be extended following a step or short run.
21. **scoot** — A short, usually backward [bkwd], slide on usually both Ft; an often straight leg sluffed jump or hop.
22. **clip** — Strike a tap on one shoe against a tap on the other shoe.

BASIC STEPS

Tap steps are common *pas* (defined dance mvmt patterns [patt's]) with established names. The term step may also apply to the basic coordination-sound (see 1.) or Step, a designated portion (usually 8 or 16 measures [M]) of a dance. The next reference categories include the most fundamental (1-4 count) basic tap steps, followed by categories listing increasingly complex steps.

23. **chug both**   Scoot fwd into chug both Ft a-s-t, usually w/ simultaneous heels.   **a1** or &**a1** (separated heels)
 (Also called **double chug**.)

24. **ball change** [b/c]   Two quick steps. That is, change [chg] wt from ball of one Ft to ball of the other.   **a1** or &**1**

25. **ball change cross-over** [b/c x-over]   {R b/c x-over bk: b/c R right [rt] x-over left Ft [L] bk:} Leap R rt, step L x bk R.
 &**1** {even rhythm} or   **a1** {duplet [dplt] rhythm, 2 quick taps}

26. **catch-step** [c/s]   (A trav'g mvmt usually performed as a b/c.) catch R, step L in desired dir. A *gallop*.   **a1**

27. **dig change** [d/c]   Two quick digs w/w.   **a1**
 NOTE: Sustained support on the heel bk edge (**heel stand**) of any shoe may separate the heel from the shoe sole. The higher the heel, the greater likelihood of damage.

28. **stamp change** [s/c]   Two quick stamps.   **a1**
 NOTE: Bold type rhythm notation (**a1** above) indicates volume (loudness) accents. This notation is optional.

29. **break-away** [b/a]   Fall into a stamp i-p, step 'away' sideward [sdwd] or specified dir.   **a**1

30. **cramp**   Step, heel on same Ft.   a1

31. **rock'n**   Heel R, snap R. **Traveling rock'n**: pivot into sdwd heeldrop then heel twist [h-t] into snap.   a1
 May bgn w/ snap depending on preceding placement.

32. **shuffle** [shfl]   A short, quick br fwd then br bk w/ the same Ft.   a1

33. **shuffle across** [shfl-x]   A shfl ending t/o x frt or x bk as specified.   a1

34. **double shuffle** [dbl-shfl]   Two shuffles [shfl's] done in quick succession w/ 4 even rhythm taps. (Also, **dbl-scuffle**, **dbl-riffle**.)
 {quadruplet [qdlt] rhythm}   a&a1 or 1&a2

35. **rattle**   Several full or partial shfl's done in quick even rhythm succession (rolling); e.g., 7-tap rattle.

36. **scuffle** [scfl]   Like a shfl but w/ a scuff fwd, br bk.   a1

37. **riff**   Striking 2 taps, br-scuff as Ft swings fwd.   a1

38. **back riff** [bk riff]   Striking 2 taps, scuff-br as Ft swings bk.   a1

39. **close riff**   Striking 2 taps, br fwd, dig w/w.   a1   (Close indicates nearness of feet.)

40. **riffle**   Like a shfl but w/ a riff fwd, br bk, done as 3 quick even taps.
 &a   1 {triplet [tplt] rhythm}

41. **4-tap riffle**   Riff fwd, bk riff.   a&a1 {qdlt rhythm}

42. **triple** [tpl]   Shfl, step.   &1 2 or usually &a1 {triplet}

43. **running triple**   Shfl, leap. &a1 (Especially several in succession producing a continuous even rhythm *roll*.)
 NOTE: Also called **double time triple** [dbl-X tpl]. Dbl-X meaning twice as fast. Easily accelerate alternating [alt'g] lead sequences [seq's] by converting steps to leaps, **running**; e.g., running (dbl-X) qdl's.

44. **quadruple** [qdl]   Shfl R, cramp R   a&a1 {qdlt}

45. **skip**   {Skip L:} hop R, step L (frequently x bk or x frt).   a1
 NOTE: The non-lead step specifies the skip, facilitating an immediate placement (location) reference; e.g., skip L x bk R.

46. **draw-back** [d-b]   Br bk R, hop L, step bk R. Br and step bkwd unless another dir is specified.
 &   a   1 {tplt}
 (Frequently, multiple draw-backs [d-b's] are done in rapid succession.)
 NOTE: When tapping speed no longer permits elevation time, all movements are made smaller, the footwork remains very close and low to the floor, and the hop is replaced by a heeldrop; thus, br-heel-step (**low d-b**). Such minimalist (sophisticated) styling can yield a flurry of taps.

47. **flap**   Striking 2 taps, a quick br-step in the same dir. Assumed fwd unless otherwise specified.   a1

48. **running flaps**   Br-leap; usually several *running* in specified dir.   a1
 NOTE: Running seq's may not be specified, but are dictated by tempo.

49. **forward flap** [fwd flap] A flap done in the dir the toe is directed; i.e., *lead* with the toe.
50. **backward flap** [bk flap] A flap done in the dir the heel is directed; i.e., lead with the heel.
    NOTE: Any type of flap may move in any one dir. For example, by turning-out R, a fwd flap R trav's rt; or, by facing (torso toward [twd]) stage left [S-L], a bk flap R x bk L is turned-out [t/o] and trav's upstage [U-S].
51. **outside flap** [o/s flap] (Working Ft raised near the supporting leg) flap sdwd away from the supporting Ft, leading w/ the outside [o/s] edge of the Ft.
52. **inside flap** [i/s flap] A flap done in the dir the inside [i/s] of the Ft is 'facing'; i.e., leading w/ the i/s of the Ft.
    NOTE: Mvmt's leading w/ the sides of the Ft may be termed **inside** or **outside**. Lead part of Ft is normally dictated by dir (flap bk), but specifying it can be useful; e.g., o/s flap R rt turned-in [t/i].
53. **swinging flap** An i/s flap done as an i/s br-leap i-p while swinging the other Ft outward (away from the supporting leg) sdwd, unless other dir's specified.
54. **leaped flap** Leap from one Ft, flapping the other to land on it, brush and landing after leap apex.
55. **slap** Flap n/w; i.e., br-tap.   a1
56. **irish** Shfl, hop, step.   a1 a2   (usually dplt rhythm, 2 pairs of taps)
57. **quadruplet irish** [qdlt irish] Irish done in qdlt rhythm.   a&a1   (4 quick even taps)
    NOTE: Any seq of taps can be presented even rhythm; e.g., qdlt shfl-b/c. Rhythm variations [var's] exist for all multi-tap steps.
58. **sliding irish** An irish w/ a ball slide during the hop. The free leg is usually lifted to high frt **passé** (ft near knee) and the i/s slide is in the dir of the lifted leg.
    NOTE: Most hops may become sluffs; try **sliding cinc's**.
59. **cincinnati** [cinc] Br bk R, hop L, tpl R x bk L.   &1 &a2
60. **pendulum cincinnati** [pend cinc] Pend R rt-diagonally-bk [r-d-b], hop L, tpl R x bk L.   &1 &a2
61. **triple cincinnati** [tpl-cinc] Br bk R, hop L, br fwd R, hop L, cinc R. a1 a2 {a3&a4} (Also, as **triple pendulum cinc**.)
    NOTE: There are many versions of cinc, all of which build from a d-b. The above terms relate the in-common br-hop.
62. **balancé** [bal] Leap R rt, b/c L x bk R - R i-p. 1 a2   Also: leap R rt, step L x bk R, step R i-p. 1 2 3
    (Space hyphen space [-] indicates additional information while continuing the step.)
    NOTE: Combining steps can yield simple common **compound steps**; e.g., hop-tpl or irish-heel-heel. The single hyphen with no spaces indicates the mvmt's are linked, becoming *step-like* or a single term (left-diag-frt). Similarly linked abbreviations represent a single step or mvmt, but must be used thoughtfully. Also, check the number of taps in rhythm; for example: tpl-cinc or p-u-irish are sgl steps, as opposed to tpl, cinc or s-p-u, irish (using separating commas) which include two steps.

BUFFALOS and BOMBERSHAYS
Buffalo and bombershay var's are among the most elementary sdwd coordinations.
NOTE: The **DISCUSSION** categories parallel **TERMINOLOGY**. Flip back occasionally. You may find something interesting.

63. **buffalo** [buff] (A helpful starting pos for youngsters is w/ free Ft flexed t/o x frt of supporting leg ankle.)
    Leap R rt, shfl L, leap L (returning to starting pos or catch L to trav rt).
        1   &a   2   {qdlt}
    NOTE: Several successive buff's x'g the stage [stg] to exit are called "**shuffle off to Buffalo**".
64. **flapped buffalo** Leaped flap R rt, shfl L, leap L (returning to starting pos or trav'g).
        a1   &a   2   {quintuplet [qnlt] rhythm, 5 even taps}
65. **doubled buffalo** [dbl-buff] Hop R, tpl L x bk R, buff R.
        1   &a2   3&a4
    NOTE: **Doubled** steps combine a basic seq plus a var of that basic, combined requiring twice the counts [ct's].
66. **baby bombershay** Stamp R t/i x frt L, step L left [lt] -- heel twist (pivot Ft w/ heel on flr) R t/o. **1** 2
    (A simplified bombershay coordination for young beginners [bgn'rs].)
    (Double [dbl] hyphen [--] or dash [–] means a-s-t.)
67. **bombershay** [bmb] O/s flap R rt – h-t t/o L, step (or stamp) L closed pos [c-p] next to (or t/i x frt) R. a1 2
68. **flapped bombershay** O/s flap R rt – h-t t/o L, i/s flap L c-p.   a1 a2
69. **5-tap bombershay** O/s flap R rt – h-t t/o L, i/s br L, heel R, step L c-p.   {a1&a2} ({ct's} in braces are even rhythm)
70. **6-tap bombershay** O/s flap-heel R rt – h-t t/o L, i/s br L, heel R, step L c-p.   {&a1&a2}
    NOTE: By adding snaps and heels, this series of bmb var's can be further extended; e.g., 7-tap, 8-tap, plus clips.

71. **rolling bombershay**   O/s flap roll change [f-r-c] R rt – h-t t/o L, i/s br L, heel R, cramp L c-p. {a&a1a&a2 }
NOTE: Bmb's frequently include a toe to heel clip; e.g., **5-tap bmb w/ clip**: o/s flap R rt – h-t L t/o, i/s br L into L toe to R heel clip, heel R, step L {a1a&a2}. There are many bmb var's.

WALKS

Stylized locomotor (trav'g) flat Ft, stepping, strolling, or running. Walk and run lead generally specifies the final supporting Ft (walking Ft) even if the other Ft makes the first tap sound; e.g., a heeldrop.

72. **walk**   Natural [nat] walk, usually w/o taps. If rhythm notated, a relaxed dig-snap.   &1 or 1 2

73. **run**   Low short leap w/ opp Ft lifted low i-p. Usually several alt'g.

74. **piqué**   [piq]   Step onto ball of Ft. Ballet technique requires a st leg step; slight plié is acceptable when tapping.

75. **pas de bourrée** [p-d-b]   Step R x bk L, step L lt, step R x frt L. A 3-step grapevine. 1 2 3   (Also, i/s p-d-b bgn's x frt.)

76. **jazz triangle**   Step R x frt L, step L lt-diagonally-bk [l-d-b], step R r-d-b.   1 2 3

77. **jazz diamond**   Step R x frt L, step L l-d-b, step R r-d-b, step L rt-diagonally-frt [r-d-f] x frt R.   1 2 3 4
(Also, fwd triangle and diamond bgn x bk into frt diag's. Any step can be modified to chg dir; e.g., diag bal's can be r-d-f then l-d-b.)

78. **march**   Lift stepping Ft past supporting calf (w/ or w/o heeldrop) into step (or cramp);
e.g., heel L into march-cramp R.   & a1

79. **strut**   Lift stepping Ft past supporting knee (w/ or w/o heel) usually w/ frt or t/i passé into step.

80. **tap strut**   Heel L – high frt passé R, tap extended tendu R x frt L, heel L – high frt passé R, step R.   a1 a2
NOTES: Above walk steps are often performed as flaps or cramps; thus, **flapped diamond**, **strut-cramp**, etc.

81. **sugar foot**   [sgr]   Steps done trav'g fwd w/ Ft t/o on the step frt, then pivot [pvt] turn-front [t/f] or t/i as other Ft steps fwd t/o (opposite [opp] hip fwd). A twist walk.

82. **shorty george**   [shorty]   (Trav'g fwd or bkwd in plié; i.e., knees bent) Ft parallel [//] t/f (not pvt'g) step R on i/s of Ft sole (ball or flat Ft instep) – *roll* onto o/s of L (knees close and swing lt), rev. An instep walk.

83. **twisting shorty**   (Ft remain //) shorty w/ slight t/i step.   (The first stylization is most common.)

84. **suzie-q**   (Trav'g rt, both Ft on flr, Ft // and close together) pivot both Ft into // heels rt, both heels twist // into simultaneous snaps rt. Toes lead if specified.   1 2
A cutie step. Often styled in plié w/ knees swinging to remain above toes – (arms [A's] pressed palms down [dn] frt w/ fingers interlaced) swing A's and/or shoulders [Sh's] opp knees dir.

85. **pigeon-toe**   (Trav'g rt, both Ft on flr) h-t t/o R into snap rt -- pvt L t/o into heeldrop L near R heel,
                      1 -- 1
pvt t/i R into heel rt – h-t t/i L into snap near R toe. (Resulting in combined taps, both Ft t/o, t/i.)
                      2 -- 2

86. **grapevine**   [gpvn]   Steps trav'g sdwd w/ the trailing Ft x'g alternately [alt'ly] x frt then x bk (or x bk, x frt).
Using the same alt'g x'g pattern, numerous steps and combinations [comb's] may be gpvn'd.

87. **flapped grapevine** [flapped gpvn]   Fwd flap R rt, i/s flap L x frt R, fwd flap R rt, bk flap L x bk R, etc. a1 a2 a3 a4

88. **ball change grapevine** [b/c gpvn]   B/c R rt x-over L bk, b/c R rt x-over L frt, etc.   a1 a2

89. **draw-back grapevine** [d-b gpvn]   (Trav'g rt) o/s d-b R rt, d-b L x bk R, o/s d-b R rt, fwd d-b L x frt R.   &a1&a2&a3&a4

90. **snake hips**   (Moderate plié L -- R rt w/ R hip up-rt) isolate [isol] hips lt drawing (or sluff) R into catch R i-p w/ (or w/o) sluff into rev starting pos w/ tap L lt. (The mvmt sinuously ripples from pelvis downward [dnwd], *pulling* legs through 1st pos Ft to chg sides [sd's]. May trav fwd or bkwd.)

91. **sluefoot**   A languid hip lead *drag* (sluff) *walk*. (R bk) lift R hip w/ knee t/o leaving tip of R toe on flr, R hip and knee lead i/s r-d-j w/ toe sluff, R knee gradually t/i into short step frt. (Also, bkwd.)
NOTE: Snake hips and sluefoot are eccentric *rubberleg* hip lead walks.

92. **trench**   (Usually from a pos of moderate plié and leaning fwd) slightly st'n [straighten] L into slide bk L, fall R i-p or trav'g in any dir; usually at running tempo.   (Also, see pickup change trench.)
NOTE: There are two common styles of presentation, side view or frt view by the audience.
Side View: Leg extends straight [st] bk w/ arched Ft (extended opposing A swing [o-A-s]).
Frt View: Leg extends x bk w/ arched Ft (dbl A swing [d-A-s] over landing Ft).
Also, c/s, trav'g rock'n, pigeon-toe roll, running steps, and trav'g waltz clog [w-c] and soft shoe comb's stylized as walks.

RIFF WALKS

Sophisticated strolling styling (low to the floor, small rapid movements) is facilitated using nearly i-p ankle coordination wherein the the riff br is done w/ the i/s of the ball tap while flexing and twisting ankle slightly t/o into o/s-bk heel edge scuff.

93. **4-tap riff walk**   Riff R, dig w/w R, snap R.   a1 &2

94. **5-tap riff walk**   Riff R, heel L, dig w/w R, snap R.   {a1&a2 quintuplet}

95. **6-tap riff walk**   Riff R, heel L, dig w/w R, snap R, heel R.   {&a1&a2 sextuplet [sxlt], 6 even taps}

96. **7-tap riff walk**   Riff R, heel L, dig w/w R, snap R, heel R, snap R. &a1 a&a2 or {septuplet [splt], 7 even}

97. **doubled riff walk** [dbl riff walk] Riff R, heel L, bk riff R x frt L, heel L, 6-tap riff walk. {&a1&a2&a3&a4 rolling rhythm}
     To repeat [rpt], replace final 6-tap riff walk <u>heel</u> w/ <u>step</u>.

98. **eccentric riff walk**   5-tap riff walk R, step L c-p, dig-snap R, b/c L c-p – R fwd (or 'stumbling' c/s).
     {a1&a2}   &   {3 &   a   4}

As with most tap steps, there are numerous riff walk var's; try bgn'g w/ heel, ending by adding a step or bk brush – experiment.

ADVANCED RIFFS

Although not walks, these riffs are here included as an extension of riff coordinations. The sd riffle and sd riff are increasingly advanced sophisticated mvmt's, using a quick o/s circular *thrown* (not sluffed) relaxed ankle control (riffing, using o/s then i/s tap edges coordination, rather than sluffing like into a wing) w/ minimal Ft and leg mvmt.

99. **side riffle**   [sd riffle]   O/s br R w/ o/s edge of ball tap, scuff R rt w/ i/s edge of heel, R ankle recoils into i/s br. &a1
NOTE: This is an intermediate technique, frequently proving helpful in developing the wing-like thrown ankle control necessary for side riffs and riffed russian eagles.

100. **side riff**   [sd riff]   Striking 3 ball taps done w/ ankle coordination similar to side riffle: 1st tap is made w/ fwd-o/s edge of ball tap as Ft trav's slightly fwd to side, 2nd tap is made w/ rearward-i/s edge of ball tap as naturally t/o Ft arcs slightly bkwd and sdwd, 3rd tap is i/s br as Ft recoils inward. &a1
NOTE: Many find sd riffs exceptionally difficult. The lower leg must control a *small outside circular thrown Ft ankle coordination*. This is generally most easily developed after wings are comfortably easy.

101. **running side riff**   Sd riff into a leap, usually alt'g several. a&a1

KICKS

Various leg swings and extensions usually incorporating tap sounds. For other leg swing and kick coordinations, see BODY POSITIONS, FEET and LEGS. Simple non-elevating (without 'jump') kicks are generally specified by kick leg, even when lead is a wt transfer, heel, or tap rather than the kick. Leaping kicks (hitch and scissor) specify the lead (running) Ft. Most kicks appear best with arched Ft ('pointed toe').

102. **pendulum**   [pend]   (Leg remains t/o from the hip and st w/ arched Ft) swing leg diagonally [diag'ly] alt'ly x frt then diag'ly open bk striking a ball tap i-p during each swing. St leg diag br's. Often done during supporting Ft hop elevation; i.e., pend bk R -- hop L.   a1
NOTE: The diag is assumed as included in the term definition (r-d-b in example), unless otherwise directed.

103. **scissor kick**   (St R lifted frt) leap R – high swing kick L frt. An extended leg frt hitch kick.
     (Frequently preceded with a swing kick (or battement [batt]) frt to establish starting pos.)

104. **side scissor kick**   B/c R rt x-over L frt, leap R rt -- raise st L lt (or low snap (quick) developpé [dev] kick L lt). a1 2

105. **eagle rock**   Side scissor kick ending dig sdwd; i.e., b/c, leap, dig.   a1 a2
     Commonly performed w/ slight body twist to face the dig and tilting (*rocking*) slightly bkwd.

106. **hitch kick**   [hitch]   (Plié L -- R frt or bk) leap R i-p -- swing (or snap kick) L in dir indicated. A catch or leap w/ a kick.

107. **4-count hitch kick**   Hitches to R -- L bk, L -- R bk, R -- L frt, L -- R high frt. 4 hitch kicks w/ last largest (high or snap).
NOTE: Emphasis on the last kick allows, by rearranging the preceding kick dir's or final action, 2-ct, 3-ct, 6-ct, etc. hitch kicks.

108. **bounce kick**   Hop L (or nat relevé [rel] into heeldrop) – batt (or grand batt) R, jump (or step) // first [1st]
     (Ft beside each other).   1   2
NOTE: Kick leg is specified. This is the most common tiller line kick, including var's **bounce developpé**, **bounce passé**, etc.

109. **fan kick**   {o/s fan kick R:} Scuff or br R into high swing kick R x frt (sometimes w/ hop) L, continue [cont] mvmt by carrying R high rt (o/s rond de jambe [r-d-j]), drop R x bk L into tap (or step, or flap).

     {i/s fan kick R:} Scuff or br R into high swing kick R rt (sometimes w/ hop L), cont mvmt by carrying R high x frt L (i/s r-d-j), drop R through [thru] 1st to bk into tap (or step, or flap).
     Also, fan kicks frequently lead into turns [tr's] (see renversé turn).

NOTE: Circular leg mvmt's fwd then to the lead side are termed **outside**: <u>outward from</u> the frt center [ctr] line of the body [f-c-l] (an imaginary vertical line dn the ctr front of the torso). **Inside** mvmt's trav from the lead side fwd x'g frt or to approximately 1st pos (<u>inward twd</u> the f-c-l).

TURNS

Fundamental, usually complete body rotations, a few w/o taps which are frequently added. Most sgl and all multiple rapid tr's should be *spotted* (see spotting).

NOTE: As w/ circling the leg, tr's are defined **outside** or **inside** depending on whether the rotation begins [bgn's] <u>outward away from the frt of the supporting leg and torso</u> (*backward tr*) or <u>into the supporting sd and f-c-l</u> (*forward tr*). Unless otherwise specified, tr's are assumed o/s. For absolute clarity use clockwise [c-w] or counterclockwise [c-c-w].

NOTE: Many tr's are more easily accomplished using A's to provide balance and initial impetus. The most common **turn port de bras** (carriage of the arms) [tr A's] seq is:

(Turn preparation [tr prep]: tr dir A 3rd frt) open (do not *throw*) frt A to 2nd into tr (impetus), trailing A to 1st (added momentum) meeting – lead A to 1st (as rotation brings trailing Hn twd lead Hn). Used w/ spotting, this port de bras facilitates multiple tr's (stationary or trav'g), speed, and improved general control.

110.	**pivot**	[pvt]	Partial (½-pvt) or complete tr i-p on (or of) the ball or, if specified, **heel pvt** on one or both Ft. Taps if specified. A pvt is not always specified, but required by stg'g; e.g., br bk into bkwd tr.
111.	**paddle**		Push. Step or flap along the circle [circ] circumference around the pvt Ft into pvt, rock, thus creating a partial tr requiring multiple paddles to complete. A multi step-pvt-rock tr.
112.	**three-step turn**	[3-step tr]	{3-step tr R rt:} (Facing D-S) step R rt twd stage right [S-R] tr'g clockwise [c-w], step L lt S-R (facing U-S), cont'g c-w (facing D-S) into step R rt S-R. (An o/s tr R.)
113.	**pas de bourrée turn**	[p-d-b tr]	{o/s p-d-b tr R:} Step R x bk L into c-w tr, step L i-p, step R x frt L finishing tr. (Try as i/s tr.)

NOTE: Unlike the trav'g 3-step tr, a p-d-b tr remains i-p.

114.	**chaîné**	[ch]	Step R rt tr'g c-w, ½-turn into step L line-of-direction of trav [l-o-d] cont'g c-w tr. &1 Usually several are rapidly seq'd keeping steps *short* (Ft not far apart) as a *chain* of quick tr's. (Also, **b/c tr**: Leap-step as a quick ch. a1)
115.	**flap turn**		Fwd flap R rt tr'g c-w, ½-tr into fwd flap L l-o-d into c-w ½-tr. a1 a2 A flapped chaîné. When rpt'd, the recurring flap R is done as a bk or o/s flap l-o-d. Any stepped tr may be performed w/ flaps; e.g., **flapped p-d-b tr**, **flapped piqué tr**, etc.

NOTE: Any 2-stepped tr may be a ch. Try **step-tt ch** (tr'g step-tt R then L), **flap-hop tr** (2 flap-hops).

116.	**buffalo turn**	[buff tr]	Leap R rt into c-w tr, shfl L while tr'g, leap L i-p completing tr. 1&a2
117.	**irish turn**		{c-w irish tr R:} Irish R completing c-w o/s ½-tr i-p, irish L completing i/s c-w ½-tr. a1a2 a3a4 May also be done counterclockwise [c-c-w] (i/s) or as a trav'g **sliding** (i/s slides same l-o-d) **irish** tr.
118.	**piqué turn**	[piq tr]	{o/s piqué tr R:} Piq R into c-w tr – L raised x bk R ankle, complete tr to land (step into) demi plié (knee bent over toes lowering heel to flr) L. 1 2 (1 2& w/ landing heel tap.) {i/s piqué tr R:} Piq R x frt L into c-c-w tr -- L raised x frt R ankle, land L in demi plié.
119.	**pirouette**	[pir]	Spin. A one Ft st leg rel tr done i-p, usually finishing demi plié 5th or w/ a step. Use tr A's. **outside pirouette** {o/s pir L:} (Demi plié 4th R bk) rel L tr'g c-w -- R x frt L ankle, land R frt. (1)2 **inside pirouette** {i/s pir L:} (Demi plié 4th R frt) rel L tr'g c-c-w -- R x bk L ankle, land R 5th bk.

NOTE: <u>Common usage</u> specifies the <u>pir dir</u>, not the support leg, making the above o/s pir <u>rt</u> and i/s pir <u>lt</u>, rather than L and L. Turn <u>to dir rt</u> vs. <u>on Ft R</u>. Any 1-Ft or 2-step tr may be i/s or o/s. Try i/s ch, flap, or buff tr's.

120.	**push turn**		{o/s push tr's L:} Pir's usually finishing demi plié 5th frt or 2nd, then the landing leg immediately *pushing* into the next rel-pir.
	Also,		Step-rock or rock into pir; i.e., a paddle full tr(s).
121.	**snap turn**		Any tr (snap piq tr, snap pvt, etc.) done very rapidly w/ quick head [H] redirection (*snap*).
122.	**paddle turn**	[paddle tr]	Flap R rt into c-w tr, fwd flap L into paddle, <u>step</u> R i-p, rpt flap-<u>step</u> 2 X's completing tr. {a1 &a 2 &a 3 &a4} (<u>Steps</u> replace the paddle rocks.)
123.	**back paddle turn**		Bk flap R into c-c-w tr, bk flap L into paddle, step R i-p, rpt flap-step 2 X's completing tr.

NOTE: Paddle tr's are paddling dbl frt essences [ess's]. See SOFT SHOE style.

124.	**sluff turn**		Any tr during which the free Ft ball tap or toe tip sluffs the flr; e.g., plq tr R – tip sluff L. {o/s **sluff pir** L:} Steps R rt - L lt, sluff the Ft together into c-w pir L -- sluff R. (The 2 steps are a prep 2nd and not part of the tr.)

125.	**compass turn**	Piq tr or pir done in a lunge (plié-relevé [p-r] support) -- free leg extended bk or sd sluffing. A lunged sluff tr.
126.	**riff turn**	Riff R x frt L into c-c-w tr, heel L, bk flap R x frt L, pvt w/ heels R-L. (for 4 ct's add: snaps R-L) &a 1 &2 & 3 & 4
127.	**saut de basque**	(Trav rt) step R rt into c-w tr, scuff L l-o-d into leap L completing tr -- R x frt L ankle. a1 2 Many var's exist; e. g., {**flap saut de basque-tt**:} Flap R rt into c-w saut de basque, tt R x bk L. a1&a2
	And,	*{**flap-shfl-p-u-c-tt tr**:} Flap R rt into c-w tr, shfl L, p-u-c R completing tr, tt R x bk L. a1 a2&a3

NOTE: *A tr'g p-u-c-maxie segment. In these two var's, find the step, brush (if not scuff), leap, and final free Ft cross.

ADVANCED TURNS

128.	**acceleration turn**	A tr or, usually, series of tr's that are accelerated during execution by quickly retracting the A's and/or free leg twd the body or shortening trav'g steps.
129.	**deceleration turn**	A tr or series of tr's that are decelerated during execution by extending A(s) and/or free leg.
130.	**riff fouetté turn**	Br bk R into c-w tr, hop L – (usually lifting R t/o knee bk), riff fwd R completing tr, heel L. &1 &a2
131.	**renversé turn**	Fwd br R to extend x frt L into o/s fan kick (A's 3rd R), hop L (arch back bk-lt) into c-w tr, step R x bk L into c-w pvt tr, heels R-L (torso upright). &1 &a2 A tr'g hopped fan kick into pvt.
132.	**barrel turn**	(C-w barrel tr: st A's 2nd, bend rt D-S) o/s pir L (bend lt D-S) into (D-S bend rt) tr finish, step R. A pir bending D-S.

NOTE: Barrel turns are performed bending and focusing dn twd the audience w/ sloping st A's 2nd throughout the tr. Increased speed and waist bend give a visual impression of torso and A's likened to a barrel being spun or rolled on edge – **barrel rolls**.

133.	**push barrel turn**	Step R S-R – L on flr (bend rt D-S), push into c-w snap pir L (maintaining D-S bend lt - rt). &(1) (Also, called a **spotted barrel turn**, meaning done in one spot; i.e., i-p.)

134.	**rolling barrel turn**	Step R S-R (bend rt D-S), heels R-L, push into c-w snap pir (maintaining D-S bend lt - rt) --
		              & a 1 (&) (silent - no taps)
		R x bk L ankle, heel L (finishing tr).
		                    2

NOTE: Although not notated, the following, as with all barrel tr's, are identified by the extended sloping A's maintaining the same angle, facilitated by bending twd facing dir.

135.	**traveling barrel turn**	Tt R x bk L into c-w snap tr, step R x frt L, step L lt. 1 & a
136.	**walking barrel turn**	Step R x frt L (bend rt), heel R, step L lt into c-w snap tr (bend lt), heel L. &a1 2 (Try several in c-c-w circle. Especially effective at faster tempo.)
137.	**hopped barrel turn**	Tt R x bk L (bend lt) into c-w barrel tr, hop L, step R x frt L (bend rt). 1&2 (Also, alt'd as **reversing barrel turns**.)
138.	**traveling hopped barrel turn**	Step R rt (bend rt), br L x bk R into c-c-w barrel tr, hop R, step L x frt (bend lt). &1&2
139.	**double barrel turn**	Any barrel turn done w/ a dbl pir (w/ or w/o tt(s), check notated rhythm).

NOTE: Many tr's can be done as barrel tr's. In a barrel roll pos, try step R x bk L into a series of rapid c-w ch's trav'g lt. Also, toe spin and heel spin.

TWISTS

Twisting seq's rotate the body (or part) to nearly opp dir's; e.g., heel twist toe or sugar Ft heel.

140.	**irish twist**	Irish R c-w ½-tr, irish L c-c-w ½-tr. a1a2 a3a4
141.	**bandy twist** [b-t]	Step R x frt L (facing S-L), step L i-p, shfl-b/c R – ½-pvt c-w (to face S-R). 8 1 a2 a3
142.	**traveling bandy twist** [trav b-t] (→ S-L) step R x frt L (face S-L), step L S-L (face D-S), shfl-b/c R x bk L - L S-L (face S-R). 8 1 a2 a3
143.	**bandy twist turn** [b-t tr]	B-t R completing full c-w tr during shfl-b/c. (If desired, <u>leap</u> i-p into rev. 8 1 a2 a3 <u>a</u>) Also, pivot, falling off a log, b/c gpvn alt'ly facing opp frt diag's or sd's, and other steps w/ rev'g twists.

ROLLS

Comb's and steps intended to replicate drum-roll or ongoing even rhythms, commonly called **rolling** steps or comb's; e.g., several rapid d-b's. See **MILITARY** style for roll cadences.

NOTE: Generally, the word **change** indicates a step coordination intended to facilitate change of support or lead Ft; e.g., b/c or flap roll change.

144.	**roll**	There are two definitions. Multiple even rhythm taps. Heel roll, 2 alt'g heeldrops, usually concluding a step; e.g., eagle roll R (eagle, heels R-L).
145.	**heel roll**	Rpt'd alt'g heeldrops from specified lead; e.g., 5-heel roll R. {1a&a2} (Or rhythm as indicated.) (Also, **snap roll** using ball taps.)
146.	**rock'n roll**	Heels R-L, snaps R-L. (Or snaps lead, depending on wt placement.) a&a1
147.	**pigeon-toe roll**	(pigeon-toe roll R rt:} Pivot t/i R into heel rt, pvt t/o L into heel next to R, h-t R into snap rt, h-t L rt into snap next to R. Trav'g rock'n roll which is a rolling var of pigeon-toe. a&a1
148.	**cramproll** [c-r]	Leap landing b/c R-L, heels R-L. Most c-r var's can bgn w/ an elevation or a step. a&a1
149.	**cramproll change** [c-r-c]	Leap landing R-L, heels L-R. a&a1

NOTE: A roll may become **roll change** [r-c] by rev'g the final pair of heeldrops, leaving the lead Ft w/w. Thus the following may become **standing cramproll change**, **flap roll change** [f-r-c], etc.

150.	**hop cramproll** [hop-c-r]	Hop R, step L, heels R-L. a&a1
151.	**standing cramproll** [standing-c-r]	Tpl R, heels R-L {a1&a2}
152.	**triple cramproll** [tpl-c-r]	Running tpl R, step L, roll R-L {a1a&a2}

NOTE: This is a time factored c-r (see time factor). Similarly, the flapped c-r appears in notes as a **double cramproll**.

153.	**flapped cramproll**	Running flap R, step L c-p, roll R-L. {a1&a2} (Also: Flaps R-L, roll R-L. {a1a&a2} check rhythm.)
154.	**traveling cramproll** [trav-c-r]	{Trav-c-r R lt:}(Trav'g lt) elevation into heel clip into b/c R-L lt, roll R-L. {a1&a2}
155.	**slap roll** [s-r]	Slap R, roll R-L. (Wt remains L. S-r-c wt rocks to heel R.) a&a1
156.	**flap roll** [f-r]	Flap R, roll R-L. (Wt rocks R then L. F-r-c wt rocks and remains R.) a&a1

NOTE: S-r versus f-r and s-r-c vs. f-r-c are examples of steps which offer styling (flow of body placement) options during similar coordination and rhythm. Try it.

157.	**nerve roll**	(In any fixed or chg'g pos's) the free leg is tensed and rapidly vibrates the Ft striking rpt'd ball or, if specified, heel or toe-taps. For sweeping mvmt's (like r-d-j) the effect can be more comfortably achieved by less rapid ankle controlled taps.
158.	**patter steps**	(Rel 2nd) alt'ly rapidly tap the balls of the Ft. This is a st leg ankle controlled running mvmt and appears somewhat like nerve rolls bouncing between R and L. Done trav'g or i-p.

CLIPS

Striking together taps, sometimes edges of shoe soles, or tap to sole edge.

159.	**toe clip**	Strike i/s toes together. If wt is on both heels, **standing toe clip**.
160.	**heel clip**	Strike i/s heels together. If standing on both Ft, **standing heel clip**.
161.	**toe to heel clip**	Strike i/s (near frt) toe of one Ft against i/s (near bk) heel of other; e.g., R toe to L heel clip.
162.	**heel to toe clip**	Strike i/s (near bk) heel of one Ft against i/s (near frt) toe of other.

NOTE: Raise struck heel or toe if necessary to avoid unwanted sluff. Leave on flr to add tap-sluff; e.g., R toe **tap-clip** L toe (tap flr into sluffed toe clip a1). Moving Ft dir may be included; e.g., R toe lt to L heel clip.

163.	**riff clip**	Strike i/s of ball then heel against i/s heel (**heel riff clip**) or i/s ball (**toe riff clip**) of other Ft; e.g., heel riff clip R to L. a1
164.	**bell**	Kick or lift t/o R rt ending w/ knee and Ft flexed, hop L t/o flexed into heel clip in air rt, land L i-p. (Frequently performed bgn'g w/ step x frt alt'g sides 1(&)a2, thus the chiming bell appearance.)

NOTE: Most clip var's may be done standing or airborne; e.g., frt hitch w/ heel clip.

PICKUPS

From one or both Ft, pickups and wings are variations w/ br's and sluffs executed unsupported, while becoming airborne.

165. **pickup** [p-u] A sgl tap struck as a br by the supporting Ft while elevating during a hop, leap, or jump.
NOTE: Although many initial p-u training techniques bgn by rocking bk on the heels then bk br'g while jumping from heels, technically correct p-u br's are done after airborne.

166. **single pickup** [p-u, s-p-u] Hop striking two taps: a p-u, then landing w/ same Ft.   a1
NOTE: This is a hop into a flap, and, like any flap, may be done in any dir; bkwd unless otherwise noted. Unlike a leaped flap, the br is done while the body is lifting, not landing. Use notation s-p-u when clarity is required.

167. **single pickup change** [p-u-c] P-u R, land L. P-u during a leap.   a1

168. **pickup change toe-tap** [p-u-c-tt] P-u-c R, tt R x bk L.   &a1

169. **shuffle pickup change** [shfl-p-u-c] Shfl R, p-u-c L. a&a1   (Also, R [shfl-p-u-c-tt] L x bk R. Added tt L x bk R. {a&ea1})
(Note the R lead and ending L tt coordination notation clarification.)

170. **double pickup** [d-p-u] Jump into p-u's R-L, landings R-L.   a&a1

171. **double pickup change** [d-p-u-c] Jump into p-u's R-L, land R. 2 p-u's, 1 landing.   &a1

172. **double pickup change toe-tap** [d-p-u-c-tt] D-p-u-c R, tt L x bk R.   a&a1

173. **pull-back** [p-b] Shfl R, p-u L.   a&a1

174. **pickup irish** [p-u-irish] Shfl R, p-u L. step R. {a1&a2}
NOTE: Nearly any elevation can become a p-u.

175. **shuffle into double pickup** [shfl-d-p-u] Shfl-p-u-c R, step L. {a1&a2} (Also, [shfl-d-p-u-tt] adds tt R x bk L. {a1a&a2})
(Because the shfl provides the first bk br while being supported L, this is a **faked** d-p-u.)

176. **double pickup roll** [d-p-u-r] D-p-u R, heels R-L.   {&a1&a2}   ([D-p-u-r-c] (roll change) is achieved by rev'g heels.)

177. **running double pickup change** [running-d-p-u-c] Fwd br R, p-u-c L.   &a1
(This is a faked d-p-u because the first br is done while not airborne. Running and riffed d-p-u-c's are often alt'd in a series i-p or trav'g.)

178. **riffed double pickup change** [riffed-d-p-u-c] Fwd riff R, p-u-c L.   a&a1

179. **double pickup grapevine** [d-p-u-gpvn] D-p-u R rt - L x frt R, d-p-u R rt - L x bk R, etc.   a&a1 a&a2
NOTE: Use o/s and i/s br p-u's. As w/ flaps, p-u br's can lead in any dir.

180. **pickup change trench** [p-u-c-trench] Trench performed substituting p-u-c for sluff-landing; sometimes with tt bk or x bk.

WINGS

Visually, a tap dance wing is a low outward leg mvmt while elevating. The primary taps source is a landing i/s flap or tpl.

181. **wing movement** [wm] With a relaxed ankle, o/s sluff R by moving R knee rt dragging and rolling
    the R Ft over o/s edge of ball tap, when Ft leaves flr rt allow Ft to level (no roll-over) and
    relaxedly *snap* t/o, causing ankle *recoil* to enable a quickly executed i/s flap. 1 a2 or &a1
NOTE: This is a training mvmt, not a wing. Practice ending w/ an i/s slap and rpt'g the mvmt seq. When relaxed, moderate tempo repetitions R and L are achieved, practice should cont alt'g lead, then by rpt'g lead w/ a hop into the sluff while facing (w/ Hn support to extend elevation time) a *dance barre*, thus becoming a wing.

182. **wing**   A wing mvmt done during a hop.   (elevating) & (sluff) a1 (flap)
NOTE: With a few noted exceptions, in this manual wings include the lead sd sluff and, like chug, include the sound as rhythm.

183. **wing change** [wing chg] Start a wing R, i/s br R, land L.   & a1

184. **swinging wings**   Alt'g wing chg's ending w/ free Ft swinging x bk supporting leg. &a1 (Try adding tt x bk. &a1a)

185. **traveling wing**   Hop R (w/ o/s sluff) raising R slightly rt while trav'g lt into i/s flap R.   &a1

186. **traveling wing change**   Hop R (w/ o/s sluff) trav'g lt into i/s br R, land L.   &a1

187. **battement wing** [batt wing] {fwd batt wing R:} Elevate into high swing kick (or gr batt) L lt – wing R, step L x frt R.
(1)   a&a   2
(To rpt: Step R x bk L, end step L x bk R; i.e., bkwd batt wing R. Usually batt 2nd.)
NOTE: Generally, fwd, bkwd, sdwd are trav'g dir's; frt, bk, sd placement pos's but may be used to clarify similar dir actions; e.g., frt fwd batt wing R (means:) frt batt L into wing R, step L frt or x frt (trav'g slightly fwd).

188. **battement wing turn** [batt wing tr] Step R x frt L into c-c-w ½-pvt into batt wing R (face U-S) ending step L x bk R into c-c-w ½-pvt. 1&a2& (Also, end step x frt into c-w ½-tr as a **battement wing twist**.)

189. **hip wing**   Wing R -- high t/o passé L, tt L x frt R.   a&a1   (Also called a **scissor wing**.)
Usually rpt'd w/ tt's alt'g x bk then x frt.
NOTE: Many wing steps can be performed substituting a p-u(s); e.g., batt p-u, hip p-u, etc.

190. **toe stand wing**   Rel into toe stand (or faked toe-stand) L x bk (or frt) R into wing R ending x bk (or frt).   (a)&a1
(A var of a hip wing wherein the wing changes bk\frt.)

191. **pendulum wing**   A pend L – wing R, usually mutiple w/ alt'g pend dir's.   a&a1

192. **rolling wing**   O/s flap R rt, i/s br L, wing chg R landing L x frt R.   {a1a&a2}

193. **rolling wing change**   O/s flap R rt, swinging flap L c-p, step R rt.   {a1&a2}
(This is not a wing, but is based on the rolling wing appearance. Both rolling wings are frequently preceded by a hop.)

194. **eagle**   Wings done w/ both Ft a-s-t, thus simultaneous R and L taps.   &a1

195. **double eagle** [dbl-eagle] Start an eagle (jump sluffing both Ft a-s-t), then i/s br's R-L, landings R-L.   &1&a2

196. **eagle change** [eagle chg] Dbl-eagle w/o last landing; sluff-br-br-land.   &1&a   (May apply to any eagle; e.g., **trav eagle chg**.)

197. **traveling eagle** [trav eagle] [Trav rt] br R rt (no R sluff), short o/s sluff L, i/s br's R-L, land R-L.   {&a1&a2} (Try x'g lands.)

ADVANCED WINGS

NOTE: The following wings and eagles usually include no starting sluff; thus are incomplete wings, but are named for appearance and coordination similarity.

198. **triplet wing**   Hop R into o/s br (not sluff) R r-d-f, i/s-bk flap R; i.e., hop into a tpl.   &a1

199. **triplet eagle**   Jump or hop R into o/s br's R r-d-f - L l-d-f, i/s-bk br's R-L, land R-L. (*interlocking* tpl's)   {ea&ea1}
NOTE: Hyphenated dir's combine as a sgl orientation; e.g., up-bk, o/s-frt.

200. **russian wing**   Hop R into scuff r-d-f, i/s-bk flap R.   &a1

201. **russian eagle**   Jump into interlocking russian wings; i.e., scuffs R-L, i/s-bk br's R-L, land R-L.   {ea&ea1}
Commonly performed in a semi-squat, intended to resemble polzounoks (a Russian folk dance step).

202. **riffed russian eagle**   Jump into interlocking fwd riffs R-L, interlocking bk flaps R-L.{eae&eae1 octuplet [oclt] rhythm}
NOTE: These latter eagles may also be performed leading w/ o/s short sluff into fwd scuffs, br's or riffs, which, as wings, most dancers find more difficult than the eagles, and are among the most challenging tap steps. The addition of sluffs requires *tighter* (closer) footwork and diminishes the forcefulness of the polzounoks kick effect. To give it a try, back to the barre.

GLIDES and TOE STANDS

The supporting Ft hopping over the other leg is commonly called a **glide**. When executed over a balancoire or batt near hip height, often called **over-the-top**. A toe stand is a visual effect flash step perceived as difficult or dangerous.

203. **step-over**   [glide]   Any of a variety of mvmt's wherein one Ft appears to momentarily support the body
(usually in tt or tendu pos x frt or bk) while the other Ft hops or falls (appears to step) over the 'supporting' ankle or Ft. Assumed a fwd step-over unless otherwise specified.

204. **hop-over**   [glide]   Any of a variety of mvmt's wherein the supporting Ft hops over the free Ft while
held raised, kicked, or passing under the hopping Ft. Fwd unless otherwise specified.
NOTE: While all glides are hop-overs, step-over elevation is subtly minimal and sustained, emphasizing an impression of 'floating' just above the flr. The specific terms provide clarity when needed.

205. **single glide**   [glide]   Step R r-d-b, tt L x frt R, R step-over L.   &1 2

206. **rond de jambe glide** [r-d-j glide] Step R r-d-b, i/s r-d-j L, R hop-over L, cont r-d-j to desired pos.   &(1) 2

207. **doubled glide** [dbl-glide] Scuff R, leap R, tt L x frt R, glide R, tt L x bk R, bkwd glide R, shims L-R, scuff L l-d-f,
                 1   &   2   3   &(4)   &   5&a 6&a 7
               b/c L lt - R x bk L, step (or lamp) L lt.   (The actual dbl-glide is counts 1 thru (4)&,
                 a   8   &   but it's a nice shim sham rhythm comb.)

208. **doubled glide turn** [dbl-glide tr] (L raised x bk R) R bk hop-over L into c-w tr, fwd scuff L U-S-L, hop R cont'g tr,
tt L x frt R (face S-L), glide R finishing tr, step L l-d-b.   {1&2&3} 4
(Consider ending w/ a *long* step L -- draw R twd L. Try as c-c-w tr.)

Page 11

209.	**running glide**	(Wt L) slide L close x frt ending sluff w/ o/s ball tap edge into, fall fwd R over L, alt several. A trench-like faked (chg'g Ft) glide, slightly straightening supporting leg after fall.
210.	**toe stand**	Any of a variety of mvmt's wherein the body is supported on the ends of the toes (tips) of one or both Ft; i.e., **en pointe**. Toe-tap into toe stand unless rel or elevation is indicated. (Also, **toe stand both**, using both Ft.)
211.	**4-tap toe stand**	Toe-tap toe stands R-L, b/c R-L. 1&a2
212.	**faked toe stand**	A toe stand pos n/w; i.e., done during an elevation, land. Starting w/ rel (&1); or tt &(1).
213.	**toe slide**	Sliding, usually fwd, in a toe stand pos n/w. (Also, **toe slide both**, using both Ft.)
214.	**toe spin**	A piq or pir in toe stand pos.

NOTE: Toe stands generally do not permit completely straightening the supporting knee; however, greater extension and pull-up improve control.

215.	**heel spin**	A piq or pir on bk edge of heel (w/ flexed Ft). A heel stand tr.

RHYTHM PATTERNS

A few terms, not herein expanded as tap dance style categories, which are based on frequently used rhythms. Following are increasingly complex steps, requiring 2M or more.

216.	**lindy**	(Trav rt) o/s flap R rt, c/s L - R rt, rock w/ steps L x bk R - R i-p.
		a1 & 2 3 4
217.	**lindy rhythm pattern**	1&2 3 4 5&6 7 8; also, 1 a2 3 4 5 a6 7 8 (Try sgr's fwd in lindy rhythm.)
218.	**charleston rhythm pattern**	Simple: 1 (2) & (34) 5 (6) & (78); Syncopated: 1(2&) a(34) 5(6&) a(78)
219.	**charleston swing**	Flap-heel R, scuff L x frt R into o/s (low or high) r-d-j, heel R, bk flaps L-R, irish L x frt R.
	swing rhythm:	a1 2 3 4 a5 a6 a7a8
	Or syncopated:	1a(&)2(&) a(3) 4 5a(&) 6a(&) {7&a8}

NOTE: Created from early 20th century ragtime music. This after count syncopated version shifts the flap emphasis to the br's.

220.	**shave and a haircut - -**	A concluding rhythm commonly ending in a pose w/ one leg and A featured. From the spoken rhythm: "shave and a haircut, six bits". 1 2&3 4(5)6 7(8)

MAXIE FORDS

A unique rhythm pattern of 7 ct's: a repeated waltz (3 ct) comb, plus an ending. Following are a few.

221.	**maxie ford** [maxie]	{**stamped maxie:**} Stamp R, shfl L, leap L, tt R x bk L, rpt, stamp. (Also, **flapped** (lead) **maxie**.)
222.	**maxie ford rhythm pattern**	**8** &1 & 2 **3**&**4**&5 **6** (silent 7). (Accents **8 3 6**.)
		Simple form: a **maxie segment** (stamp-shfl-leap-tt) comb, rpt or rev, a finishing mvmt.
223.	**waltz clog maxie** [-w-c-maxie]	W-c-t-s's R-L, step R. 8&1&2 3&4&5 6(7) (Sgl t-s's unless otherwise specified.)
224.	**hopped maxie**	Step R, shfl L, hop R, tt L x bk R, rev, step R. 8&1&2 3&4&5 6(7)
225.	**irish maxie**	Step R, irish L x frt R, rpt, step R.
		8 a1a2 3a4a5 6(7)

NOTE: The 'accents' may simply be rhythmic, not dynamic (loud).

226.	**turning maxie**	A maxie R w/ a c-w tr during each segment; e.g., **turning irish maxie, turning p-u-c maxie**, etc.
227.	**pickup change maxie** [p-u-c-maxie]	Flap R, shfl-p-u-c-tt R x bk L, rpt comb, flap R. (or bgn flap-heel)
		a8 {a1 &a 2} a3{a4&a5} a6 (7)
	Or,	Flap R, b/c L-R, dig L, br bk L into p-u-c-tt R x bk L, rpt comb, flap-b/c R. (More complex var.)
		a8 &a 1 a &a 2 (&) a3&a4a&a5(&) a6 a7 (8 ct's of tapping)
228.	**double pickup maxie**	[d-p-u-maxie] Lamp R, shfl-d-p-u R x bk L, rev comb, lamp R.
		8 a1 &a2 3 a4&a5 6 (7)
229.	**hip wing maxie**	Flap R, hip wing R into tt L x frt, hip wing R into step L x bk (no tt), rpt comb, dbl-eagle R.
		{a8 a&a 1 a&a 2} {a3a&a4a&a5} a&ea6 (7)

NOTE: Separated clusters of taps can provide the broken rhythm necessary to achieve the 8 3 6 emphasis.

TAP DANCE STYLES

There are many tap dance styles (as opposed to individual performer/choreographic styles) based largely on music and appearance. Most in the dance field include waltz clog, buck, soft shoe, shim sham, and rhythm as essential tap training styles, considering military and eccentric steps nearly as important. Although any dance steps may be used, the following style listings highlight a few examples of steps largely, sometimes exclusively, associated with that style.

NOTE: Tap styles are often blended: Rhythm Buck (see SHOWOFF), Soft Shoe Eccentric, Shim Sham Military, etc.

TIME-STEP STYLES

While many styles include occasionally performed time-steps [t-s's], buck and waltz clog routines [rout's] nearly always include them. Generally, t-s's are structured to change lead; however, included below are suggestions for retaining lead if desired.

NOTE: Time-steps originated as a method for dancers to establish a meter ($^4/_4$, $^3/_4$, etc.), tempo, and style (buck, soft shoe, waltz clog, etc) for cooperative performance with musicians or other dancers – "setting the time". The standard buck time-step Step format is 3 time-steps (6M) plus a time-step break (2M). There are hundreds of t-s's.

WALTZ CLOG TIME-STEPS

Waltz clog styling is $^3/_4$ meter, moderate tempo, primary accent on count [ct] 1, commonly used for simple vernacular clog, swagger, strolling, and couples song and dances, and is dominated by even, duplet, and triplet rhythms.

230. **single waltz clog time-step** [s-w-c-t-s] Step R, shfl L, b/c L-R.
   waltz clog time-step rhythm pattern: 1   a2   a 3   (Often even rhythm at slower tempos. 1&2&3)
   A w-c-t-s is assumed sgl unless a dbl, tpl, or qdl time factor (see BUCK TIME-STEPS time-step rhythm pattern below) is specified, replacing the step. Also, performed twisting from sd to sd or as complete i/s or o/s tr's. Rpt'g var's include ending flap, tpl, or cramp L on a3 or &a3; or tt R x bk L on 3.
   NOTE: Although there are many clogging styles, in this manual "w-c" and most "c-t-s" abbreviations reference waltz clog. Many w-c-t-s's have been created, including:

231. **hop clog time-step**   [hop-c-t-s]   Hop R, shfl L, b/c L-R.   1 a2 a3

232. **doubled clog time-step**   [-d-c-t-s]{s-d-c-t-s:} S-w-c-t-s R, hop-c-t-s R.   1a2a3 4a5a6

233. **toe-tap clog time-step**   [-tt-c-t-s]   {s-tt-c-t-s:} Step R, shfl L, hop R, tt L x bk R.   1 a2 a3

234. **roll clog time-step**   [-roll-c-t-s]   {s-roll-c-t-s:} Step R, tpl L, heels L-R (or R-L into rpt).   1 &2&a3

235. **close riff clog time-step** [close-riff-c-t-s] (Strolling or skating style) close riff R, step L, shfl R x frt L, cramp R.   &a1 a2 a3

236. **double triple clog time-step** [-d-t-c-t-s]   {s-d-t-c-t-s:} Step R, tpl's L-R. {1 &a2 &a3} (Yes, t-d-t-c-t-s is just 3 tpl's.)

237. **double triple roll clog time-step** [-d-t-roll-c-t-s] {s-d-t-roll-c-t-s:} Step R, tpl's L-R, heels L-R (or R-L).
   {1   &a2 &a3   & a}
   (Try above dbl-tpl-c-t-s's w/ all steps x frt or bk.)

238. **strolling clog time-step**   [strolling-c-t-s]   Shfl R (or x frt), hop L, flap-heel R, step L c-p (or close x bk or fwd), flap-heel R.
   &a   1   a& a   2   &a 3

BUCK TIME-STEPS

Buck styling is $^4/_4$ (occasionally $^2/_4$), minimum 140 [met] (140 ¼ notes or metronome beats per minute) moderate to very fast tempo, building from even rhythm phrases usually bgn'g on count 8 w/ primary accent on ct 1, includes a liberal mix of even, duplet, triplet, and quadruplet rhythms, mostly low (non-elevated) steps, and is very energetic, frequently *hard driving*.

NOTE: Standard basic (simple) buck time-steps are comprised of a bgn'g (traditionally shfl, hop), a **time factor** (described next), and an ending (most commonly flap, step).

239. **time-step rhythm pattern** 8&1 2&3& Ct 1 is a rhythm (not volume) accent, interrupting a repeated dominantly even rhythm seq. There are four basic time factors: sgl, dbl, tpl, and qdl. Many t-s var's are possible using these basic time factors. In this manual, t-s's are buck unless otherwise specified.

240. **single time-step** [s-t-s]   Shfl R, hop L, step R, flap L, step R.
   8&   1   2   &3   &
   NOTE: *Single* is the *time factor* term used with a variety of time-steps wherein the mvmt immediately following the hop (or heel) is a sgl tap, a step usually falling on ct 2.

241. **double time-step** [d-t-s]   Shfl R, hop L, flap R, flap L, step R.
   8&   1   &2   &3   &
   NOTE: The dbl generally follows the hop as two taps, a flap falling on ct's &2, thus maintaining the even rhythm.

242. **triple time-step** [t-t-s]   Shfl R, hop L, tpl R, flap L, step R.
   8&   1   &a2   &3   &   NOTE: The tpl time factor follows the hop as a triplet.

Page 13

243. **quadruple time-step** [q-t-s] Shfl R, hop L, qdl R, flap L, step R. A quadruplet rhythm qdl.   8&1 a&a2 &3&
   NOTE: When time factor is not specified, assume sgl unless rhythm notates otherwise. Most t-s's are designed to reverse; however, if the same side lead is desired, replace the flap-step w/ a tpl or flap-heel.

VARIOUS BEGINNINGS

More var's of the above basic t-s's are easily achieved by changing the bgn'g and/or end. Following are a few examples.

244. **scuff time-step** [-scuff-t-s] {s-scuff-t-s:} Scuff fwd R, hop L, step R, flap L, step R.   8 1 2&3&
   Frequently done scuff x frt into o/s r-d-j w/ the time factor ending behind the supporting Ft, emphasizing side to side twisting or facilitating full o/s or i/s tr styling; e.g.:

   {d-scuff-t-s:} Scuff R x frt L (facing l-d-f), hop L, bk flap R, flap L x frt R (facing r-d-f), step R i-p.
                  8   1   &2   &3   &

   Or, {d-scuff-t-s c-w tr:} Scuff R x frt L (facing l-d-f) into o/s r-d-j, hop L, bk flap R x bk L into c-w tr, bk flap L, step R x frt L (finishing tr; or end step x bk into rev tr).

245. **riff time-step** [-riff-t-s]   A scuff time-step bgn'g w/ a riff rather than a scuff.   a8 1 2&3&

246. **scuffle time-step** [-scfl-t-s]   {s-scfl-t-s:} Scuffle R, hop L, step R, flap L, step R.   8&1 2&3&   (Scfl replaces shfl.)

247. **riffle time-step** [-riffle-t-s]   {s-riffle-t-s:} Riffle R, hop L, step R, flap L, step R.   a8&1 2&3& (Bgn's w/ riffle.)

248. **stomp time-step** [-stomp-t-s]   {s-stomp-t-s):} Stomp fwd R, br bk R, hop L, step R, flap L, step R.   8&1 2&3&
   (Also, starting w/ dig, **dig time-step**.)

249. **toe-tap time-step** [-tt-t-s]   {Sgl toe-tap t-s (s-tt-t-s):} Shfl R, hop L, tt R x bk L, step R, flap L, step R.
                                          8&   1   &   2   &3   &

   NOTE: -tt-t-s is sometimes called an **english time-step**.
   Also: The hop may become a cramp by adding a heeldrop upon landing, done as a slide, or as a s-p-u.

VARIOUS ENDINGS

The following examples are time-steps incorporating tpl-step, cramp, and wing mvmt endings. By changing time factors, bgn'gs, and endings hundreds of buck time-step and rhythm var's are easily created from the basic buck t-s patt.

250. **double triple time-step** [d-t-t-s]   Shfl R, hop L, tpl R, tpl L, step R. (A t-s w/ a tpl replacing the flap.)
                                    8&   1   &a2 &a3   &

   The 2 tpl's have 2 rhythm interpretations, separated ((a)&a2 (a)&a3) and even ({&a2&a3}). The latter is the smoother t-s rhythm, the rhythmically broken former emphasizes the &'s.

251. **stomp cramp time-step** [-stomp-cramp-t-s]   {s-stomp-cramp-t-s:} Stomp fwd R, br bk R, hop L, step R, flap L, cramp R.
                                                                    8   &   1   2   &3   &a

   The above s-stomp-cramp-t-s varies the bgn'g and ending as does the s-stomp-wm-t-s listed next.

252. **stomp wing movement time-step** [-stomp-wm-t-s]   {sgl:} Stomp fwd R, br bk R, hop L, step R, flap L, wing mvmt R.
                                                                    8   &   1   2   &3   a&a

   (Also called a **stomp wing time-step**.)
   Other variations: Swap the ending step to flap &a or substitute tpl, qdl, p-u-c, etc.

BUCK TIME-STEP BREAKS

Generally, breaks [brk's] are the last phrase (2M-4M) of a dance Step. T-s breaks are t-s variations intended to emphasize, frequently w/ a closing rhythm or dynamic accent, the changing (*breaking off*) of an established t-s rhythm or visual coordination patt.

253. **single time-step break** [s-t-s - brk] Shfl R, hop L, step R, flap L, step R, shfl L, hop R, flap L, b/c R-L.
                                         8&   1   2   &3   &   4&   5   &6   &7

   A sgl time-step break is composed of a sgl time-step followed by the **break combination** [brk comb]. Any time factor (sgl, dbl, etc.) or t-s can precede the brk comb. The following brk comb's are lead L to facilitate comparison using various t-s's R.

254. **basic buck time-step break comb**   [- brk] Shfl L, hop R, flap L, b/c R-L.   (Brk comb's alone are also called **half brk's**)

255. **double triple break combination**   [- d-t-brk] Tpl's L-R, step L.
                                  4&5 &6&   7

256. **triple-triple break combination**   [- t-t-brk] Tpl's L-R-L, step R.
                                     4&5{&a6&a7}   &

   Also, the final tap may be optionally syncopated:. 4&5{&a6&a7a}(&), permitting a rhythm hesitation ((&) rhythm shading) before continuing. For a dynamic accent, end w/ a stamp or stomp.

257. **draw-back break combination** [- d-b-brk] 2 d-b's L-R, stamp L.
                  4&5 &6& 7

   Also, **syncopated-d-b-brk** [- sync-d-b-brk] 2 d-b's L-R, step L, stomp R. 4&5 &a6 &7
NOTE: D-b brk's are commonly found in rhythm and buck rout's. There are probably as many buck brk's as buck time-steps.

Time-step Break Notation

Although appearing confusing, time-step plus brk comb notation is logical (the spaced hyphen continues the step); e.g.:
    R d-scuff-t-s - d-t-brk = Dbl scuff t-s R, dbl-tpl brk comb L. 8 1&2&3& - 4&5&6&7
    L t-stomp-t-s - t-t-brk = Tpl stomp t-s L, tpl's R-L-R, step L. **8**&1&a2&3& - 4&5&a6&a7&

MORE BUCK TIME-STEPS

Following are a few *freestyle* (non-basic) *complex structure* time-steps which illustrate the range of possible originality.

258. **flap roll change time-step** [-f-r-c-t-s] {(Dbl) d-f-r-c-t-s:} Bk flap R, bk f-r-c L, bk flap R, dig L, bk flap L, dig R,
                   &8 a&a1 &2 & 3& 4

   br bk R, heel L, f-r-c R. (Try chg'g the dir's of any or all flaps.) (A non-waltz -c-t-s.)
     & 5 &6&7

A t-s with no hop or heel before the time factor. Also performed bgn'g with the last f-r-c, returning the time factor to ct 2.

259. **bill robinson time-step** [-b-r-t-s] {(Tpl) t-b-r-t-s:} Step R x frt L, hop R, shfl-b/c L x bk R - R i-p, stomp frt L, br bk L,
                 8   1 &a 2&   **3** &

   hop R, tpl's L-R, shfl L x frt R.
    4 &a5 &6& 7&

Usually performed as a tpl t-s, this is a var of a stomp-t-s with the time factor following the second hop and being 1 ct early (normally ct's 2 or 6). Also, note the rhythm shading (subtle chg) from &a to 2&, then &a5 to &6&.

260. **fred astaire time-step** [-f-a-t-s] {d-f-a-t-s:} Scuff R, hop L, flaps bk R-L, step R, scuff L x frt R into slow c-w tr to U-S,
               8 1 &2 &3 & 4   (5-6)

   b/c L-R completing c-w tr (arching back), step L. (A scuff t-s var w/ an accelleration tr ending.)
    & 7   &

261. **cubanola**   {Sgl cubanola:} Tpl R, shfl L, 2 b/c's moving rt (Ft do not x), hop R, step L , tpl R.
             8&1 &2 &3 &4   5 6 &7&

NOTE: A *traveling time-step*. Increase trav w/ tpl's and hop sdwd and step x. Any time-step can trav by x'g, redirecting, or substituting trav'g mvmt's. Notice that ct 6 is the 2nd M equivalent of the usual time factor location ct 2.

262. **cross bar**   Hop R, shfl L, hop R, shfl L x frt R, hop R, tpl's L i-p - R x frt L, L shfl-p-u-c-tt R x bk L.
             8 &a 1 2&   3 &a4 &a5 &6 &a 7

   (This is used as both a buck and rhythm t-s.)

263. **interlocking time-steps** Any of a variety of patt's wherein two or more dancers simultaneously perform the same or
   different time-steps, each starting his comb on a different ct (**offset**) of music, generally within a 2M
   reference phrase. The resulting rhythms may be compared to singing in rounds.
NOTE: Any comb(s) may be interlocked. The offset (separation) is 1 ct, unless otherwise specified.

OTHER COMMON STYLES

Current frequently encountered styles.

264. **sophisticated**   Subtle, little mvmt. Whether slow or fast, feet remain low to the floor and mostly close to each other,
            w/ few tr's and minimal trav.

265. **song and dance** A performer's personality style. Usually, a thematic vocal verse and chorus with staging or simple
            choreography, followed by a chorus of dance. (Also, see banter.)

266. **ballroom**   A duet derived from ballroom styling, usually costumed in formalwear.

267. **tiller**   A *precision* (synchronized) line of dancers, emphasizing drill-like and high kick seq's.

268. **production**   A complex performance. Whether an entire show or single dance, includes any or all: theme/story,
            large cast, sets, involved stg'g, multiple dances, extended length, scene changes, special effects.

269. **vernacular**   National or regional popular dance styles interpreted by tapping; e.g., Latin, Dutch, Country Clog.

BUCK and WING

Buck and wing styling is $^4/_4$, fast to very fast tempo, phrased from ct 8 with primary accent on ct 1 or 2, intended to exhibit speed with complex footwork, often heavily accented using buck time-steps, pickups, wings, and showy flash steps.

RHYTHM

Rhythm styling is $^4/_4$, moderate to fast tempo, often phrased from syncopated pre-count a1 or &a1, utilizing a broad mix of rhythms including tight (closely spaced taps) clusters, rhythm shading, and frequent syncopated accents off the music ct, while exhibiting easy skill and, usually, mobility during trav'g, tr'g, elevated, and advanced techniques. Commonly arranged to swing or bouncy foxtrot music, it is ideal for faster hat and cane, stop time, and sophisticated rout's. Potentially the most interesting tap dance style, especially for soloists.

SOFT SHOE

Soft shoe styling is $^4/_4$, slow to moderate tempo, starting from primary accent ct 1 or &1, dominated by duplet and triplet rhythms performed in a fluid, leisurely manner. Excellent for song & dance, banter, couples, sand dance, and other extended body line, prop, and gently animated performance pieces. Originally in leather (*soft*, not being wood) soled shoes without taps.
NOTE: Most traditional soft shoe steps bgn w/ a step (ct 1), but flap (&1) lead rhythm has become most common.

270. **single front essence** [ess]   O/s flap R, fwd flap L x frt R, step R i-p.   &1 &a2; or {even rhythm a1&a2}

271. **doubled front essence** [dbl ess]   Sgl ess R, o/s flap L l-d-b, step R i-p, fwd flap L x frt R, step R i-p.
&{1&a2   &a   3   &a   4}

272. **soft shoe essence combination** [ess comb]   Sgl ess, rev, dbl ess. May be either **front essence combination** or **bk ess comb**.
&1&a2 &3&a4 &{5&a6&a7&a8}   a1a2a3a4a5a6a7a8
NOTE: The frt ess comb is the **soft shoe essence rhythm pattern** used w/ many soft shoe comb's and serves as a t-s.
Frt ess's can also be done w/ flaps x bk (**ess x bk**) as can bk ess's (**bk ess x frt**) w/ flaps x frt (not swinging flaps).

273. **single back essence**   [bk ess]   Bk flap R x bk L, b/c L lt - R i-p.   a1 a2

274. **doubled back essence** [dbl bk ess]   Swinging flaps R - L - R, b/c L lt - R i-p.   a1 a2 a3 a4

275. **virginia essence**   [v-ess]   O/s flap R, close riff L x frt R, step R i-p.   &1 &a2   (Also, **v-ess comb**, similar to frt ess comb.)

276. **traveling essence**   [trav ess]   O/s flap R, bk flap L x bk R, step R rt, i/s flap L x frt R, step R rt,
bk flap L x bk R, step R rt. &{1&a2&a3&a4}   (A dbl frt ess gpvn or, if specified, c-p w/o x'g.)

277. **soft shoe time-step** [-soft-shoe-t-s]   Step R, shfl L x frt R, shfl L lt, b/c L lt - R i-p, i/s flap L x frt R, step R. (Note dbl ess rhythm.)
{1   &a   2&   a   3   &a   4}
NOTE: The sgl, dbl, tpl, or qdl time factor falls on ct 1, no hop.

278. **soft shoe time-step break** [soft-shoe-t-s-brk]   Sgl ess R, shfl-hop-tpl L x bk R, qdlt irish R x bk L, flaps L-R, s/c L-R.
{a1&a2   &a 3 &a4}   a&a5   a6 a7   **& 8**

279. **back essence break** [bk-ess-brk] Bk flap R x bk L, o/s br L lt, b/c L lt - R i-p, tpl L x bk R, rev & - - 3 2 X's, o/s br R, b/c R rt - L i-p.
{a1   &   a2   &a3   &a4&a5 &a6&a7   &   a 8}
NOTE: The above are two 2M dedicated soft shoe brk's. The 2nd M of the soft-shoe-t-s-brk (qdlt irish, 2 flaps, s/c) frequently appears as a brk comb. As with all styles, there are numerous soft shoe brk comb's, time-steps, and t-s brk's.
Also, see fwd and bk paddle tr's. Try soft shoe steps in firm leather soled *soft shoes*.

SHIM SHAM

Shim sham styling is $^4/_4$ or $^2/_4$ meter, moderate to faster tempo, starting ct 8, often w/ strongly accented even ct's, even and duplet rhythms, having low, close, largely i-p or sdwd staging.

280. **shim**   Dig frt R, bk flap R c-p.   8&1 {even rhythm}

281. **shim sham**   [sham]   Shim R, step L, shim R,   {8&1 2&3}

282. **shim sham comb** [shim sham]   2 shims and 1 sham; e.g., shims R-L, shim sham R.
8&1 2&3 {4&5&6&7}   (Basic **shim sham rhythm pattern**.)

SHIM SHAM COMBINATIONS

There are many shims and shams which, once specified, form shim sham comb's w/ associated rhythm patt's.

283. **'tack annie**   [annie}   O/s flap R rt, tap L c-p, rev 2 X's, step L, b/a R - L lt.
&8   1   &23 &45   a (&6)   & 7
There are several common variations of "attack Annie", usually with accented taps. For this version the shim is flap-tap, the sham, flap-tap-step-b/a.

284.	**shuffle double pickup grapevine shim sham**	Shfl-d-p-u R - L x frt R, irish R x frt L, rev.
		a8 &a 1 a2a3 a4 - - - 7
		Shfl-d-p-u R - L x bk R, rpt 2 X's ending x frt then x bk (gpvn), irish R x bk L.
		a8 &a 1 a2&a3 a4&a5 a6a7 (A 4M gpvn shim sham comb.)
285.	**stamp step shim sham**	Stamp R r-d-f, step L c-p bk R, rpt, step R, irish L x frt R, step R. Rev 2M.
		8 1 **2** 3 4 a5a6 7 **8** - - - 7
		Stamp R r-d-f, irish L x frt R, step R, rev. Rpt 1ˢᵗ 2M.
		8 a1a2 3 4a5a67 **8** - - - 7

NOTE: The stamp step shim sham illustrates creating an 8M shim sham Step from a 2M shim sham comb.
    Consider: 1ˢᵗ 2M is a shim sham comb (shim: stamp, step; sham: step, irish, step).
              Last 4M is a shim sham comb (shim: stamp, irish, step; sham: 1ˢᵗ 2M).
              Arguably, this is a full Step (8M) shim sham comb (shim: 1ˢᵗ 2M; sham: last 4M).
              3 different shim sham comb's built by expanding the stamp-step and step (or stamp)-irish-step seq's. Interesting, eh?
              (Try starting with 2 baby bmb's rather than diag stamp-step's.)

MILITARY

Military styling is ⁴/₄ or ²/₄ meter, usually 90-130 met, dominated by drum cadence (rpt'd patt) rhythms, often characterized by stylized marching drill comb's and/or a stiff military-like toy soldier appearance. See rolls. Ideal for patriotic and tiller themes.

286.	**cramproll cadence**	3 separated c-r's R, march R-L. a&a1 (2) a&a3 (4) a&a5 6-7 (8)
287.	**cramproll pivot cadence**	C-r R, step bk R into c-w ¼-pivot, step L c-p, rpt comb, rpt thru ct 3, scuff R frt S-L, hop L,
		a&a1 2 3 (4) a&a567(8) a&a1 2 3 a (4) &
		step bk R, ¼-pivot D-S -- step L lt S-L, step R c-p. (Note <u>syncopation</u>.
		5 (6) -- 6 7 (8) Also, try c-c-w using fwd steps.)
288.	**drum flap**	Shfl, hop, flap. {a1 & a2} (Also, **drum slap**: shfl-hop-slap.)
289.	**drum flap cadence**	Drum flap R, flaps L-R. {a1&a2} a3 a4; or w/ flap-heels {a1&a2&a3&a4&}

Many more military cadences and comb's exist. Listen to marching band cadences, especially swing cadences, then experiment.

NOVELTY STYLES

Tap styles infrequently performed, often growing from unique personal abilities, or offering non-usual novelty performances.

290.	**challenge**	A mock tap competition between dancers, or a rhythm/tempo contest between dancer and drums.
291.	**jazz-tap**	Jazz dance technique w/ tapping, performed wearing softer soled jazz-tap shoes.
292.	**classical**	Accompanied by classical music and including tapped var's of ballet pas. Frequently performed in low heeled shoes and occasionally in ballet costume. However, "classical" steps are more often included in non-classically styled routines.
293.	**sand dance**	A low soft shoe (no metal taps) performed on sand scattered over the stage, distinguished by numerous sluffing/sliding mvmt's generating unique swishing and crunching (try a chug) sounds.
294.	**novelty**	The general category for a wide range of less common prop, costume, setting, and effects performance themes or motivations; e.g., chair or stair dance, pistols or drum sticks rhythm props, 'peg-leg', garbage can lid 'shoes', unruly 'shadow' duet, or chasing a contrary follow 'spot'. Pointe and acro-tap were novelties once popular enough to be included as training styles.
295.	**pointe**	Usually non-classical theme, performed entirely en pointe in pointe slippers with custom taps.
296.	**acrobatic-tap**	Usually a flash-buck or eccentric routine interspersed with acrobatic "tricks".

ECCENTRIC

Eccentric styling may be any meter or tempo, may include strongly characterized or comedic styling, frequently incorporating exaggerated leg and arm mvmt's portraying falling, wobbling, flailing *crazy legs*, and/or 'jointless' and shaky *rubberlegs*.

297.	**falling off a log** [log]	(A's extended 2ⁿᵈ, usually Sh's remain facing D-S while focus [F] and hips twist)
		leap R, tpl L x bk R – hips and kicking st R S-L (tilting slightly bkwd),
		8 &a1 (1)
		leap (or fall) fwd R (hips D-S), leap (or step-over or fall) L x frt R (hips S-R, bending slightly fwd).
		2 3

NOTE: This is an eccentric buff / hitch kick var interpreted as an off balance log rolling contestant. 8&a1 **half log** [½-log] also appears as a shuffle off to Buffalo, in hitch kick var's, and leads into tr's, glides (see below), etc. Bgn w/ hop to rev.

298. **falling off a log turn** [log tr]   Leap (or fall) R x bk L into c-w tr (arching slightly bk-rt), tpl L to face S-L -- kicking st R
                                           S-L, finish as log.   8&a1 2 3   (Especially effective following a log.)

299. **log glide** Leap R, tpl L x bk R -- facing and kicking st R S-L (A's moving freely, tilting slightly bk),
                             8   &a1
                          glide L over R (twist c-w to S-R, bending slightly fwd). (Try w/ an over-the-top into a log tr.)
                          (2)   3

300. **leg spin** (Standing L keeping knees close but not touching, slight tilt fwd, st A's 2nd, and noticeably moving only the R lower leg) i/s br R x bk L, circ R up x bk (R Ft to rear-lt of L hip), R passes behind hips to rear-rt of hips, R Ft circ's dn-rt to starting pos. (Br impetus into quick circle.)
NOTE: Leg spins are generally performed facing D-S, providing the audience a view of a revolving lower leg (*rubberknee*) effect, frequently done w/ a supporting leg hop (a) landing before each br.   a1 a2 - - - -

301. **wiggle sticks** (Rel t/i toes close) sluff t/o demi plié 5th R bk, sluff to starting pos, sluff t/o 5th R frt, sluff to starting pos &1&2. 5th pos w/ both heels a&(a)1a&(a)2 or separated heels 5th ea&(a)1ea&(a)2.
       Or,   (From starting pos) pivot L t/o w/ heel L -- sluff R 5th bk, snap L t/i -- sluff R to starting pos, rev. (Whether all sluffs or w/ distinct taps, the coordination is t/i rel 1st, t/o demi plié 5th, invert.)

302. **legomania** Pivot L t/o -- t/o R knee and swing R Ft behind L knee, pvt L t/i -- t/i R knee near L knee and swing R Ft rt, rpt t/o w/ R Ft x frt L knee, rpt t/i. (1&2&)   (or w/ heels L)

303. **sailor rock** (R t/o p-r 5th frt -- R hip lifted rt and L leg st w/ Ft flat), heel R w/ flat Ft on flr into st leg -- L p-r (rev'g flat/p-r pos's). (Usually two or more are alt'd in various rhythms.)1
     Also,   (Styled diag'ly:) w/ R hip r-d-f (tilt slightly l-d-b), L hip l-d-b (tilt r-d-f).

304. **flea hop** Swing (or br) R rt (R st or open passé) -- slide L rt (tilt body lt), step R c-p (upright). 12 or a12
                         Also, fwd\bkwd or opp'g diags as specified.

305. **knee split jump** A comedy jump during which the knees remain close while the lower legs split frt -- bk.
                        (Although usually performed w/ no added taps, the comic appearance encourages listing in this category.)
Also, see sugar Ft, shorty george, suzie-q, pigeon-toe and roll, snake hips, sluefoot, hitch kicks, eccentric riff walk, bell.

RAILROAD

Railroad styling is $^2/_4$ or $^4/_4$ meter, fast tempo, strongly accented rpt'g mostly even cluster rhythms, mimicking steam locomotive sounds with rout's frequently growing from a "take a trip" theme. This is introduced as an example of a once popular style with unique thematic, visual, rhythmic, and choreographic objectives.

306. **railroad series** [r-r-4, r-r-6, etc.]   Based on shfl-b/c (railroad-4), 4 taps performed even rhythm.   &1&2
                          Add b/c's to extend the base r-r-#; i.e., r-r-6 = shfl-b/c-b/c, r-r-8 = shfl-b/c-b/c-b/c, etc.
NOTE: The r-r-series appears as preschool training numerical terminology (see **ALTERNATE TERMINOLOGY**, NUMERICAL, 4 and 6). Representative of railroad style steps, it is intended to mimic the clattering of railroad cars at full speed and the excitement of a high speed cross country journey. Sequences with repeating and varying r-r-# yields a cont'g patt (i-p or trav'g) with subtle audio shading (the shfl) indicating regularly spaced track irregularities; e.g., r-r-4, r-r-6, r-r-6, rpt all. In sd view, a line of dancers sd circ'g horz D-S fore-A's and exaggerating the shfl w/ higher lifted Ft before 1st b/c suggest piston driven 'wheels'. Tapping on and off wood 'suitcases' adds tonal variation. Another use of the r-r-series is as a subdued group [grp] background rhythm behind a featured performer.
Also, see chug (locomotive start and acceleration), sluff (steam release sound), trenches, hitch kick, running and trav'g steps.

BODY POSITIONS

The following positions and actions, usually without tap sounds, are useful when describing tap dancing. Some are French ballet terms used throughout theater dance. Note: Most anatomic abbreviations begin with an upper case letter; A, F, Ft, H, Hn, L, R, Sh.

307. **Right** [R], **Left** [L]   Right or Left indicated part of the body (Ft, A, hip, etc.). Ft/leg unless otherwise specified.

308. **both** R and L a-s-t (Ft/legs or A's/Hn's); e.g.; h-t both. (Also, when stg'g, Both partners.)

309. **placement** Location(s) of a part(s) of the body, indicating support, balance, line, and possibly momentum dir.

310. **pull-up** By *lifting* and ctr'g the rib cage and upper torso, the ctr of gravity is raised, permitting improved balance and subsequent directionality. Most dance flows from a pulled-up carriage of the body.

311. **carriage** General body control and appearance.

312. **movement** [mvmt]   A noticeable chg in body pos.

313. **lead** Start; e.g., body part doing 1st mvmt or dir of mvmt, usually a Ft or leg. Also, 1st step of a comb.

314.	**preparation**	[prep]	A pos or mvmt intended to facilitate doing the following mvmt(s).
315.	**into**		Indicates a preceding mvmt blends with the next mvmt as though part of it; e.g., step R into c-w tr. Words: from, start, to, at, thru, on, and end are similarly useful when specifying a seq; e.g., from 2nd; to C-S; end ptnr's lt.
316.	**recover**		Return to previous pos.
317.	**hold**		Pause rhythm or briefly maintain a pos or delay the next mvmt. Rhythm in parentheses; e.g., 12(3)4.
318.	**pose**		Sustain a pos; commonly as a background or at the conclusion of a dance.
319.	**body line**	[line]	Body shape. Appearance of the arrangement of the body or specified part(s); e.g., extended leg line.
320.	**upright**		Torso vert, not bending at waist. Standing upright, unless otherwise specified.
321.	**bend**		Torso folded from waist, unless other part of body is specified.
322.	**tilt**		With spine relatively st, torso is angled, not vert. (May apply to other parts of body.)
323.	**lean**		Sufficient torso tilt or bend to indicate the need for directional support.
	NOTE: Bend, tilt, and lean are comfortably noticeable unless specified more extreme.		
324.	**sway**		Slight sd bend, usually w/ sdwd mvmt or trav, then st'n to upright w/w.
325.	**focus**	[F]	The dir the face is toward. (Not the same as facing.)
326.	**spotting**		To focus l-o-d or twd finishing dir before finishing tr's, thus permitting accurate directionality.
	NOTE: This is achieved by looking in the desired dir as the tr is begun, holding the F during the early portion of the tr, then quickly rotating (*snap*) the H to refocus in the desired dir before finishing the tr. (Generically, *snappy* mvmt's are quick.)		
327.	**isolate**	[isol]	Move specified body part(s) without visually influencing other body lines.
328.	**interlocking**		Similar mvmt's or steps seq'd by offset (delayed) repetition or alt'g leads; e.g., s-p-u's and landings during a d-p-u, flaps in russian eagles, or offset t-s's by multiple dancers.

FEET and LEGS

329.	**low, mid, high**		Ft/leg lift: near the flr w/ reduced buoyancy (heels, not hops), vs. knee level, vs. higher leg mvmt's and/or elevations.
330.	**close, short, long**		Ft/leg placement: near, vs. notably separated, vs. widely separated. (May apply to other anatomy.)
331.	**flat foot**	[flat]	Ball and heel taps of a Ft on the flr; i.e., no rel.
332.	**arched**		Ankle bends Ft dnwd w/ arch of Ft curved (*pointed*), extending the leg line in indicated dir.
333.	**flexed**		Bend ankle upward [upwd], bringing Ft perpendicular to shin. (May also apply to wrist/Hn.)
334.	**tendu**		Stretched. Ft is arched w/ toe touching flr, usually w/ st t/o leg. A tap if rhythm is notated.
335.	**closed position**	[c-p]	Ft and/or leg(s) touching or close, usually close // 1st. (Close means near, closed may touch.)
336.	**open position**	[o-p]	Ft and/or leg(s) separated and legs not x'd. (May also apply to A's.)
337.	**first position**	[1st]*	Ft beside and near each other.
	(NOTE: Ft pos numbers* may also apply to A's (see ARMS and HANDS). Numbered Ft and A pos's are more liberally interpreted (freestyled) for tap and may appear more nat than ballet pos's.)		
338.	**second position**	[2nd]*	Ft noticeably separated sdwd.
339.	**fourth position**	[4th]*	Ft noticeably separated frt and bk.
340.	**fifth position**	[5th]*	Ft near each other frt and bk.
341.	**parallel**	[//]	Pos's and mvmt's, whether on the floor or elevated, done with both Ft/knees directed in the same dir, usually fwd; i.e., Ft parallel with each other. Most non-x'g and non-sdwd tapping is done //.
342.	**turn-front**	[t/f]	Ft/knee(s) directed fwd.
343.	**turn-out**	[t/o]	Leg pos's and mvmt's with the hip(s), knee(s), and possibly toes rotated outward, directed sdwd.
344.	**turn-in**	[t/i]	Pos's and mvmt's with the knee(s) and/or toes directed inward twd or across the ctr of the body.
345.	**natural**	[nat]	A personally comfortable pos, requiring no exaggeration.
346.	**natural turn-out**	[n-t/o]	A personally comfortable t/o, not as extreme as encountered in ballet.

#	Term	Abbr.	Definition
347.	**cross** or **across**	[x]	Crossing frt or bk of the vertical [vert] center line of the performer's body.
348.	**cross-over**	[x-over]	A trav'g seq, usually sdwd, ending w/ legs x'd.
349.	**heel twist**	[h-t]	(Flexed Ft pos w/ heel on flr) pivot the Ft t/o or t/i as directed.
350.	**rock**		(Ft on flr) a subtle wt transfer from one Ft to the other, or to different part of Ft. Taps included if specified; e.g., (Ft 2nd) rock heels R-L. 1 2
351.	**plié**		Bend the knee(s), generally over the toes. **Grand** [gr] (large) **plié** lifts the heels while the upright body lowers near the floor. In **demi** (half) plié the knees bend about 90°, the heels remain on the floor. Grand plié only if specified. Most tapping is done w/ a **natural plié**, less than demi.
352.	**relevé**	[rel]	Rise. Lift the heel(s) while supported on the ball(s) of the Ft w/ supporting leg(s) st. Most tapping is done w/ a **natural relevé**, heels comfortably lifted.
353.	**plié-relevé**	[p-r]	A nat plié and relevé, usually w/w. A deeper plié if specified.
354.	**land**		Finish a step or mvmt in plié. Most tap elevations end p-r, large elevations and some tr's, demi plié.
355.	**lunge**		Various pos's wherein one leg in noticeable plié takes most or all wt, usually while other is extended.
356.	**draw**		Moving a Ft on the flr, usually inward twd the supporting Ft, w/o sound.
357.	**rond de jambe**	[r-d-j]	Circle of the leg. Usually from or thru 1st, Ft is carried on or above the flr circularly fwd - 2nd - to bk (o/s r-d-j) or bkwd - 2nd - to frt (i/s r-d-j). May be partial; e.g., o/s r-d-j to 2nd.
358.	**passé**		Passed. Free Ft moves past or is held near the supporting leg, between ankle (low) and knee (high).
359.	**battement**	[batt]	A moderate to high (**grand battement** [gr batt]) st leg lift from a c-p, usually returning to a c-p.
360.	**swing kick**		Ft moves thru 1st or 5th into batt, returning to an o-p.
361.	**balancoire**		St leg swing from a lifted leg pos.
362.	**developpé**	[dev]	Develop (extend). (From passé) st'n the leg in the indicated dir. If necessary, bgn w/ passé.
363.	**snap kick**		Passé, quick developé, quick recovery to passé; a fast lower leg kick w/ *snappy rebound*.
364.	**tuck**		Bend twd body. Ft near buttock(s), unless props or other anatomy or pos is specified.

ARMS and HANDS

#	Term	Abbr.	Definition
365.	**port de bras**	[A, A's]	Carriage of the A's, their pos's and mvmt, frequently specified as numbered pos's.
366.	**first position**	[1st]*	A's extended fwd from sternum, curved inward, finger tips slightly separated. (A's dn-frt: **low 1st**.)
367.	**second position**	[2nd]*	Curved A's extended to both sd's near Sh level. (NOTE: All A pos numbers* may also apply to Ft.)
368.	**third position**	[3rd]*	Specified curved A overhead [over-H] -- other A 2nd. (**Low 3rd** or **3rd frt**: specified A dn-frt or 1st.)
369.	**fifth position**	[5st]*	Curved A's extended slightly fwd over-H. 1st pos high frt. NOTE: The ballet stipulated curved A shape may be otherwise specified; e.g., st A's 2nd.
370.	**jazz second**	[jazz 2nd]	A's 2nd with elbows bent down and jazz Hn's palms frt.
371.	**V-arms**	[V-A's]	St arms over-H w/ flat Hn's palms in and wrists flexed slightly bk (sdwd). (Also, **V-A's frt**.)
372.	**opposing arm swing**	[o-A-s]	A's swing dnwd then in opp dir's, one fwd while the other bkwd, usually opp to leg pos's. If specified, x frt--bk w/ bent elbows; a relaxed **crossed o-A-s** [x-o-A-s].
373.	**double arm swing**	[d-A-s]	Both A's swing dnwd then to the same side, usually over the supporting leg.
374.	**extend**		Nat'ly, comfortably straighten indicated A or leg.
375.	**reach**		Fully extend (elbow, wrist, and fingers alligned) A(s) in indicated dir(s).
376.	**flexed**		Bend wrist, bringing bk of Hn toward A unless otherwise specified. (May also apply to ankle/Ft.)
377.	**press**		With Hn flexed, fully extend A(s) in indicated dir(s). A flexed reach.
378.	**present**		Extend A in specified dir w/ palm up. An "it's your turn" gesture. Both A's if specified.
379.	**neutral shoulder position**	[n-Sh-p]	Closed Hn (not tight fist) near frt of Sh.
380.	**flat hand**	[flat Hn]	Fingers extended and together.
381.	**jazz hand**	[jazz Hn]	Fingers extended and spread; i.e., a palm-viewed large Hn.

382.	**vibrate**	Jazz Hn rapidly alt'g wrist twist dir's. Rev'g semi-rotary vibration. (Other part of body, if specified.)
383.	**interlaced**	St fingers of 1 Hn between those of the other, thumbs by forefingers. Frequently pressed palms dn.
384.	**scissor**	A's x (**scissor x**) and/or *slice* (**scissor open**) open dnwd frt. Usually x then open in seq. **Scissor front** is horz about waist high w/ palms dn.
385.	**tiller arms second**	A's 2nd w/ Hn(s) on top of or behind adjacent dancer(s) Sh(s). Ends of line A usually st A 2nd.
386.	**tiller arms back**	A's or Hn's x backs of adjacent dancer(s). Ends of line Hn usually on sd of waist.
387.	**scarecrow arms**	A's Sh level 2nd, elbows bent 90°, both fore-A's dn, flat Hn's palms bk.
388.	**railroad arms** [r-r-A's]	(A's Sh level 2nd, elbows bent 90°, fore-A's up and dn, flat Hn's palms frt--bk) opp fore-A's swing fwd vert'ly alt'g up\dn; e.g., R up -- L dn, R dn -- L up, etc.
	Also,	**pend-r-r-A's**: (scareceow A's) pendulum swing fore-A's sdwd then inward (out\in).

Also, see turn port de bras and INTRODUCTION TO PARTNERING.

GENERAL TAP TERMS

Commonly used terms not directly related to other listed categories.

389.	**dance type**	Dances grouped by similar function (type of dance); i.e., ethnic, folk, ballroom, theatrical.
390.	**dance form**	Subdivisions of a dance type by unique structural (form/appearance) or historic characteristics; e.g., American Indian versus African ethnic, or tap vs. ballet.
391.	**technique**	Physical skills: mobility, steps, prop handling, etc.
392.	**style**	Appearance. A set of distinct technical and aesthetic characteristics establishing a recognizeable uniqeness of dance or dancer. **Dance styles** are subdivisions of a dance form; e.g., Hopi hoop dance vs. Sioux fancy shawl dance, or soft shoe vs. buck and wing. **Step styles** are different movement interpretations of dance steps. **Personal styles** feature distinctive performance or choreographic characteristics.
393.	**choreography** [chor]	Composing dance. Generally, a complex *freestyle* arrangement of dance steps, staging, and music which requires performer interpretation or builds from a performer's personal style.
394.	**set**, **set on**	Present chor and establish performability. (Also setting, a performance location 'decorated' w/ furnishings - sets.)
395.	**narrative dance**	A story dance, progressing through associated events to a conclusion.
396.	**banter**, **patter**	An ongoing dialog, usually comedic, between dancers while dancing.
397.	**shading**	Subtle changes in tap volume, rhythm, or audio frequency or quality (type of sound}.
398.	**hoofer**	An accomplished tapper, especially rhythmically, often noted for 'unique' comb's or *footwork*.
399.	**trademark**, **signature**	Personal style identifier. An often repeated mvmt, step, style, rhythm, stg'g, prop, and/or costume.
400.	**shine**	Displaying exceptional dance skill and personality. An exciting performance – "put some shine on your shoes".
401.	**flash step**	A dance step intended to impress the audience, frequently by repetition. Flashy *show-off* steps.
402.	**break-out**	While performing, leaving a group to solo.
403.	**backup**	*Background* dancers, *backing* or *supporting* a soloist by encouragement or redundant rhythm or mvmt.
404.	**freestyle**	Adlib. Extemporized tapping or prepared choreography *freely* organized, dominated by non-common complex steps and nonrepetitive structures.

ARRANGEMENT TERMS

Most tap dancing is structured in association with musical accompaniment, closely relating dance and music structure terms.

DANCE STRUCTURE

The following terms aid in understanding the construction of tap dances.

405.	**sequence**	[seq]	Mvmt's or sounds which immediately follow one another.

406.	**pattern**	[patt]	A foundation (serves as a pattern) seq of mvmt's or rhythm; e.g., a basic step, often used or familiar rhythm, trav or stg'g shape. Long established patt's are considered **standards**, often referenced.
407.	**step**		A defined mvmt or mvmt sequence; a named dance pattern; **pas**.
408.	**combination**	[comb]	A seq of steps.
409.	**segment**		A notable, repeating, dominant, usually unnamed comb within a step or longer comb.
410.	**phrase**		A 2M to 4M comb usually synchronized w/ a musical accompaniment phrase.
411.	**Step**		A division of a routine, usually composed of four phrases totaling 8M or 16M in length, frequently, like much music, incorporating formal repetitive structures (See break, simple Step formats below).

NOTE: Choreography is usually presented to dancers in numbered short portions, Steps, identified herein with upper case "S".

412.	**section**		A functionally or stylistically separate portion of a choeographic piece; e.g., vamp, stop time section, or soft shoe before segue to buck.
413.	**routine**	[rout]	A prepared simple dance, largely or entirely organized using common steps and formats, intended to be performed rote w/ little or no interpretation. May refer to any often rpt'd excercises. A simple performance rout is composed of 6 (waltz) to 8 Steps w/ or w/o entrance or exit.
414.	**interlude**		A brief (2M-8M) change in mood (dance and/or music); e.g., comedy interlude; 4M waltz interlude.
415.	**break**	[brk]	A change from established patt(s). Usually the 4th phrase of a Step and often used in multiple Steps.

NOTE: Simple Step structure formats include:
- Phrase *A*, rpt or rev *A* 2 X's, brk *B*; structure referenced as *AAAB*.
- Phrase *A*, a different phrase *B*, rpt or rev *AB* (no brk); referenced as *ABAB*.
- Phrase *A*, a different phrase *B*, rpt or rev *A*, brk *C*; referenced as *ABAC*.
- Phrase *A*, rpt or rev *A*, a different phrase *B*, rpt or rev *B* (no brk); referenced as *AABB*.

416.	**entrance**	[ent]	Moving onto the performance area.
417.	**exit**		Leaving the performance area.
418.	**accent**		A tap emphasized either by rhythmic separation (**rhythm accent**) or by being noticeably loud (**dynamic accent**). A dynamic accent unless otherwise specified (may be printed bold **&8**).
419.	**rhythm**		Flow of emphasis. Spacing of the beginning pulse (*attack*) of each of a seq of sounds, including pulse strength (accent). Variously categorized as smooth vs. broken, clustered and intermittent, or evenly spaced and on the musical ct's (*on the beat*) vs. sync'd with shifting accents before or otherwise *off the beat*, etc.
420.	**repeat**	[rpt]	Duplicate the preceding or specified mvmt's or comb w/ the same lead.
421.	**reverse**	[rev]	Duplicate w/ opp lead, usually including opp associated body dir's rt and lt (not frt or bk). May be alt'g; e.g., rev 3 X's.
422.	**alternate**	[alt]	A specified series of rev's, lead chg's, or opposite placements or dir's; e,g,, alt frt\bk 6 X's.
423.	**invert**	[inv]	Rev w/ opp frt\bk, fwd\bkwd; e.g., flap-heel R, fwd br L, inv (bk flap-heel L, bk br R).
424.	**variation**	[var]	A different version of an established mvmt, step, comb, or dance.
425.	**times**	[X's]	Multiples; e.g., 2 X's, 4 X's.

MUSIC STRUCTURE
Music and rhythm related terms useful for tap dancing.

426.	**count**	[ct]	Primary rhythm value in music, evenly counted "1 2 3 4" etc., usually a quarter note of time spacing. Rhythmic ct fractions are notated: &, a, e. See meter below and **SIMPLE RHYTHM NOTATION**.
427.	**note**		A unit of music duration or rhythm spacing. On a *music staff* it also locates sound frequency. Duration of notes are specified as fractions of a $^4/_4$ measure; i.e.; $^1/_8$ $^1/_4$ $^1/_2$, etc., thus allowing melodic and rhythmic notation.
428.	**measure**	[M]	Basic grouping (measurement) of rhythm or music (ct's or notes). A <u>*whole* note</u> = <u>1</u>M of $^4/_4$ time.
429.	**time**	[X]	The flow of music or rhythm measured in *counts of music/rhythm* during a specific period, usually a musical measure or phrase. Musical time is not directly related to any clock and duration varies with tempo. (See meter and metronomic beat below.)

430.	**meter**	*Musical time* (full ct's) contained in a M, defined by the **time signature** fraction which specifies the note value which receives 1 ct of rhythm time under the number of ct's included in a M of music.
	Examples:	$^4/_4$: The $^1/_4$ note receives 1 ct of time, each M of music includes 4 ct's of time.
		$^3/_4$: The $^1/_4$ note receives 1 ct of time, each M of music includes 3 ct's of time.
		$^6/_8$: The $^1/_8$ note receives 1 ct of time, each M of music includes 6 ct's of time.
431.	**phrase**	A recognizably complete rhythmic or musical seq, usually 2M or 4M in length. Commonly a verbal phrase or sentence (line) of song lyrics. (Also, see DANCE STRUCTURE.)
432.	**movement**	A distinct and separate section of a lengthy musical composition.
433.	**tempo**	The counted speed of music or rhythm. **Up-tempo** means faster.
434.	**metronomic beat** [met]	Tempo in ct's per minute, as established by a metronome. Through meter, here time meets the clock.
435.	**accelerando**	A gradual tempo increase.
436.	**ritardando**	A gradual decrease in tempo.
437.	**half-time** [½-X]	Half tempo. 1 ct of action every 2 ct's of music.
438.	**double time** [dbl-X]	Twice the established tempo; twice as fast. 2 ct's of action per 1 ct of music.
439.	**chord**	A sgl separated music sound of any duration, usually composed of three or more audio frequencies.
440.	**pick up**	Intoductory few notes or chords.
441.	**introduction** [intro]	A musical phrase(s) introducing a musical composition and leading into the verse or first chorus. It may serve to alert performers and/or provide entrance accompaniment.
442.	**vamp**	A repetitive musical phrase indefinitely repeated until the dancer is ready to bgn.
443.	**verse**	Story. One or more vocal phrases, following the intro, which establish a song theme and lead into the chorus. Multiple lyric verses expand the story.
444.	**chorus**	The primary *musical theme* of a *musical composition*, usually 32M in length. Most tap rout's are based on 2 choruses (64M). Also, a rpt'd vocal 4-16M phrase concluding each of several verses and often intended for group (chorus) participation.
445.	**bridge**	A 4M to 8M phrase between cont'g choruses or musical pieces, often transitioning by implementing a change of musical style, key, tempo, instrumentation, meter, etc. Sometimes, the 3rd 8M phrase of a chorus before repeating the 1st 8M melody.
446.	**segue**	A direct transition between ongoing different pieces of music.
447.	**tacit**	Silent. Little or no instrumentation; usually featuring tapping.
448.	**stop time** [stop-X]	A chorded (fragmented) instrumental pattern. During the tacit *gaps*, tap rhythms are featured, sometimes repeating, varying, or challenging the instrumental rhythms.
449.	**fade**	Gradually reduce music volume, usually to silence. (Also, decrease stg lighting intensity.)
450.	**tag**	An appended phrase (usually 2M-4M) concluding a piece of music. May serve as an exit or segue.
451.	**button**	A single note or chord concluding a piece of music - "button it up". Or multiple; e.g., **dbl button**.

SIMPLE RHYTHM NOTATION

The simple form of rhythm notation used herein is not always accurate. Consistently accurate notation is possible using Labanotation or other music score notation, but is far less convenient. Most tap rhythm is a sequence of unsustained audio pulses – taps. The following abbreviated system is easily notated, read, and is usually functionally accurate, but requires some personal interpretation.

TYPES of RHYTHM
Common descriptions of rhythm include:

452.	**even**	Evenly spaced rhythm emphasis.
453.	**duplet, triplet**, etc.	Separated even rhythm groups of 2, 3, etc.
454.	**rolling**	Ongoing rapid even rhythm.
455.	**uneven**	Rhythm flow w/ changing rhythm seq's.
456.	**broken**	Fragmented (having gaps) rhythm.

457. **syncopate** [sync]   Rhythm emphasis immediately before or after a ct.
458. **cluster**   A distinctive rapid <u>rhythm</u> seq, dominantly even rhythm and may be rpt'd. This is a seq of <u>sounds</u> which may be duplicated using different comb's of steps, starting ct, and/or shifted accents.
459. **rhythm shift** [shift]   Rearranging a rhythm patt or relocating emphasis or starting ct of an established comb. A cluster example: **1**&a2&a3 4, later rpt'd 8&a**1**&a**2** 3.   (Also, see STAGING ARRANGEMENTS, shift.)

RHYTHM SYMBOLS

Indicating ct fractions eases identifying the intended sound pattern. Symbols locate the flow of the attack (the beginning of separate sounds/actions) between silence or different actions during a M or phrase of counts.

($4/4$ meter musical spacing equivalets = $1/\#$ note).

( )	silent rhythm ct or ct's; action(s), if any, are without dance sound	
1 2 3 etc.	count	(= $1/4$ note)
&	$1/2$-count	(= $1/8$ note)
a	$1/4$-count	(= $1/16$ note)
e	$1/8$-count	(= $1/32$ note)
i	$1/16$-count, rarely encountered	

RHYTHM NOTATION

The format used herein notates rhythm under or following mvmt notation. Effective notation frequently requires arranging symbols to 'look like' sound patterns.

&1&2   Even rhythm; equally spaced sounds. (Also, see using *braces, **FORMATTING** below.)
a1 a2 or 1a 2a Duplet rhythm; sounds grouped in pairs.

The following triplet notation appears to occur in the last half of each ct, but may be interpreted as evenly ct distributed.

&a1   Triplet; 3 quick even sounds separately grouped per 3: &a2 &a3 &a4.
&a1&a2&a3   Multiple successive triplets are generally interpreted as rolling. (See d-t-t-s as an example of rolling vs. separated triplets.)
a&a1 or 1&a2   Quadruplet; 4 quick even sounds.   (The different notations indicate bgn'g and end ct's.)

Following is where interpretation becomes necessary.

ea&a1 or 1a&a2 {quintuplet}; 5 very quick even sounds (or a&ea1, etc.).   (Note {quintuplet} even rhythm braces.)
ea&ea1 or 1a&ea2 {sextuplet}; 6 very quick even sounds (or 1ea&a2).   (Within braces, all three rhythm notations are the same – even.)

Generally, 7 or more taps per ct will, of tempo necessity, be performed rolling.

FORMATTING

Whether notated under the steps or phrased after a step sequence, more accurate rhythm notation is achieved by:

Separating non-even seq's of taps: a1&a2 {quintuplet} versus a1 &a2 duplet then separated triplet rhythms.
Group by rhythm fragment: a1 2a 3&a4 5a& 6 7&8.
$1/4$ and $1/8$-count rhythm may be more accurately specified using (silent) place holders; e.g., a5ea(&)6 vs. a5(&)ea6.
Bold rhythm notation indicates dynamic (loud) accents : **8**&1&2 3&**4**&5 6(**7**).
   (This is optional notation, but may add clarity, especially when the movement is not normally a loud tap.)
Notating rhythm directly below specific taps or mvmt's is most accurate.
*Specifying within braces {ct's} even rhythm seq's or as {even, qdlt, rolling, etc.} improves interpretation accuracy.
Unspaced hyphens: 1-2-& indicate a single continuing sound or action; e.g., sluff 1-2-3.
Spaced hyphens: 1 - - - - - 8 indicate a span of ct's, not rhythm.
Dbl hyphen or dash: --, – indicates actions using the same ct(s); i.e., a-s-t.
Rhythm cluster may be bounded by upper case letters: A→ ←A defines a cluster; A: :A indicates repetition.
   e.g., &1&2 C→{3&a4} (&){5&a6a} ←C(&)78 C:{1&a2}(&){3&a4a}:C 5&6 (7) a8

STAGING TERMS

Staging is planned locations and trav, referenced using performance areas, body dir's, and location relationships and shapes. The bottom of most staging sketches is assumed D-S, audience view of the presentation.

STAGE AREAS

There are 9 general, 4 intermediate, and 3 off-stage area references and 8 numbered dance (ballet) stage directions. Once downstage is specified, these do not change for a performance area. Other staging references follow.

```
                        Backstage
         ┌──────────────────────────────────────┐
         │ U-S-R          U-S           U-S-L   │
         │   4             7              3     │
         │              U-S-C                   │
         │ S-R                            S-L   │
off S-R  │  8    C-S-R   C-S    C-S-L    6      │  off S-L
         │                                      │
         │              D-S-C                   │
         │   1             5              2     │
         │ D-S-R          D-S           D-S-L   │
         └──────────────────────────────────────┘
                        Audience
```

460. **center stage** [C-S]   The center portion of the performance area.

461. **downstage** [D-S]   The front of the stg, nearest the center of the audience.
     NOTE: Early Euopean stages were raked (sloped toward the audience), thus *down* and *up* stage.

462. **upstage** [U-S]   The back of the performance area, farthest from the audience.

463. **downstage center** [D-S-C], **upstage center** [U-S-C]   Area between center and downstage or upstage.

464. **stage left** [S-L]   When facing D-S, the performer's lt.

465. **stage right** [S-R]   When facing D-S, the performer's rt.
     NOTE: All stg dir's relate to the performers' activities, thus their rt and lt as they confront the audience.

466. **center stage left** [C-S-L], **center stage right** [C-S-R]   Area between center stage and stage left or right.

467. **upstage left** [U-S-L], **downstage left** [D-S-L]   The up and downstage S-L corners and diagonals.

468. **upstage right** [U-S-R], **downstage right** [D-S-R]   The S-R corners and diagonals upstage or downstage.

469. **Cecchetti stage directions**   A directional number system (#1-8) used in ballet and other theater dance forms. Begins D-S-R, c-c-w numbering corners then "walls" of stg. (See above stage sketch.)

470. **onstage**   The performance area, visible to the audience.

471. **off-stage** [off-stg]   Any portion of the stg not part of the performance area.

472. **backstage**   The off-stage area beyond U-S. Commonly, also off S-R and S-L.

BODY DIRECTIONS

In addition to up and down, there are several direction references relating body placement, mvmt, and/or trav. These are not fixed stage directions, but rather depend on the dir the body is facing prior to change.

473. **front center line** [f-c-l]   An imaginary vertical line dn the ctr frt of the torso, which defines the facing dir of the body, as well as, inward and outward mvmt's.

474. **face, facing**   Dir of the frt of the torso; or, if the Sh's and hips are not allligned, the dir of the frt of the hips. (Not the same as focus. Also, may be any specified anatomy; e.g., palms facing bk)

475. **front** [frt], **forward** [fwd]   In front of the performer, move forward from the frt.

476. **back** [bk], **backward** [bkwd]   Behind the performer.

477. **side** [sd], **sideward** [sdwd]   Relating to the performer's side.

478. **right** [rt], **left** [lt]   Sideward, the performer's right or left.

479. **right diagonal front** [r-d-f], **right diagonal back** [r-d-b]   Performer's frt or bk right diagonals.
480. **left diagonal front** [l-d-f], **left diagonal back** [l-d-b]   Performer's left diag's frt or bk.
    NOTE: The above diag's usually reference **open diagonal** pos's, not crossing the f-c-l.
481. **in place**   [i-p]   Without relocating. Usually referencing current Ft or support location.
482. **up**, **upward** [upwd], **down** [dn], **downward** [dnwd]   Significant vertical mvmt.
    NOTE: Although used interchangeably, when clarity is adviseable, rt, lt, sd, up, dn are most accurately terms of placement;
    ----ward references mvmt; e.g., step frt, trav fwd.
    Various compound dir's are hyphenated; e.g., swing kick into o/s r-d-j to dn-bk; reach up-rt; i/s-bk flap.
    Also, see x, x-over, i/s, o/s, c-w, c-c-w. Many consider twists and turns (facing changes) staging.

STAGING ARRANGEMENTS
A short list of the many terms identifying and describing fixed and trav'g arrangements of or by performers.

483. <u>**Boy**</u>, <u>**Girl**</u>, <u>**Group #**</u>, etc.   [<u>B</u>, <u>G</u>, <u>Grp #</u>]   Specifies performers. (Applies generally when normally formatted, grp, girls, etc.)
484. **preset**   Locate before specified action(s) in fixed pos(s) or pattern(s); e.g., preset 8 <u>G</u>'s C-S circ (Hn's on hips, face c-w) R c-p t/i p-r n/w.
485. **travel**   [trav, →]   Directionally relocate body; e.g., trav S-R; → c-c-w circ.
486. **staging**   [stg'g]   A pattern of placement or trav on the stg.
487. **blocking**   Moving thru the stg'g patt, usually to establish it.
488. **marque**   Physical or mental review of the stg'g, usually including *walking thru* the dance steps.
489. **line-of-direction**   [l-o-d]   An established or specified line of trav, either st or complex.
490. **up-line-of-direction**   [u-l-o-d]   Return along an established l-o-d.
491. **horizontal**   [horz]   Lateral (S-R «--» S-L) stg trav or patt. Also, a level mvmt.
492. **vertical**   [vert]   Depth (U-S «--» D-S) stg trav or patt. Also, lifted or lowered.
493. **tiller line**   Usually horz line, often w/ performer's Hn's (A's) sdwd on adjacent Sh's or x backs.
494. **staggered**   Multiple lines offset with all performers visible from D-S; e.g.,   ° ° ° ° °
     3 staggered lines of 5.   ° ° ° ° °
                                 ° ° ° ° °
495. **merge**   Combine multiple individuals or lines into a stg'd shape, commonly one line from staggered lines.
496. **shift**   Move past, usually sdwd. Pass an adjacent dancer, 1 person (if a line) or as specified.
    Often, both dancers shift in opp dir's (**opposing shift**).   (May also apply to rhythm.)
497. **consolidate**   Complete a stg'g arrangement, usually visually clarifying a patt; e.g., consolidate circ.
498. **circle**   [circ]   Usually each performer trav's, bgn'g arc U-S, in a personal circ, not following others.
499. **eddie leonard**   Tr'g comb's done while trav'g in a circ; i.e., a circ of tr's.

INTRODUCTION TO PARTNERING
When the dancing of two or more dancers is personally interassociated, their dance relationship becomes unified as partners, often requiring interrelated staging. When a couple, the male frequently aids the female. Following are a few partnering related terms.

500. **partner**   [ptnr, <u>P</u>]   One of usually two (rarely more than four) dancers, each of whose dancing depends on the other(s).
501. **couple**   A pair of ptnr's; <u>B</u> and <u>G</u> unless otherwise specified.
502. **cavalier**   Ptnr who escorts and supports, presenting and displaying his ptnr. Assumed the male of a couple.
503. **overhand**   [o-Hn]   Place Hn palm dn, usually on ptnr's Hn, A, or leg.
504. **underhand**   [u-Hn]   Place Hn palm up, usually on ptnr's Hn, A, or leg.
505. **arch arms**   [arch A's]   With ptnr, join and raise Hn's over-H. One A each unless both A's specified.
506. **link**   Mutually join i/s of A's; e.g., link fore-A's, or link elbows.
507. **support**   A pos, usually w/ Hn(s), intended to maintain or move ptnr by balancing, turning, or lifting.
508. **pass**   Escort. Appearing to move ptnr by chg'g relative pos's (pass x bk) or support Hn's (pass lt to L Hn).

509.	**pull**, **push**	Usually w/ Hn, providing mvmt impetus. The pos may be used w/o actually providing assistance.
510.	**waist support**	Hn grip, usually both, on sd's of ptnr's waist, usually from behind (**back waist support**) w/ fingers fwd, thumb on back. Most common lift support.
511.	**front lift**	(Bk waist support, B behind) <u>Both</u> demi plié, <u>G</u> jumps vert'ly or slightly bk – <u>B</u> lifts bringing Hn's over chest into, vert'ly lift <u>G</u>'s waist above his Sh's, gently return <u>G</u> to standing or other specified pos. The basic lift. Displays the <u>G</u> thru a seq of elevated pos's i-p or while <u>B</u> trav's.
512.	**hip lift**	(<u>G</u> close rt) <u>B</u> pliés, hip low against <u>G</u>'s, (R A x <u>G</u>'s back, R Hn grasps <u>G</u>'s R waist a-s-t <u>G</u>'s L A x bk <u>B</u>'s Sh's or neck and grasps his L ribcage or Sh), <u>B</u> st'n legs into lift (tilt lt) supporting <u>G</u> on rt or r-d-f of hip – <u>G</u>'s legs to specified pos's; e.g., tuck Ft – knees l-d-f.

CLARIFICATIONS

It may seem ridiculous to define as dance terminology such words as back, front, down, and up. However, reading **ALTERNATE TERMINOLOGY** reveals many common words being ambiguously applied, many for over a century. An objective of this work is to elliminate confusion; to <u>know</u> that up-bk means lifted (or raised) rearward, not upstage.

In this publication the selected terms are defined as working tap vocabulary. Simpler definitions are commonly used; e.g.,

bandy twist	B/c x-over, ½-pvt.	a1 (2)
paddle turn	Step fwd R into pivot c-c-w tr, rock L, rpt step-pivot (finishing tr).	1 (2)
shim sham	Stomp frt R, sluff R c-p w/w, rev stomp-sluff 2 X's, step L, stomp-sluff R.	12 34 56&78

Neither the movements nor rhythmics are particularly interesting. Similarly, a maxie segment is often called a maxie ford or maxie turn, ignoring the maxie ford rhythm pattern.

The objective of the featured terminology is to provide a non-contradictory vocabulary with balanced consideration for tapping, moving, and understanding.

Slashed abbreviations are of three types:
2 sgl tap Ft chg's (b/c-like)	b/c, d/c. s/c, c/s, b/a
"with" related	w/, w/o, w/w, n/w
f-c-l related	t/f, t/i, t/o, i/s, o/s

Back slash:
do\undo	release\relink elbows
alt	fwd\bkwd

TERMINOLOGY INDEX

The TERMINOLOGY INDEX format is: **term**, *is found following* terminology number *or* heading *on* page number

4-count hitch kick, 107 pg. 6
4-tap riff walk, 93 pg. 6
4-tap riffle, 41 pg. 3
4-tap riffle eagle, 202 pg. 11
4-tap toe stand, 211 pg. 12
5-tap bmb w/ clip, 71 pg. 5
5-tap bombershay, 69 pg. 4
5-tap riff walk, 94 pg. 6
6-tap bombershay, 70 pg. 4
6-tap riff walk, 95 pg. 6
7-tap riff walk, 96 pg. 6
accelerando, 435 pg. 23
acceleration turn, 128 pg. 8
accent, 418 pg. 22
acrobatic-tap, 296 pg. 17
across, 347 pg. 20
alternate, 422 pg. 22
arch arms, 505 pg. 26
arched, 332 pg. 19
baby bombershay, 66 pg. 4
back, 476 pg. 25
back essence across front, 272 pg. 16
back essence break, 279 pg. 16
back essence combination, 272 pg. 16
back flap, 50 pg. 4
back paddle turn, 123 pg. 7
back riff, 38 pg. 3
back waist support, 510 pg. 27
backstage, 472 pg. 25
backup, 403 pg. 21
backward, 476 pg. 25
balancé, 62 pg. 4
balancoire, 361 pg. 20
ball change, 24 pg. 3
ball change cross-over, 25 pg. 3
ball change grapevine, 88 pg. 5
ball change turn, 114 pg. 7
ballroom, 266 pg. 15
bandy twist, 141 pg. 8
bandy twist turn, 143 pg. 8
banter, 396 pg. 21
barrel roll, 132 pg. 8
barrel turn, 132 pg. 8
basic buck time-step break comb, 254 pg. 14
battement, 359 pg. 20
battement wing, 187 pg. 10
battement wing turn, 188 pg. 11
battement wing twist, 188 pg. 11
bell, 164 pg. 9
bend, 321 pg. 19
bill robinson time-step, 259 pg. 15
blocking, 487 pg. 26
body line, 319 pg. 19
bombershay, 67 pg. 4
both, 308 pg. 18
bounce developpé, 108 pg. 6
bounce kick, 108 pg. 6

bounce passé, 108 pg. 6
Boy, 483 pg. 26
break, 415 pg. 22
break combination, 253 pg. 14
break-away, 29 pg. 3
break-out, 402 pg. 21
bridge, 445 pg. 23
broken rhythm, 456 pg. 23
brush, 6 pg. 2
buck and wing styling, BUCK & WING, pg. 16
buck styling, BUCK TIME-STEPS, pg. 13
buffalo, 63 pg. 4
buffalo turn, 116 pg. 7
button, 451 pg. 23
carriage, 311 pg. 18
catch, 16 pg. 2
catch-step, 26 pg. 3
cavalier, 502 pg. 26
Cecchetti stage directions, 469 pg. 25
center stage, 460 pg. 25
center stage left, 466 pg. 25
center stage right, 466 pg. 25
chaîné, 114 pg. 7
challenge, 290 pg. 17
change, 143 pg. 9
charleston rhythm pattern, 218 pg. 12
charleston swing, 219 pg. 12
chord, 439 pg. 23
choreography, 393 pg. 21
chorus, 444 pg. 23
chug, 19 pg. 2
chug both, 23 pg. 3
cincinnati, 59 pg. 4
circle, 498 pg. 26
classical tap, 292 pg. 17
clip, 22 pg. 2
clog, WHAT IS, pg. 1
close (footwork), 330 pg. 19
close riff, 39 pg. 3
close riff clog time-step, 235 pg. 13
closed position, 335 pg. 19
cluster (rhythm), 458 pg. 24
combination, 408 pg. 22
compass turn, 125 pg. 8
compound step, 62 pg. 4
consolidate, 497 pg. 26
count, 426 pg. 22
couple, 501 pg. 26
cramp, 30 pg. 3
cramproll, 148 pg. 9
cramproll cadence, 286 pg. 17
cramproll change, 149 pg. 9
cramproll pivot cadence, 287 pg. 17
cross, 347 pg. 20
cross bar, 262 pg. 15
crossed opposing arm swing, 372 pg. 20
cross-over, 348 pg. 20

cubanola, 261 pg. 15
dance form, 390 pg. 21
dance style, 392 pg. 21
dance type, 389 pg. 21, 391 pg. 21
deceleration turn, 129 pg. 8
demi, 351 pg. 20
developpé, 362 pg. 20
dig, 9 pg. 2
dig change, 27 pg. 3
dig time-step, 248 pg. 14
double arm swing, 373 pg. 20
double barrel turn, 139 pg. 8
double button, 451 pg. 23
double chug, 23 pg. 3
double cramproll, 152 pg. 9
double eagle, 195 pg. 11
double pickup, 170 pg. 10
double pickup change, 171 pg. 10
double pickup change toe-tap, 172 pg. 10
double pickup grapevine, 179 pg. 10
double pickup maxie, 228 pg. 12
double pickup roll, 176 pg. 10
double pickup roll change, 176 pg. 10
double riffle, 34 pg. 3
double scuffle, 34 pg. 3
double shuffle, 34 pg. 3
double time, 438 pg. 23
double time triple, 43 pg. 3
double time-step, 241 pg. 13
double triple break combination, 255 pg. 14
double triple clog time-step, 236 pg. 13
double triple roll clog time-step, 237 pg. 13
double triple time-step, 250 pg. 14
doubled, 65 pg. 4
doubled back essence, 274 pg. 16
doubled buffalo, 65 pg. 4
doubled clog time-step, 232 pg. 13
doubled front essence, 271 pg. 16
doubled glide, 207 pg. 11
doubled glide turn, 208 pg. 11
doubled riff walk, 97 pg. 6
down, 482 pg. 26
downstage, 461 pg. 25
downstage center, 463 pg. 25
downstage left, 467 pg. 25
downstage right, 468 pg. 25
downward, 482 pg. 26
draw, 356 pg. 20
draw-back, 46 pg. 3
draw-back break combination, 257 pg. 15
draw-back grapevine, 89 pg. 5
drum flap, 288 pg. 17
drum flap cadence, 289 pg. 17
drum slap, 288 pg. 17
duplet, triplet, etc., 453 pg. 23
dynamic accent, 418 pg. 22
eagle, 194 pg. 11
eagle change, 196 pg. 11
eagle rock, 105 pg. 6
eccentric riff walk, 98 pg. 6
eccentric styling, ECCENTRIC, pg. 17

eddie leonard, 499 pg. 26
en pointe, 210 pg. 12
english time-step, 249 pg. 14
entrance, 416 pg. 22
essence across back, 272 pg. 16
even rhythm, 452 pg. 23
exit, 417 pg. 22
extend, 374 pg. 20
face, 474 pg. 25
facing, 474 pg. 25
fade, 449 pg. 23
faked, 175 pg. 10
faked toe stand, 212 pg. 12
fall, 17 pg. 2
falling off a log, 297 pg. 17
falling off a log turn, 298 pg. 18
fan kick, 109 pg. 6
fifth position (arms), 369 pg. 20
fifth position (feet), 340 pg. 19
first position (arms), 366 pg. 20
first position (feet), 337 pg. 19
flap, 47 pg. 3
flap roll, 156 pg. 9
flap roll change, 149 pg. 9
flap roll change time-step, 258 pg. 15
flap saut de basque toe-tap, 127 pg. 8
flap turn, 115 pg. 7
flap-hop chaîné, 115 pg. 7
flapped, 80 pg. 5
flapped bombershay, 68 pg. 4
flapped buffalo, 64 pg. 4
flapped cramproll, 153 pg. 9
flapped diamond, 80 pg. 5
flapped grapevine, 87 pg. 5
flapped maxie, 221 pg. 12
flapped pas de bourrée turn, 115 pg. 7
flapped piqué turn, 115 pg. 7
flapped strut, 80 pg. 5
flash step, 401 pg. 21
flat foot, 331 pg. 19
flat hand, 380 pg. 20
flea hop, 304 pg. 18
flexed (foot/ankle), 333 pg. 19
flexed (hand/wrist), 376 pg. 20
focus, 325 pg. 19
forward, 475 pg. 25
forward flap, 49 pg. 4
fourth position (feet), 339 pg. 19
fred astaire time-step, 260 pg. 15
freestyle, 404 pg. 21
front, 475 pg. 25
front center line, 473 pg. 25
front essence combination, 272 pg. 16
front lift, 511 pg. 27
<u>Girl</u>, 483 pg. 26
glide, GLIDES and, pg. 11
grand, 351 pg. 20
grand battement, 359 pg. 20
grand plié, 351 pg. 20
grapevine, 86 pg. 5
<u>Group #</u>, 483 pg. 26

half break, 254 pg. 14
half log, 297 pg. 17
half-time, 437 pg. 23
hamp, 14 pg. 2
heel, 8 pg. 2
heel clip, 160 pg. 9
heel pivot, 110 pg. 7
heel riff clip, 163 pg. 9
heel roll, 145 pg. 9
heel spin, 215 pg. 12
heel stand, 27 pg. 3
heel to toe clip, 162 pg. 9
heel twist, 349 pg. 20
high (footwork), 329 pg. 19
hip lift, 512 pg. 27
hip wing, 189 pg. 11
hip wing maxie, 229 pg. 12
hitch kick, 106 pg. 6
hold, 317 pg. 19
hoofer, 398 pg. 21
hop, 11 pg. 2
hop clog time-step, 231 pg. 13
hop cramproll, 150 pg. 9
hop-over, 204 pg. 11
hopped barrel turn, 137 pg. 8
hopped maxie, 224 pg. 12
horizontal, 491 pg. 26
in place, 481 pg. 26
inside (of foot), 52 pg. 4
inside (rond de jambe), 109 pg. 7
inside (turns), TURNS, pg. 7
inside fan kick, 109 pg. 6
inside flap, 52 pg. 4
inside piqué turn, 118 pg. 7
inside pirouette, 119 pg. 7
interlaced, 383 pg. 21
interlocking, 328 pg. 19
interlocking time-steps, 263 pg. 15
interlude, 414 pg. 22
into, 315 pg. 19
introduction, 441 pg. 23
invert, 423 pg. 22
irish, 56 pg. 4
irish maxie, 225 pg. 12
irish turn, 117 pg. 7
irish twist, 140 pg. 8
isolate, 327 pg. 19
jazz diamond, 77 pg. 5
jazz hand, 381 pg. 20
jazz second (arms), 370 pg. 20
jazz triangle, 76 pg. 5
jazz-tap, 291 pg. 17
jump, 13 pg. 2
knee split jump, 305 pg. 18
lamp, 15 pg. 2
land, 354 pg. 20
lead, 313 pg. 18
lean, 323 pg. 19
leap, 12 pg. 2
leaped flap, 54 pg. 4
left, 478 pg. 25

Left, 307 pg. 18
left diagonal back, 480 pg. 26
left diagonal front, 480 pg. 26
leg spin, 300 pg. 18
legomania, 302 pg. 18
lindy, 216 pg. 12
lindy rhythm pattern, 217 pg. 12
line-of-direction, 489 pg. 26
link, 506 pg. 26
log glide, 299 pg. 18
long (footwork), 330 pg. 19
low (footwork), 329 pg. 19
low draw-back, 46 pg. 3
lunge, 355 pg. 20
march, 78 pg. 5
marque, 488 pg. 26
maxie ford, 221 pg. 12
maxie ford rhythm pattern, 222 pg. 12
maxie segment, 222 pg. 12
measure, 428 pg. 22
merge, 495 pg. 26
meter, 430 pg. 23
metronomic beat, 434 pg. 23
mid (footwork), 329 pg. 19
military styling, MILITARY, pg. 17
movement (body), 312 pg. 18
movement (music), 432 pg. 23
narrative dance, 395 pg. 21
natural, 345 pg. 19
natural plié, 351 pg. 20
natural relevé, 352 pg. 20
natural turn-out, 346 pg. 19
nerve roll, 157 pg. 9
neutral shoulder position, 379 pg. 20
note, 427 pg. 22
novelty, 294 pg. 17
offset, 263 pg. 15
off-stage, 471 pg. 25
onstage, 470 pg. 25
open diagonal, 480 pg. 26
open position, 336 pg. 19
opposing arm swing, 372 pg. 20
opposing shift (staging), 496 pg. 26
outside (of foot), 52 pg. 4
outside (rond de jambe), 109 pg. 7
outside (turns), TURNS, pg. 7
outside fan kick, 109 pg. 6
outside flap, 51 pg. 4
outside piqué turn, 118 pg. 7
outside pirouette, 119 pg. 7
overhand, 503 pg. 26
over-the-top, GLIDES and, pg. 11
paddle, 111 pg. 7
paddle turn, 122 pg. 7
parallel, 341 pg. 19
partner, 500 pg. 26
pas, 407 pg. 22
pas de bourrée, 75 pg. 5
pas de bourrée turn, 113 pg. 7
pass, 508 pg. 26
passé, 358 pg. 20

patter, 396 pg. 21
patter steps, 158 pg. 9
pattern, 406 pg. 22
pendulum, 102 pg. 6
pendulum cincinnati, 60 pg. 4
pendulum railroad arms, 388 pg. 21
pendulum wing, 191 pg. 11
personal style, 392 pg. 21
phrase (dance), 410 pg. 22
phrase (music), 431 pg. 23
pick up (music), 440 pg. 23
pickup (tap), 165 pg. 10
pickup change maxie, 227 pg. 12
pickup change toe-tap, 168 pg. 10
pickup change trench, 180 pg. 10
pickup irish, 174 pg. 10
pigeon-toe, 85 pg. 5
pigeon-toe roll, 147 pg. 9
piqué, 74 pg. 5
piqué turn, 118 pg. 7
pirouette, 119 pg. 7
pivot, 110 pg. 7
placement, 309 pg. 18
plié, 351 pg. 20
plié-relevé, 353 pg. 20
pointe tap, 295 pg. 17
port de bras, 365 pg. 20
pose, 318 pg. 19
preparation, 314 pg. 19
present, 378 pg. 20
preset, 484 pg. 26
press, 377 pg. 20
production, 268 pg. 15
pull, 509 pg. 27
pull-back, 173 pg. 10
pull-up, 310 pg. 18
push, 509 pg. 27
push barrel turn, 133 pg. 8
push turn, 120 pg. 7
quadruple, 44 pg. 3
quadruple time-step, 243 pg. 14
quadruplet irish, 57 pg. 4
railroad arms, 388 pg. 21
railroad series, 306 pg. 18
railroad styling, RAILROAD, pg. 18
rattle, 35 pg. 3
reach, 375 pg. 20
recover, 316 pg. 19
relevé, 352 pg. 20
renversé turn, 131 pg. 8
repeat, 420 pg. 22
reverse, 421 pg. 22
reversing barrel turns, 137 pg. 8
rhythm, 419 pg. 22
rhythm accent, 418 pg. 22
rhythm shift, 459 pg. 24
rhythm styling, RHYTHM, pg. 16
riff, 37 pg. 3
riff clip, 163 pg. 9
riff fouetté turn, 130 pg. 8
riff time-step, 245 pg. 14

riff turn, 126 pg. 8
riffed double pickup change, 178 pg. 10
riffed russian eagle, 202 pg. 11
riffle, 40 pg. 3
riffle time-step, 247 pg. 14
right, 478 pg. 25
Right, 307 pg. 18
right diagonal back, 479 pg. 26
right diagonal front, 479 pg. 26
ritardando, 436 pg. 23
rock, 350 pg. 20
rock'n, 31 pg. 3
rock'n roll, 146 pg. 9
roll, 144 pg. 9
roll change, 149 pg. 9
roll clog time-step, 234 pg. 13
rolling, ROLLS, pg. 9
rolling barrel turn, 134 pg. 8
rolling bombershay, 71 pg. 5
rolling rhythm, 454 pg. 23
rolling wing, 192 pg. 11
rolling wing change, 193 pg. 11
rond de jambe, 357 pg. 20
rond de jambe glide, 206 pg. 11
routine, 413 pg. 22
run, 73 pg. 5
running, 43 pg. 3
running double pickup change, 177 pg. 10
running flaps, 48 pg. 3
running glide, 209 pg. 12
running side riff, 101 pg. 6
running triple, 43 pg. 3
russian eagle, 201 pg. 11
russian wing, 200 pg. 11
sailor rock, 303 pg. 18
sand dance, 293 pg. 17
saut de basque, 127 pg. 8
scarecrow arms, 387 pg. 21
scissor (A's), 384 pg. 21
scissor cross, 384 pg. 21
scissor front (A's), 384 pg. 21
scissor kick, 103 pg. 6
scissor open, 384 pg. 21
scissor wing, 189 pg. 11
scoot, 21 pg. 2
scuff, 7 pg. 2
scuff time-step, 244 pg. 14
scuffle, 36 pg. 3
scuffle time-step, 246 pg. 14
second position (arms), 367 pg. 20
second position (feet), 338 pg. 19
section, 412 pg. 22
segment, 409 pg. 22
segue, 446 pg. 23
sequence, 405 pg. 21
set, set on, 394 pg. 21
shading, 397 pg. 21
shave and a haircut - -, 220 pg. 12
shift (staging), 496 pg. 26
shim, 280 pg. 16
shim sham, 281 pg. 16

shim sham combination, 282 pg. 16
shim sham rhythm pattern, 282 pg. 16
shim sham styling, SHIM SHAM, pg. 16
shine, 400 pg. 21
short (footwork), 330 pg. 19
shorty george, 82 pg. 5
shuffle, 32 pg. 3
shuffle across, 33 pg. 3
shuffle double pickup grapevine shim sham, 284 pg. 17
shuffle into double pickup, 175 pg. 10
shuffle off to Buffalo, 63 pg. 4
shuffle pickup change, 169 pg. 10
side, 477 pg. 25
side riff, 100 pg. 6
side riffle, 99 pg. 6
side scissor kick, 104 pg. 6
sideward, 477 pg. 25
signature, 399 pg. 21
single back essence, 273 pg. 16
single front essence, 270 pg. 16
single glide, 205 pg. 11
single pickup, 166 pg. 10
single pickup change, 167 pg. 10
single time-step, 240 pg. 13
single time-step break, 253 pg. 14
single waltz clog time-step, 230 pg. 13
skip, 45 pg. 3
slap, 55 pg. 4
slap roll, 155 pg. 9
slide, 20 pg. 2
sliding cincinnati, 58 pg. 4
sliding irish, 58 pg. 4
sliding irish turn, 117 pg. 7
sluefoot, 91 pg. 5
sluff, 18 pg. 2
sluff pirouette, 124 pg. 7
sluff turn, 124 pg. 7
snake hips, 90 pg. 5
snap, 10 pg. 2
snap kick, 363 pg. 20
snap roll, 145 pg. 9
snap turn, 121 pg. 7
soft shoe, WHAT IS, pg. 1
soft shoe essence combination, 272 pg. 16
soft shoe essence rhythm pattern, 272 pg. 16
soft shoe styling, SOFT SHOE, pg. 16
soft shoe time-step, 277 pg. 16
soft shoe time-step break, 278 pg. 16
song and dance, 265 pg. 15
sophisticated, 264 pg. 15
spotted barrel turn, 133 pg. 8
spotting, 326 pg. 19
stage left, 464 pg. 25
stage right, 465 pg. 25
staggered, 494 pg. 26
staging, 486 pg. 26
stamp, 4 pg. 2
stamp change, 28 pg. 3
stamp step shim sham, 285 pg. 17
stamped maxie, 221 pg. 12
standards, 406 pg. 22

standing cramproll, 151 pg. 9
standing cramproll change, 149 pg. 9
standing heel clip, 160 pg. 9
standing toe clip, 159 pg. 9
Step, 411 pg. 22
step (basic movement), 1 pg. 2
step (pas), 407 pg. 22
step style, 392 pg. 21
step-over, 203 pg. 11
step-toe-tap chaîné, 115 pg. 7
stomp, 5 pg. 2
stomp cramp time-step, 251 pg. 14
stomp time-step, 248 pg. 14
stomp wing movement time-step, 252 pg. 14
stomp wing time-step, 252 pg. 14
stop time, 448 pg. 23
strolling clog time-step, 238 pg. 13
strut, 79 pg. 5
style, 392 pg. 21
sugar foot, 81 pg. 5
support, 507 pg. 26
suzie-q, 84 pg. 5
sway, 324 pg. 19
swing kick, 360 pg. 20
swinging flap, 53 pg. 4
swinging wings, 184 pg. 10
syncopate, 457 pg. 24
syncopated draw-back break combination, 257 pg. 15
tacit, 447 pg. 23
tack annie, 283 pg. 16
tag, 450 pg. 23
tap, 2 pg. 2
tap strut, 80 pg. 5
tap styles, TAP DANCE STYLES, pg. 13
tap-clip, 162 pg. 9
tapping, WHAT IS, pg. 1
taps, WHAT IS, pg. 1
tempo, 433 pg. 23
tendu, 334 pg. 19
third position (arms), 368 pg. 20
three-step turn, 112 pg. 7
tiller, 267 pg. 15
tiller arms back, 386 pg. 21
tiller arms second, 385 pg. 21
tiller line, 493 pg. 26
tilt, 322 pg. 19
time, 429 pg. 22
time factor, BUCK TIME-STEPS, pg. 13
time signature, 430 pg. 23
times, 425 pg. 22
time-step, 239 pg. 13
time-step rhythm pattern, 239 pg. 13
tip (of toes), 3 pg. 2
toe clip, 159 pg. 9
toe riff clip, 163 pg. 9
toe slide, 213 pg. 12
toe slide both, 213 pg. 12
toe spin, 214 pg. 12
toe stand, 210 pg. 12
toe stand both, 210 pg. 12
toe stand wing, 190 pg. 11

toe to heel clip, 161 pg. 9
toe-tap, 3 pg. 2
toe-tap clog time-step, 233 pg. 13
toe-tap time-step, 249 pg. 14
trademark, 399 pg. 21
travel, 485 pg. 26
traveling bandy twist, 142 pg. 8
traveling barrel turn, 135 pg. 8
traveling cramproll, 154 pg. 9
traveling eagle, 197 pg. 11
traveling eagle change, 196 pg. 11
traveling essence, 276 pg. 16
traveling hopped barrel turn, 138 pg. 8
traveling rock'n, 31 pg. 3
traveling wing, 185 pg. 10
traveling wing change, 186 pg. 10
trench, 92 pg. 5
triple, 42 pg. 3
triple cincinnati, 61 pg. 4
triple cramproll, 152 pg. 9
triple pendulum cincinnati, 61 pg. 4
triple time-step, 242 pg. 13
triplet eagle, 199 pg. 11
triplet wing, 198 pg. 11
triple-triple break combination, 256 pg. 14
tuck, 364 pg. 20
turn port de bras, 109 pg. 7
turn-front, 342 pg. 19
turn-in, 344 pg. 19
turning irish maxie, 226 pg. 12
turning maxie, 226 pg. 12
turning pickup change maxie, 226 pg. 12
turn-out, 343 pg. 19

twisting, 139 pg. 8
twisting shorty, 83 pg. 5
underhand, 504 pg. 26
uneven rhythm, 455 pg. 23
up, 482 pg. 26
up-line-of-direction, 490 pg. 26
upright, 320 pg. 19
upstage, 462 pg. 25
upstage center, 463 pg. 25
upstage left, 467 pg. 25
upstage right, 468 pg. 25
up-tempo, 433 pg. 23
upward, 482 pg. 26
vamp, 442 pg. 23
variation, 424 pg. 22
V-arms, 371 pg. 20
V-arms front, 371 pg. 20
vernacular, 269 pg. 15
verse, 443 pg. 23
vertical, 492 pg. 26
vibrate, 382 pg. 21
virginia essence, 275 pg. 16
virginia essence combination, 275 pg. 16
waist support, 510 pg. 27
walk, 72 pg. 5
walking barrel turn, 136 pg. 8
waltz clog maxie, 223 pg. 12
waltz clog styling, WALTZ CLOG, pg. 13
waltz clog time-step rhythm pattern, 230 pg. 13
wiggle sticks, 301 pg. 18
wing, 182 pg. 10
wing change, 183 pg. 10
wing movement, 181 pg. 10

ABBREVIATIONS INDEX

Most abbreviations may become plural, or vary tense or form by ending: 's, 'd, 'g, 'ly, 'n , 'r, 'rs. They may also be expanded when hyphenated with other words or syllables; e.g., fore-A, over-H.

The **ABBREVIATIONS INDEX** format is: [abbreviation], *is found following* terminology number *or* heading *on* page number

[-], 62 pg. 4
[--] or [–], 66 pg. 4
[- brk], 254 pg. 14
[- d-b-brk], 257 pg. 15
[- d-t-brk], 255 pg. 14
[- sync-d-b-brk], 257 pg. 15
[- t-t-brk], 256 pg. 14
[→], 485 pg. 26
[&, a, e, i], 459 pg. 24
[(*silent counts*)], 459 pg. 24
[//], 341 pg. 19
[-], 19 pg. 2
[{*even rhythm*}], 459 pg. 24
[½-log], 297 pg. 17
[½-X], 437 pg. 23
[1st] (arms), 366 pg. 20
[1st] (feet), 337 pg. 19
[2nd] (arms), 367 pg. 20
[2nd] (feet), 338 pg. 19
[3rd], 368 pg. 20
[3rd frt], 368 pg. 20
[3-step tr], 112 pg. 7
[4th], 339 pg. 19
[5st] (arms), 369 pg. 20
[5th] (feet), 340 pg. 19
[A, A's], 365 pg. 20
[**a1**] (bold rhythm notation), 28 pg. 3
[alt], 422 pg. 22
[alt'ly], 86 pg. 5
[annie], 283 pg. 16
[arch A's], 505 pg. 26
[a-s-t], 13 pg. 2
[b/a], 29 pg. 3
[b/c], 24 pg. 3
[b/c gpvn], 88 pg. 5
[b/c tr], 114 pg. 7
[b/c x-over], 25 pg. 3
[**B**], 483 pg. 26
[bal], 62 pg. 4
[batt], 359 pg. 20
[batt wing], 187 pg. 10
[batt wing tr], 188 pg. 11
[bgn], TAP TERMINOLOGY, pg. 2
[bgn'rs], 66 pg. 4
[bk], 476 pg. 25
[bk ess comb], 272 pg. 16
[bk ess x frt], 272 pg. 16
[bk ess], 273 pg. 16
[bk-ess-brk], 279 pg. 16
[bkwd], 476 pg. 25
[bmb], 67 pg. 4
[br], 6 pg. 2
[brk], 415 pg. 22
[brk comb], 253 pg. 14
[-b-r-t-s], 259 pg. 15

[b-t tr], 143 pg. 8
[b-t], 141 pg. 8
[buff], 63 pg. 4
[buff tr], 116 pg. 7
[c/s], 26 pg. 3
[c-c-w], 109 pg. 7
[ch], 114 pg. 7
[chg], 24 pg. 3
[chor], 393 pg. 21
[cinc], 59 pg. 4
[circ], 498 pg. 26
[close-riff-c-t-s], 235 pg. 13
[comb], 408 pg. 22
[cont], 109 pg. 6
[c-p], 335 pg. 19
[c-r], 148 pg. 9
[c-r-c], 149 pg. 9
[C-S], 460 pg. 25
[C-S-L], 466 pg. 25
[C-S-R], 466 pg. 25
[ct], 426 pg. 22
[ctr], 109 pg. 7
[c-t-s], 230 pg. 13
[c-w], 109 pg. 7
[d/c], 27 pg. 3
[d-A-s], 373 pg. 20
[d-b], 46 pg. 3
[d-b gpvn], 89 pg. 5
[dbl bk ess], 274 pg. 16
[dbl ess], 271 pg. 16
[dbl-buff], 65 pg. 4
[dbl-eagle], 195 pg. 11
[dbl-glide], 207 pg. 11
[dbl-glide tr], 208 pg. 11
[dbl-riffle], 34 pg. 3
[dbl-scfl], 34 pg. 3
[dbl-shfl], 34 pg. 3
[dbl-X], 438 pg. 23
[-d-c-t-s], 232 pg. 13
[dev], 362 pg. 20
[diag], 102 pg. 6
[dir], 6 pg. 2
[dn], 482 pg. 26
[dnwd], 482 pg. 26
[dplt], 56 pg. 4
[d-p-u], 170 pg. 10
[d-p-u-c], 171 pg. 10
[d-p-u-c-tt], 172 pg. 10
[d-p-u-gpvn], 179 pg. 10
[d-p-u-maxie], 228 pg. 12
[d-p-u-r], 176 pg. 10
[d-p-u-r-c], 176 pg. 10
[D-S], 461 pg. 25
[D-S-C], 463 pg. 25
[D-S-L], 467 pg. 25

[D-S-R], 468 pg. 25
[-d-t-c-t-s], 236 pg. 13
[-d-t-roll-c-t-s], 237 pg. 13
[d-t-s], 241 pg. 13
[d-t-t-s], 250 pg. 14
[eagle chg], 196 pg. 11
[ent], 416 pg. 22
[ess], 270 pg. 16
[ess comb], 272 pg. 16
[ess x bk], 272 pg. 16
[F], 325 pg. 19
[-f-a-t-s], 260 pg. 15
[f-c-l], 473 pg. 25
[flapped gpvn], 87 pg. 5
[flap-shfl-p-u-c-tt], 127 pg. 8
[flat Hn], 380 pg. 20
[flat], 331 pg. 19
[flr], 8 pg. 2
[f-r], 156 pg. 9
[f-r-c], 149 pg. 9
[-f-r-c-t-s], 258 pg. 15
[frt], 475 pg. 25
[frt ess comb], 272 pg. 16
[Ft], 1 pg. 2
[fwd], 475 pg. 25
[G], 483 pg. 26
[glide], 203, 204, 205 pg. 11
[gpvn], 86 pg. 5
[gr batt], 359 pg. 20
[gr], 351 pg. 20
[Grp #], 483 pg. 26
[grp], 306 pg. 18
[H], 121 pg. 7
[hitch], 106 pg. 6
[Hn], 16 pg. 2
[hop c-r], 150 pg. 9
[hop-c-t-s], 231 pg. 13
[horz], 491 pg. 26
[h-t], 349 pg. 20
[i/s], 52 pg. 4
[i/s flap], 52 pg. 4
[intro], 441 pg. 23
[inv], 423 pg. 22
[i-p], 481 pg. 26
[isol], 327 pg. 19
[jazz 2nd] (arms), 370 pg. 20
[jazz Hn], 381 pg. 20
[L], 307 pg. 18
[l-d-b], 480 pg. 26
[l-d-f], 480 pg. 26
[line], 319 pg. 19
[l-o-d], 489 pg. 26
[log], 297 pg. 17
[log tr], 298 pg. 18
[low 1st] (arms), 366 pg. 20
[low 3rd], 368 pg. 20
[lt], 478 pg. 25
[M], 428 pg. 22
[maxie], 221 pg. 12
[met], 434 pg. 23
[mvmt], 312 pg. 18
[n/w], 3 pg. 2

[nat], 345 pg. 19
[n-Sh-p], 379 pg. 20
[n-t/o], 346 pg. 19
[o/s], 51 pg. 4
[o/s flap], 51 pg. 4
[o/s] (side of shoe), 51 pg. 4
[o-A-s], 372 pg. 20
[oclt], 202 pg. 11
[off-stg], 471 pg. 25
[o-Hn], 503 pg. 26
[o-p], 336 pg. 19
[opp shift], 496 pg. 26
[opp], 81 pg. 5
[over-H], 368 pg. 20
[P], 500 pg. 26
[paddle tr], 122 pg. 7
[patt], 406 pg. 22
[p-b], 173 pg. 10
[p-d-b], 75 pg. 5
[p-d-b tr], 113 pg. 7
[pend cinc], 60 pg. 4
[pend], 102 pg. 6
[pend-r-r-A's], 388 pg. 21
[piq tr], 118 pg. 7
[piq], 74 pg. 5
[pir], 119 pg. 7
[pos], 8 pg. 2
[p-r], 353 pg. 20
[prep], 314 pg. 19
[ptnr], 500 pg. 26
[p-u], 165 pg. 10
[p-u-c], 167 pg. 10
[p-u-c-maxie], 227 pg. 12
[p-u-c-trench], 180 pg. 10
[p-u-c-tt], 168 pg. 10
[p-u-irish], 174 pg. 10
[pvt], 110 pg. 7
[qdl], 44 pg. 3
[qdlt irish], 57 pg. 4
[qdlt], 34 pg. 3
[qnlt], 64 pg. 4
[q-t-s], 243 pg. 14
[R], 307 pg. 18
[r-c], 149 pg. 9
[r-d-b], 479 pg. 26
[r-d-f], 479 pg. 26
[r-d-j glide], 206 pg. 11
[r-d-j], 357 pg. 20
[rel], 352 pg. 20
[rev], 421 pg. 22
[-riff-t-s], 245 pg. 14
[riffed-d-p-u-c], 178 pg. 10
[-riffle-t-s], 247 pg. 14
[-roll-c-t-s], 234 pg. 13
[rout], 413 pg. 22
[rpt], 420 pg. 22
[r-r-], 306 pg. 18
[r-r-A's], 388 pg. 21
[rt], 478 pg. 25
[running-d-p-u-c], 177 pg. 10
[s/c], 28 pg. 3
[scfl], 36 pg. 3

[-scfl-t-s], 246 pg. 14
[-scuff-t-s], 244 pg. 14
[sd], 477 pg. 25
[sd riff], 100 pg. 6
[sd riffle], 99 pg. 6
[sdwd], 477 pg. 25
[seq], 405 pg. 21
[sgl bk ess], 273 pg. 16
[sgl ess], 270 pg. 16
[sgl], 1 pg. 2
[sgr], 81 pg. 5
[Sh], 84 pg. 5
[sham], 281 pg. 16
[shfl], 32 pg. 3
[shfl-d-p-u], 175 pg. 10
[shfl-d-p-u-tt], 175 pg. 10
[shfl-p-u-c], 169 pg. 10
[shfl-p-u-c-tt], 169 pg. 10
[shfl-x], 33 pg. 3
[shift (rhythm)], 459 pg. 24
[shim sham], 282 pg. 16
[shorty], 82 pg. 5
[S-L], 464 pg. 25
[-soft-shoe-t-s], 277 pg. 16
[soft-shoe-t-s-brk], 278 pg. 16
[splt], 96 pg. 6
[s-p-u], 166 pg. 10
[s-r], 155 pg. 9
[S-R], 465 pg. 25
[st], 92 pg. 5
[standing-c-r], 151 pg. 9
[stg], 63 pg. 4
[stg'g], 486 pg. 26
[-stomp-cramp-t-s], 251 pg. 14
[-stomp-t-s], 248 pg. 14
[-stomp-wm-t-s], 252 pg. 14
[stop-X], 448 pg. 23
[strolling-c-t-s], 238 pg. 13
[s-t-s], 240 pg. 13
[s-t-s - brk], 253 pg. 14
[s-w-c-t-s], 230 pg. 13
[sxlt], 95 pg. 6
[sync], 457 pg. 24
[t/f], 342 pg. 19
[t/i], 344 pg. 19
[t/o], 343 pg. 19

[thru], 109 pg. 6
[tpl], 42 pg. 3
[tpl-cinc], 61 pg. 4
[tpl-c-r], 152 pg. 9
[tpl-pend-cinc], 61 pg. 4
[tplt], 40 pg. 3
[tr A's], 109 pg. 7
[tr prep], 109 pg. 7
[tr], 109 pg. 6
[trav b-t], 142 pg. 8
[trav eagle], 197 pg. 11
[trav ess], 276 pg. 16
[trav], 485 pg. 26
[trav-c-r], 154 pg. 9
[t-s], TIME-STEP, pg. 13
[tt], 3 pg. 2
[-tt-c-t-s], 233 pg. 13
[t-t-s], 242 pg. 13
[-tt-t-s], 249 pg. 14
[twd], 50 pg. 4
[u-Hn], 504 pg. 26
[u-l-o-d], 490 pg. 26
[upwd], 482 pg. 26
[U-S], 462 pg. 25
[U-S-C], 463 pg. 25
[U-S-L], 467 pg. 25
[U-S-R], 468 pg. 25
[V-A's frt], 371 pg. 20
[V-A's], 371 pg. 20
[var], 424 pg. 22
[vert], 492 pg. 26
[v-ess comb], 275 pg. 16
[v-ess], 275 pg. 16
[w/], 2 pg. 2
[w/o], 19 pg. 2
[w/w], 8 pg. 2
[w-c], 92 pg. 5
[-w-c-maxie], 223 pg. 12
[wing-chg], 183 pg. 10
[wm], 181 pg. 10
[wt], 1 pg. 2
[x], 347 pg. 20
[X], 429 pg. 22
[X's], 425 pg. 22
[x-o-A-s], 372 pg. 20
[x-over], 348 pg. 20

DEVELOPING PERSONAL TECHNIQUE

Tap dancing should be interesting to hear, enjoyable to watch, and comfortable to perform. Once a student is familiar with basic steps routines, training needs to include some attention to improved sound clarity and ease of movement. Some initial considerations:

Although sluffs and slides are legitimate tap sounds, the vast majority of taps should be *sharp*, *clear*, and *clean* (obviously separated from other taps). Taps should be clearly heard, not excessively loud, the majority performed with minimal floor contact. At any tempo, clean taps should be struck instantaneously, not slid along the floor, with successive tap sounds not adjoined. Unless performing a sand dance, *sluffy* tapping is not desireable.

Rhythmics need to be accurate, coordinated with the accompaniment and consistently patterned. If simple duple rhythm (a1 a2 etc.) cannot be reliably performed ending on the musical count, shifted and increasingly complex rhythms are unlikely to be reliable. Consistency begins with flaps and triples *marched* at slower tempos, then *run* at faster tempos starting before and ending on the musical count. Once simple rhythmics are dependable, begin on the count, then experiment with mixed rhythms and syncopation, seeking reliable repetition. Mentally 'hear' the rhythms.

Volume accents should be selectively controlled (shaded). A basic awareness exercise is to sequence a phrase of taps (as simple as snaps or shuffles) on the musical count, initially done with all the same volume 1 2 3 4 5 6 7 8, then accent (make louder) the primary counts (first of each measure) **1** 2 3 4 **5** 6 7 8. Each successive 2M shifts the accent 1 count 1 **2** 3 4 5 **6** 7 8 1 2 **3** 4 5 6 **7** 8 etc. As with music, loud is not better, controlled variation is. Keep in mind that most tap combinations are rhythm accented, not dynamically accented. Continuous pounding is not tapping, it is noise. As with syncopation, selectively place dynamic accents, arranging interesting rhythm emphasis.

Buoyancy is the foundation of *easy* tap movement. Nearly all tapping is done in relevé with the knees slightly bent while supported on the ball of one foot at a time. Balancing and moving in plié-relevé needs to <u>be</u> comfortable to <u>look</u> natural. Do not tap flat footed with heels resting on the floor – even most supportive heeldrops and stamps are sustained less than a count before heels leave the floor. Spend tap time on the balls of the feet, using the arms to comfortably counterbalance your body as you move. Moving in tap shoes should feel easy and appear to float, even when performing twists, turns, elevations, large movements, or most eccentric combinations.

Quicken leg/ankle coordination. Technique development requires replacement of larger, slower leg/knee movements with smaller, quicker ankle/arch movements. Begin by practicing ankle shuffle coordination, not merely forward\backward, but also sideward, diagonally, and, with a slight lower leg swing, in small circles. Relaxed, flexible, quick, accurate ankle coordination is a valuable asset. As tempos increase, nearly all movements must be compacted. A dig becomes an in place ankle flex, a riff is created with a quick twist of the ankle, a hop becomes a heeldrop, etc. When needed, economize movement while maintaining tap clarity. Established slower styling and an extended body line are easily recovered when desired.

Expand your step repertoire. The steps and tap styles herein listed are a solid beginning but far from a complete catalog. The sequel, adds early 20th century fad styles (Cakewalk through Boogie) and Latin (Flamenco through Calypso) styles; as well as, an expansion of basic steps including additional approaches to time-steps and wings. Still to come are jigs and hornpipes, country clog, up-tempo sophisticated, jazz-tap, etc. There are thousands of tap steps and variations, dozens of tap interpreted dance styles. I hope you will enjoy exploring them.

However,

Dancing is moving. The primary purpose of theater dance training is improved coordination, including traveling. Theater dancing is intended to entertain, to be interesting; both audibly and visually when tapping. As with other theater dance forms, use the stage, cover area, don't get stuck in one spot.

The single greatest improvement results from expanded overall dance and associated skills. Ballet is the foundation of all aesthetic movement. Jazz and modern dance encourage experimentation with personal and musical styles. Ballroom, folk dance, and character dance study offers partnering and characterization experience. Acrobatics permit expanded eccentric styling and surprise unique staging. Cane and hat handling, juggling, maracas, cape, and many other props open new audio and action opportunities. Tapping is only the beginning.

Finally, the performance is the thing. Whether the objective is professional performance or personal satisfaction, when a natural appearance results from natural movement, it is time to attend to interpretation. Consider and experiment with every aspect of presentation that increases performer and viewer enjoyment. This is where the student becomes the dancer.

APPLICATION EXAMPLE

Communication is the reason for terminology. Pursue accuracy. Anytime you are talking tap and you sense confusion, seek immediate clarification. Understanding is communication. The greatest value offered by language is the storage and transport of ideas – writing. To access the wealth of tap dance ideas, you will need to read dance notes. Although there are written references from the 18th century, since 1930 thousands of routines have been preserved, a legacy untouchable by video or word of mouth. This is the archived history of tap dancing. An increasing interest in tapping eventually leads to reading tap notes; composing dances to writing them.

Actually, this entire book is an example of terminology and notation. To illustrate a common routine notation structure, following is an introduction and entrance Step for a training soft shoe. Note left column accompaniment references.

INTERMEDIATE RHYTHM - SOFT SHOE

An interesting performance soft shoe with varied staging and interspersed surprise syncopation.
Music: 4M intro + 2 choruses, relaxing $^4/_4$ meter, about 120 met   Choreography: Terry Dill

INTRO

4M   Wait off S-L.

STEP ONE - ENTRANCE

    (Face and trav C-S) flap-heel R (face U-S), tt L x bk R, flap-b/c L (face D-S), flap R l-o-d into c-w tr, L shfl-p-u-c-tt R x bk L,
                 a1   a   2   a3 a4   a5   {a6 & a 7}
    step R U-S (face S-R).
2M   && (8)
    Flap L lt, bk ess's R–L (st A's 2nd), (slight bend lt-bk, bk paddle tr L w/o lead flap L -- bkwd c-w tr:) bk flap R, step L i-p,
       a1   a2a3   a4a5   {&a   6
    rpt flap-step 2 X's (end facing S-R).
2M   &a 7 &a8}
4M   Rpt above 4M (end facing D-S).
8M   (Where is the lead flap for the bk paddle tr?)

NOTATION FORMAT

There are three general format structures for dance notation: horizontal, vertical, and simple paragraph. There are several variations of horizontal and vertical, but in general:
    horizontal is a sentence structure,
    vertical is a multi-column structure (see **Recognize anything?**, page78),
    simple paragraph structure lists a Step of steps and staging (few rhythm or music references) per paragraph (page 77).

The choreographic notation horizontal format used here is quite efficient, requiring less paper than vertical, and has several user advantages.
    1. Readable left to right by dance phrase or combination.
    2. Efficiently spaced, allowing easy flow of reading analysis, more visually compact than vertical, with
    3. Visually inclusive rhythm notation.
    4. Easy choreographic structure analysis with evident Step, phrase, combination, steps.
    5. Music phrase location. (For live accompaniment, sequentially number the music measures, paralleling the score.)
    6. Coordination flow analysis (body support and staging).
    7. Appropriately located supplemental information.
    8. Accurate rhythm location (usually under specific action).
    9. Space available for annotation or revision.

THE PARTS   {see above example}

After the composition title {**INTERMEDIATE RHYTHM – SOFT SHOE**} is an introductory statement {An interesting performance . . . .} providing a perspective of the what, why, and special requirements (if any) of the piece.

Next is intended accompaniment {Music:} (left) and source {Choreography:} (right). The music phrasing progresses down the left side of the notes including a total {**8M**} for each Step or interlude.

Each dance Step or music interlude {**INTRO**} is a subtitled paragraph and may include expanded identification {**STEP ONE – ENTRANCE**} or be followed by an introductory statement {none above}. These paragraphs are subdivided into phrases notated as sentences.

The dance steps are arranged: step, lead, location (placement) {tt L x bk R}, plus supplemental body {(st A's 2nd), (slight bend lt-bk, . . .)}, travel, or other movement information {(. . . bkwd c-w tr)}, usually in parentheses. Supplemental information preceding a step(s) {Face and trav C-S)} usually provides preparatory guidance, trailing information {(face U-S)} is for inclusion or completion of the step. Occasionally a pre-combination explanation is useful. Ending with a colon {(. . . bkwd c-w tr:)} indicates that it relates to the notes which immediately follow. A period concludes each dance phrase {(end facing S-R).}. An occasional NOTE: {none in example} can be inserted between Steps or phrases. A NOTE: provides expanded production or performance information: added details, alternate staging, set or scene changes, lighting cues, etc. A routine conclusion is indicated; e.g., **FINIS** (see **ROUTINES** for further examples.).

READING NOTES

-Begin at the beginning: title, introduction, music, choreographer. Get a feel for the piece. Next, check the technical level. Read the step sequence, analyzing your understanding of its performance difficulty. Continue through the notes until assured that your analyses are reasonable.

Back to the beginning to add staging. Visualize the travel, rotation, and facing sequences. Mentally or physically marque the combinations, acquiring an understanding of the choreographic flow. If there are coordination problems, reanalyze the notes. Even while seated, footwork and placement can be sensed. Always keep in mind possible interpretation problems. Terms may be differently defined or be new to you, steps varied, notation may include typographical errors, be a different format or layout, or character or choreographic style may influence body placement. (ALTERNATE TERMINOLOGY may prove helpful.)

Once a few phrases move comfortably, include the rhythm. Again, rhythm notation varies with source and step interpretation. One of the advantages of knowing the writer's material, from notes or performance, is an expectation of his established personal style, step selections, and rhythm structures. Marqueing should now include rhythm flow. Check accompaniment for tempo, music style, and title. 120 met is 2 counts per second. "One one-thousand , two one-thousand" is a handy mechanism worth practicing. It can serve as a basis for estimating tempo and is usually suitable for initial rhythm marqueing. Future marqueing should approach a working tempo.

If you are not familiar with the titled music, make an effort to hear an instrumental arrangement, preferably that listed. Initially notice meter and melodic rhythm, then any countering harmony or bass rhythms. If a song, the lyrics may clarify characterization, mood, or even some specific points of action or rhythm emphasis.

Repeat the above process as you procede through the routine. Hopefully, it will yield some new dance insights, ideas, combinations, steps, or prove worth developing for class or performance. Ultimately, if performed, it is your decision to attempt rote duplication or adapt it to your personal needs or taste. In either event, credit the original source. It is common courtesy.

VIDEO vs. NOTES

For new choreography, why waste time with terminology and producing notes? Just make a video. It's faster, and you can see everything. Think so?

View a tap video, several times. Perform the tapping from memory, while watching, or did you take notes? How about the staging? Are you sure of each step? Which part? Does it sound correct? Tap with the video. OK, but can you discriminate your taps? Is it comfortable to perform? Is there something different about the styling? Is it personal or integral to the routine? Better check movement throughout the entire video again. Although some terms are different, the included verbal instructions help, but what is a 5-tap wing? Slow the video. What's the ankle doing? Try again. Well, it gets by. Is that combination repeated in Step Three? Is the Step Seven break a variation combining breaks from Steps Four and Five? Back up the video, then jump to Step Seven. Are you sure of the combined sequences? So you think that should be changed. Hope you remember the change and where to insert it. Now try the routine without the video. Think you have it? Have you saved enough time, yet?

To answer the initial question: well composed notes include more functional information available relatively quickly, being easily sequenced and cross referenced. Video has learning values, illustrating presentation and choreographic style, skill level, and performance effectiveness. Even for sophisticated tapping, video provides an immediate appreciation of interesting syncopation, yet notes clarify footwork. When creating new material, notes are far more easily recorded, reviewed, and revised - the only way to go.

WRITING NOTES

The purpose of this book is communication, the production of unambiguous descriptions of tapping useable to accurately recreate coordination, rhythm, staging, and style of a step, combination, or tap dance.

When creating new material, jot down key ideas as they coalesce. Annotate changes as they become relavent. When done with the session, review the notes, confirming sufficient clarity for your future interpretation. Personal notes can be sloppy, but unreferenced for a significant time, what originally was obvious may no longer be. Greater detail is always helpful, and for others, essential.

Notation builds from feet and steps; coordination from placement (movement direction and support). Write a phrase of steps with leads. If staging or style are not crucial, continue building phrases to complete a Step. Now, SEE the Step. Add staging with necessary styling (facing, arms, focus, isolations, characterization, etc.). Next, HEAR it and notate rhythm at accurate locations or as rhythm phrases. Notate enough material to establish choreographic continuity. Proof to elliminate errors. Allow the piece, and the notes, to develop through each choreographic session until done. Notate a first 'final' draft for easy recollection.

Eventually, an archival copy should be rendered. Unlike personal notes, archival notes should be understandable by anyone. Here is the hard part, frequently made easier by waiting a day. FORGET THE ROUTINE. The next reading is a communication proof. Marque the notes as literally written, then REMEMBER AND COMPARE. Do the notes describe the dance? Reread and clarify the questionable documentation. If in doubt, tap the notes (not what you remember) for comparison. Repeat the process until satisfied. Wait a few days then proof again. It is likely you will find the return justified.

If you find a volunteer, have them interpret the notes. Discuss any questions or performance variance, improving notation clarity. This requires effort but assures improved communication and reproduction worthy of your choreography.

A PERSONAL ASIDE

As a teenage dance student and teacher in the post vaudeville 1950s, the best source of dance material was motion pictures and television. I always carried a pocket notebook and pen (still do) and, in the dark, would blind-notate steps and combinations while viewing. The practice proved invaluable and I occasionally revive it.

Flip back to ROUTINES and try the initial analysis approach described in the first paragraph of READING NOTES.

A DISCUSSION

Following is an assortment of tapping perspectives and challenges, as well as, information useful to any theater performer plus a few interesting backstories. Instructors may find items worth inserting into their classes. Much of the steps and combinations information has been derived from post-1920s dance notes, the dates frequently guesstimated. Tap dancing should be interesting, and is, more so than you may be aware. As you have the opportunity, view the referenced and other motion picture performances. If any challenges are confusing, skip them. After more tapping experience, give them another try. Let's find out what you know and more you can discover by discussing tap.

For help, see the following **DISCUSSION ASSISTANCE**.

TAPS and STANCE

Why tapping?
Ask any youngster newly donning his first tap shoes – noise is fun! "Life is rhythm" is equally simplistic, but sound is interesting and making it viewably surprising can be fascinating, even inspiring. If you haven't already tapped, give it a try. You'll likely like it.

Accurate sloppiness:
Most tap terminology is rooted in European folk dance and Southern American Negro social dance. The words scuff, sluff, shuffle, slap, and flap are associated by non-tappers with sloppy footwork. Most were applied to 18th and 19th century pre-tap social and performance styles danced in clogs, or even barefoot. (For example, shuffle is derived from African sluffing walks; slaps were brushes, becoming early vaudeville slang for clog shoes.) For tapping, these, as all terms, are accurately defined movements, yielding clear, predetermined actions and sounds.

Tap-Twisters:
Flat footed flaps suffer from sloppy sluffy feet.   Rat-tat-tat-tat two twin toe-tip toe taps.

Fill in using the following (each insert is used only once):
   back   ball   does   doesn't   heel   one   one   plié-relevé   raised   stamp   stomp   stood on   tip   toe   two

Each tap shoe includes _____ taps, the _____ or _____ tap under the toes and the _____ tap. Most tapping is done while supported on _____ foot. The free foot is _____ near the supporting leg. Usually, in order to have a foot free to move, when one foot is _____ _____, the other foot is lifted. Most tap sounds are made by striking _____ tap at a time. Different parts of the taps may be used. For example, a toe-tap is a striking of the _____ of the toe, and a dig strikes the _____ edge of the heel. Some tap movements are different because they do or don't accept weight. A step _____ take the weight, while a ball tap _____. A few tap sounds, such as _____ and _____, are made using two taps at the same time. The proper supporting stance is with the supporting leg heel raised and knee slightly bent, a _____, which permits nearly continuous bouncing on one or between feet.

With a shine on your shoes:
By 1805, English inventors had patented leather preparation processes using variously linseed oil, lampblack, enamels, etc. to produce low maintenance waterproof glossy finishes ideal for shoes. Established as "the" dance shoe finish during vaudeville (an 1870s ad offered clogging shoes (oxfords) for $10) black patent leather was replaced in the 1950s by more durable vinyl fabric (the patent finish cracked). Black patina tap shoes remained the shiny attention getting standard through the 1960s when matte black, then white, silver, and tan vied for color popularity. By 2010 the 150 years standard had been replaced by matte black and assorted tans.

BASIC SOUNDS and COORDINATION

It takes two:
All listed **BASIC SOUNDS** are single, except one. Which requires 2 different sounds? _____

Select landing relationships (2 per | line):

	same foot / change feet / both feet	ball tap(s) / flat foot
leap	/ /	/
hamp	/ /	/
lamp	/ /	/
catch	/ /	/
jump	/ /	/
fall	/ /	/

Let them be heard:
Thomas Edison's 1894 Kinetoscope was supplemented (1895) with recorded cylinder sound projected through a horn – hand-cranked "peepshow talkies". In 1906 Lee de Forest invented the audion (triode vacuum tube) used to amplify telephone signals. Western Electric acquired development rights resulting in improvements by 1912 permitting the growth of commercial radio from the early 1920s. Warner Brothers and Western Electric's 1925 experiments led to a New York City 1926 early talking picture "short" Warner theater trial. The audience response, influenced by radio entertainment, encouraged further film application development.

Following Warner Brothers 89 minute 1927 partial talky *Jazz Singer* (including some dialog and 6 songs sung by Al Jolson) implementing Bell Telephone Laboratory Vitaphone 16″ sound-on-disc synchronized phonograph record technology, 20th Century Fox followed (*Sunrise*, 1927) using German technology Movietone, an optical sound track on the film accurately paralleling the images. M-G-M in 1928 produced *The Broadway Melody*, released February 1929, the first feature length musical-comedy motion picture with fully integrated sound. By 1930 the entire industry was transitioning, providing movie-goers with vocals, music, and even taps*.

Just as radio spurred development of microphone technology (beginning with E. C. Wente's 1916 condenser mic), talkies in theaters required improved quality higher volume speakers. The 1925 electromagnet controlled diaphragm speaker ushered in the union of audio and video, eventually known as AV technology. M-G-M was not satisfied with theater sound. John Hilliard from the studio worked with James B. Lansing (later JBL Corp.) to create higher clarity two-way (separately designed bass and treble frequency range) speaker horn drivers (electromagnet/diaphragm components). The Shearer Horn was established in 1936 as the Cinema audio standard until replaced in 1945 by the Altec-Lansing The Voice of the Theatre larger, louder, clearer horn array units**. M-G-M's initial 1930s improvement motivation – clearer dance taps reproduction.

(*For insights into early sound films technology, filming techniques, and resultant motion picture developments, see *The Movie Musical from Vitaphone to 42nd Street*, compiled by Miles Kreuger.)

(**The Alnico V (aluminum, nickel, cobalt, iron alloy) permanent magnet core driver provided quicker diaphragm response.)

Keep in - - -
Unlike a heel lead "walk", "step" nearly always means changing lead onto the ball of the foot, even if the heel is next lowered. The required lifting of the foot coordination may explain such expressions as "high stepping" and as a synonym for stairs.

From the bottom up:
Match the best associations:

fall	replace and kick
catch	airborne
hitch	drop
leap	replace

Tappin':
Just as there are three different definitions of "step" (see **BASIC STEPS** introduction), this manual includes the basic pas plus what three other uses of "tap"?

_____
_____
_____

Move it:
Fundamentally, dance follows movement. It has been said that a dancer is distinguishable in public by the way she moves. Functionally, the opposite is correct. Movement skills (range and ease) determine dance-ability. Noticeable is the natural efficiency of dance (especially ballet) technique. The **BASIC SOUNDS** actually present only a few sounds, but all are different coordinations.

Word-link puzzle:
The terms needed can be found in BASIC SOUNDS AND MOVEMENTS in the TAP TERMINOLOGY.

```
            _ h _ _
              _
          _ _ _ _         _
                          j
        b _ _             _
          _               _ _ _ _
          _
          _ _ _           _ _
          _               _
          _ _ _           _ _ _ _
                          _
                          _
```

BASIC STEPS

Stepping out:
Shuffle, walk, buck, dance, move, hoof'n, pattern, jazz'n, roll, step about, and others have been generic terms meaning a tap step(s). A vocabulary of dance steps is the source of movement experience. Widening that experience brings new skills and creative opportunities. Seek new steps and variations, the words of the language that is dance.

More than one step for tap-kind:
According to *Jazz Dance* by Marshall and Jean Stearns, from Giouba, an African dance, Southern Negroes developed Juba, a call-and-response circle dance. A man from the circle would call out the name of a dance characterization ("Yeller Cat, Long Dog Scratch, Blow Dat Candle Out", etc.) then performed by two dancers inside the circle. When concluded, the shout "Juba, Juba" led the dance repetition by the circle of men, followed by a call for a different step. Because drum use by African slaves was generally forbidden, rhythm was maintained by clapping and body slapping – patting Juba. "These characteristics are a fair list of the major Afro-American traits in the blend of vernacular dance.": circle dance, characterization, challenge, spontaneous rhythms, and freestyling. From such community dancing grew the steps, and a few of the structures and names, which became tap dancing.

By the 1840s Master Juba (William Henry Lane) was established as America's leading dancer. His unique appearances as a Negro without black makeup in Caucasion blackface minstrel shows testifies to his professional and popular status. Building from clog-jig dances he created a style duplicated and thus credited as establishing the first tap steps still in use.

Name the steps described as:

shfl, shfl	_____	br-scuff fwd	_____
brush bk, hop, step bk	_____	scuff fwd, br bk	_____
shfl, hop, step	_____	brush bk R, hop L, tpl bk R	_____

Some assembly required:

Match the best relationships between first and second column lists.

basic sounds	2M or more
basic steps	2M, 4M
complex steps	foundation coordinations
combination	sequence of steps
phrase	64M, 96M
Step	1M or less
routine	8M, 16M

It's classified?

The **TERMINOLOGY** categories are intended to group associated concepts by increasing complexity. Some categories may be incorrectly assumed to classify all included items; however, many terms could fall into several categories. For example, trenches are a runing eccentric coordination which can be performed with p-u-c's or as glides.

Why terminology?

Relying on the simplest basic coordinations provides accurate but messy communication. An example (using 5 tap terms and 2 directional abbreviations):

Brush bk, hop, step, brush bk, hop, step, brush bk, hop, shfl, step, shfl, hop, step, shfl, hop, step, leap sdwd, shfl, step, shfl, hop, step, shfl, step, shfl, step, shfl, step, step, step.

Proponents of few tap terms (as few as 7*, usually 2-3 dozen) claim simplicity is easier. Compare to the previous:

2 d-b's, cinc, 2 irishes, buff, irish, 3 tpl's, b/c.

Simplicity isn't easier, clarity (brevity with accuracy) is.

(*A very limited terms list example: brush, step, flat, toe, heel, jump, stand.)

Various compensations have been attempted, including:

underlined step or specified Ft in parentheses means no weight	stamp = stamp; <u>stamp</u> = stomp; stamp (R) = stomp R
step in parentheses means no weight change	(flap) = slap
added explanation	step flat (loud) = stamp; brush with heel = scuff

If the coordination is repeatedly used, define it as a term. (See **ROUTINES**, <u>Shim It Up</u>, pre-entrance NOTE.)

It could be worse:

Following are non-vocabulary tap notes samples.

Taps employed:	THHHT	= 5-tap riff walk	("toe, heel," etc.)
	RtD LtD RhD LhD	= c-r R	("R toe dn," etc.)
Number of taps:	1+3+4	= buff, shfl-b/c	(see **ALTERNATE TERMINOLOGY, NUMERICAL**)

The above are confusing and very coordination limited. Kahnotation, developed by the master tap instructor Stanley Kahn, is a symbolic tap shorthand indicating use of taps, weight placement, and excellent rhythm notation. Although not audio inclined, Labanotation provides a very detailed full body movement staff. Neither of these abstact systems are terminology based, requiring considerable learning effort.

A great value of terminology is easily related abbreviation notation. Many approaches exist. One of the simplest is ellimination of all vowels: brsh, shffl, trpl. This can quickly become problematic and self-limiting: mxfrd (maxie), rsh (irish), pckpchng (p-u-c).

Or something <u>else</u>:

You would expect a tap class to be organized around tap steps and tapping techniques. Paul Draper began his practices with at least 30 minutes of ballet barre while wearing tap shoes. Many of the ballet exercises incorporated taps, concentrating on placement, clarity, and ankle control.

In a 1958 *Dance Digest* interview, Draper indicated "the fundamental ways to make sounds" included "slaps, shuffles, heel-drops, ball changes, wings, pullbacks, nerve taps". He believed tap steps to be few and limited, requiring ballet and other dance techniques to choreograph "movement" to which "sounds" could be added – <u>tapped</u> dancing

Make up your mind:

Various descriptions of complex steps like falling off a log offer not only several differing movement sequences, but varying language (verbal and written), even from the same source. The usual reason is undefined foundation (basic) movements, the roots from which tap terminology grows.

Each following line is from notes of a single routine, yet includes different descriptions producing the same rhythm and weight placement.

Flat ft ~ stamp (no wt)	= stomp
step ~ hit toe ~ tap toe	= step
flap ~ slap ~ toe slap ~ brush step	= flap
heel ~ heel drop ~ cramp	= heel
toe tp bk ~ toe pt tapbk ~ toept tapbk	= tt x bk (Obviously similar, but consistency would eliminate confusion.)

In <u>Choreo Shuffle</u> (Ch-300LP) Bill Graham includes: ball step, ball ball, step ball, ball change, and step step with the same weight change and even rhythm – a b/c.

Sometimes similarly applied terms discriminate coordination but lack definition, like "heel drop" meaning dig with weight vs. "dig" without. Flat foot clog stylist Willie Covan's teacher convention notes include such confusion. Sluffs include "slide" ending with weight and "drag" ending with lifted foot. He evidently found this differentiation useful and used it consistently, but without reader awareness it could be confusing. His 1949 Willie Covan Strut routine is preceded, "Explanation of step, means ball of foot. Explanation of slap, means flap." And at end, "For further explanation of these steps, please contact Willie Covan." Possibly a response to comments from readers of his earlier notes.

A mind made up:
Farruca 1949 notes by Lola Montes begin with several definitions including, "CHUG -- Push front part of foot forward along floor several inches and drop heel of same foot." No confusion there.

And from (1940s) Allan MacKenzie Side Riff Routine, "Explanation of Terms, Side Riff – consists of 3 taps executed in 2 actions. 1st tap is made with outside edge of sole as foot travels out to side. 2nd tap is made with inside edge of sole as part of same action. 3rd tap is made by brushing foot in. Keep knee and ankle relaxed."

Too many, too few:
Read: "Small brush bk. R-step R-small brush bk. L-step L-shuffle step R-heel drop R-heel touch L in front-small brush bk. L-step L-heel touch R in front-brush bk. R-heel step R-step L-brush step bk. R-heel touch L in front-small brush bk. step L-scuff R" a&a1&2&3&4&5&a6&a7&a8. From Eva Varady Begin the Beguine STEP IV, this break is an unnecessarily challenging quick read – too many similar step, brush, heel references, too few discriminating steps. Translate this phrase into clearer language.

From this list   ball change   cramp   flap   irish   quadruple   shuffle   triple:
   The two most used duple rhythm tap steps are s_____ and f_____.
   Select 3 more terms that begin with a shfl: _____, _____, _____
   Two quick steps are called a _____. A step-heel is a _____.

Can you tap this combination?
Shfl R, b/c R-L, rpt shfl-b/c, 2 flap-b/c's R-L, 3 irishes R-L-R, stamp fwd L, step R. Rev all.
An obvious duplet dominant 4M in $^4/_4$ meter. How would you rephrase the rhythm for 8M of waltz?

Unscramble:
f i f r   _____   t a r l e t   _____
l p m a   _____   p h t s e c c t a   ____-____
t l e s e h i w t   ____ ____   a u p q d e u r l   _____

Regarding flaps:
Although flaps can move in any direction, each flap can go in only _____. To permit efficient movement, flaps may move in the direction of any part of the foot. Which part of the foot leads forward, backward, outside, inside flaps? _____, _____, _____, _____ A leisurely br-step is a walking flap. When done running, what must the step become? _____ What action makes a swinging flap unique? _____ A _____ is like a flap without transferring weight.

Why?
Traditional tap step origins and definitions tend to be personal, at broadest, regional or trend related, often changing over time. Basic steps terminology has often been dictated not by coordination, but by such vagaries as direction or exact rhythm. Some notes specify any successive 2 steps as b/c, while others require their occurrence within 1 count &1 and still others as a duplet a1 to avoid listing as two steps. Jimmy Sutton's notes are an example: "Repeat all but substitute a flap for the Brush step L back at 'a1'." For many dancers a flap must be duple rhythm, otherwise it is a brush-step. Some view flaps as exclusively forward, other directions being brush-step, thus the quote.

Even a simple brush can be directionally defined. From Jack Stanly's Soft Shoe Eccentric: "brush L ft fwd, scuff L ft fwd (Riff)" is followed by "flap R ft (out to R side, at same time kick L out to L side), spank L ft (in place to R ft), step on L ft (in close to R ft)". Both brush and flap (vs. spank and spank-step) coordinations are discriminated. Confusing, eh?

Stage Arts '77 Teacher's Dance Notes include Dani Lagervall (Blue Finger Lou, Step Three) and Lynda Gache (Stompin At the Savoy, Step One) distinguishing flap as toe lead and back flap as simply "brush bk": "step right brush bk. ball chg left brush heel step r" (i.e., step R, bk flap-b/c L, br R, heel L, step R   2&3&4&5&), which also is the notation for bk br: "flap r brush bk. l drop r heel" &1&a.

Most tap steps default to fwd lead unless otherwise defined or directed. There are so many ways to vary even a simple shuffle or flap that unless frequently used (scuffle, dbl-shfl, slap, swinging flap) it is usually least confusing to build from the most basic term; e.g., bk flap R x frt L.

Build it and they will - - - :
While all steps are built from the **BASIC SOUNDS AND MOVEMENTS**, complex steps are built from more **BASIC STEPS** coordinations and concepts. Increasingly varied and complex similar coordination can be developed as movement/terminology Series. B/c moves as c/s, travels as gallops or b/c x-overs, turns as a b/c tr, becomes heels as d/c, flat as s/c, and is abrupt as a b/a. This is a Basic Series, built from the simplest pair of audio weight changes. Added complexity can yield, b/c gpvn, sd scissor or eagle rock, add

heels for c-r, brush into paddle or ess's, even d-p-u and eagle landings are the original coordination. Similar coordination series can be constructed from shfl, flap, and with elevations, turns, rolls, p-u's, t-s's, etc. Such Technique Series are useful training tools, clarifying coordination/rhythm similarities vs. differences, and, with logical terminology, aid in understanding such associations.

Basically most:
How many of the 40 listed **BASIC STEPS** are comprised only of one or more step(s) and/or brush(s)? _____
How many more if hop(s) and/or leap(s) are included? _____ more
Now include heel(s) and scuff(s). _____ more
What **BASIC SOUNDS AND MOVEMENTS** are needed to include the remaining **BASIC STEPS**?
_____

Its time had come:
When considered necessary, choreographers define their notated steps, perhaps for the first time.

The 1937 Chicago Association of Dance Masters convention notes include a Bobby Rivers tap routine <u>Floating Rhythm</u> preceded by, "Note: In order to execute this dance properly and also to aid the teachers in reading these notes, a new term has been created, called 'Scuffle'. It is the same as 'Shuffle', only instead of a forward brush, the heel digs into the floor for the first beat". He also comments, "A new style of dancing designed to keep all foot movement as close to the floor as possible. Special attention should be given to the rhythms, as this is rapidly becoming a more important factor in dance today". The complexities of rhythm tap were maturing.

Elmer Wheatly's 1940s <u>Swing Classic</u> Step VII includes: "Hop L., brush R. fwd., step on R. heel (close riff), step L. in place a&a1". Although not in a soft shoe routine, this is a variation of what step? _____

<u>Rhythm Dance</u> (1940s) by Billy Moyer begins, "Shuffle riff" "ea1". In a Hanf routine <u>It's All Right With Me</u> (Hanf Record #1015) is explained, RIFF SHUFFLE: "A close shuffle with a heel scuff between the fwd. and back brushes. It is a fwd. brush – a scuff – and a back brush.". What one word basic step is described? _____

1966 Eva Varady "Broadway Rhythm" STEP VIII: "close riff (brush fwd. R toe – heel touch R)".

Although appearing earlier, in 1951 <u>You Do Something to Me</u> (Hoctor Record #DH-1722), Danny Hoctor felt the need to asterisk then begin the post-routine glossary, "*LAMP – A combination of a leap and a stamp. Leap to Flat foot with opposite foot off the floor". In other notes Danny defined hamp. Perhaps overdoing it, Betty Hoctor in 1968, "Talk to the Animals" clarified duple rhythm steps as "B.C." (b/c). Again, in the 1980 Dance Caravan – Stars manual, <u>I've Got Your Number</u> (#H-2836) ends (after stamp R) "Do a br bk R as you (This is known as a Pick Up Change) Leap L - &, Hldrp L – A, Toe pt tap R in bk – 2". Did you notice a rhythm notation is missing?

Although most basics had been widely recognized since the 1940s, even the most common (including irish, riff, and waltz clog time step) some writers believe require explanation. Ron Matty's 1974 *ABC's of Tap* technique album notes begin one flap exercise "This movement without weight is usually called a 'slap'". In <u>Sweet Seasons</u> (1976) Bonnie Lee Ratzin inserted descriptions of buffalo and cramproll, still occasionally defined in workshop notes.

For 50 years, beginning in the 1940s, over a dozen companies, including Hanf and Hoctor, published music recordings prepared specifically for theater dance training. Many came with dance notes (class technique or routines) arranged for the accompaniment. These significantly aided in spreading and standardizing dance terminology.

Says who?
From 1930s and '40s notes, a few more examples of in-line definitions.

"scuffle step (scuff L heel fwd, brush back L, step L), (a2a)"	Bobby Rivers	<u>A Study In Modern Rhythms</u>
"st. R st. L st. R st. L (patter) 1&a2	Helyn R. Flanagan	<u>Wahoo Western</u>
"Brush L. back (&) Stamp L. (1) Stomp R. (no wt.) (&)"	J. Allen Mackenzie	<u>Riffs and Sluffs</u>
"Step L. back (7) Touch R. toe across in ront of L. (&) Hop L. fwd. over R. (8)"	J. A. M.	same
"Step L, shuffle R, ballchange RL, stamp R (bandy twist) (1&2&3-4)"	Johnny Mattison	<u>Mattison Rhythm No. 1</u>
"cramp roll (toe toe heel heel)	Jill Davison	<u>Wheels and Whirls</u>
"Step forward on ball of R foot & twist foot ('Sugar') 7"	Jill Davison	<u>Wheels and Whirls</u>
"Maxie Ford Turn R (Stamp R-shuffle L-leap to L-hit R toe back-Step R) 9 & 10, 11, 12"	J. D.	same
"Shuffle R – hop L – step back on R (Irish)"	J. D	same
"3 step walking turn to R (R-L-R)"	J. D	same
"4 buffaloes with R: Shuffle step R. (X B. of L.), step L. to L. &a1, 2" rpt 3 X's	Virginia Self	<u>Gingerbread Boys</u>
"(One buck time step with R.:) Brush R. back, hop L. &1 Shuffle step R. in rear &a2 Flap L. fwd, step R. in rear &3&, hold 4	Virginia Self	<u>Chefs</u>
"5 tap riff: Toe tap L. (X B. of R.), scuff L. heel fwd. &a Drop R. heel, step on L. heel to L., drop L. toe 3&4"	same	
"Stamp R fwd. (no weight), brush R. back, hop L., flap R., flap L. extending R. out to R. side, brush step R. in to L. (wing time step)."	Elmer Wheatly	<u>Drum Beat</u>
"Shuffle R., hop L., step back R., brush L. fwd., ball change L.R. (single time step) 8&1,2,&3&"		same

Page 44

Look at that:
Some terms have obvious visual origins (x-over, draw-back, pend, pigeon-toe). A few may require some explanation.

- balancé — Balance between feet, rock. Various folk and period dance examples led to current ballet and ballroom use.
- break-away — An abrupt change of direction. From a closed position, ballroom partners separate. It's possible that the term historically links to the 'tack annie final tug.
- shim sham — Jumble, a mess, shamble (clumsy walk), confusion.
- cross bar — A folk dance term for crossed legs.
- legomania — High kicks, probably from late 19th century foot-above-the-head leg lift novelty acts. The current coordination was perhaps inspired by Tyrolian and similar lifted foot slapping folk dances.
- sugar foot and suzie-q — Sugar footing is slang for acting 'sweet' (being romantically inclined). From 1920s-1930s fad dances interpreted both terms as "girlie" steps, appearing cute, still leading to frequent pre-school dance use.
- flea hop — Variation from pre-1920 Carolinas Negro bouncy "shag" dancing (step-hop, rev, 2 steps) early shades of Jitterbug.
- English time-step — Inserted tt inspired by Irish Step Dance (see Wild-n-Irish routine).
- wiggle sticks — Associated with 1920s Charleston, but with a possible Hornpipe precedent as alluded to by James Sutton (1930s) in "Shore Leave (Sailor Eccentric)" STEP FOUR: "Jump on both feet with R crossed front of L (using a sliding effect of feet rather than a quick 'jump'), Jump with both feet apart (still using the sliding effect), Jump with both feet together (still using the sliding effect)". Wiggle sticks with little wiggle.

Incidentally, a frequent appearance of 'longer' pendulums with hops is in pointe tap routines.

Crazy:
According to Hanf in an eccentric routine "Satan Takes A Holiday" (Hanf record #544 side B) (probably 1950s):

Step 1: "LEG-O-MANIA – Place R Ankle B of L Knee with R Knee straight out to Rt. – L toe turned to the Rt. – Pivot ¼ to the Lt. – R ankle Front of L Knee – R Knee turned to the Lt. & L toe turned Diag. to the Lt. – Pivot ¼ to the Rt. – Body and Knee Stiff – Kick R out to the Rt. – In this position Drop R Foot (Flat) – REVERSE THE LAST FOUR COUNTS". A R ankle wrapping around L knee approach with snap developpé.

Step 8: "KEEP KNEES TIGHT TOGETHER DURING THE FOLLOWING TWO MEAS.- Jump up with R foot Fwd. and L foot Back – Land on both feet (together) – Jump up with R foot B and L foot Fwd. – Land on both feet (together)". Name the step.

Step 9: "FLEA HOP - - - -: - Weight on L – Flex R knee and slide L foot to Rt. – Step R – REVERSE & REPEAT (No Wt. on last ct.) – Weight on L – Flex R knee and slide L foot to the Rt. – Step R". Passé flea hops rt-lt, dbl flea hop rt.

7 (or 5) come 11 (or more):
There are various approaches to riff walk series. Al Gilbert (*Dance Magazine* April 1967) "Variations in Riffs" built from a

5-tap riff walk R (riff ,heel, dig, snap)
6-tap riff walk: , heel R
7-tap riff walk: , roll L-R
8-tap: , snap R
9-tap: , snaps L-R
10-tap: , heel R
11-tap: riff R, heel L, bk riff R, heel L, 5-tap riff walk

Then cont'g through 16-tap by following the 11-tap riff walk first 6 taps with above 6-tap (making a 12-tap dbl'd riff walk), 6-tap+7-tap (=13-tap), etc. This could go on forever.

So many riffs, so few descriptions:
Sometimes there is an overabundance of "common useage". Many choreogaphers note "four tap riff" as a universally understood term which, as being a riff walk, it is. The problem is that defined versions include:

riff, step, heel   riff, heel, step   riff , heel, dig w/w   riff, dig, snap   riff, b/c   riff, bk flap x frt.

A Billy Moyer routine Rhythm Dance is chock-full of riffs. In his routines most variations are described, but several terms are not defined, including: slap riffs iea1 (done in a circle), shuffle riff ea (without weight), double shuffle riff iea7& (no weight), leap riff ea (into step), back sole riff "(2 times)" &6 (no weight), and twist riff ea&7&a (ends with weight).

A clue is combinations like "riff R, flex R, riff R" 2e&3e (perhaps riff, bk br, riff) indicating low, close, compact coordination.

Analysis is an educated guess posing an interesting puzzle. Logically, slap riffs may be riff, i/s-fwd flap done as a riff walk. Scuffle or ankle controlled brush fwd, bk scuff might be the shuffle riff. Double shuffle riff coordinates easily as riffle, riff (think dbl shfl: riff, bk br, riff). Three sequenced leap into riff-land are probably running, like running flaps. The back sole riff may be a double tap back brush or ball then heel clips during a back leg swing, but "(2 times)" remains confusing. Twist riff could be a close riff or 6-tap riff walk ending with trav'g rock'n. Oh well, there's no reason Sherlock Holmes should have all the fun.

Auld tap syne (old tap since):
Many now less used tap terms repeatedly appear in notes from the 1920s onward. Translate these to **TERMINOLOGY** terms.

    paddle wheel turn _____   shuffle riff _____
    change kick _____   step flat _____
    double wings _____   twist step _____
    heel jab _____   toeback _____
    cross steps _____   click _____

They are all listed in **ALTERNATE TERMINOLOGY**.

Back to basics:
In *Sweetheart of the Campus* (1941) Ruby Keeler performs swing and boogie numbers composed largely of basic steps, combinations, and staging, including pull-bk's, maxies, and an eddie leonard. If you have the opportunity to watch the film, identify the many steps and patterns as they are performed.

BUFFALOS and BOMBERSHAYS

Vaudeville, a classification of variety shows, is an aberration of "vieux de Vire" (vaudevire), the veterans (experts) of Vire, associated with popular satirical songs from the Vire Valley in Normandy, France.

As an American outgrowth of local pub shows, specialty acts (magicians, jugglers, acrobats, singers, dancers, comics, actors, etc.) began traveling regionally in the 1870s. Popularity encouraged development of vaudeville theaters, then chains of such venues, featuring acts eventually maturing into polished national and international tours popular into the 1930s. Many of these variety performers were the foundation talent for Broadway, motion pictures, radio, and television.

Many tap terms were created and became commonly used by dancers interassociating during vaudeville tours. Ideas were exchanged, steps 'stolen', dance and personal styles established. Reinterpretation and communication of steps and combinations required a common vocabulary, much of which is still in use.

Buffalo, New York was a principal variety circuit booking center for touring shows. The shuffle off to Buffalo exit is attributed (1880s) to Pat Rooney when a Buffalo theater stage manager refused him an exit blackout. The cincinnatti purportedly was originated as a tap step – guess where.

Which tap step is named for a state _____; which four for countries _____, _____, _____, _____; which for a pilot _____? It is not difficult to figure out many of the tap terms which honor performers.

Bombs away!
The German *bombershay* – bombe (bomb) shay (carriage), a traveling explosion – is interpreted as a stamp or toe to heel clip while moving. Another vaudeville coordination, the baby bombershay appeared in ragtime (music) fad dances (short-lived social dance styles) of the early 1900s, reappearing in later "fads".

The interpretation may be less explosive, as in Dorothy Donelson's (1940s) <u>Ghost Dance</u> Step III: "Brush step R in to L: Step &a2 (Bombershay)". Inside flap, rather than outside.

Or may begin with the accent, as in Jimmy Sutton's (1940s) <u>Tap Impressions</u> Step 1 break: "Buck R fwd (L ft back of R calf) (8) Flap L to L (twisting R toe to R) (and 1) Brush step R (in) (and a) Step L (2)", the chug ("Buck").

WALKS

Takes the cake:
The military sounding tap "strut" actually derives from a 19th century festive competition wherein the showiest, elegant, most original "walk" competitor was awarded a cake. Minstrel shows expanded the cakewalk strut into an entrance/exit parade, popularized in the early 1900s as a fad dance.

A walk on the wild side:
Many 1940s and '50s dance convention notes provide step and terminology definition insights. In the 1947 Chicago National Association of Dance Masters 34th annual convention manual, Jimmy Sutton's <u>Minstrelette</u> includes "(Riff as follows) Brush L diag fwd L, Scuff L heel diag fwd L, Step on L heel, Drop ball of L", a 4-tap riff walk. Following were 5-tap and syncopated riff walk variations.

Effective riff walks are sophisticated walks. While walking at moderate tempo, include an occasional 4-tap riff walk without affecting stride or overall appearance. Include more, then 5-tap, 6-tap, etc, always maintaining a natural stroll.

Step Two <u>Struttin' Along</u>, for students "5 to 8 years", NADAA 1949 notes by Agnes L. Ward, includes "Brush R ft inward - step R in place. Reverse and repeat alt. ft doing 8 times in all. This movement resembles 'Snake Hips'." Or swinging flaps if leapt.

In <u>Highland Swing</u> she specifies "Exit R doing 'Sugar Foot'. Stepping fwd alterrnate ft on balls of ft and twisting knees out on each step." Sounds about right. Try it. Notice how the back foot counter twist naturally occurs. Exagerate it for styling.

Do it with - - - - -:
Many dance terms specify more than coordination or rhythm, they include a visual specification – style. Stepping aesthetically varies significantly as a sugar foot, strut, shorty george, sluefoot, or walk.

Restyling a step can be as simple as changing movement allignment or size. Compare:
    (Trav sdwd) 4 b/c's close //   vs.   as an expanded (cover some ground) twisting b/c gpvn.

What is now a *step* sometimes was popularized as a personal signature or short routine. Many tap steps originated within other dance forms and types from ethnic and folk, through ballet and jazz, to ballroom and fad dances. Derived from a Southern Negro style, ladies reportedly swooned during Earl 'Snake Hips' Tucker's 1920s performances, well before Elvis.

The shorty george is traditionally attributed to 'Shorty George' Snowden of 1920s-'30s Lindy Hop fame. The Lindy Hop (remember that lindy rhythm pattern?) was the original version of the Lindy (or Swing) which was popularized after Charles Lindberg's 1927 premiere transatlantic solo flight to Paris. Sugar foot and suzie-q (a 1937 fad) are other *walks* associated with the Lindy Hop.

Try shorty georges as cramp, flap, tpl, or wing mvmt.

Some argue that suzie-q first appeared as a bombershay variation. Try a baby bombershay with h-t L t/o during – stamp R t/i x frt, t/o pvt R (not h-t) into t/i step L short lt.

Performed as a sluff walk, shim sham patterns often appeared as a vaudeville finalé routine, curtain call, or exit, sometimes with audience participation. Popularized during the '20s and '30s, with added shoulder shaking, as the Shim Sham Shimmy (often attributed to Leonard Reed*), it later became another step incorporated into Jitterbug, then finally returning as a routine, the Lindy Line Dance, sometimes partnered. (*From a 1988 interview with Rusty Frank in *Tap* Reed contradicted "we didn't do the shakin' ").

Find "slue" (slew) in a dictionary: swing, twist, skid, veer. Sluefoot – 19th century mariners' slang for clumsy (associated with turned-out feet) – was performed in minstrel shows then popularized in vaudeville as a rubberlegs comedy sketch (brief dramatic scene) step and incorporated into eccentric tap routines. The 1955 <u>Slew Foot</u> number, featuring Fred Astaire and Leslie Caron, in *Daddy Long Legs* was choreographed as a 1950s teen fad dance. The original leisurely walk styling was reconstituted as upbeat kicky bounce, but the core sluff walk pattern occasionally appears, and it's a great duet.

There's always another riff walk:
The variety of tap step variations can seem infinite. Alfred Lloyd (1930s) supplemented the beginning and end: shfl, heel, 6-tap riff walk, tt. Billy Moyer (1940s) "riff L to heel, drop L toe, L heel, L heel" "iea&8" is a hesitation walk. If a riff leads to travel, look for a riff walk.

KICKS

Put a hitch in your get done:
Johnny Boyle ends a 1940s clog routine, "jump onto R kicking L fwd – hitch kick to L ft, wait – hitch kick to R ft – bend L knee & slam L fwd." 345(6)7. Decisive "4-ct" hitch kick finish with emphasis down rather than up.

Just for kicks:
For each kick, select the best beginning and end leg and foot or two feet position relationships. (4 per line)

	Begins				Ends		
	Open / Close	On Floor / Off Floor		Open / Close	On Floor / Off Floor
battment	/	/		/	/
swing kick	/	/		/	/
balancoire	/	/		/	/
devellopé	/	/		/	/
snap kick	/	/		/	/

There's flapping and flapping, wings and wings, eagles and eagles:
A side scissor kick or eagle rock (another teens to 1920s fad dance) commonly includes low frt scissor A's opening to 2nd, emphasizing the leg line and reminiscent of the fad dance flapping arms eagle wings. Converting the leap to a hop provides the opportunity for wing taps, or jump into an eagle, or make it a battement wing, often accompanied by A's swinging overhead then down.

Actually, there is another wing, the stage sides (S-R, S-L) entryways between the side drapes (tormenters/ legs).

The eagle has landed:
Early 20th century fad dances included over two dozen animal characterizations derived from American Negro dances. The aviary group included Chicken Scratch, Pigeon Wing, Turkey Trot, Buzzard Lope, and Eagle Rock featuring knee lifts, hopping, front/back rocks, hand fluttering, high/low side waving arms, and thigh slapping. In *Jazz Dance* by Marshall and Jean Stearns, a 19th century observer noted "Pigeon Wing, a scraping and sometimes shaking from one foot to the other with fluttering arm and hand motions like a bird trying to fly". In 1968 <u>Cavalcade of the Dance</u> (HLP 4061) Michael Dominico interprets "The Eagle": "Hands waist high, R side of body - - - Hands used with broken wrists - - - like a bird: Heel dig R - &, Wave down: Drop toe R – 5, Wave up: Step L - &", rpt 2 X's ending tap L, "Dig heel L – 1 (L hand above head R hand down, B.C. RL - &2", {even rhythm} heel L into rev, (cont alt'g A's) heel R, dig-snap L, rev, dig L &3&4&5&6&7. An erratic comic walk. Lift the feet, exagerate the characterization.

Eventually becoming: 1964 *Dance Caravan U.S.A., Students – Stage Arts* Vol. Five includes Ruth Cater's <u>Spirit of Youth</u> (Statler #453) Step One "(eagle rock) leap R to R, step L x'D front of R, leap R to R, heel dig L to L" &1&2. A homogenized simplification of earlier stylings. Quite a change, however - - -

About 1914 Harry Harshfield created a newspaper cartoon strip *Abie the Agent* featuring Abe Kabibble. The name became associated with a comic musician Ish Kabibble (Merwyn Bogue) who portrayed a dim witted character who personified his stage name Yiddish source, translated "What, me worry?". Vaudeville references to the abe kabibble dance step define the current eagle rock.

Another example coordinatively en route is found in the 1916 *Dances Drills and Story Plays* by Nina Lambkin. Described under "Sailor's Hornpipe" "Fifth Figure: Scissors step.": "Jump in half stride. Jump and cross feet. Repeat." A side scissor without kick. Also, "Fourth Figure: Twisting Step." "Heels and toes close together, move sideward left four counts by moving toes to left, then heels."

Name that step. _____

Kick that bell:

One 1940s definition of bell is a hitch front with heel clip, perhaps associated with the following. Lift R fwd as a swing kick (prep), br bk R into, p-u-c L i-p -- L into swing kick bk, inv (br fwd L, fwd p-u-c R into frt swing kick). Bell kick is a comedy running-d-p-u-c var during alt'g frt\bk hitches. The coordination is tricky, although similar to running-d-p-u-c: br bk R, p-u-c L (lift L bk), br fwd L, frt p-u-c R (lift R frt). Faked d-p-u-c's bk\frt {&a1&a2}, legs swinging bk\frt. Try it.

TURNS & TWISTS

It's everywhere, it's everywhere!!

To change facing dir on a supporting foot, turn with both feet on the floor, or turn out or in, a p-r foot requires the omnipresent pivot, the most frequent twisting mvmt. Usually not notated, nearly every tap comb naturally requires spontaneous pivots. Check it out.

Tap-Twister: Better barrels begin by being bendy.

Twists or turns?

OK, a turn is a rotation, a twist reverses direction. Why is a ½-pivot a turn and a heel pivot a twist? The concept underlying the terms is purpose, specific rotation position vs. noticeable change of direction. Most turns, even partial, must end toward a predetermined direction, while most twists need display only a noticeable directional change. Stand and twist the hips, turn the head.

Around you go:

Most tap turns are derived from ballet turns. A few, like the barrel turn, more likely derive from folk dance, such as a similar Flamenco waist-bent delayed torso snap roll turn executed with arms close to the torso.

Many basics easily become tr's: irish, bandy twist, etc. Try tr'g: cinc   bal   w-c-t-s   and others.

Or combining:

PDTA (Professional Dance Teachers Association) 1965: Bob Audy's <u>Once In Love With Amy</u> Step 8 includes "Making one turn to R on L - - push off with R - &, Step L in place – 1, While turning - - tap R 3 Xs - &a2 (Nerve taps), Repeat &3 & a4, Repeat &5 & a6, Repeat 7 – 8". B/c into bkwd push tr's w/ 3-tap nerve roll.

That's right?

Right and left turns can be ambiguous. Referring to backward turns (thumb pointing backward over specified shoulder – righthand/lefthand), the terms also specify anatomy and both body and stage directions. "Turn right" confusion is easily avoided by using i/s or o/s, c-w or c-c-w.

Along with tr dir's, what other 2 types of mvmt's may be specified i/s or o/s? _____, _____

Where did that come from?

Vaudevillian Jack Wiggins (early 1900s) is credited with popularizing the Bantam Twist (like the rooster), possibly the forerunner of the bandy twist which is credited to Jim Bandy, another vaudeville dancer.

Step 8 of Billy Clower's <u>Avalon</u> (1953): "8 – leap R (to R) &a – shuffle L **Buffalo R** 1 – step L (X bk. of R) 2 – leap R (to R) 3 – leap L (X frt of R) 4 – leap R (to R) **Falling Off Log R**".

Try a buff R ending hitch x frt (leap, shfl, catch), hitches frt then bk while tr'g rt.   or

Do a buff R. Do a bandy R. Now do a buff into a b-t. Rpt ending the buff w/ st R x frt L, then the two b-t steps x frt. What step preceded the shfl-b/c? _____   or

Consider a baby bombershay followed by a shfl-b/c. Bandy twists (side to side) may be performed very subdued, beginning with a little-or-no t/i step near the frt of the supporting Ft, then a fall into a buff, enlarge to ½ then full tr's, expand with hitch kicks to become falling off a log, log tr, rev'g tr, add an over the top. Whew!

A confusing Willie Covan turning hitch kick version: (trav lt) "Step back R L step L, step R and scissors cross R F over L F double turn." Can you figure out this log var? _____
(Covan's R and L indicate body and stg dir's.)

Obviously, there are multiple possible inspirations and approaches to creating a bandy twist or falling off a log. Build an eccentric comb from b-t's, log's, buff's, and hitches. Did you create a new step? Put together a log rolling Step. Make it look precarious (while staying on your feet).

By the way, did you locate the w-c-t-s in the b-t? Could the b-t be a $^4/_4$ var of the $^3/_4$ t-s?

Roll out the barrel, we'll all have a barrel of rolls:
In *Summer Stock* (1950) Gene Kelly performs a dining room table to floor number to "Dig, Brother, Dig" closing with a demonstration of barrel roll variations.

ROLLS & CLIPS

Zapped:
While jazz and modern are technically defined as unrestricted theater dance forms, tapping is surprisingly broadly sourced.

Having viewed a Flamenco performance, it is easy to attribute many tap dancing rolls and close coordinations to the Spanish folk dance form. In so doing an unexpected history influences tapping. Associations reach back to Roman Empire dances later blended when migrations brought Indian Gypsy and Middle Eastern ethnic influences to join African Moorish styles in Spain. There, individuals musically interpreted their passions and sorrows through spontaneous cooperative creations by musician (usually guitarist), vocalist (often adding clapping counter rhythms), and dancer (zapateado styles). Rooted in the Spanish zapato (shoe), zapatear (strike with shoe), the folk dance styles were, by the 17th century in southern Andalusia, enhanced using castanets, permitting exceptionally complex polyrhythmics. Introduced into the West Indies and Mexico, Flamenco, like Irish jigs, influenced early American tap. Now an acknowledged dance art, Flamenco is largely a commercial character dance form, rarely presented unrehearsed, yet still interpreting its original sensual intensity.

Spanish folk dance, especially from the northern Basque region adjacent to France, is characterized in ballet. Which term is listed in this **INDEX**? _____ Which (not in this **INDEX**) is associated with a yellow brick road? _____

Cramped:
The simplest cramproll coordination, 2 consecutive cramps, often appeared in pre-1950 tap notes; e.g., Billy Moyer "step R, heel R, step L, heel L (cramp roll style)" "iea6". It is, however, an awkward roll coordination, especially up-tempo, and has since been predominantly replaced by interlocking cramps. Prove why for yourself. Paul Draper's 1978 book *On Tap Dancing* includes both descriptions.

Tap-Twister: Regularly rolling rhythms ripple repeatedly.

Let 'er roll:
Extended roll rhythms are usually achieved using non-roll steps, like running tpl's. What steps would you use as various 2M rolling rhythm phrases?

Merrily we - - -
Paradiddle is a percusionist term for a specific drumstick technique pattern: RLRR, rev {1a&a2a&a} roll.

Heel R, dig L, bk flap L. a1&2   or (scuffle-cramp)

Paddle and roll ("paradiddle") is a shim commonly associated with sophisticated rhythm styling. Dig-br bk (scuffle) is the "paddle", step-heel (cramp) is the "roll", permitting a double paddle (heel-dig-br bk-dig-br bk-flap a1&2&3&), a dbl roll (scfl, 2 cramps, step), or similar var's. The term has been applied to any or all shims, shams, and shim shams. Build it into a shim sham. Several step and rhythm var's exist. Create a few.

Try the dig w/w as a bk paddle tr.

Tanglefoot:
Often meaning heel twist, here is another interesting rolling pattern. A 2M version:

Step R c-p, dig-snap L lt, rpt, step R c-p, step-heel L lt t/i, h-t t/o L into snap, rpt step-dig-snap 2 X's, s/c R-L (&1&2&3&4a&a5&6&7&**8**).

Or, according to John Manning in his 1936 routine <u>Tanglefoot</u>:

(Trav'g lead sdwd, Hn's on hips) scfl-heel-step, flap x bk, rpt seq 2 or more X's {even rhythm}, add any ending if desired. Tanglefoot is a sdwd patt performed as a slow (soft shoe) sophisticate strut w/ Hn's on hips or a fast roll, often with h-t before flap.

Road less taken:
An interesting variation is from <u>Close Rhythm</u>, Johnny Mattison, Step Three:
- "1& -   two tap riff fwd with R (brush and heel scuff fwd with R)
- a   -   twisting on ball of L turn L heel towards R and drop L heel
- 2& -   two tap riff back with R (heel scuff back and brush R back)
- a   -   twisting on L heel, turn L toe towards R and drop on ball of L
            repeat 1&a2&a"

A 4-tap riffle during trav'g rock'n. Nicely styled roll.

Clipped:
The Lancashire Clog from northwestern England, is heel-tap-rich and often viewed as the primary source of toe and heel clips. A possibly authentic example is the stub toe walk: heel R – raise R toe, L heel to R toe clip, snap R, step L x frt, R toe to L heel clip, step R x bk L (&1&2&3).

An advantage of clog soles is easier, clearer sole clips. Another approach is a vaudeville reference to, "metal strips on the sides of his shoes".

From Johnny Boyle's <u>The American Clog Dance</u> Step 4:

" 1   2 &   a   3   4   & 5   &
ball L – ball change R L – heel drop L – ball R – click heels together center – land R L – brush L heel with R toe in crossing –
     6   &   7   &   8   &
hop L – brush L heel again with R toe to original position – hop L – ball R – heel scuff L with wgt – heel scuff R with wgt –
           1   & 2   &   3 &
snap toe togerther standing on heels – toe drops L R – heels click standing on toes – drop L R heels in place –
                4   &   5   &
click L toe to R heel in crossing back – hop R – click L toe again to R heel into original position – hop R –
                      6 &   7   & a   8
heel stands L R toes turned up – snap toes together – toe drops L R – heels click wgt on toes".

"Heel scuff" is dig, the pair a d/c, later notated "heel stands". "Ball" avoids flat foot.
What 3 terms are used for clip? _____, _____, _____
Which heel clip is elevated? _____
Try it soft shoe, making sole edge clips, then with taps. Definitely more challenging. Tappers favoring clips frequently locate their taps along the inside edges of soles and/or heels, facilitating easier contact.

Triple roll:
The term appears in several contexts including any rolling combination ending with a triple. More often:
rolling tpl's; tpl, step, roll; or rolling tplt's (see next item).

3, 4, or more:
Rolls are sometimes described by the number of taps per music count. The following rhythm notation is fragmented by step.
Running tpl's produce (&a1) a triplet roll   {&a1 &a2 &a3 &a4 &a5 &a6 &a7 &a8}, or
                       (a&a1) quadruplet roll   {10 tpl's, flap: a&a 1a& a2a &a3 a&a 4a& a5a &a6 a&a 7a& a8}, or
                       (ea&a1) quintuplet roll   {13 tpl's, leap: ea& a1e a&a 2ea &a3 ea& a4e a&a 5ea &a6 ea& a7e a&a 8}.
Try each with music then combine 4 or more of each roll in sequence. Quintuplet footwork timing may seem a bit tricky, but moving the shading emphasis (the leap) adds interest. Just maintain cleanly separated taps and even rhythm within each "---plet" cluster.

PICKUPS & WINGS

Once a young fellow who tapped
Sluffed sideways into a flap
That's an interesting thing
I'll call it a wing
With both feet, an _____, perhaps.

Pick a pickup:
Which type of actual pickup?	Types
d-p-u	single
pull-back	single change
shfl-d-p-u	double
p-u-c-t-t	double change
d-p-u-r	
p-u-irish	
p-u-c-trench	
d-p-u-c	

A study in pickups:
Singin' in the Rain includes "Moses Supposes" wherein Donald O'Connor and Gene Kelly provide an ongoing exhibition of pickup variations. Also watch for O'Connor in his slapstick (physical comedy) eccentric "Make 'em Laugh" (by Louis DaPron), including pratfalls (faked falls) and a knee split jump.

Is it or isn't it?
Faked pickups are a long established tradition. They usually reference legitimate p-u steps, being named for similar coordination (appearance) and/or rhythm; e.g., shfl-d-p-u. Technically a pickup begins <u>after</u> the supprting foot is "picked up", <u>airborne</u>. Into the early 1940s, many routine notes began p-u's, while supported in plié, with a free foot brush lead for added lift <u>before elevating</u>, a "brush, leap" as a "pickup" (change); e.g., "Step L Pull Bk R bk of L" &a1 which is actually step L, running bk flap R. Even in 1987 "stomp R, double pull bk R".

Originally, any quick sideward leg swing was commonly called a wing, becoming a wing movement. Interestingly, few notes misname faked wings (like rolling wing change) although several difficult variations were performed - try a snap kick during a wing or wing change.

Self defining:
Eva Varady's "Broadway Rhythm" includes "brush R-up to R-side in seconde pos., hop L-step R-in front of L" - - - - " (For more advanced students a wing may be substituted for the hop)". And from Ann Dansetts <u>Advanced Soft Shoe</u> Step Five break: "Hop back L, picking up extra sound on hop."

Described are what wing and p-u steps? _____, _____

What's the flap about?
A pickup, like a flap, can be executed in any one direction leading at any angle by the foot. Functionally, a pickup is an airborn flap as specified in a Billy Clower 1956 routine "I Know That You Know" distributed for Russell Record #R5: "shuffle L, flap bk. R (grab-off)" repeated three times. The quote describes what step? _____

GLIDES & TOE STANDS

2 '- -teens' terms:
Often attributed as a Toots Davis trademark from the 1910s, making it "over the top" (running glides) and keeping low while moving "through the trenches" (trenches) were battle phrases popularized as tap steps during WWI. Did you notice that running glides coordination is trench-like?

Make it look easy:
The most abused, and so recognized, tap steps are glides. Ann Dansetts' <u>Advanced Soft Shoe</u> (1940s) Step Three, "Jump (or fake) 'over the top' to R". Faked over-the-tops are so common they are functionally the standard presentation. For the audience to appreciate the proper technique, provide them a view of the <u>over</u>, not around. Skill is displayed by ease of execution, <u>glide</u>, don't strain.

Similarly, pendulums, especially several performed facing D-S, must be swung diagonally to present the namesake image. High speed leg spins are most effectively obvious facing D-S and easiest with st A's 2nd, F D-S, tilting slightly fwd to minimize torso and emphasize action leg, with low hops adding rhythm interest.

To the pointe:
An early pointe tap-buck Fred Astaire training routine was so well done that it was incorporated into his and Adele's early vaudeville act. Some reviews compared his skills to the finest ballet dancers. The 1925-1935 fad style appeared in vaudeville, films, and dance studios; where youngsters with underdeveloped feet (skeletal and muscular) tapped en pointe.

Careful:
Toe stands, as with any en pointe (support on toe tip) technique, should be attempted only when foot extension, strength, and body placement are reliable. While properly fitted boxed (reinforced toe) tap shoes help maintain extended toes during toe stands, box rigidity prevents complete shoe shaping and usually indicates insufficient foot strength. For the visual effect, there are *faked* toe stands.

RHYTHM PATTERNS

It's about time:
In its simplest form rhythm establishes meter and tempo. To know the when of music, begin with the bass rhythm – the count starts there.

<u>Taps</u> or rattles:
Tap <u>rhythms</u> are determined by clearly separated taps. Early attempts to impress audiences with rapid tapping included washers, bottle caps, and coins nailed to the arches of the soles. In the 1850s the Worrell sisters, Irene, Jennie, and Sophie, created a unique design of hollow clog heels each containing a tin box loaded with two bullets, creating a rapid-fire rattle. Loose metal insert "jingle" taps are now rarely used by tappers, but remain the standard for country-western cloggers.

The silent tap:
Rhythm exists because of silence. Lacking clear gaps between sounds generates the monotony of continuous noise.

The primary and secondary accents for nearly all dance music are counts 1 and 3. To add interest, some tap styles intentionally precede or move (syncopate) the common accents, anticipating or countering (opposing) the music. An obvious example is the maxie rhythm pattern: 8&1&2 3&4&5 6 with rhythmically primary accents 8, 3, and 6. By establishing an unexpected accent pattern, most listeners still "hear" (7), the tap that isn't there.

Similarly, separated stop time music chords mentally evoke an unbroken familiar melody, and its rhythm.

Many dance notes have no indicator for a (*silent*) ct or hold. When notes include more ct's of rhythm than taps from steps, check for a notation error or a rhythmically notated sustained pos before the next tap.

There is another silent tap. Leather shoe bottoms are required to accept screws or tacks holding metal dance taps. Most student tap shoes include synthetic heels, necessitating nailing a $1/8''$ thick leather overlay, called a tap, to the plastic heel. This is the fourth use of the word tap. Add a tap to the tap to tap taps (metal to overlay to dance making sounds).

His name was Max:
Most named tap rhythm patterns are derived from dance styles or associated music: charleston, military, shim sham, etc. An early 20th century popular vaudeville tap quartet, The Four Fords, included brothers and sisters Edwin, Max, Dora, and Mabel. Max is credited with creating the oft encountered namesake rhythm pattern. Although a clog pattern, maxies are commonly used with all tap styles, and probably originated from waltz clog time-steps being incorporated into $^4/_4$ meter buck and rhythm routines. Try it, then see waltz clog maxie. Max did not originate the rhythm. Spanish character dance students will recognize: stamp, 2 claps, rev, stamp, clap <u>1</u>23<u>4</u>56<u>78</u>.

Name these rhythm patterns:
1a2a3 4a5a6
1&2 3 4 5&6 7 8
8&1&2 3&4&5 6 (7)
&1&a2 &3&a4 &5&a6&a7&a8

8&1 2&3 4&5&6&7
8&1 2&3& 4&5 6&7&
1 2&3 4(5) 67 (8)
a1&a2 a3 a4 a5&a6 a7 a8

Fascinating rhythms:
Do 16 runs on the balls of your feet. The rhythm was probably even 1&2&3&4& - - -. Try 8 b/c's. Probably duplet gallops a1a2 - - -. Repeat the experiment with slow or walking vs. running flaps. The landing coordination drives the rhythm. Hear and "feel" the difference between even and duplet rhythms.

Rhythm these rides:
An old memory aid (mnemonic) for buck time-step rhythms is the "buggy ride" series.
"thanks, for the buggy ride" = br bk, heel, step, flap, step (s-t-s var rhythm) 8 1&2&3
"thank you for the buggy ride" = " , flap, " (d-t-s var) 8&1&2&3
"thank you for the fast buggy ride" = " , tpl, " (t-t-s var) 8&1&a2&3
There are several variations.

That's not the same?
A rhythm shift is an emphasis change within a repeated pattern.
Rhythm shift is a dual concept, meaning either or both:
    (1.) changing the established rhythm of a sequence of similar steps
    (2.) changing the emphasis within an established rhythm pattern
How?
    (1.) Irish R x frt L, 2 heels R a1a234, rev 5&a67(8)&, rpt 2M. Same steps modified using qdlt irish and sync'n.
    (2.) R flap-b/c, tt L x bk R, step L a1a234, R flap-s/c, rpt tt-step a5**a**678. Same rhythm sequence, added accents.

Why? Because the duality often appears combined.
    (1.+2.) R flap-b/c, tt L x bk R, step L, R flap-s/c, tt L x bk R, stamp L.
        a1 a2(&) a (3&) a (4) {a5&**a** 6} (7) **&** (8)

Even a simple rhythm change may create the emphasis change. From <u>Showoff</u> Step 6, first phrase: f-r-c R rt, br bk L, heel R, tt L x bk R, heel R {&1&2&3&4}, rev comb {a5&a6}a7 (&)a, step R 8.

Cluster? Segment?
Cluster and segment are not beginner tap (even adult) concepts, but eventually prove useful. Cluster is often confused with even rhythm or segment. Being a rapid sequence, a rhythm cluster may be rolling, or more commonly include some even taps, although not required. A repeated sequence usually shorter than a phrase, it can be a segment of a longer combination, but may be repeated as a different set of steps, not a repeated segment composed of the same steps. A cluster is NOT a step combination, it IS a rhythm pattern. The concept is useful when defining unusual or complex rapid rhythms which are repeated; especially when the starting count is shifted or the cluster is performed using different step combinations. The isolated rhythm cluster can be practiced as a sound pattern then applied using any required combination or from any phrase count. Think clustered (group of) taps, segment (portion) of a combination.

This cluster/segment example is the second pickup change maxie variation (page 12), a duplet triplet quadruplet a8 &a1 a&a2 or quintuplet quadruplet {a8&a1} a&a2 cluster maxie segment used twice.
    Flap R, b/c L-R, dig L, br bk L into p-u-c-tt R x bk L, rpt comb,   flap-b/c R.
      a8   &a   1   a   &a 2 (&)   a3&a4a&a5(&) a6 a7
A cluster {a1&a2}(&)a(3&)a4, applied to different combinations, repeats as {a5&a6}(&)a(7&)a8.

F-r-c R rt, br L x bk R, heel R, tt L x bk R, heel R, flap L lt, br R x bk L, heel L, tt R x bk L, stamp R, step L c-p, stamp R.
    {a1&a   2}   (&)   a (3&)a   4 (&) {a5   &   a   6}   (&)   **a**(7&) a   **8**

Some notes are divided by segments or clusters rather than phrases. Danny Hoctor's <u>Lover</u> Step Five is divided: 5. (ct's 1-3) 5a. (4-8) 5b. (4-8), to be performed: 5., 5a., 5., 5a., 5., 5b., 5., 5a., 5., 5c. (4-8) 5d. (1-8), 5e. (1-8). In <u>Sunny Side of the Street</u> his Step Five was 5. (ct's 1-2) 5a. (3-5&), performed: 5., 5a., "Reverse and alternate 5a. 8 times in all as you travel fwd to S-L – 6&7&,8& – 1&2&,3& –", etc., "3&4&,5& , Heeldrop R – 6, Stamp L – 7 hld 8".

Another tpl, dbl, sgl:

The listed lindy rhythm pattern is actually a triple lindy ballroom rhythm, three action counts before partners "break-away", releasing a hand to rock back in opposite directions. Most theater dance lindys are the more interesting triple. The original ballroom Lindy (Swing) rhythm is 3 or 6 music ct's (slow, slow, quick, quick). The 6 ct non-traveling single Lindy basic is: step side, free Ft twd supporting Ft, rev, step x bk (releasing 1 hand), step-rock i-p   1(2)3(4)56. Double Lindy: step sd, tap c-p, rev step-tap, rock break 123456. The tpl: sdwd step-catch-step, rev, brk   1&23&456. Placing the brk after each tplt converts the ballroom 6 ct's to the common theater dance 4 ct's yielding the listed (tpl) lindy rhythm pattern   (1&234 5&678).

Pure poetry:

Irish R, flap L lt, hold
3 flap-steps (wiggle your hips)
Step-flap-step, shfl-hop, tpl lt
2 swinging flaps, 2 claps, that's that.
Try it. It is tappable and you get to applaud yourself.
Because most tapping is musically phrased, many rhythm patterns are noticeably melodic, spoken steps even poetic.

Shave and a crew cut:

Like footwork standards, familiar rhythms are often juggled. Lindy 1&234 becomes 123&4 and shave and a haircut 12&34 (5)67(8) performed with the hold shifted: jump, d-p-u, hold, scuff, hop, stomp extended frt   12&a3(4)567(8).

A taste of syncopation:

Some define syncopation as rhythm emphasis before a count, especially 1 or 3 (a12a34), but relocating emphasis can yield far more interesting rhythms. Simple flap-step syncopation may be significantly varied. Rhythmically count each phrase then tap it.

A.	8 flap-steps	&1 2 &3 4 - - - 8	even rhythm &1, on the ct	not very exciting	2 ct rhythm
B.	2M	a12(&) a34 - - - 8	a duplet a1, leading syncopation	better	2 ct rhythm
C.	2M	a1a(&2) a3a(&4) - - - 8	a triplet, leading and trailing sync'n	rushed	1 ct "
D.	2M	&1a(&2) &3a(&4) - - - 8	duplet 1a, trailing sync'n	delayed 'hiccup'	1 ct "
E.	2M	a1(&)a(2) a3(&)a(4) - - - 8	a duplet and a delayed ½ 'duplet'	skip and 'stumble'	broken 2 ct

Tap at slow then moderate tempos, rhythms sequence: A. 2 X's, 1 each B. - C., A. 2X's, 1 each D. - E. (4M). Rpt several X's.
Tap B., C., D., E. several times letting the rhythm shading "become natural".

In sync:

The basic Charleston {step, kick frt (opposing A reach up), step, tt bk (bend fwd, rev reach twd flr)} establishes mvmt for the simplest 4 ct's per 2M phrase. Don't fight the notation rhythm. Listen to a few versions of the title line rhythm of the song "Charleston".

Tap-Twister: Swinging syncopated certainly satisfies.

Music to their ears:

Leading composers and lyricists produced original music for many film musicals. Fred Astaire introduced many popular songs as dance themes, resulting in his recording dozens of 78 and 45 rpm phonograph record titles and LP (long playing) albums from 1923 through 1975. During 1936-7 NBC contracted him to reprise his hits as host of The Packard Hour, a 39 week season variety show. The live radio broadcasts included guest stars and were attended by public audiences. Along with comedy sketches and music, Fred tapped, restricted to a 4´ x 4´ mat next to a microphone. The studio and radio audiences were delighted; however, as noted in his autobiography *Steps In Time*, "there wasn't much I could do in the way of steps, especially, because my regular style was to cover ground and also get off the floor and up in the air a lot. Here I found that the only effective steps for radio were those with a lot of taps close together - - - - - If you got off the floor there was just nothing." With no rehearsal time while filming *Shall We Dance*, "I would ad lib each dance and hop into a finish step when I knew I was about twelve bars or so from home", selecting from his repertoire of a dozen "sustaining exhibition tap steps". Even a few of his recordings included tap inserts; other tappers recorded full routines.

It is noteworthy that Astaire copyrighted 20 tunes, most with lyrics by collaborators. Four were used in stage shows.

TAP DANCE STYLES

are distinct when specific steps, music, and rhythms combine to create a unique appearance and "sound". The evolution of these characteristics is, at best, blurred, but the following is worth considering.

Earliest?

"The Wing" has been claimed as the earliest tap forerunner American Negro dance. Originally a South African war dance, it was Americanized as the "break down" by Southern Caucasian and Negro minstrels, most notably the 1880s team Jim McIntire and Tom Heath. Slower barefoot slap, pat, and patter all male circle dance versions have been associated as the source of stop time, challenge, syncopated buck, and buck and wing stylings. This anthology links early speed and originality, sometimes wildly ad lib, by slave competitors (even while head balancing a jar of water) to establishing fast buck; while the slower styles generated soft shoe. Birmingham, Cincinnatti, and other breakdown variations were incorporated into theater dance; while Scottish and English round dance versions helped form American Country-Western (e.g., Louisiana breakdown) and some square dance steps. Breakdown spontenaiety may be the origin of terms (although not their definitions) such as: break, break-out, break-away. And you thought break dancing was a recent phenomenon.

Another view:
Excerpted from *Dance Digest* March 1958:
By 1800, "levee dancing" had been incorporated by minstrels to be popularized in the 1830s by performers such as Zip Coon and Jim 'Crow' Rice. Irish clog dancer Barney Williams' 1840 U.S. visit inspired lower leg auditory buck leading to late 1800s military stiff "rhythm contests of speed and clarity"* encouraging raised pedestal (2′ square) dancing novelty acts, most notably Henrey Dixey. The 1902-03 New York Theater Roof featured "Ned Wayburn's Minstrel Misses", blackface chorines performing "graceful feminine" hybrid "tap and step dancing", the first public use of the dance form name.

Terms developed: levee dancing, then step dancing becoming buck and wing, with an "eccentric slower form", soft shoe presented with "humorous, leisurely delicacy". There is an 1880s painting *Dancing For Eels* illustrative of the challenge for rewards practical function of levee dancing.

There are other chronicles.

(*Rhythm judges evaluated sound from behind a drape or under the stage, without viewing the contestants.)

An American first:
During the 1700s through 1800s, an intermingling of European and African dance styles gradually metamorphosed into the first American theater dance form – tap.

Initially, Southern Negro slaves copied Irish jigs, British hornpipes, even formal ballroom dance steps, endowing them with African dance rhythm complexity and jubilant styling. Although often a community activity, soloists improvised the creation of new patterns which, when frequently copied, became established steps. Jigging contests helped popularize the clogging style, early 1800s traveling medicine and gilly shows spread the influence of new style variations, with later 1800s minstrelsy bringing them north to build an established 20th century vaudeville dance form. Waltz clog, buck and wing, and soft shoe became formalized as song and dance, then expanded as eccentric, military, and a multitude of specialty/novelty acts. By the 1930s performers ongoingly exchanged ideas (Harlem Hoofers Club, later Copasetics) establishing a common vocabulary of steps, even routines. With popularity legitimatized in 1930s Broadway revues, tap began its dominance, firmly established as THE musical theater dance form, a new uniquely indigenous genre.

Perspective:
According to Aubrey Haines "Tap Dancings' Facts and Figures" article in April 1959 *Dance Digest*, in the U.S. in 1935 were:

    16,000 dance teachers   2 million dance students, 60% attending tap classes averaging 69¢
    $ll million spent on dance shoes $20 million on recital costumes
    one taps manufacturer sold 50,000 taps plus 25,000 pre-attached to shoes
    representing overall a $68 million industry   DURING THE DEPRESSION

A taps manufacturer noted a 280% annual production increase in 1934, plus another 400% in 1935.

Step! Thief!
The history of tap includes many sources from European, African, North and Central American, even Mid Eastern and Asian cultures. Creating new from previously blended steps and styles has been a recognized tap tradition. The Harlem 1920s Hoofers (social) Club was specifically created for the meeting of hoofers to gossip, exchange steps, and challenge for bragging rights. The 1949 instituted Copasetics added the promotion of tap dancing, and is still offering lecture-classes and videos. The Hoofer Club unofficial credo: "Thou shalt not copy each others steps, exactly".

The History of Taps:
Dance rhythms made using bare feet have many ethnic origins. Firmer shoe/boot soles and heels permitted greater loudness with comfort, yielding more rhythmically complex "foot dancing". During the 19th and 20th centuries maturing footwear and music development inspired a widening spectrum of tap styles.

Clogging:
Before there was dancing with taps, audio shoe rhythms were made using wood (frequently maple) soled shoes initially designed as protection from rough weather and rougher terrain. From Colonial times, American dancing included the Irish and English jigs and hornpipes of clog shod British sailors; however, French, Swiss, German, and Baltic folk clogging also immigrated. Dutch clogs were danced in hollowed all-wood shoes. Some Spanish zapateado (liberally defined "shoe dancing") boots and shoes included nails imbedded near the front of the soles and back of the heels – a precursor to metal taps.

Developed in thick-soled, heavy shoes, tap dance clog styles (waltz clog, buck and wing, etc.) are generally interpreted as bold, loud, frequently pounding, and rhythmically redundant – in no way subtle.

Soft shoe:
Hardier sole leather and improved public walking environments brought to the stage lighter, firm leather soles permitting easier, smoother movement and more subdued sounds. Although the relaxed style was also performed in clog shoes, soft shoes encouraged the execution of an array of elevations, kicks, turns, sluffs and slides with a tempo suitable to display extended body line – picture dancing. The most unique example, swishing sounds facilitated by a layer of sand scattered on the stage – sand dancing.

A gentle, nostalgic, romantic style excellent for relaxed duets (*Me and My Shadow*, *Strolling Through the Park One Day*) or hat and cane manipulations, including time for shadow duet synchronization or magic cane illusions.

Try clog and soft shoe, even sand dance styling (outdoors), wearing smooth-soled shoes (no taps).

Buck:
An antiquated term for male, once applied to "wild" undisciplined older boys and young men (young buck). The performance style originated and was early developed in Southern Negro medicine, gilly (traveling wagon), and minstrel shows. Various taps, including instep nailed jingling washers, were used from mid 19th century minstrelsy onward, with faster tap dance styles (not clog) dominating 1920s vaudeville. Adding arced metal wear protectors to the front edge of leather soles and back edge of heels introduced higher pitched audio clarity. As the arcs became half-moons and various placements permitted different floor contact points, new tap coordinations and tighter (faster, compactly clustered) sound combinations were discovered, leading to the evident desireability of specifically designed dance taps. Late 1920s patents by several inventers included William John Haney who arranged their Broadway exhibition in *No No Nanette* (1925). The 1930s into the '50s was the final transition period when vaudeville and film performances included Bill Robinson in front mounted clog "split-soles", Frank Condos with steel plates, Paul Draper using personally shaped and attached crescents, and a growing list of performers switching to various enlarged, thickened, louder aluminum alloy dance taps. By the early 1950s tappers could choose from several shapes, alloys, and designs, including built-in "floating" jingles, pointe slipper taps, and the tap that changed the industry – Tele Tone. The unique Tele Tone light weight shallow hollowed air pocket design permitted full coordination with exceptionally *sharp* (short, clear), separated tap sounds at floor level, improving stage audio output and micophone pickup (input) for live television and consistent recording.

Now, most tap routines are buck or rhythm-buck, up-tempo, busy-tap styles building from even rhythm time-steps through a liberal mix of strongly accented duple and syncopated patterns. Additionaly, showing off with pickups, wings, turns, trick steps, and rapid travel heightens audience excitement.

Incidentally, the gray marks on most dance studio floors are aluminum alloy scuffed from taps. The objections of mothers to student practice tap scuffs on house floors motivated, in the 1960s, the invention of split (2 pieces alligned to inside and outside sole and heel edges) Kalo nylon dance taps which were fine for practice but did not provide performance pitch, resonance, or volume and were never widely used.

And while we're at it - - -
Shim sham:
A heavily accented *floor* (low, without elevation) sophisticated clog style, performed dominantly in place or sideward.

Like falling off a log, 'tack annie is an action characterization. Traditionally, the alternating, non-traveling sideward movements represent a woman struggling to free herself from the custody of police "attacking Annie", frequently beginning the struggle with the break-away on ct's &8.

Rhythm:
This most complex style grew from the expanding rhythmics of buck and wing combining with the movement freedom of soft shoes into tapping. Encouraged by Swing music, easy sophistication expanded to rolling double time, or even rhythms interspersed with varied syncopation, all while ranging the stage. Technically and personally, rhythm tap became tap dancing, ideal for exhibition of personal skills and style.

Clap-tap:
Bill Robinson's tapping was variously described as "hammering" and "delicate", distinctly conflicting qualities. His clogs were custom built with a wood heel and front sole, leaving a flexible leather arch (the original split-sole dance shoe) enabling easier plié-relevé. Fastened from the tip only to the ball of the foot, the slightly loose clog sole freely resonated each tap, allowing, like a piano pedal, clamped sharp and/or louder or higher frequency slightly sustained off-the-floor tones. Additionally, he shaded his tap volume and rhythm sequences. His signature stair dance was performed on a unit designed to produce a different frequency from each step, combining features permitting an exceptional range of audio capability. Fred Astaire is quoted "He plays tunes with his feet as effortlessly and accurately as a fine drummer plays a snare drum."

Properly mounted, Tele tone taps can produce a similar metallic response. Audio reflective sounding boards, firmly tacked to the shoes, are overlaid with hollow taps mounted using a loosened, tone-adjustable point and two firmly attached base screws. Taps remaining on floor vs. immediately freed permit achieving loud clapping or subtle higher pitched resonance.

For the *Broadway Melody of 1936*, Bill Morgan of Capezio created for Eleanor Powell the Femme Oxford with inlaid taps within the outer of 2 soles, maintaining taps and soles at the same support level. Neat.

In the 1950s Paul Draper purchased 6 sets (75¢ per set) of taps at a time. Tapped by a hammer while hanging from string, allowed selection of pairs with the desireable mated frequency/resonance (tone). Hearing of this, a taps manufacturer volunteered to customize matched sets ($25).

Buck up:
While the Southern origin of the buck style is unquestioned, the source of the applied term is arguable. Of the several possibilities (including slang for a wearer of buckskin or 'uncivilized' male), many scholars assert the West Indies association of Negro slaves viewing Irish buccaneer jig dancing "buc dancers" as the likely importers of the rhythmic speed and term to America. Historically, the earliest consistent definition is male.

In the beginning:
The popularization of vaudeville personalities established many styles, steps, and tap terms.

Buck & wing, the union of flat foot clog (buck) with hopped sideward foot shaking taps (pigeon wing), is sometimes credited to James McIntyre, an 1880s clogger.

'King' Rastus Brown, an early 20th century flat foot master clogger, commonly "broke off" a series of time-steps with an improvised break. His inventive repetoire, including buck, cakewalk, cane, Irish jig, sand, stair, and stop time, encouraged 'King' being frequently credited with establishing (some claim creating, or at least formalizing) the buck time-step.

Break time:
The term chain break seems to have two nearly opposite meanings. After a sequence of similar combinations, like buck time-steps, a chain break is a variation that ends the rhythm/movement linkage. By repeated use during a routine, the same (or similar) break(s) links the pattern/style/intent of the routine; e.g., a simple waltz clog. Break the chain, or link the Steps. In both cases the breaks are usually a common (relatively standard) structure.

The ~~old~~ ancient soft shoe?
It has been facetiously argued that ethnic and folk stamping dances in leather soled footwear preceded clog soles, making soft shoe the earliest tap style. More appropriately, in America for some of his early 1900s routines, George Primrose exchanged his Lancashire Clog soles for leather, receiving credit for this theater dance innovation.

The essence of an essence:
The essence has many historic credits. Originally performed $^6/_8$ in minstrel shows, the term was well established by the 1850s, becoming George Primrose's waltz clog variations, George F. Moore's soft (non-clog) version, W. W. (Billy) Newcomb's named "Quintessence" style, and more. In the 1870s Eddie Girard included in his clogging act "The Essence of Old Virginia", a smoothly flowing dance performed to popular Southern music. The style gradually refined into soft shoe, including Eddie Leonard's specialty, the Virginia essense. With its many variations, it may be the earliest professionally popular complex step to be sustained to the present.

Essence means intrinsic quality. In its several forms, the soft shoe essence is indeed that. From the simplest step with rocking ball change, the extended arms and legs, smoothly flowing coordination, and relaxed rhythms all typify soft shoe styling. Like a buck time-step, the presentation of an essence instantly conveys the stylistic intent of the performer.

Beginning with step-b/c, how many sgl, dbl, and comb ess's can you create? Don't forget bk ess's, tr'g ess's, and try mixing frt and bk ess's in comb's, varying lead dir's, or restyling; e.g., parallel sdwd as sways.

Transition?
Early 1900s Jack 'Ginger' Wiggins' soft shoe style included acrobatic splits, "balletic" extended and arched body line (including a step he called "pull it", reportedly a 'tack annie variation), visually interesting steps (bantam and tango twists), elevated, and up-tempo traveling combinations. Possibly early shades of rhythm tap and step terminology.

An uplifting experience:
Early performance buck clogging tended toward pounding Irish origins: non-traveling (static), and composed of simple bold coordinations and rhythms at about 110-130 met. The entertainment value lay with the inclusion of song and dance staging, comedy patter, and novelty gimmicks. During the 1920s John W. Bubbles (born John Sublett) developed a style emphasizing:
1. more relaxed relevé, buoyancy, and travel,
2. tighter clusters with novel, more subtle use of heel and toe taps,
3. up-tempo "4 to a bar" (dbl-X $^2/_4$) with extended (4M-8M) phrases of increased rhythm/accent shaded complexity.

His expanded staging with a rapid flow of unexpected sound sequences thrilled audiences and amazed contemporary tappers. Bubble's personal style may be responsible for significant revisions in rolls and riffs, being often credited as the Father of Rhythm Tap. *Varsity Show* (1937) includes solo Bubble's, duet with vaudeville partner Ford Lee 'Buck' Washington, and a typical Busby Berkeley finalé. Well worth viewing.

Timing can be everything:
Tempo limits or expands styling opportunities. The even rhythms, heavier accents, and limited travel of shim sham and buck are largely the result of fast tempos. Although up-tempo syncopation characterizes sophisticated rhythm tap, even slight speed reduction enhances rhythm variation while permitting more interesting staging. Slower tempos encourage more expansive soft shoe body line or more personal waltz clog partnering.

Presentation style can vary as easily as changing tempo. Compare:

(Slow, romantic, arm-in-arm stroll fwd) w-c-t-s's R-L, scuff-dig w/w R x frt L, step L close-bk R – o/s r-d-j R into p-d-b.
              1&2&3 4&5&6 1 2   3   4 5 6

(Up-tempo tough guy Bowery clog) w-c-t-s's R-L, scuff R x frt L, hop L, dig w/w R x frt L, stamp L – lift R knee frt (fists on hips, tilt slightly bk), b/a R-L lt (A's open).   1&2&3 4&5&6 1 2 3 **4** (5) **&**6

Stick it:
In dance parlance pegs or sticks are legs. What step emphasizes this association? _____

"Stick it", "nail it", or "peg it" encourages the successful accurate performance of an especially difficult combination; e.g., multiple wings or turns – "lick it and stick it".

Theater slang and humor are frequently dangerously ambivalent. "Take the stage" does not result in a strained back. "Hit your mark" mildly entreats the performer to arrive at a specified stage location sometimes marked with colored gaffer tape, and there perhaps, "strike a pose". "Break a leg", "knock 'em dead", and "kill 'em" wish the performer onstage success.

Another, "make a leg", describes flatteringly posing a girl's leg. For dance, think closed or crossed position plié-relevé n/w.

What other 2 listed steps stem from "leg"? _____, _____

Factor it in:

A factor is a part which determines the finished whole. Many add the <u>double triple</u> as a natural extension of the 4 foundation time-step time factors. Most frequently presented as: shfl, hop, <u>tpl</u>, <u>tpl</u>, flap 8&1{&a2&a3&a}, this uses <u>dual time factors</u> (2 tpl's) with a flap ending.

As noted in **TERMINOLOGY**, cincinnati builds from draw-back (sometimes called pull back). Billy Clower in (1953) <u>Avalon</u>, Step 5 names: "& - brush bk. R 1 - heel drop L &a - shuffle R 2 - Step bk R" a "Triple Pull Bk. R", a close cinc.

You may encounter time factors more often than you expect. As with cramprolls, some dancers apply them to non-time-steps, making doubles versions of, among other steps, d-b's and cinc's by ending flap (not step), adding a tap while remaining i-p.

dbl-d-b	br bk, hop, flap	a&a1	dbl-cinc	br bk, hop, shfl, flap	&1a&a2
qdl-d-b	br bk, hop, qdl	a1a&a2	qdl-cinc	br bk, hop, shfl, qdl	&1a&a2a&
			or	br bk, hop, qdl	&1a&a2

Tapping, clogging, or - - -

Astaire was an avid drummer, incorporating his skills into several film numbers. The best is "Great Work If You Can Get It" in *Dansel In Distress* with a sticks and feet taps and traps (drum set) arrangement. Astaire's opening solo in *Gay Divorcee* is a clog styled soft shoe emphasized during a tacit break.

Wearing roller skates, Fred and Ginger coasted through a skate-tap routine in *Shall We Dance**, as did Gene Kelly down a street during "She Likes Me" in *It's Always Fair Weather*. "I'd Rather Be Blue With You Than Happy With Somebody Else" is more title than tapping, but an enjoyable comic skate-tap by Barbara Streisand and chorus near the beginning of *Funny Girl*.

With a right foot tap shoe and a wood left lower leg, Clayton 'Peg Leg' Bates tapped <u>and</u> clogged through his routines.

Marylin Miller on Broadway, as well as, Dick and Edith Barstow in *The Gem of the Ocean*, and even children tapped en pointe in pointe slippers. The novelty appeal was less coordination (movement was very limited) than daring-do. Routines, performed entirely en pointe, bounced down and up stairs and one-footed across the stage. In 1959 Robert Joffrey included in *A la Gershwin* a toe-tap, "My One and Only".

You decide what to call clanging and clomping in such footwear as garbage can lids.

(*As noted in the book *Starring Fred Astaire*, "Let's Call the Whole Thing Off" was no minor novelty number. It required 32 rehearsal hours then 4 days and 80 miles of skating during 30 takes (filmed performances) to provide 2½ minutes of film. There's no record of accumulated falls or bruises.)

The same Stanley Green and Burt Goldblatt book also enumerates the Astaire golf novelty "Since They Turned Loch Lomond into Swing" as requiring 10 days, 80 hours with a thousand tee and iron shots as preparation for 2½ days of filming. The 3 minutes of screen time in *Carefree* includes 16 swings. I wonder how many golf balls were used and whether they were all blocked as intended. Prop and novelty numbers can be time consuming production head-(and otherwise)-aches.

Shim and sham and shim and . . . . :

Tap dancers Danny Hoctor, Jules Stone, and Bob Kimble in the mid 1950s created Dance Caravan, which became an annual national tour of three day workshops presenting a faculty of nationally recognized dancers and instructors. Danny collected tap steps, claiming to have accumulated hundreds of shim shams, maxis, and time-steps. They appear frequently in his routine notes. Several **TERMINOLOGY** category listings conclude indicating many more exist. Something familiar in a routine may be a different shim sham or riff walk or time-step or . . . . . Watch Lawrence Welk Show reruns for Arthur Duncan's mostly buck performances, including time-step variations followed by buck breaks.

Dance Caravan U.S.A., Students – Stage Arts, Vol. 16 manual, pp. 56-60 <u>Doin' the New Lowdown</u> (A Tribute to Bill Robinson), is a sampler of Hoctor's buck time-steps and breaks collection. Dance Caravan was created to bring dance convention workshops to underserved areas while promoting the training aid recordings published through the founders' respective companies: Hoctor, Statler, and Kimbo Records. Classes included a variety of dance forms technique and routines prepared for students and instructors. Attending dance instructors received a selection of recordings and books of notes representing the workshop materials intended to be implemented in studio classes and recitals.

Incidentally, Arthur Duncan's national television career was launched on the 1952-1954 Betty White Show. Some Southern stations refused to air the series with a Negro appearing weekly, but White didn't buckle.

Give it a shove:

Replacing the irish with a snap kick and step x front converts a "shoveling" stamp step shim sham into "push and cross": stamp, step, rpt, stamp, kick, step x frt, step – another shim sham commonly performed with scissor or press down arms over the stamps.

Toot, toot:

In *The Harvey Girls*, Ray Bolger's dance party appearance includes a soft shoe-rhythm-eccentric number. Look for flea hops, patter steps, a couple of maxies, tapped pas de chats ("cat steps", a double passé leap), and his naturally comedic personal style. The film's musical theme ("On the Atcheson, Topeka, and the Santa Fe") permits several tapless railroad style dance and staging inserts.

Various railroad effects rhythms can be achieved using different basic steps.
　　　Shim-step, rpt, 2 shims, 2 steps. {8&1& 2&3& 4&5 &6& 7&}
　　　However, western flyer is a railroad combination with a track imperfection rhythm "hiccup". Scuffle-cramp (paddle and roll), flap-step, b/c. 8&1& a2&3&.
　　　Listen to the combinations. Do you hear the different sound quality of the digs and scuffs?
　　　Try flapped patterns using flap-heel, flap-step, flap-tpl, f-r-c, etc. Seek a subtle audio quality shading in each combination; not louder, just different. What term suggests a steam locomotive starting to move? _____

A style?

The January 1958 Assoc. Dance Teachers of Southern California meeting included "Authentic Irish Reel Tap" by Bobby Root.
　　　As with other tap terms, tap styles often arise from frequent use then fade when less popular. A few evolve, like flat foot clog becoming sophisticated tap. Acro-tap, pointe tap, and stair dance are actually novelty performance styles, not distinct technical divisions of the dance form. When popular they were sufficiently distinct to be readily identified, even advertised. Flat or sophisticated describe personal styling, while Russian or song and dance are character or theme based. Why a "style" is named can be confusing, this may help:

Tap <u>Dance Styles</u>	feature distinctive tap steps, music/rhythm, and staging.	(shim sham, military, etc.)
	Dance form styles are widely established and persistent, lasting many decades, making them a necessary technical element of tap knowledge.	
Tap <u>Novelties</u>	are tap styles with a gimmick added.	(soft shoe as sand dance or acro-buck)
	Exhibition of added dance skills to tapping.	
<u>Novelty Styles</u>	are "you gotta have a gimmick" with taps added.	(pointe or pedestal tap)
	Short-lived exploitation with no associated tap steps of intrinsic technical value.	
<u>Prop Dances</u>	any tap style being identified by costume, prop, or set piece(s).	(soft shoe <u>or</u> rhythm hat and cane
	Added handling, not step skills.	or stair dance)
<u>Characterizations</u>	represent impersonations or personalities.	(vernacular, comedy patter, etc.)
	All about who, with limited technical training expansion.	

　　　Even picking a subcategory can be tricky. Consider a country bumpkin doing a rubberleg hoedown, sailor doing a gob hat prop hornpipe, schoolgirl hopscotch jig, or ballroom tap with a hat tree partner. Again, as with step names, a dance description best builds from the foundation tap dance style, expanded for clarity; e.g., eccentric hoedown. Incidentally, the above Irish reel tap was likely a variant of Irish clog incorporated into country-western tap.
　　　Out of vogue does not mean out of use. Class studies and excellent performance pieces can be built from an Irish jig, sailor hornpipe, stair number, or railroad production. 21st century styles? Perhaps hip hop tap, electronic tap, rap tap, or stepping – if they persist.

You gotta have a gimmick:

Stop Flirting in London in 1923 was a spectacular hit. After one of their numbers, Fred and Adele Astaire teased the audience by repeatedly circling the stage with a high-stepping pantomime of tandem bicycling. The audience roared at their blase´ extended exit and the Oompah Trot was born. The step didn't spread but the team carried it back to New York to revive as the run-around, reestablishing their trademark Broadway exit.

Who's eccentric?

　　　A general reference to unusual performances, eccentric steps were derived from folk, fad, characterizations, prop, and novelty sources. Clogging on a pedastal, faux scratching the Itch (an Afro-origin fad dance), or Buddy and sister Vilma Ebsen's rope dance all fit the definition but yielded no exclusive tap techniques. Even the grotesque and unique, such as contortionist tap (feet tapping around the performer's head on the floor) or the elegantly costumed with feather fans Harriet Hoctor's deep backbend bourree's, continue to broaden use of the term. However, hornpipes and comedy characterizations did encourage teetering, sliding, and the flying limbs necessary for sailor rocks, flea hops, and logs. But it was Earl 'Snake Hips' Tucker's pelvic and others' interpretaions as rubberleg acts that engendered the most flamboyant steps, alligning eccentric largely as updated rubberlegs and overt comedy styling.

I get a kick out of you:

　　　Lines of cloggers can be traced back to folk dance (Irish, German, etc.) and minstrel (early 19th century blackface all male) variery shows. All girl chorus lines appearing in Southern Negro vaudeville and European cabarets from the 1850s were not always well coordinated. In Manchester, England in 1889, John Tiller introduced a troupe of kicking tappers who synchronized their leggy "Fancy-Dancing" rhythm by linking arms. Their popularity engendered the formation of a dance school which produced additional troupes, spreading the style in Europe, and eventually to the *Ziegfeld Follies of 1922*. The precision staging concept was copied and in 1925 Russell Markert introduced the 16 member Missouri Rockets to St. Louis. In 1931 the group moved to New York City and doubled in size to become the Roxyettes at the Roxy Theater. John D. Rockefeller hired Samuel 'Roxy' Rothafel as part of the creative team which engendered Rockefeller Center, highlighted by Radio City Music Hall. The "Worlds Largest Theater Stage" (144´ x 66´) 12/27/32 opening program included the Roxyettes – opening act was the Berry Brothers, on the bill was Ray Bolger. The 1933 first *Radio City Christmas Spectacular* featured the renamed Radio City Rockettes and their holiday trademark "Parade of the Wooden Soldiers".
　　　Even a physically linked tiller line has an end-to-end synchronization limit. Most are 12 to 24 girls, Rockettes 36, with a historic Tiller Girls record of 40.

I tap every day 'cause I gotta
Even though I'm told I should'nt oughta
I need help, plainly
But doc's book says lamely
Diagnosis: I got legomania.

POSITIONS

Bigger is lefter:
Notating L ft lead in upper case and R ft lower case elliminates redundent lead references.
    irish FLAP ballchange shuffle PICKUP CHANGE SHUFFLE LEAP toe-tap

Match the opposites:

arched	o/s
t/o	c-p
rel	t/i
i/s	plié
o-p	flexed

What you see is:
Which positions/movements mimic:
- log rolling _____
- railroad signal _____
- shaky hand _____
- struggling captive _____
- pushing _____
- leg tremor (1 leg) _____
- (2 legs) _____

Last stand:
Each following combination is lead R. Which is the final suporting Ft?
- Shfl, heel, step, shfl-b/c. _____
- Flap, heel, irish x frt, f-r-c, cinc. _____
- Log, stamp fwd into c-w shfl-b/c ½-tr. _____
- Shfl, wing chg, hip wing, tt. _____

The buck* starts here:
For most tapping the free foot moves from a raised position near the supporting leg ankle. However, other starting pos's have long been recognized: Johnny Boyle (1940s) "Triple L raising R ft front buffalo style". When introducing some steps, presetting a starting position is helpful (back flap, back essence). Many steps require a starting position. Describe them for:

- chug _____
- snap kick _____
- scoot _____
- swinging flap _____
- suzie-q _____
- snap _____
- sluff _____
- heel _____
- heel twist _____
- there are several more.

(*Buck is an outdated term for chug.)

Viva la French:
Ballet is the technical foundation of all aesthetic movement. Derived from European period dance (codified 16th century aristocratic social dance) early ballet performance technique was first codfied in Italy and France. During the 18th century, dance masters from the Parisian Académie de Danse (founded 1661) traveled throughout Europe, spreading the established training system, including the rules of movement, body positions, steps, and language of the techniques. All subsequent theater dance eventually blended, in varying degrees, with this foundation and continues to utilize the mostly French terminology.

Also, see the following **RHYTHM NOTATION, On the <u>beat</u>** (page 74).

To a French language student the ballet term en face may be confusing. The French definition is "opposite", in ballet "face the audience" (D-S). Understanding that a performer en face is facing opposite that of the audience justifies the seeming conflicting definitions. The more accurate term is de face, "full face" (facing) toward the audience. All right ballet students, how many different French ballet terms appear in the **TERMINOLOGY INDEX**? _____

Here are a few more:
    coupé = cut (catch)   en de dans = i/s   en de hors = o/s   entournant = tr'g   pas de deux = steps for two (duet)   fermé = c-p

List other ballet terms which could accurately replace terms used by tappers.

Look at me!
Theater dance is peformance dance, intended to visually entertain an audience. Tapping does not exclude the need to present interesting pictures – body line. As the tapping requires less concentration, consider your appearance: arms, torso, legs, head, even shoulders, hands, and facial expression. Mostly, enjoy your dancing, allowing the audience to see and experience your pleasure and satisfaction.

Picture this:
Occasionally only a picture can provide the required new or nuanced body line. Billy Glower's 1951 <u>Jealousy</u> tango tap notes include many stylized tango ballroom positions among the 12 pages of 355 photographs depicting the appearance of each tap step.

GENERAL TERMS

Personal? style:
Personal style can be elusive. Obviously, Astaire and Hines dance very differently. Even Fred and Gene Kelly don't move the same – or do they? In the 1946 *Ziegfeld Follies*, in their only film duet, they are a compatible surprise in "The Babbitt and the Bromide", ranging from jazzy comedy to smooth elegance with nearly parallel flow. Reprising the 1927 Broadway *Funny Face* number by Fred and sister Adele, perhaps their characters as two old friends, recurrently brought together over decades, explains their mutual ease and obvious enjoyment. A passing note. In 1957, after 30 years, *Funny Face* was hybrided with other scripts as an Astaire movie without "The Babbitt and the Bromide".

Sometimes the characterization takes over, like the Fred Astaire and George Murphy duo class act fencing with canes slapstick in "Please Don't Monkey with Broadway" in *Broadway Melody of 1940* – elegant slapstick.

Even gender need not discriminate. Observe Vera Ellen and Fred Astaire in *Three Little Words*.

It's mine:
Every tap dancer eventually selects a favorite tap style, buck time-step, shim sham, rhythm pattern, combination, and warm up exercise indicative of his personal style. Broadly categorized, hoofers tend toward sophisticated material while dancers select buoyant larger actions. Bobby Root's style is indicated by his recommended warm up riff: heel L, 5-tap riff walk R, heel L, bk flap-heel R, dig L, bk br L {1&a2&a3&a4&a}; a rocking hesitation walk. Start slow then gradually accellerate to improve subtlety and ankle control.

Make it personal: Number an item in each column best associated with the dancer.

The Guys: (5 radically different styles)

Dancer	Style	Personal Association	Appeared With	Motion Picture
1. Bill Robinson	__ athletic & jazzy	__ ballroom popularizer	__ Jerry Mouse	__ *White Nights*
2. Fred Astaire	__ eccentric & comedic	__ H--, H--, and Dad	__ Mikhail Baryshnikov	__ *Singin' In The Rain*
3. Gene Kelly	__ easy & ambling	__ Bojangles	__ Shirley Temple	__ *The Harvey Girls*
4. Ray Bolger	__ percussive	__ umbrella dance	__ Ginger Rogers	__ *The Little Colonel*
5. Gregory Hines	__ smooth & wide ranging	__ rubberlegs	__ Judy Garland	__ *Daddy Long Legs*

And the Gals:

Dancer	Style	Personal Association	Appeared With	Motion Picture
1. Eleanor Powell	__ lithe and energetic	__ Busby Berkeley	__ Donald O'Connor	__ *Footlight Parade*
2. Ann Miller	__ "favorite dance partner"	__ Rockette	__ Lucille Ball	__ *Lady Be Good*
3. Ginger Rogers	__ athletic	__ million dollar legs	__ James Cagney	__ *Easter Parade*
4. Ruby Keeler	__ "world's fastest tapper"	__ top hat & tails	__ Mickey Rooney	__ *On the Town*
5. Vera-Ellen	__ rapid turn sequences	__ Best Actress Oscar	__ Buddy Ebsen	__ *Shall We Dance*

Which guy tap danced 4 of these gals across the screen? _____

For a greater appreciation of the style differences, view the films.

Sophisticated and/or sophistication?
Following Step One of syncopated heel rolls in <u>A Study In Modern Rhythms</u>, Bobby Rivers adds: " NOTE: This step should be done in a very sophisticated manner, with as little movement as possible. Arms at sides or behind back with hands clasped."

A sophisticated tap style should not be confused with personal sophisticate styling, a calm, formal, even aloof "upper-class, classy" appearance presented as a "class act". An elegantly costumed performance neither requires nor excludes compact footwork. Sophisticated buck is often presented in top hat and tails, while evening gown and tuxedo ballroom tap usually includes very unsophisticated partnered lifts and floor covering travel. See the internet *Tap Dance Improvisation, Live In The Greene Space* for an excellent demonstration of sophisticated freestyle self-challenge by Savion Glover. Frequent close-ups and clear audio permit insights into ankle control, four taps frequencies, and shading of rhythms, volume, and tap contact point sound sources. Watch for subtle stylings and listen for rhythm variations of many common steps and combinations.

By 1920 the natty Eddie Rector's graceful "stage dancing" style was established and copied. While usually tuxedo costumed, class act was a general term for any elegantly presented usually male duet or trio, like the two Charles' double, 'Cholly' Atkins (Atkinson) and (Charles) 'Honi' Coles, noted for their gracefully synchronized slow motion soft shoe.

Or just the personality. From *Jazz Dance*, a 1916 early vaudeville review of Adele and the 17 year old Fred Astaire: "--- it could be wished that the young man gave up the blasé air which he carried constantly with him. He is too young for it and deceives no one." Later descriptions of Fred included "lack-a-daisical" and having a "gift for wry humor", a relaxed persona which never changed.

Freestyling:
Freestyling offers an opportunity for individuals to shine, restricted only by the accompaniment and their skills. An a cappella challenge can be uniquely exciting, with each round driving the challengers creatively ever deeper into their repetoire of subtleties and tricks. A group challenge may be rotational, each participant ending his turn "handing off" a pattern for the next challenger to build on before presenting new material. It is interesting to note that such unrestricted displays tend to be mostly metered $4/4$, confirming the natural human need for regulated rhythmics.

Play me a riff:

A music riff is a repeated pleasant musical theme. A tap riff is commonly followed by a heel, producing a pleasant flow of frequencies. Add a dig, snap, etc. and repeat a few as a redundant rhythmic easy stroll.

Riffles are small waves, often melodious ripples, created in shallow water. Repeat riffle-heel several times as quadruplets. Do you think the rolling frequency change is rippling? Just a thought.

Although largely ignored, frequency shading, like dynamics, is an essential part of tap audio. What you hear is more than what you notice.

Shim shading:

Shading may include any one or combination of subtle changes in rhythm, volume, frequency, or other tap sound qualities. Compare shims: scfl, step; shfl, step; scuff, heel, step; dig, bk flap. Do 2 of each in sequence. Similar, but subtly different.

Dances like a dream:

Most find quiet is conducive to creativity. During an interview, Bill Robinson admitted "I dreamed that I was dancing before some important person in some foreign country. I remembered what I dreamed and worked it out for the stage." In *Top Hat* (1935) the "Top Hat, White Tie, & Tails" closing shooting gallery concept (first used in the 1930 revue *Smiles*) was conceived by Fred Astaire years earlier at 4:00 a.m. while in bed.

The art of tap:

Too frequently, even professional tap performances are just another routine. Tap dancing can render genuinely entertaining listening, tapping, and pleasantly unexpected motion, dancing. Properly planned choreography can produce elegance or comedy, evoke patriotism or pathos, even portray romance or complex personalities.

In 1952 Morton Gould created *Tap Dance Concerto* in collaboration with Danny Daniels, who performed it widely in the U.S. and Europe. Louis DePron also often featured this 20 minute melodic-rhythmic tour de tap – the only symphonic work composed for orchestra and tap dancer. Gould and Daniels again in 1956 joined creativity for the shorter *Hoofer Suite*.

Paul Draper was an exceptional stylist. Billed as the "aristocrat of tap", his concerts included choreography inspired by classical, character, popular, and jazz music. In the 1935 revue *Thumbs Up* he performed "Words Without Music", an a cappella tap romance scene. His 1959 New York City YM-YWHA concert was reviewed: "The second section of the *Sonata*, entitled "Softly", was without doubt the finest creation of his career. The audience rendered fully earned bravos. - - - - The house was reluctant to let him go."

Probably the finest eccentric tap stylist, Ray Bolger's lanky physique, high kicking limberness, and rubberlegs bafoonery unfolded a flowing succession of visual humor. (Remember the *Oz* Scarecrow?)

At Home Abroad, another 1935 revue, featured a spy sketch in which Eleanor Powell tapped code. In *Ship Ahoy* (1942) an extended tacit break permits a reprise using Morse code. What's the message, Scouts?

Arguably, *Top Hat* was the first musical to fully integrate songs and dances into the story. Composer Irving Berlin was present at all production conferences, resulting in all songs being created to achieve script and scene continuity. The first half of *Top Hat* is probably the best film example of contiguous integration of scene action, story continuity, dialog, songs, music, and tapping; including a hotel room Sand Man sand dance and a rhythm interplay of Fred's feet in the boot of a hansom cab with horses hooves on the pavement. Director Mark Sandrich noted, "If any of them (songs) had to be eliminated - - - - dialogue would have to be substituted".

In *The Sky's the Limit* Fred Astaire goes on a "One for My Baby" binge, including an atop-a-bar sandless sand dance with a concluding frustration release glass disaster.

In 1989 Thomas 'Tommy' Tune performed as tapping guest artist during a *Tribute to Fred Astaire* Boston Pops concert. Unfortunately, he was restricted to a platform far too small to adequately illustrate the wide ranging Astaire style.

Acting is convincingly representing a character and situation. Gene Kelly believed any character can be interpreted through dance and took a 1940 opportunity to prove it. In a Broadway musical based on a William Saroyan play and John O'Hara novel, Kelly's portrayal of Joey Evans in *Pal Joey* was a breakthrough dramatic musical role. Bouncing the audience through a disquieting evening in a twisted world of seedy characters and amoral behavior, what might be considered the first melancholy musical brought Kelly to the attention of Broadway and Hollywood producers, leading to his first film studio contract.

More recent, *Tap* (1989) is the dramatic story of a contemporary hoofer (Gregory Hines) seeking an honest income in a society with little interest in tap performers. Along with Sammy Davis, Jr. and Savion Glover, there are opportunities to taste the stylings of Steve Condos, Jimmy Slyde, Harold Nichols, 'Sandman' Sims, and Bunny Briggs among others.

Curiouser and curiouser:

There is a difference between originality and peculiar.

During the *Thoroughly Modern Millie* movie, a single ladies rooming house persnickety elevator frequently requires tapping to persuade it to function. It seems equally responsive to triples, buck and wing, rattles, and a Chinese sand dance.

And the award for the slowest waltz clog ever filmed goes to: Susan Sarandan in *Elizabethtown*, performed as a new tap student at her character's deceased husband's memorial supper.

Many film plots have been segued using a romantic or stage performance tap scene. Probably the strangest is a bowling alley mood/time transition by a kidnap victim (Christina Ricci) in *Buffalo 66*.

As a spiritual demonstration, in *The Golden Child* a brief unsynchronized "Puttin On the Ritz" is performed by a mystically animated Pepsi can.

THE MOVIES

Thank you!
Our treasury of tap videos is largely the successful film musicals by M-G-M, 20th Century Fox, RKO, Warner, Paramount, Columbia, and their progenitors. From the late 1920s into the 1950s dozens of films were produced featuring or otherwise including tap dancing. The result is a library of performances illustrating some of the finest in tapping.

Studio creation stories began with the 20th century, building largely from small production and/or distribution companies. The following thumbnails provide some insight into the film industry.

By the end of the 19th century, penny arcade amusements included hand cranked flip-card and photograph peep show machines (Mutoscope, etc.). Motion pictures, the outgrowth of the Thomas Edison Company's 1891 camera and 1896 Vitascope projector patents, by 1907 were being viewed at over 2500 nickelodian "houses" charging 5 to 10 cents admission. The first films from Edison's West Orange, NJ laboratory were soon joined by productions from an assortment of mostly East Coast and European (using equipment similar to Edison's) directors. The 15 to 20 minute black and white silent "flicker picture" novelties fascinated audiences. In 1908 the Edison Company, with several other film equipment patent holders, formed the Motion Picture Patent Trust, attempting to standardardize the American technologies, reduce foreign imports, and licensing all use of their film products, from filming through viewing. To avoid East Coast licensing law suits, independent directors began moving production to the Los Angeles area. When, in 1915, the federal courts elliminated the broad scope of the MPPT attempted monopoly, producers-directors expanded film length (multi-reel) and entertainment value while theater owners improved viewing facilities. The industry exploded, with theater chains being supplied by associated studios producing year-round thanks to the West Coast climate. It was the onset of the Wild West of film studio development.

Chained:
It is a common belief that motion picture studios always controlled the movie industry. Initially, theater chains, needing films and having the money, dominated production trends. The earliest successful 1880s early Broadway, New York and other metropolitan theater owners expanded to other cities, eventually developing chains of theaters, accomodating performer, even entire show, tours. Early motion picture theaters developed from these nickelodian, vaudeville, and "variety" houses, some of which, like Loew's, Keith, and Orpheum, spanned several states. By the late 1890s flickers closed many vaudeville shows. By the 1910s movie theaters were being built, many including stages suitable for live performance preceding a 1920s transition from vaudeville to motion picture entertainment. Check your local theater history. It likely includes some of the following names.

Edward Albee and Benjamin Keith used their youthful 19th century circus experience as a foundation for museum shows (a mix of circus side show exhibits and variety performers) which springboarded them into vaudeville. By 1925 the Keith-Albee chain was 400+ East Coast and Midwest theaters. Their 1927 merger with Martin Beck's Orpheum Circuit united 700+ theaters in the U.S and Canada, eventually linking to RKO.

The oldest of the American theater chains was started by Marcus Loew (penny arcade operator). Joined by Adolph Zukor and others, the 1904 purchase of a nickleodeon was the first of many acquisitions. Within a year Loew had become the independent owner of several theaters as the People's Vaudeville Company, providing live and one-reeler entertainment. 1910 brought Loew's Consolidated Enterprises, merging with Zukor and Joseph and Nicholas Schenk (amusement park operators). Its 1919 purchase added the failing Metro Pictures to other acquired entertainment companies reorganized as Loew's Inc. Ongoing expansion included M-G-M.

What's in a name:
We are accustomed to the names of the major motion picture production companies, giving little thought to their origins. A motion picture company minimally requires three things: production, distribution, theaters. The formation of the successful motion picture corporations is a story of intermingled acquisistion of, or access to, these three essential elements. Although media companies continue to be traded and consolidated, the long established pattern began with the competitive muddle of the originals.

Pathé, the world's second oldest (1896) major film production company, originated in Paris. Initially importing into the U.S., it was producing films in Jersey City, NJ by 1914. By the early 1900s it was the world's largest producer of films and motion picture equipment and a large manufacturer of phonograph cylinders, later records. Absorbed into RKO the brand ceased in 1931.

Starting 1909, the varied scenic selection around Fort Lee, NJ attracted film-makers', filming in giant greenhouses, creating America's first motion picture capital. In 1911 Nestor Studios of Bayonne, NJ moved to California, becoming the first Hollywood film company. William Selig (previously magician and minstrel show manager) in 1896 was making films in Chicago. Beginning in 1908 Selig Polyscope Co. transitioned to Edendale as the first Los Angeles film production company. Relocating in 1915 to an expanded East Los Angeles location, the action film company site included outdoor space for over 700 animals and was known as the Selig Zoo. When film production ended in 1918, the animal facilities became an amusement park and zoo.

In 1905 two Chicagoans, Carl Laemmle (clothing store manager and nickelodeon operator) and Aaron Jones formed Laemmle Film Service as a film exchange network supplying theater owners. Independent Motion Picture Company was created in 1909 to produce films in violation of the MPPT. The 1912 merger of IMP with five New York film companies became – borrowing a pipe-fitting company's name - Universal Film Manufacturing Co. with Laemmle president and leading to a move to California becoming Universal Studios with Hollywood and San Fernando Valley locations. Combined as Universal City in 1914 on a 230 acre chicken farm, the complex remained the world's largest until M-G-M's 1925 expansion. A silent film tour was 25¢; a dozen eggs, 5¢ more. The 1913 Hollywood population was 5,000.

The British (1897) Marconi Co. provided wireless (radio) telegraphy communication between ships and with shore stations. The 1899 expansion as American Marconi offered the opportunity for David Sarnoff to learn the radio business. Marconi policy was to manufacture and lease equipment and provide company trained operators, maintaining complete system control. After W.W.I the U.S. Navy objected to foreign control of defense communication, leading to an arrangement whereby General Electric purchased (1919) American Marconi and the patents necessary to operate the company as Radio Corporation of America headed by David Sarnoff. After unsuccessful attempts to convince the RCA board of directors to try transmitting entertainment to the public, Sarnoff in July 1921 stategically distributed receivers to New York area bars and theaters, then broadcast live the "Fight of the Century" Jack Dempsey vs. Georges Carpentier world championship boxing match to 300,000 listeners. The huge public response requesting similar programs, within months generated the establishment of broadcast stations with GE/RCA becoming the principal producer of radios (1922 Radiola, $25) for the exploding home radio market. In 1926 RCA spun-off NBC (National Broadcasting Co.) developing a national network of affiliated stations and, after W.W. II, led television broadcast development.

Formed by Harry Aitken and others in 1906, Western Film Exchange (Milwaukee) in 1912 merged with Thanhouser Film Corp. and American Film Manufacturing Co. (founded 1910) as Mutual Film. Future associations with D.W. Griffith and Charlie Chaplin led to the development of several picture companies including Triangle (originated by D.W. Griffith and Mack Sennett) and Keystone (home of the comedy cops). Chaplin's 1916 $670,000 film contract was a world record.

Robertson-Cole, a British import/export company, in 1920 created Robertson-Cole Studios in Pacific Palisades CA as an import movie outlet and U.S. production facility. From it (1922) the Film Booking Offices of America (FBO) was founded with the studio as a subsidiary, shortly thereafter being run by Pat Powers. Joseph P. Kennedy acquired FBO in 1926.

Radio Corporation of America controlled the rights to the General Electric developed Photophone film audio strip technology. However, most major studios had already committed to the 1926 AT&T/Western Electric ERPI (Electrical Research Products Inc.) licensed syncronized sound system. In 1927 Pathé and DeMille's Producers Distributing Corp. (1924) joined the KAO (Keith-Albee-Orpheum) theater chain, accessing Pathé's Culver City studio production output. David Sarnoff of RCA convinced Joseph Kennedy (FBO) to underwrite consolidation with Pathé-KAO forming Radio-Keith-Orpheum Corp. (RKO) with RKO-Pathé and Radio Pictures providing an outlet for Photophone. By the early 1930s RKO was acquiring additional theaters.

An interesting tidbit is that RKO was an early Walt Disney distributor. RKO ceased production in 1957.

While, in 1912, the merged Carl Laemmle (Independent Motion Picture Co.) and Pat Powers (Powers Motion Picture Co.) vied for leadership of the newly generated Universal, Lewis J. Selznick (jeweler), on the pretext of peddling his wares, invaded the embattled N.Y. Universal offices as an undeclared hiree of either contender. By the time Laemmle was victorious over Powers, Selznik had sereptitiously learned enough about the film business to form World Films with Arthur Spiegel of Chicago. Ejected by Spiegel, Selznick formed Selznick Productions (1917). That year Zukor induced Selznick to sell him half the Selznick company and rename it Select Film Co., one of several lines Louis B. Mayer, over the years, distributed out of Boston. Within months Mayer abondoned Select and bought back into and assumed control of American Feature Films and Metro of New England. By 1918 Mayer abandoned Metro to join Nathan Gordon (Boston penny arcade operator) as Gordon-Mayer Film Exchange linking to the First National Exhibitors Circuit.

(If you think this is confusing, you're right, and there's more.)

Early films were dominantly 1 or 2-reeler slapstick comedies or serial "cliff-hanger" adventures. In 1913 Jessie Lasky (vaudeville cornet player) and his brother-in-law, Samuel Goldfish (glove salesman, born Schmuel Gelbfisz), joined writer-stage director Cecil B. DeMille as the Jesse L. Lasky Feature Film Co. (later Paramount Pictures), with the objective of converting "literature" to feature-length film (photoplays). None had movie experience. In a rented barn they produced the first 6-reel (264 scenes) Hollywood movie, *The Squaw Man*. In 1916 Goldfish left Feature Film to join Edgar and Archibald Selwyn, combining names as Goldwyn Pictures. Preferring a more impressive moniker, Goldfish in 1918 became Goldwyn. Louis B. Mayer (American Film Co.) with Al Lichtman, and others in 1914 formed Alco Film Corp. a production and distribution pool which arranged with other distributors to finance producers at $15,000 per picture for a 50/50% split. In 1915 Alco transformed into Metro Pictures Corp. in California. Louis B. Mayer Pictures Corporation leased production space from William Selig through 1918 during construction, on adjacent purchased property, of new studios which opened January 1919. About the same time Samuel Goldwyn acquired the Culver City former Triangle Pictures studio for his productions. To ensure a steady supply of new films, Loew's Metro was merged (1920) into the Loew's theater chain. The 1924 Loew's expansion acquiring Goldwyn Corporation required a studio head and Mayer, with the understanding that his name would prominently introduce each film, agreed, joining the new Metro-Goldwyn Corp. Part of his January 1926 contract renewal included completion of the new, and continuing, name Metro-Goldwyn-Mayer Corp.* (M-G-M). Used by Goldwyn Corp. since 1916, the M-G-M lion logo inspiration was credited as being the Columbia University mascot. Louis B. Mayer probably locally associated Leo.

(*Samuel Goldwyn was never a part of the corporation which continues to feature his name.)

The earliest flickers, made by dozens of entrepreneur producer film companies, were commonly sold to distributors by the foot (.10 per foot is often mentioned), encouraging longer, more interesting content. The distributors were free to hawk the films however they could arrange, leasing or sale. With the spread of nickelodeons and increased film use in vaudeville theaters, the growing market led to regionally franchised distribution and the need for more product which encouraged production financing by distributors and theater (especially chain) owners. The underwriting contracts and expanding market left ever more profits with the middle-man distributors. As a protest against erratic distribution contracts and resultant low producer revenues, in 1919 Mary Pickford, Douglas Fairbanks, Charlie Chaplin, William S.Hart, and D. W. Griffith formed United Artists. Over time, many non-studio (independent) producers used U.A. facilities. By 1919 over 100 motion picture studios were located in the Los Angeles area. Hollywood population was 35,000. United Artists was the original Disney distributor.

William Fox's 1904 purchase of a Brooklyn nickleodeon led, by 1914, to his contracting with the Balboa Amusement Producing Company for exclusive distribution of their film prints. He also purchased the New Jersey Éclair studios, becoming the Box Office Attractions Co. while continuing to add vaudeville-movie theaters. Early West Coast development included (1919) William Fox's Fox Films first studio on the Selig lot next to Mayer, followed in the 1920s by the acquisition of an outlet chain of theaters. In 1932 Louis B. Mayer's son-in-law Bill Goetz was leaving Fox and Darryl Zanuck and Joseph Schenck were leaving Warner. Mayer, with Nicholas Schenk (Joseph's younger brother at Loew's), financed in 1933 Twentieth Century Co. with Twentieth Century Pictures making films using Samuel Goldwyn's studios and releasing through United Artists, effectively competing with Loew's and M-G-M. The 1934 refusal by Mary Pickford to negotiate U.A. stock sales led Twentirth Century to negotiate and (1935) merge with the bankrupt Fox Film Corp., becoming 20th Century-Fox, thus acquiring a theater chain.

In 1907, theater operator William Hodkinson of Ogden, UT became MPPT regional distribution manager, establishing Progressive Pictures and the profitable distribution format still in use. Adolph Zukor (New York furrier and penny arcade operator) imported (1912) European films as Famous Players Film Co. with distribution by Hodkinson who, in 1914 becoming disenamored of MPPT links, sought new affiliations. Inspired by his sketching a new mountain peak logo brought to mind a New York City apartment house, resulting in his company's name change to Paramount Pictures. In 1915 Zukor and Jesse L. Lasky Co. productions of Hollywood sold their companies to Paramount, their shares giving them control of Paramount stock. A 1916 Zukor-Lasky merger, to eliminate their competition for top stories and actors, unified the companies. Through the 1920s Zukor developed Publix Theatres Corp. (including the 1926 purchase of the Balaban & Katz chain) into a 2,000 screen outlet into which Lasky added Vitaphone. The current Paramount studios opened in 1926 on 26 acres, eventually expanding to 65. In 1939 Gary Cooper, at $482,819, was America's top wage earner.

26 independent theater chains (600 cinemas) in 1917 formed First National Exhibitors' Circuit as a distribution company for such producers as Mary Pickford and Charlie Chaplin, as well as, underwriting film producers in competition to the increasingly powerful Zukor. Reincorporated in 1919, Associated First National Theatres (and Pictures production company) had grown to the largest national chain (5,000 theaters). As First National Pictures, it began in 1924 producing from a new 62 acre Burbank studio while still distributing for others.

The four Warner brothers (Albert, Harry, Jack, Sam) opened their first theater in New Castle, PA in 1903, adding (1904) Duquesne Amusement and Supply for film distribution. Opening a Sunset Blvd. studio in 1918 led to the 1923 founding of Warner Brothers Pictures and the 1924 purchase of the Vitagraph Company (1897 Brooklyn) as national distributors. With spectacular early talkies success (1926 Vitaphone), Jack had accumulated the majority of First National stock by 1928, naming Darryl F. Zanuck National's manager. The 1929 purchase of the Mid-west Skouras Brothers theater chain as part of the Warner Bros. Theater Circuit led to the acquisition of First National with combined Warner-First National film credits into the 1940s.

In 1918 Harry and Jack Cohn with Joe Brandt created C.B.C. Sales Film Corp., an economy film production (Hollywood) and distribution (New York) company, renamed Colombia Pictures Corp. in 1924. In 1927 Frank Capra joined Columbia and directed a legacy of award winning hits, boosting Columbia's income and industry status. The corporation owned no theaters.

 1924 Big Three: First National, M-G-M, Paramount
 1927 Big Five: plus Producers' Distributing, Universal
 1928 Big Six: Fox, M-G-M, Paramount, RKO, Universal, Warner

Technicolor (1916) dominated the film industry until 1955. Frequently enhancing dance production musical inserts beginning in the 1920s, full-color saw much wider use after the 1930s depression*. By the late 1940s, improved lower cost color technology established color as the cinema standard.

(*The 1929 Warner-First National *On With the Show* was advertised as "The first 100% Natural Color ALL SINGING PRODUCTION".)

Although first appearing in 1897, widescreen movies were popularized during the 1920s. Several lens technologies (Fox Grandeur, Natural Vision, Fathom Screen, Realife) developed until the depression forced production economization. From the 1940s Vista Vision, Panavision, and Cinemascope combined with color and improved sound to bring a vibrant history of an array of lavish musical cinema excitement.

 1944 Big Five theater owners: Loew's, Paramount, RKO, 20th Century-Fox, Warner

This is a mild version of early American film history. There are many books presenting the gritty conflicts, a good start being *Hollywood Raja*, the Louis B. Mayer biography by Bosley Crowther.

At various times several of these film corporations included live theater, phonograph, radio, and other entertainment subsidiaries, a trend consistent with their current international relationships with television, the internet, and theme parks.

Check 'em out:

Tap dancing was popularized by vaudeville then vigorously promoted by the motion picture industry. During the 1930s into the 1950s most featured film performers (stars) were contracted to motion picture studios. Not only were top stage tappers featured in films (frequently tailored to their talents) but budding studio contract (training and performance control exchanged for a guaranteed salary) talent deemed suitable for musical roles received classes in acting, singing, and dancing – ballroom and tap. Additionally, studios sought novelty tap acts, as well as, a range of choreographers and music, providing a broad video sampling of tap stylings.

Motion picture performances provide excellent demonstrations of techniques, styling, and staging. Note music and choreographic trends associated with movie release dates. Following are a few style studies of featured performers and choreographers as filmed tap numbers, most internet viewable. Watch and listen.

Date (Studio)	Performers	Film	Accompaniment	Choreographer
1929 (MGM)	various	*Broadway Melody*	various	various

First talky and tap musical includes tiller and pointe tap (pend, log). First Best Picture Musical Academy Award.

1929 (MGM)	various	*Hollywood Revue*	various	various

Less a dance film than, with *Broadway Melody*, the standard for the rash of following film musicals. The list of early MGM stars includes several later popular on radio and even television. Original premiere of "Singin' In The Rain".

1930 (RKO)	Bill Robinson	*Dixiana*	medley (including stop time)	Bill Robinson

Film debut. A lazy feather duster opening transitions into a relaxed stairway number with a shave-and-a-haircut finish. Listen for some early unintended sluffiness; watch for eagle with quasi-legomania comb.

1933 (WB)	Sammy Davis, Jr.	*Rufus Jones for President*	multiple	probably Sammy Davis, Sr.

Film debut routines by 7 year old Sammy include buck standards, toe stands, vaudeville styling.

1933 (WB)	Ruby Keeler	*Forty-Second Street*	"Forty-Second Street"	Ruby Keeler

Keeler's solos represent "theater" (musicals) buck and wing clog of the period. Seek the 1932 color clip.

1933 (RKO)	Fred Astaire, Ginger Rogers	*Flying Down to Rio*	"Carioca"	Astaire with Hermes Pan

A light comedy Latin ballroom tap duet established a new standard for film tap partnering. The duo's film debut.

1934 (WB)	Bill Robinson	*King For A Day*	multiple	Bill Robinson

A spectrum of historical material, from a minstrel show format to vaudeville. Lots of standards.   uncredited

1934 (RKO)	Fred Astaire, Ginger Rogers	*Gay Divorcee*	"The Continental"	Astaire & Pan

Pick-a-style two step, Latin, swing arrangment, plus waltz when reprised. The mixed rhythm music earned composer Con Conrad and lyricist Herb Madgidson the 1st Academy Award presented for Best Original Song.

1935 (Fox)	Bill Robinson	*In Old Kentucky*	sophisticated buck; w-c medley	Bill Robinson

Excellent display of easy style, including a few enlightening close-ups. Dbl-shfl's into rattles and a log exit.

1935 (RKO)	Bill Robinson, Jeni LeGon	*Hooray for Love*	"Living in a Great Big Way"	probably Robinson

An easygoing duet and closing Robinson solo. Many standard rhythm patterns and associated combinations.

1936 (MGM)	Ray Bolger	*The Great Ziegfeld*	"She's Not My Girl"	probably Bolger

Eccentric spectrum includes nerve rolls, patter steps, slow motion side split and recovery, and trademark flapped pas de chat.

1936 (MGM)	Eleanor Powell	*Born to Dance*	"Rap-Tap On Wood"	Dave Gould

Too simple a number for Powell, but indicative of 1930s choreography.

1936 (Para)	Louis DaPron, Eleanor Whitney	*Three Cheers For Love*	"Swing Tap"	Daniel Dare or DaPron

Includes a taste of the DaPron classical tap trademark.

1937 (Fox)	Geneva Sawyer, Bill Robinson	*Café Metropole*	various	probably self

Duets deleted from film. Caucasian Sawyer (Shirley Temple's tap instructor at Fox) performed in Negro makeup.

1937 (RKO)	Fred Astaire, Gracie Allen, George Burns	*Damsel In Distress*	"Put Me to the Test"	George Burns

Whisk broom number; originated by a friend in vaudeville, was restaged by George.

1938 (Ind)	probably a Tyler twin	*Swing*	"Bye Bye Blues"	self

Stop time buck & wing. Note hip wings, p-u trenches, and outside of foot sluffed trenches (faked running glides?).

1939 (MGM) & (WB)	Judy Garland & Mickey Rooney			

Unlike Fred and Ginger, they started as teen child stars performing duets (some tap) in 10 films (1937-1948).

1941 (MGM)	Berry Brothers	*Lady Be Good*	"Lady Be Good", "Fascinating Rhythm"	Berry Bros.

Vaudeville novelty acro-tap trio James, Nyas, and Warren. Also, Eleanor Powell: fouetté, pigeon-toe roll, and more.

1941 (Fox)	Hermes Pan (uncredited), Betty Grable	*Moon Over Miami*	"Kindergarten Conga"	Hermes Pan

A ballroom swing-Latin duet. Also a Nick and Steve Condos (Condos Brothers) rhythm number.

1943 (Fox)	Nicholas Brothers	*Stormy Weather*	"The Jumpin' Jive"	self

The Fayard & Harold Nicholas famous jump into splits stair descent. More Bill Robinson.

1944 (RKO)	George Murphy, Constance Moore	*Show Business*	"It Had to Be You"	Nick Castle

Easy going fun song and dance soft shoe duet.

1944 (Col)	Rita Hayworth, Phil Silvers, Gene Kelly	*Cover Girl*	"Make Way For Tomorrow"	Gene Kelly

Hayworth's voice is dubbed but she and Phil can tap. Watch for Kelly's windows reflections "Alter-Ego Dance".

1946 (WB)	Condos Brothers	*The Time, the Place, and the Girl*		self

The Nick and Steve Condos slip and slide signature style with a touch of fun with wings.

1948 (Fox)	Dan Dailey, Betty Grable	*When My Baby Smiles At Me*	"By the Way"	Seymour Felix
1947 (Fox)	" "	*Mother Wore Tights*	"Kokomo Indiana"	" "

The first, a real soft shoe, on a stage with a burlesque runway. The second, a late vaudeville styling.

Date	Performer(s)	Show/Film	Number	Choreographer
1949	Gene Kelly, Vera-Ellen	*On The Town*	"Mainstreet"	Gene Kelly

Traditional soft shoe with lots of standard steps.

| 1953 (Fox) | Donald O'Connor, Vera-Ellen | *Call Me Madam* | "It's a Lovely Day Today" | Robert Alton |

Ballroom styled romantic soft shoe.

| 1954 (MGM) | Gene and Fred Kelly | *Deep In My Heart* | "I Love to Go Swimmin' With Wimmen" | Gene Kelly |

The only feature film duet by the Kelly Brothers who performed together before Gene's early Broadway career.

| 1956 (theater) | Atkins & Coles | at the Apollo Theatre, Harlem | "Come On Let's Dance" | Atkins & Coles |

Song and dance class act smooth rhythm duet.

| 1956 (NBC) | Louis DaPron, Vera-Ellen | *Perry Como Show* | "That Old Soft Shoe" | Louis DaPron |

Watch for the easy-to-miss Step of sand dance.

| '50s (CBS) & '60s (ABC) | Clayton 'Peg Leg' Bates | *Ed Sullivan Show* | | self |

22 performances – more than any other Sullivan Show performer.

| | Arthur Duncan | *Lawrence Welk Show* | | self |

With occasional exceptions, Duncan's many appearances illustrate the often unavoidable bandstand staging limitations.

| 2001 (MGM) | Gregory Hines | *Bojangles* | | Henry LeTang |

'20s vaudeville into '40s film, a fragmented evolution of tap technique and styles. Watch the closing stair dances.

| 2016 (theater) | Rockettes | *Christmas Spectacular* | "Ragdoll Dance" | Julie Branam |

Syncronized line alphabet blocks dance box number at Radio City Music Hall.

The most evident trend is that tapping matured into the 1950s, becoming smoother (more natural) while more technically and spacially expansive. The traditional strolling vaudeville and sophisticated hoofer clog routines transformed into set consuming and down-the-street broadly resourced dancing with taps. For a 50 year perspective of M-G-M musicals, watch the 1974 *That's Entertainment*.

I did that:

Choreographic styles are frequently as distinctive as performer styles. More film references:

Date	Choreographer	Film	Noteworthy
1929 (MGM)	George Cunningham	*The Broadway Melody*	Earliest sound musical choreography, first of title series.
1934 (WB)	Allan Foster	*Gem of the Ocean*	Novelty stair dance pointe tap featuring polzounoks, russian wings, wing chg's.
1935 (WB)	Busby Berkeley	*Gold Diggers of 1935*	"Lullaby of Broadway" narrative production.
1935 (RKO)	Fred and Hermes	*Top Hat*	A film-stage male dance chorus production.
1942 (WB)	LeRoy Prinz	*Yankee Doodle Dandy*	Early Broadway to Hollywood styling.
1943 (MGM)	Bobby Connolly	*I Dood It*	Eleanor Powell novelty lariat dance. Also, Buck and Bubbles.
1945 (Col)	Jack Cole	*Eadie Was a Lady*	"The Greeks Never Mentioned It", "I'm Gonna See My Baby"

The intermixed dance forms (here modern, jazz, tap) common to Cole's style.

1946 (Col)	Hermes Pan	*Thrill of Brazil*	An Ann Miller tailored routine, 6 min's, 125 tr's.
1954 (Fox)	Robert Alton	*There's No Business Like Show Business*	O'Connor & Mitzi Gaynor jazzed-up tap standards.
1950s (CBS)	June Taylor	*Jackie Gleason Show*	Frequent appearances by tiller June Taylor Dancers.

Kaleidoscope effect (overhead camera view of synchronized dancers lying on their backs) premiered in film by Berkeley.

| 1984 (Ind) | Henry LeTang | *Cotton Club* | Includes "Sheik of Araby" typical group challenge. |

The above are only a small sampling of recorded tapping. Others are referenced throughout this **DISCUSSION**. To acquire a perspective of the performance context, occasionally take time to view an entire film.

We did that:

The most prolific and enduring tap choreography film collaboration was Fred Astaire and Hermes Pan. From 1935 through 1968, 14 films included joint choreography. While Astaire always set his final material, Pan was often instrumental with concepts (Astaire credited him as his "ideas man"), styling (jazz, character, etc.), and "lifts and other gymnastic aspects" (Fred's description). Additionally, he frequently set on choreography and rehearsed Astaire's film partners, dubbed their taps, and occasionally, even filled (appeared) in the dance cast.

Such an alliance is not unique. Stanley Donen impressed Gene Kelly as a chorus boy in two of Gene's early Broadway musicals. Moving to Hollywood shortly after Kelly, Donen was hired as an assistant during the filming of *Cover Girl*, the first of several joint choreographic/directoral efforts.

Song and dance man:

George Burns and Gracie Allen were a well established vaudeville comedy team before becoming stars of radio, film, and television. While preparing to shoot (film) *Damsel In Distress*, George told Fred Astaire about a novelty whisk broom number available from a fellow vaudevillian. Fred and Hermes Pan liked George's demonstration, performance rights were arranged, and Burns restaged "Put Me to the Test" as a trio. In his usual wry humor George noted of Fred "He picked it up real fast, that boy's a pretty good dancer".

Give them some credit:

It requires a sizeable swarm to prepare and present a professional production, especially a motion picture musical. Even a simple dance recital needs some preparatory and backstage help. Whether being on stage or reading production credits, it is useful to understand the language and be aware of the function of:

Producer — selects story, including approach (concept), contracts production business with help from attorneys and agents: financing, writers, filming locations, director, composer, leads (primary characters performers), etc.

The executive producer has responsibility for the motion picture, assisted by associate/assistant producer, consulting producer, line producer, etc., any of which may be multiple (co-producer).

Director — determines scene (performing area) and performers' appearance, prepares performers, and, with help of casting directors (dance, vocal, extras, etc.), makes most cast and filming personnel selections.

As with producer, assistant, and co---, the term director may be liberally applied. There may be other production units with assisting directors including 2nd unit director, location directors*, music and dance directors, scenic director, and, when needed, other directoral craft specialists (see below).

(*Motion picture musicals are usually shot (filmed) on a soundstage (constructed) set in a soundproofed building or backlot (studio outdoor sets) designed for filming. Sometimes a different location (away from the motion picture studio) is required.)

Author/Libretist/Story Consultant — with executive story editor and manuscript supervisor, provides the book (story), treatment (extended synopsis), scenario (detailed outline) of the plot, and/or situational idea for producer preview consideration. Studio readers, familiar with film script and production requirements, may be hired to research and recommend suitable stories.

Screen Writer/Dramatist/Scenarist/Script Writer — converts the book/plot into a screenplay/script including written dialog, staging; as well as, character, costume, and scene descriptions.

Composer/Lyricist — provide the music/lyrics. Performance numbers and situational (plot supporting) music may be arranged from various sources by a music supervisor, but original songs and film score (theme and background music) are usually by a composer/arranger who may also serve as conductor.

Choreographer/Dance Director — creates and sets production and ancilliary dances, synchronized staging, and featured dances not choreographed by the performers.

Cast — performs the show. Some leads may have understudies or stand-ins for chorus rehearsals or stunt doubles for dangerous action scenes. Also, supernumeraries/extras (non-speaking background) and bodies (ill, injured, and corpses).

Makeup — prepares the casts' facial/head appearance, assisted by stylist/hair dresser, wig maker, and makeup effects artist.

Costumer/Costume Designer/Costume Coordinator (Mens/Womens) — selects or designs and prepares, with tailors, seamstresses, and milliners, the performance costumes. The wardrobe department/wardrobe mistress maintains, delivers, and collects in-use costuming.

Designer/Scenic or Set Designer — plans the appearance of the set or location and, with the set crew (carpenters, electricians, etc.), scenic artist (paint backgrounds), wood workers and sculptors (artistic set pieces), and set dresser/decorator (selects and arranges furnishings), prepares it for rehearsal, performance, and, with script supervisor, maintains visual continuity (appearance consistency throughout filming).

Lighting Director — plans production lighting and supervises equipment use.

Stage Manager — helped by the stage crew, controls flow of performance scenes (sets, curtains, lighting, sound, etc.).

Cinematographer/Camera Director — with stage manager, lighting director, color consultant, and cameramen, selects and arranges camera equipment, placement, and shots (graphic inclusion and quality; e.g., closeup or diffused image) and helps plan lighting and microphone locations. Multiple film units may be dispersed for location shooting.

Sound Director/Recording Director — with sound engineer and recordist arranges for and records audio on set.

Arranger/Orchestrator/Music Arranger/Vocal Arranger — with the help of score editors provides the show score (sheet music).

Music Director/Conductor — rehearses and conducts (leads) the musicians and vocalists.

Production Manager — responsible for budget.

Production Supervisor — oversees production progress.

Production Secretary — maintains all production documentation.

Post Production Coordinator — integrates editing, titles and credits, video and audio masters, final production records, and other pre-release activities.

Editor/Film Editor — with director, selects and cuts (sequences) from footage (all original film) the portions which become the motion picture. Film/video technicians provide reels/DVD's of recent unedited (dailies, rushes) shooting for director/producer viewing. The cutter/video mixer adjusts and composites (combines) video sources during editing.

Sound Editor — with director, arranges (selects and balances relative volumes), cuts (deletes and sequences), and synchronizes and dubs (adds) sound sources to coordinate with the video. In sound studios, a recordist acquires post-filming music, vocals, taps, etc. as multi-channel (microphone sources) sound tracks for editing and dubbing. The sound mixer/technition adjusts and blends multi-channel recordings into final film channels. The composer/conductor may participate in final music mixing.

Music Supervisor integrates background and featured music for sound track.

Distribution and Promotion Offices prepare trailers (brief excerpts from upcoming films), advertising, posters, interviews, and coordinates film bookings to distributors and theaters.

Craft Specialists Frequently, when several personnel are assigned to a specialty, a Supervisor, Director, or Head is credited; e.g., Green Screen Supervisor, or simply Construction (crew chief).

Graphic Artist, Sketch Artist, Colorist, Photographer, Video, Montage Editor, Effects Animator, etc. produce various art pieces, titles and graphic film effects, and promotional graphics.

Concept Artist/Sketch Artist provides, story board (production sequence) sketches, and design models.

Dialog Coach/Dialogue Director assists performers with script delivery (spoken presentation), especially unfamiliar languages or dialects.

Foley Artist/Sound Designer/Sound Consultant creates and adds sound effects during filming or editing. A dance foley dubs taps.

Property Master/Prop Man acquires, builds, and maintains hand use items and smaller set pieces.

Special Effects Artist/Engineer provides a versatile range of visual effects and props; e.g., self-opening door, animated body parts, or a robot. Using vastly more realistic computer generated imagery (CGI), most film and many stage effects are no longer "mechanicals".

Armorer/Weapons Master trains users and maintains weaponry (bladed, firearms, etc.).

Fight Choreographer plans and rehearses cast fight scenes, training performers when necessary.

Stunt Coordinator plans, prepares equipment, and rehearses stunt personnel (frequently costumed to impersonate other cast members – stunt doubling) to present potentially dangerous scenes.

Pyrotechnic Coordinator plans and coordinates smoke, fire, and explosion effects.

Specialty Coordinator/Expert Advisor/Technical Advisor/Consultant provides expert topical (military, foriegn customs, etc.) information during script preparation and filming.

Animal Handler/Trainer

Responsibilities may overlap (stunts-pyrotechnic-special effects) requiring a Team Coordinator or interlock (sets-props-weapons-fight choreographer) Fight Coordinator. Filming a scene may require over 100 personnel. It's no wonder motion picture credits – most stipulated by personal and union contracts – now commonly span 5 minutes or more.

This is not the end of the personnel list. Additional crew include:

Technical Crew Construction Engineer, Electrical Engineer, etc. may be required for major projects or repairs.

Gaffer/ Light Crew/Electric lighting and electrical technician(s). Maintain lighting instruments, control follow spotlights, and operate light control console (light board).

Grip mechanical rigging technician.

Key Gaffer, Key Grip crew foreman for their operation.

(The term key may apply to any industry foreman; e.g. key recordist.

Best Boy/Best Man second in command after key gaffer, key grip.

Sound Crew maintain and operate microphones, booms, and audio console.

Dolly Grip/Boom Operator operate camera and microphone trolleys, dollies, and booms.

Drivers of specialty equipment (ship, locomotive, armored vehicles, earthmovers, cranes, etc.) or are location shuttle personnel.

Research may be anything from architecture or attire through terrain or meteorology to history, personal habits, or language deemed useful to the script or director.

Assistants Python Wrangler cable and utilities technician.

Child Wrangler/Animal Wrangler (just what it sounds like).

Numerous other assistants inhabit the production world. Many are personal assistants, responsible to one cast member or production person. Others serve as liaisons between various offices and staff; while some provide semi-specialized services such as estimate script film time and footage per scene dialog (read or count words), musical number, or other planned action.

Interns, apprentices, and "go-fors".

Location Manager/"Fixer" logistical support.

Also, scouts with advance parties/crews search for and prepare the location(s) prior to filming personnel arrival.

Craft & Maintenance Services film technicians, equipment and technology licensing, patent credits (sound processing, lenses, color processing, etc.) and copyrighted brand names, and rental/supply companies; transportation, catering and medical services; insurance and union representatives, custodial, and other outside (non-studio) services and agents.

Various other credit titles may appear. Production credits may include studio and other filming locations, underwriters (frequently several film companies share costs), music, and archival source and non-commercial contributor "Thank You's".

It takes a crew:

Fixed camera locations prevent sustained close-ups of traveling dancers. A camera, cameraman, and possibly a lens focus puller (to "zoom" closeups) on a dolly (perhaps with crane) guided by tracks permit vibration free controlled angle "long tracking shots" like Gene Kelly's "Singin' In the Rain" street splash.

Lady Be Good included a progressive four scene production beginning with Eleanor Powell tapping backward upstage through a crowd of overlapping drapes and baby grands. Throughout the scene an off-camera crew pulled drapes and shifted pianos, clearing a path for Eleanor.

Into focus:

To focus is to establish a point of attention. Setting stage lights includes focusing, a minimum two step process. Each lighting instrument is first directed toward the area to be covered by light, then the internal reflector and/or lens(es) adjusted for coverage diameter and illumination intensity from center to edge of lighted circle. Light up your face when you focus toward your audience.

Movie magic:

Similar to Gene Kelly and his cartoon buddy, Fred Astaire, during his "Shoes With Wings On" cobbler number in *Barkleys' of Broadway*, was joined by a shelf of disembodied tapping shoes. Each scene was created using different techniques, then combining (compositing) images from separately filmed sources. The *Anchors Aweigh* Gene and Jerry dance lesson required 10,000 cartoon images and two months to achieve the 4 minute screen duet which includes Jerry Mouse dancing around Gene and between his legs – no mean trick in 1945. As a director, Kelly intentionally stretched the technical boundaries of filmed dance. *Cover Girl* provides a uniquely complex filming/effects traveling duet when Gene dances with his, sometimes challenging, alter ego – himself. In 1951 Gene Kelly received a special Oscar for "brilliant achievement - - (in) - - choreography on film".

Real time:

Dances are usually filmed in continuity (without breaks) using several angles, commonly 3 camera positions: A, B, C. Several takes may later be edited into the final screen version. For his dances, Astaire assisted in editing decisions, insisting that the film copy appear to be from a single take, guaranteeing movement continuity no matter the camera angle.

Flub-a-dub-dub:

Dubbing is the addition of sounds to recorded audio. In *Lady Be Good* (1941) Eleanor Powell, during a novelty number with Buttons, a terrier, does a series of walk-overs, the first two including taps while she's inverted. It is confusing because Eleanor frequently set her choreography and reportedly always dubbed her taps. Who got creative, Ms. Powell or the sound editor?

However, Sammy Davis Jr.'s dual six-shooters number in *Robin and the 7 Hoods* (1964) intentionally featured 11 and 12 shots. He must have used revolvers left over from those 1940s endless-shots Westerns.

Have you noticed that by the 1940s tappers traveling across a motion picture set sustain consistent taps volume without echoes? Many tap numbers were filmed without taps. Dance music and vocals were recorded prior to filming; however, like background music and narration, the taps were post-filming dubbed in an echo free sound recording studio while viewing a screened (projected) video of the dance. Unfortunately, the small recording area excludes much of the tonal subtlety (like a stair dance) of the original performance. Dubbing taps requires some special skills and is frequently done by a chorus dancer, not the screen performer. "Singin' In the Rain" was purportedly dubbed in a tray of water by Gwen Verdon.

Earlier films usually live recorded music and taps with the orchestra many yards from the dance floor. Listen to Fred Astaire's "I Won't Dance" from *Roberta* (1935). The range and reverberation of tap sounds is evident, as is the orchestral distance.

Compose a combination of tap turns. Tap the combination without the turns. You could have dubbed an audio track.

Bang/clap:

When video and audio are separately recorded during a shoot, a method is needed to resynchronize them on film. Through the early 1960s this was done by identifying the production, director, date, scene, and take information on a hand-held chalk board (slate) with a top hinged clapstick. Similar information led the audio taping. To begin a take, the cameras and audio recorder would roll (begin recording) and a director's assistant would announce the identifiers then bang the clapper in front of a camera. Later mixing required holding the audio of the identified recording at the "bang", to be started when the "clap" appeared in the video.

Since the late '60s synchronization has been achieved by electronic time code, allowing multiple cameras and other equipment to share accuracy to a fraction of a second. Current clapperboards include a video readout panel displaying whizzing film frames/time.

A patriotic flying leap:

The oft ignored story behind *Flying Down To Rio* is that it was a promotional film for Pan American Airways and Franklin Roosevelt.

By the early 1930s Pan American (1927), thanks to assorted federal assistance, had acquired mail routes throughout Central and South America. Coming to the Presidency in 1933, Franklin Roosevelt wanted to expand U.S. influence across the hemisphere. With larger passenger aircraft becoming available, Pan Am began promoting south of the border tourism. One of the board members, Merian Cooper, an RKO producer, concieved using films to stimulate public interest. The first major success was 1933 *Flying Down To Rio* (Fred and Ginger's* first outing) with a closing seaplane shot likely Pan American's new Southern Clipper**.

The excitement of a romantic, colorful, gay trip south culminating with a South American girl (Delores del Rio) falling in love with and marrying a North American boy (Gene Raymond) neatly tied up the North/South link symbolism of the pitch.

(*The Astaire-Rogers duo was established by the overwhelming success of their Carioca number. Additionally, the music associated with additional South American romance films propelled the popularity of Latin rhythms and accompanying ballroom styles (rhumba, tango, cha-cha, etc.).

**The 1932 Sikorsky S-40 had a passenger capacity of 38, the previous model only 8.

Incidentally, Charles Lindbergh, as a test pilot, proved the feasibility of several new Pan Am routes.)

Watch Out ! !

For *Top Hat* Ginger Rogers overrode director Mark Sandrich's "Cheek to Cheek" proven gown choice for a new blue feather-covered creation being assembled. Not ready for rehearsals, Ginger appeared feathered to film the dance. Initially, a few feathers dropped from the costume, with turns and lifts yielding a blue flurry in the air, on Fred, the cameras, and throughout the set. Several attempts reduced molting to a filming-acceptable level. Four days later Ginger received a small box containing a gold feather bracelet charm with a note: "Dear Feathers, I love ya! Fred". Between Fred, Hermes Pan, and Ginger the affectionate nickname stuck. While there are several versions of the incident, Fred Astaire's autobiography *Steps in Time* provides an enjoyable account in the chapter "Feathers".

Even when planned, costumers do not always appreciate their influence on dancers. In *Follow the Fleet*, "Let's Face the Music and Dance", Ginger wore a 25 pound beaded gown. Not only did the full skirt and heavily beaded forearm drape sleeves tend to unbalance her during turns, but on the first take, Fred didn't duck and was smacked in his jaw and eye by a pound of beads. Twenty more takes, until 8:00 p.m., produced no faultless performance. You can watch this assault. Rushes included a camera angle that hid the initial sleeve slap, leaving the first performance in the film.

In *Broadway Melody of 1940*, "Between You and Me" was to end with Eleanor Powell and George Murphy sliding down a steep ramp. The concept was modified after technical advisor Arnold Gillespie's demonstration culminated in a broken leg.

Eleanor was less fortunate in 1943. During an *I Dood It* lariat dance rehearsal an entangling fall rendered her unconscious.

You Were Never Lovelier included a Fred Astaire audition scene in the office of supper club owner Adolphe Menjou. The tirade of taps leads Astaire onto Menjou's desk, supplementing his taps with cane raps on the desk and Menjou's head, leaving him, during one take, noticeably stunned.

Can't win them all, or can you?

During Adele and Fred Astaire's successful Broadway run of *Funny Face*, they were invited (1928) to Paramount to screen test for the possible film version. Fred's autobiography notes only that "The deal never materialized, for some reason or other." Rumors long persisted that Fred's first screen test report included (*Dance Digest* 1959) "can't act", "slightly bald", "can dance a little". RKO production chief David Selznick in 1932 was slightly more positive. "I feel, in spite of his enormous ears and bad chin line, that his charm is tremendous." *Dancing Lady* (M-G-M 1933) through *Silk Stockings* (1957) established Astaire as the most prolific dance lead in Hollywood history (31 musicals), along the way introducing and recording over 130 songs.

How did I get here?

Gene Kelly relished doing his own film stunts (watch *The Pirate*). An ardent athlete, he was noted for his film industry personnel (including Bob Fosse in his tap dancing days) inducted home volley ball games. Gene drove for excellence, sometimes including "ringers" from nearby college teams. He was infamous for his aggressive play. Matches could become fierce, leading to bruised, exhausted players. A few weeks before *Easter Parade* filming was to commence, Gene's competitive drive earned him a fractured ankle. To the infuriated M-G-M head Lious B. Mayer, Gene suggested Fred Astaire, Mayer telephoned Fred, Fred confirmed Gene's concurrence, and Astaire abandoned retirement.

The film included another substitute, Ann Miller, replacing the pregnant Cyd Charisse.

What other holiday film featured Fred Astaire? _____

That stinks!

The Hollywood Revue of 1929 premiere at Grauman's Chinese Theatre in Los Angeles concluded with an orange blossom finalé enhanced by ventilating perfume into the auditorium.

Coming down hard, and fast:

Motion picture musicals have always been expensive, especially with multi-star and large production number casts and sets.

Through the 1940s nearly every town had a movie house, city downtowns several, plus many neighborhoods a convenient theater with Saturday morning kids' features.

The diminishment of the major studios began when 1946-7 federal anti-trust suits divested them from their theater chain ownerships. With theaters independently operated came the end of lucrative studio block booking (several or annual output, including only one or two choice films) and packaged A (featured) plus B (low budget secondary) movies with shorts (newsreels, cartoons, etc.), dropping revenues 25%. The end of studio exclusive star system contracts (M-G-M boasted "More stars than there are in heaven.") opened agent negotiations for higher salaries. Post WWII national optimism and returning servicemen family-building expenses precluded the American need for a weekly film fantasy boost. During 1946-9 Britain, France, and Italy, intending to aid domestic film development, instituted protectionist 25% film import taxes. The 1947-1948 House Unamerican Activities Committee (HUAC) Hollywood hunt for Communist sympathizers forced the industry blacklisting of many professionals who turned to independent production. The 1950s household TV invasion didn't help, leaving studio budgets significantly reduced, forcing fewer, less opulent, mostly Broadway proven musicals.

Frequently ignored in tap histories were the changing trends in popular music and theater dance. As early as the 1936 Broadway *On Your Toes*, George Balanchine's "Slaughter on Tenth Avenue" ballet set a new course for musical theater dance. By the late 1940s freestyle ballet and modern (*Oklahoma* 1943, *Brigadoon* 1947) were dominating Broadway musicals with early jazz appearing in more films and on 1950s TV. Even Gene Kelly's spectacular (17 minute, 5 weeks in preparation, $450,000) 1951 *American In Paris* award winning finalé freestyle ballet managed only a brief 5 man tap sequence. The overwhelming stage (1957) and film (1961) successes of *West Side Story* nearly doomed tap musicals. Even Astaire and Kelly's late 1950s into '60s films were largely non-tap.

Swing syncopation or upbeat Foxtrot are the preferred music styles for tapping. The electric guitar and redundant "3 chord" ease of rock amplified into an untappable explosion with the 1950s introduction of moderately priced over-loud portable sound systems. The 1970s-1980s saw a major revival of 1940s style tap musicals (*No, No Nanette* 1971 (Ruby Keeler revival), *Irene* 1973 (Debbie Reynolds Broadway debut), *Bubbling Brown Sugar* 1976 (Bill Robinson style revival), *Dancin'* 1978, *Sugar babies* 1979 (burlesque outright fun with Ann Miller), *42nd Street* 1980, *Sophisticated Ladies* 1981 (danceable Duke Ellington music), and *Me and My Girl* 1986-9) bringing tap performances to a new generation of audiences. But by the 1990s commercial tap had become largely "heavy on the hoof" (the louder, the better) tedium, without interesting combinations, body line, staging, or complex rhythmics.

The commercial market has slumped, but tap (occasionally well done) continues to pop up on Broadway (*42nd Street* reprised 2001 and 2017) and in films (shades of Fred Astaire, Gene Kelly, and zapadeado in *La La Land*, 2016). Far more importantly, the dance form, properly presented, remains an essential movement/rhythm/style element of dancer development.

More to come:
The included anecdotes and vignettes are only a smattering of the rich history of tap dance in films and on stage. Much more is internet available with additional pre-tap silent and early sound films restoration continuing. Hopefully, more written archives will become similarly available. Do some browsing. Resourcing can prove entertaining, and ultimately enlightening.

ARRANGEMENT TERMS

Give me a break:
The tap term applies to both brk comb (usually 1M) and Step brk (usually 2M). Various styles (buck, soft shoe, waltz clog, military) include widely used dedicated breaks, while others do not. Fran Scanlan in <u>The Shim-Sham</u> (1940s) to break off 6M of 8&1 2&3 4&5&6&7 defined "SHIM-SHAM BREAK" as: tpl R, tap L frt, step L c-p, tap R frt, leap R rt, tap L rt, hold, rev leap-tap. 8&1 2 3 4 5&(6)&7, changing both rhythm and movement pattern from sideward to front. Danny Hoctor ("Shim Sham", Danro #964) included breaks: step, b/c, 2 skips x bk, steps sd - fwd, b/a sync'd 1a23&(4)a567**a**8; and stamp, 2 steps, (tr) shfl-b/c, 2 steps **1**2**3**a4a567(8 tr'g).

It's not difficult to determine the function of a phrase that begins with a style standard, but ends differently styled. From Micheal Dominico's <u>Soft Shoe</u> (1950s) Step III: "Flap R, flap L, (across R), step R, shuffle L, hop R, shuffle L, step L, shuffle R, hop L, step R, (behind L) flap L, flap R, B.C. LR. &1&a2&a3a&a4&a5&6&7&8". This is a rhythm variation of what step? _____

The simplest dance/music definition of break is change. What changes with:

t-s-brk	break-away	drum break
tacit brk	break-out	rehearsal break
musicians' break	Step brk	career break

Dance vs. Music:
Match the most closely related notation/term from each pair of columns.

<u>Dance</u>	<u>Music</u>	<u>Dance</u>	<u>Music</u>
Step	intro	rout	verse & chorus
( )	8M	hold	stop time
ent	tag	flash step	vamp
exit	tacit	song & dance	2 choruses

Four little words/abbreviations:
Consider:
    Shfl-b/c R 2 X's, *shfl R, hop L, tt R x frt L, flap-b/c R.   &1&2 &3&4 &5&6 &7&8
    Rev.
    Alt *M2 2 X's.
    Rpt 1st 2M.

Not enough praise can be lauded upon rpt, rev, alt, and their invaluable sidekick X's. Their inestimable value to verbal and notational efficient clarity cannot be overstated.

Hyphenated notation may be similarly used, but more thoughtfully. Do these notation pairs specify the same comb?

shfl-b/c 2X's	_____	shfl-b/c-b/c	2 step-heels	_____	step, step, heel, heel
flap-b/c's L-R	_____	flap-b/c L, flap-b/c R	riff-heel-step-heel-step	_____	riff, heel, cramp, step
dbl-shfl-p-u-c	_____	dbl-shfl, p-u-c	flap, hop 2 X's, scfl 2 X's	_____	flap-hop, flap-hop, dbl-scfl

If in doubt, rhythm notation or following weight placement usually clarifies intent.

Mirror, mirror:
View an inverted comb in a studio mirror. Try this.
>(Face mirror) sgl ess R. (Back to mirror) rpt.
>(Face mirror) sgl ess R, bk flap L into sgl ess L – R x bk. (A frt ess x bk.)

The horizontally "flipped" combination is the visual effect sought by inverting a comb.

Upside down, not backward:
While occasionally handy, the fifth repetition aid, invert, is rarely used, lacking suitable combinations. However, opposing frt/bk, fwd/bkwd step directions combinations can be interesting.
>f-r-c R rt, bk flap L x bk R, step R x bk L, inv. (f-r-c L lt, fwd flap R x frt L, step L x frt R)
>(c-w tr's) flap R, shfl-b/c L x frt, invert. (still tr'g c-w: bk flap L, shfl-b/c R x bk)

The travel sequence is not change, just the body directions. Brew up a few more.

Doubled:
A double step includes two of the same step (dbl-shfl, d-p-u). A doubled step includes the basic step and a variation of equal length - a double length step variation.
>Notate then name as an abbreviation the doubled steps based on:
>cinc _____ _____
>frt ess _____ _____
>buff _____ _____
>w-c-t-s _____ _____

Double has been applied meaning both. The term both indicates a-s-t; e.g., chug both; or both heels 3X's (123).
The concept is expandable: dbl button (2 ending chords), tpl snap kick (snap kick 3 X's), qdl pir.

The Need For Speed:
Although clarity and rhythm are the primary objectives of tapping, eventually this question will arise. No matter the answer, there will be disagreements about the limit, but the exploration can be fun.

First: Only clearly rendered taps are to be counted. (Not sluffy or rattling from jingle taps.)

Second: Calculation. A metronome set to 60 beats per minute is an ideal clock, measuring 5 to 10 seconds per test. Otherwise, a clock or watch.

Third: Plan a fast-taps combination. Running triples or quadruples provide an easy initial rate. Progress through higher tap density patterns experimenting with various steps (d-p-u roll; dbl riff walks; running d-p-u-c's; running side riffles or riffs; etc.) most suitable to your skills.

Fourth: Count the taps in the combination. Repeat the comb for 10 seconds, multiply combination taps times combination repetitions then divide by 10. Average several tests.

Most intermediate students combining cramprolls with double pickups, heels, and snaps should average 6 - 9 taps/second. Similarly, using side riffles or triplet wings ending each with heels can yield 10 - 14. Higher rates (up to 38) have been claimed, yielding a rhythmless buzz challenging a snare drum roll. Ann Miller's publicity claimed 500 taps per minute. Paul Draper rated himself at 64 taps per 5 seconds.

A simple composition or:

material	steps and Steps	set	several routines
a dance	(*I hope so*)	suite	short sequence of linked dances
a piece	a single dance	a work	"significant" composition or show
a number	sequence in a program	performance	dance(s) for an audience
a turn	a sequenced number	recital	simple performance of dances
opener	first number in a show	act	a scene or sub-theme of a program
closer, finalé	last number in a show	program, bill	performance list
spot	brief appearnce or number	concert	formal, usually non-comedic program
fill (fill in)	scene change number	show	scripted (bgn'g, middle, end) program
bit	comedic skit-like piece	ballet	an all dance performance, often a story
interlude	transitional performance, often comedic	production	complex show
flash act	novelty number	musical	music dominated production
routine	repeated performance piece		

So much for simple, and there are more terms for "a dance".

In good measure:
Measures are usually formatted to identify either phrase length or musical score location. Most dance notes indicate phrase length (2M, 4M) and Step length (<u>8M</u>, <u>16M</u>). When accompaniment is sheet music, it may prove useful to reference score location (M1-2, M3-6, etc.) with Steps still being totalled (<u>8M</u>). (See <u>New Soft Shoe</u>.)

RHYTHM NOTATION

This is hard:
Rather than bold rhythm counts (a**1**) indicating a dynamic accent, some notes use:
- ^ (caret) before or after; e.g., a^1 or a1^
- underlined ct; e.g., a<u>1</u>
- or marked hard or <u>H</u>; e.g., a<u>H</u>1.

This is harder:
Occasionally, dance rhythm will be discussed or notated as musical notes rather than counts of time. While interpreting as pulses a series of flagged orbs (with or without musical staff) is challenging, including a few interspersed eighth or dotted sixteenth rests further complicates. Music students, pick a moderately complex rhythm dance phrase and try it.

Here's the bottom line. Music notes and rhythm counts serve different functions. Notes represent time sustained; counts, time when struck – duration vs. separation.

Countless:
Many pre-1930 tap notes are without rhythm notation. While many combinations, depending on style, seem obviously even, duplet, triplet, time-step, waltz clog, or shim sham, we will never know the choreographer's intent. Unfortunately, even as late as 1949 Willie Covan's University of the Arts, NADAA (National Association of Dance and Affiliated Arts) routines include no rhythm notation.

----let it be:
Ending a numeric tap term "let" or abbreviation "lt" (duplet/dplt) indicates a cluster of evenly spaced sounds. How many taps does each abbreviation specify?

qdlt ____   splt ____   tplt ____   oclt ____   qnlt ____   sxlt ____

Simply notated:
Fran Scanlan's First Step of <u>Sophisticated Soft Shoe</u>, includes "brush R, scuff R, step R (fwd to heel), toe drop R, heel drop R, (the counts 'a6&a7' make a quintuple step)". The rhythm of this variation of what step can be more easily clarified how?

step? _____   notation? _____

I got - - - - - - :
Notate 2 significantly different comb's suitable for the phrase
&1&2 3&a4 5 6 7&8

In a dance studio with mirror, sequence the 2 comb's. Notice the change in appearance, though not rhythm. With a partner, perform them simultaneously in opposing order, then interlocked with differing rhythm or accent offsets. Compare with performing one combination repeated in unison. There are several simple ways to spice up a combination or routine.

Buddy, do you have the time?
Sometimes not. <u>A Study In Modern Rhythms</u>, Bobby Rivers (1940s) Step Seven: "scuff R toe and heel fwd, (a). NOTE: This toe and heel scuff is done so rapidly that it falls on the single count 'a'."

Put in order from briefest to longest spacing within a ct:
a   e   l   i   &   ____ ____ ____ ____ ____

Make it ct:
When a rhythm notation seems confusing, slow the tempo then begin by ct'g or finger tapping, 1 2 3 etc. Continue ct'g, adding the fractional rhythms a ct or two with each repetition, until the pattern is complete, "feels right", and you mentally "hear" it.

Try the following:
a1 &2 &a3 4a(&) {5a&a6} {a7&a8}

Which are:
As defined, classify the following as **E**ven, **D**uple, **B**roken, **S**yncopated rhythm.

| rolling | ____ | { } | ____ | dbl ess | ____ | r-r- | ____ |
| maxie | ____ | irish, flap-b/c | ____ | a1 2 3 a4&a5 6 7 a8& | ____ | shim sham comb | ____ |

There's always another way:
For the following comb, notate 2 different rhythm phrases, including a (*hold*) in one.
Chug, shim, flap, hop, tpl, b/c, lamp.

Seq the comb's noticing the rhythm flow. If you would like a different rhythm, change it. How about changing the stg'g? Try a different meter.

Why double time?
In the military double time means jog, running twice the march tempo. Some dance notes similarly apply the term, indicating running movements, not the tempo.

Actually, dbl-X requires <u>dancing double the music tempo</u>, essentially performing <u>twice the dance content</u> than at normal tempo. Dbl-X is usually notated sgl-X but includes 2 X's the steps and rhythm per musical phrase, as below:

    Single-time (normal):
        2 s-t-s's R-L.
  2M   8&12&3& 4&56&7&
    Double time:
        (Dbl-X) 4 s-t-s's R-L-R-L.
  2M   8&12&3& 4&56&7& 8&12&3& 4&56&7&
    (4M of dance during 2M of accompaniment.)

Dazzle the audience with an unexpected torrent of taps.

When reading routine notes, the left column accompaniment phrase references are useful, indicating whether the term is intended to mean running steps vs. twice as many per phrase.

Depending on music tempo, triple-X and quadruple-X are possible; however, the terms frequently reference triplet and quadruplet rhythm, not performance tempo.

Gene Kelly and his brother Fred, claiming that they would do their routine single, then double, then triple time, acquired an audition with Cab Calloway. Their abilities so impressed Calloway that they got the job performing with the band and, under the band's, their first marquee listing – The Kelly Brothers

On the <u>beat</u>:
In 16th and 17th century court dance manuals (*Orchesography*, Arbeau, *Nobilta di Dame*, Caroso) rhythm was specified by matching "figures" (combinations of dance steps) to required accompanying music (Galliard, Minuet, Pavane, etc.). The 18th century standardization of music notation led, by the 19th century, to movement notes appearing on or below music staffs (*Stenochorégraphie*, Saint-Léon, *Grammar of the Art of Dancing*, Zorn), permitting greater creativity with accuracy. In the early 20th century Rudolf Laban developed a vertical music staff representing the center line of the body outward, thus vertically indicating by position and length, the relative start, duration, and end of movements by each part of the body. While Labanotation accuracy permitted copyrighting (initially 1952 – four years after its Broadway premiere – Hanya Holm's *Kiss Me Kate* choreography manuscript was added to the Library of Congress card catalog, #DU30088, Class D) the symbolic complexity required significant training, restricting use to few in the dance field. Throughout, dance classes and rehearsals included spoken rhythms, usually by counting time with tempo emphasized by the instructor's cane <u>striking</u> the floor (see Degas' *The Ballet Class*), easily understood by dancers and accompanist. Although video now provides an accurate record, only printed notes allow reliably preserved portable study with easy revision or quick notation of an inspiration, even staging, body line, characterization, or costume sketches.

Dance figures (pas, meaning stride) could be specified simply: "step forward, touch foot forward"; or as complex as several measures of "movement about" the room – both, as now, called steps.

The beat goes on:
A pounding action, a "beat" of rhythm has many definitions, too many. A sharp sound, a tap sound, a count of rhythm, an accent, regular rhythm pulses, etc. leaves the word undefined. For this writing, the term is avoided and replaced by rhythm notation of the beginning (attack) of sounds. Most musicians acknowledge beat as the counting action of a conductor's baton – the upbeat between or preceding a count or emphasized count of the music; downbeat on the count, emphasizing beginning a movement, phrase, or measure.

Unless talking to a jazz musician. Then upbeat means faster, syncopated, or "jazzy"; while downbeat music is "low brow" (non-classic), blues, popular ("get down") styles. 1930s and '40s jive (slang) was so oblique and convoluted that, frequently, only "cats, in the know" (aficionados) understood it.

"5 6 7 8"
Unless specified or otherwise evident, most tap accompaniment is $^4/_4$, naturally phrasing combinations in 8 counts. So dominant is this pattern, that other meters are commonly choreographed "in eights": $^2/_4$ by 4M phrases, $^6/_8$ by 4M phrases of "1 ct" eighth note triplets (effectively $^2/_4$ – see <u>Wild-n-Irish</u>). This was not always the case. Routine notes into the 1930s were counted by M (12341234). Try that with a Step of $^2/_4$ and notice how quickly phrasing is lost.

Playtime:
Because basic buck time-steps are so easily varied and ubiquitous, they are often not identified or even noticed. For example: flap, 2 shfl-b/c's, shfl-hop, step, tpl &8&1&2&3&4&a56&a7. Even slight variations can yield something interesting; i.e., dig-snap-t-s: dig w/w, snap, step, hop, step, flap-step or insert a b/a or c-r. Try building a few different, 2M, 3M, and 4M t-s's, brk's, and brk comb's.

Natural phrasing:
If asked, most would define music as a tune. Perhaps it is more fundamental.

Without counting, in $^4/_4$ meter even rhythm, tap: r-r-4, r-r-6, r-r-8, cont rpt'g all or part of the comb until it "feels like" the end of a phrase (2M, 4M, 6M, etc – you decide). Try 2-3 times to confirm your "sense of timing". Now count it.

Phrases are naturally self constituted. Whether fluid poetry, music, dance, whatever rhythm content or length, they tend to continue to an obvious conclusion, constituting a recurrent "musical" pattern – the underlying structure which delimits the tune.

STAGING

Expanding their world:
The limited mobility of early film equipment required that dancing be presented from a single perspective as though on stage. Adding cameras provided differing angles, but most dance focus remained downstage with interruptive foot closeups and non-dance "dramatic" cuts. Fred Astaire choreographed for "natural" camera "views" of his surroundings (the set) filmed full-frame (full-body) with no cutaways, establishing the fast moving, wide ranging, multi-directional non-downstage continuous view choreographic style which transformed motion picture tap. As choreographer and director, Gene Kelly similarly staged many dance numbers, emphasizing uninterrupted action (long tracking shots) traveling along varying routes through expanded settings.

Down where?
Not all performance areas are enclosed rectangles. Thrust (extending into the auditorium) or round (largely or entirely surrounded by audience) configurations encourage multi-direction performance. Cast/director/crew communication still requires establishing D-S.

Staging or dancing?
"Moving to music" does not qualify as dancing any more than the marching of a company of soldiers led by a band. Jerome Robbins' choreography imbued every action scene, from opening credits to finalé, functionally creating an intermittent jazz ballet propelling *West Side Story*. An opposing approach by Gower Champion throughout the Broadway *Hello Dolly* staged the scene transitions simply, using musically coordinated walks and background cast activities to sustain the pace of the show. Contrast both to the often ignored *Singin' In the Rain* Gene Kelly, Cyd Charisse tap narrative "Gotta Dance", an all dance production.

During the 1930s and '40s Busby Berkeley choreographed film dance numbers including Ruby Keeler tap. He also directed several films. However, Berkley is much better known for his trademark production numbers featuring large, frequently complex, high, curving, even rotating sets filled with 30 to 50 chorus dancers, often equipped with outsized props and unique costumes, producing flowing images while utilizing simple movements. Sometimes they danced. Technically, Berkeley was a dance director. His forté was selecting camera angles which impressively presented his staged fantasies. During preparation of 29 year old Gene Kelly's first film *For Me and My Gal* (1942) non-dancer director Berkeley early realized Kelly was better suited to choreograph his solos and duets with co-star Judy Garland. As was frequently the case for self-choreography, Kelly was not credited. Also worth watching, the title song and dance soft shoe duet by Judy and Gene.

How much do I have?
Space may dictate a performance. Nightclubs and ballrooms typically included a small stage/bandstand, but if occupied, the tapping was on the waxed ballroom floor. From the 1920s into the '50s many dance band appearances included a vocalist(s), sometimes a dancer(s). The dance presentation may offer the latest ballroom steps, an exhibition ballroom routine, and/or a tap number. A cramped vs. slippery area frequently determined which.

The endless frontier:
Most dancers want more space to travel. Eddie Leonard (Lemuel Toney), an early 20th century minstrel soft shoe expert, is noted for his solution. What is it? _____

Another example, the Charles 'Honi' Coles stroll. Demonstrated starting as a c-c-w circle of easygoing walk, skip, c/s, and riff variations blending into alternating horizontally staged oscillations of traveling rock'n, crossing cramps, bombershays, and shim shams.

Move it:
Sure, there are traveling time-steps, but most time-steps are performed in place. That does not preclude their moving like Fran Scanlan's 1930s <u>Beginners Buck Dance</u> entrance.

"The Half Break Time Step
Start at R of stage and travel to the center
Shuffle R-hop L-step R-shuffle step L-shuffle R-hop L-step R-shuffle step L." 8&12&3&4&56&7&, rpt 2 X's.
"The Chain Break
Shuffle R-hop L-step R-shuffle step L-shuffle step R-shuffle step L-step R" 8&12&3&4&5&6&7
This chain break is repeated through the routine, except Step Eight.

Try it stepping forward. How about twisting U-S\D-S or backing on stage with steps x back? Moving t-s's can add interest without abandoning style.

Up\Down, Right\Left, Front\Back, In\Out, On\Off:
These terms have unique stage definitions which may confuse neophyte performers. For example, in and out do not reference doors, nor on/off lights.

Traditional European stages are raked (gently sloped) downward toward the audience, improving the audience's view of all performers and making upstage literally higher than downstage. These long established terms apply to all stages, even those not raked. Stage directions are a performance aid, thus usually referencing, when facing downstage, the performer's right, left, front, and back. "Auditorium" right and left reference audience view directions and, in much of Europe, stage right and left are the director's view from the auditorium. It is noteworthy that up and down also refers to sound and lighting intensity - up is more, down is less; while, in and out indicates whether fly batten (cable supported overhead pipes) attached scenery or drapes have been lowered into the visual stage scene or raised out of audience view. Generally, sets, props, and performers moving across the stage from or to offstage are referenced as moving on or off stage.

Raked stages can initally be a problem for unaccustomed dancers, but are adjusted to with experience. None the less, many European ballet company rehearsal rooms have raked floors dimensioned to match their home stage.

Stages are potentially dangerous areas. Overhead (flown) are large, heavy set drops (scenery) and draperies, lighting instruments are high amperage and very hot, blackouts and follow spots can be temporarily blinding, and stepping over the lip (downstage stage edge) may result in a fall into the orchestra pit (area between front of stage and audience seats).

Don't stare at a follow spot, focus just above the audience. Unless assigned to do so, never touch any stage equipment. While on stage, know the stage periphery, side pathways (wings), sets, and performers locations. During a blackout stay put until work lights (low intensity lighting permitting safe stage activity) are up. "Heads up" warns of overhead flys being brought in (lowered). When warned, look for and avoid them. Finally, locate emergency exit stage doors. Although, rarely needed, they are an important safety route.

About face:
When C-S facing as specified, relate stage dir to indicated body dir:
- When facing D-S, bk _____, l-d-f _____.
- When facing S-R, lt _____, frt _____.
- When facing S-L, l-d-b _____, r-d-f _____.
- When facing U-S, r-d-b _____, rt _____.

You danced where?
OK, so many dancers tapped on tables; but - - -

Street dancing (outdoors) has long been an income source for the needy hoofer, with the unique button-covered-costumed buskers* being an established English tradition. (*Roaming entertainers who pass a hat for viewer donations.)

Shirley Temple joined Bill Robinson for a stair dance in *Little Colonel*.

Gene Kelly sloshed along a rain-drenched sidewalk and water-filled curb gutter in *Singin' In The Rain*.

It gets wetter. In *Broadway Melody of 1938* Eleanor Powell and George Murphy end a number neck deep in a pond.

Pedestal dancing, a fad novelty, was Honi Coles' 6′ high first job (with the Miller brothers) at the Lafayette Theater, NYC in 1931. During his early career, Paul Draper performed club shows atop a 2′ diameter round marble-topped 2′ high pedestal.

In *Stormy Weather* the acro-tap duo Nicholas Brothers, Fayard and Harold, leapfrogged down stairs landing in full splits then rising without hand assistance.

In *Yankee Doodle Dandy* Jimmy Cagney danced off the walls of the stage proscenium arch. The Nicholas Brothers went further in *Down Agentine Way*, running up a wall into a back somersault ending in a split. (Don't try this at home - - or elsewhere.)

A Damsel In Distress, "Stiff Upper Lip" featured Fred Astaire, George Burns, and Gracie Allen tapping through a fun house, maneuvering ski boards, opposing conveyers and turn tables, and being distorted in warped mirrors. Built around Gracie's "naïve" humor, the Hermes Pan comedy number concludes with a reenactment of Fred and sister Adelle's signature Broadway exit gag, the run-around.

Three Sailors and a Girl included Gene Nelson "In Love to Stay" tapping in an auto repair shop, on and between car lifts with bouncing transitions in and out of the three grease pits, presumably trampoline equipped. In *Tea For Two* Gene's version of a stair dance included tapping on a window sill and up and down a banister.

In *Royal Wedding* Fred Astaire and Jane Powell tapped and slid, not always on their feet, on a rocking boat deck*; a good preparation for Fred later dancing up and down walls and across the ceiling of his hotel room. Figure out how.

(*Aboard the ocean liner Aquatania enroute to London for their 1923 opening of *Stop Flirting*, Fred and Adele agreed to participate in a traditional passenger charity show. Their performance took place on a waxed ballroom floor while "following seas" rock-and-rolled the liner. The audience appreciation of the resultant comic fiasco was the inspiration for the *Royal Wedding* number.)

Franklin Roosevelt's February 4, 1936 birthday radio address from the Oval Office was preceded by an FDR requested brief performance by his guest, Ginger Rogers.

More who than where, WWII name dropping. *Royal Wedding*, set in London, had cast as Fred's love interest Sarah Churchill, former Prime Minister Winston's daughter.

Between 1991-1995 Savion Glover made several tap dancing appearances on *Sesame Street*. Wearing a mo-cap (motion capture) suit, he also served as the dance movement prototype for the animated *Happy Feet* star Mumbles.

Dance flooring:
Performance floors have long been the touring dancer's greatest unwanted surprise. An uneven, damaged, paint-covered, or slippery surface prevents reliable presentation and may endanger the performer. Pre and early vaudeville "stages" were frequently rough surfaced or the ground. Clog dancers countered with tap mats (typically, 5′ to 6′ lengths of ¼" thick x 1" wide hardwood slats glued to canvas of desired length) unrolled to provide wood on wood rhythms. Used over "dead" (non-resonating) concrete surfaces, wood mats remained available into the 1980s.

Popularized in the 1960s, vinyl roll-out flooring has provided a nearly universal solution. Although early floorings were thick, bulky to haul, heavy to handle, and slow to aclimate (after transport, comform to theater temperature and stage contours), now lighter $1/16$" to $1/8$" thick, quick-laying rolls accompany most dance and musical theater companies. The matte surfaces are neither slippery nor tractive and the thinnest sheets smoothly contour, accurately transferring tap and zapateado forces to underlying stages with no functional change in audio pitch or volume. Because of portability, many dance schools now use them for studio classes and theater recital. General purpose floorings, having been joined by models variously laminated two-color reversible, under-padded for ballet and modern, hard-surfaced to reflect taps, fiberglas dimensionally stabilized, and custom graphic imprinted as graphic ground cloths, have established synthetic theater floorings as ubiquitous in the field.

By the numbers:

Historically attributed to Enrico Cecchetti, Italian founder of a method of ballet training (Cecchetti school of ballet), the stage c-c-w directions of 4 corners (#1-4) and 4 sides or walls (#5-8) simplify notation but limit accuracy. Most ballet body positions are limited by specified technique to these 8 primary body directions. However, stage positions and movement frequently require interpretation of the diagonal numbers. Consider, from location #1, numbering travel to C-S-L or U-S-C.

You may encounter other numbered stages in ballet notes. The English Royal Academy of Dance (RAD) begins with D-S (#1) c-w specifying sides, then corners from D-S-L (#5). The Russian school of technique also begins D-S then simply sequences c-w.

NOTATION SAFARI

For decades dance teacher organizations, independent workshop sponsors, dance record publishers, dance teachers, and other choreographers have published and personally notated libraries of class, routine, and production dance. Exploring this vast terrain can be challenging but reveals sources of steps, terms, styles, and communication formats; as well as, some interesting dance material.

Take note:

Gene Kelly's mother, Harriet, insisted that her five children receive dance and music lessons. The 1924 season closing production at the Nixon Theater, in hometown Pittsburgh, headlined Eddie Foy and the Seven Little Foys. When hurricane-like weather prevented their timely arrival, the amateur performance veterans, the Five Kellys, were hired, proving to be a popular temporary replacement, starting the family's limited professional career. From 1929, during the Depression, Gene and brother Fred supplemented family income by performing a song/dance/master of ceremonies/magic act intended to extend onstage time and income. Their bookings (hired performances) afforded back stage opportunities to resource new dance material. According to Alvin Yudkoff in *A Life of Dance and Dreams Gene Kelly*, "He and Fred worked out their own method of notating a visiting professional's tap routine when something really new was presented. In a Kelly-invented choreographic shorthand Gene would sketch out eight bars and Fred would take down the next eight. Then they would watch the next two or three performances making corrections and improving their notes, until they felt they 'had' the routine."

Very old notes:

From the Stearns' book *Jazz Dance*, in 1789 as Friday in *Robinson Crusoe* at the Southwark Theatre in Philadelphia, John Durang introduced blackface dance by inserting a Hornpipe into the story. The first six of 22 Steps are described:

"1. Glissade around (first part of tune).
2. Double shuffle down, do.
3. Heel and toe back, finish with back shuffle.
4. Cut the buckle down, finish the shuffle.
5. Side shuffle right and left, finishing with beats.
6. Pigeon wing going round."

Notice the mixture of indigenous, clog, and ballet terms.

Early tap dance notes were exclusively personal, not intended for use by others. By the 1920s exchangeable notes were becoming commonly used by performers, choreographers, and instructors. Over the next 20 years notation syntax and structure consolidated into a few continuing standard formats.

Paragraph format:

A version of mixed horizontal-paragraph format notes is 1949 "Bong Boogie Rhythms" by Nick Castle for Ann Miller in *Thrill of Brazil*, Step Six.

"Step fwd. on left, step in back on ball of right foot, broad ball change L-R, bringing left to side (second position). Stamp fwd. L; repeat all starting R. (ct. 1&a2&3&a4&) . . . . 2 Meas.

Step back on left, brush right back, heel L, step back on right, brush left back, heel right, step back on left, stamp R, stamp L (second position). Strut walking fwd. swagger style, R-L-R-L. . . . . 2 Meas.

REPEAT ALL REVERSING TO RIGHT . . . . <u>4 Meas.</u>
8 Meas."

Interpretation: Although not specified, the 1st M is rpt'd. The 2nd phrase is likely {1&a2&a3} **a4** 5 6 7 8.

Recognize anything?

As an example of vertical column notation format, here is a 1947 description by Jimmy Sutton, <u>Fast Flash</u> Step Three.

"STEP THREE

Hop L	(8)	
Shuffle step R (x'd bk of L – raising L foot up in fr of R – i.e. Buffalo)	(and a 1)	
Flap L	(and 2)	
Flap R	(and 3)	
Drop L heel	(and)	
Drop R heel	(4)	
Brush L (back)	(and)	
Hop R	(5)	
Step L	(and)	
Stamp R flat (x'd fr of L, toe Of R twisted to L or "turned in")	(6)	
Step L to L (twisting R toe to R)	(and)	
Brush R (in)	(7)	
Repeat cts "6 and"	(and 8)	2 meas
Brush R back	(and)	
Buck L fwd	(1)	
Double shuffle R	(and a 2 and)	
Pickup change L to R	(a 3)	
Reverse cts "and a 2 and a 3"	(and a 4 and a 5)	
Shuffle R	(and 6)	
Pickup change L to R	(and a)	
Tap L toe (x'd back of R)	(7)	2 meas
Repeat all (starting "jump to flap L")	(and 8)	<u>4 meas</u>
		8 meas"

To the right, rewrite this Step, simplifying by notating as steps you can identify. "Buck" is a chug.

Don't get crossed up:

The usual b/c x-over coordination is: leap sd, step x (frt or bk). While this can be expressed in detail, the established coordination frequently permits simpler notation.

                b/c R rt x-over L bk
                b/c R x-over bk
   (known R lead)   b/c x-over bk

The above 3 notations signify the same most common coordination. However, the format does allow for varied coordinations.

Interpret:
- (available lead) b/c x-over (end either frt or bk)
- (available lead) b/c i-p x-over frt (c/s ending x frt)
- (available lead) b/c x-overs frt - bk - frt (gpvn)

Being creative is fine, just remember the essential requirements: lead, dir, x'g pos(s).

Now see this:

Some notes begin every tap term upper case:
   Flap R, Step back L, Hop L, Shuffle-step R cross back, Bandi twist L, Single time step break L.
It clearly separates each step including supplemental information.

Call to order:

Dance notes tend to build from the general to the specific. As indicated at the beginning of **TAP TERMINOLOGY**, the recommended syntax sequence is:

   (prep, trav) quantity over 1 step lead dir placement (body, finish)

However, the arrangement is flexible, the objective being clarity.

Write the following steps information (found between commas), seeking clarity.

R irish frt x	_____
L-R fwd c/s	_____
into f-r-c U-S face L ½-pvt ( )	_____
R-L-R tr p-d-b c-w	_____

In cases of complex (often hyphenated) steps it may prove clarifying to begin by specifying a lead and conclude by indicating the final action foot; e.g., R shfl-hop-tpl-tt L x frt. Always keep in mind that unlike you, those reading your notes have no prior understanding of your intent. Avoid confusion.

There has to be an easier way (quotes from notes):

Examples, from various 1936-1995 tap routine notes, include pre-term glimpses and/or indication of notation variety and often unnecessarily confusing complexity. Simplify and clarify these descriptions:

"jump to R foot (FLAT FOOT)" _____
"quickly leap R in place" _____
"jump to flap" _____
"dig R – dig L – dig R – dig L" _____
"heel of L hand pushing" _____
"hands to chest frt" _____
"fingers spread wide – palms toward audience" _____
"R ft. front of L calf" _____
"drop R heel eight times sliding fwd on R" _____
"keeping knee st. brush R to L" _____
"brush L forward, wing R" _____
"slide back with seven running steps" _____
"step back R ft crossed behind L, step L to side, step R front of L, travel to L on this movement" _____
"extend L diag fwd L (no sound)" _____
"leap R in place, raising L off floor fwd" _____
"shuffle jump, drop heel" _____
"brush toe in, heel rest" _____
"brush R (b)-brush L (b) land on R step L" _____
"step → on R (fall)" _____
"shove fwd both toes simultaneously knees bent" _____
"stub R heel against L toe" _____
"travel R by turning both toes inward then outward" _____
"move to the R – drop RL heels – drop RL toes" _____
"wing L (bringing R through passe x frt)" _____
"jump to heel roll a&a1" _____
"slide R across in front – land on L _____
"leap R to R – close L in front of R (like a glissade)" _____
"step R x frt of L, step L bk, step R to R, step L fwd" _____
"lift R ft behind L knee. twist R ft to Rt. R knee turned in touching L knee. twist R ft to L knee. R knee out AST." _____
"off the ground outside barrel" _____
"click AST hop on L and lift R" _____
"step R – step L – step R – step L. do these last 4 steps as a twist" _____
"arms in opposition across body" _____
"(flap R) cramp roll RLRL &1&a2" _____
"raise L knee to L as you slide on R to S-L" _____
"bring both together with dragging motion on floor" _____
"step on flat of L ft. – step on flat of R ft. &8" _____
"brush step back on R ft. across in front of L" _____
"step L (fwd over R)" _____
"fast steps high on toes" _____
"Arms stretched out shoulder high – hands dangling" _____
"arms out to low 2nd" _____
"arms in 2nd, hands down, elbows up" _____
"touch R toe (&), scuff R (a), drop L heel (1), step on R heel (&), drop R toe (2)" _____
"step L to side, step R across front, glissade LR closing R in back, step L to side, step R across front, glissade LR closing R in back" _____
"opposite ft. and direction" _____

More complex statements:

"Scuff R fwd in a semi-circle to R" _____
"scuff R, step (B) R (x F of L)" _____
"step fwd on R ft, kick L leg fwd & circle it ard in frt of R, jump up in air & land on L ft" _____
"raise front part of foot off floor, heel resting on floor, then turn foot to right and drop front part of foot" _____
"shuff R step pull bk L behind R" _____
"drop R L heels (rocking body first back then fwd)" _____
"drag R up to L (making a definite scraping sound on the floor), transfer weight to R foot" _____
"do two essence steps back, to L then to R side" _____
"continue turning left as you shuffle R, pickup L, land on R, touch L toe across behind R" _____

Page 80

"lunge R to R, spin in place on R, AST drag L toe as in figure skating" _____
"buck for'd on both feet, pull knees back" _____
"slap L into cramp roll dropping R heel first 5&a6" _____
"jump to L clicking heels together, coming down in cramp-roll" _____

Chaos:
Reproduced as published in 1980, including rhythm notation placement.
"ST R L R-DIG LF BK-BCLR-STEP L TO L
  1 &2&3 &4 &5 6   & 78"
The rest of the routine is readably notated, but this phrase is chaos. Any ideas?

X + 2y + z(H) =
a combination. As with algebra, chemistry, computer programming, or baking, dance notes are a formula/algorithm/recipe to be assembled. Accuracy produces prescribed results; experimenting, a new brew.

Although tap notation has clearly improved since the 1930s,
since the late 1950s terminology use has stagnated. Most writers assume readers to be ignorant of even the basics (irish, buffalo, cramproll, 3-step turn) avoiding terms which include more than two taps – Gates: "triple (shff-step)". The unnecessarily wordy result is inevitably clumsy and inefficient. At its best, tap notation should flow from and to the mind with no more complexity or delay than marqueing the same material being set by a demonstrator. Build a tap vocabulary and use it. An easier exploration makes for a more enjoyable adventure.

FINALÉ

Tap happy:
What do you enjoy about tapping?   What, about tapping, do you find interesting?

Which tap step do you think is the wildest?   Which step is the most fun?

What's the silliest tap term?   Which step do you find most balletic?

Which tap style do you most enjoy?   Which tap performers do you enjoy? Why?

Categories:
Specify the category of terms referred to by each set of associations.
- sgl, dbl, tpl, qdl _____
- soft shoe, r-r, eccentric _____
- buck, shim sham, and waltz styles _____
- bgn'g + sgl, dbl, etc. + end _____
- U-S, D-S-L, S-R _____
- rt, bk, x frt, l-d-b _____
- 4/4, 6/8, 3/4, 5/4 _____

Phff or shfl:
Have you noticed that most abbreviations are 4 letters or less and are term beginning letters or phonetic representations?
   cinc   ess   patt   seq   trav   batt
   Pronounce:
   brk   fwd   mvmt   sgl   wt   gpvn
Separator connected single letters represent words or syllables.
   d-b   c-r-c   u-l-o-d   o/s   w/w   C-S-R

Riddles:
What tap expressions may be implied from:
- table light _____   draws a circle _____
- shakey dowels _____   quiet footwear _____
- chainé of wild bovines _____ sweet feet _____
- barber shop _____   reptile pelvis _____
- he plows _____   ding dong _____
- S N's _____   bouncing insect _____
- tangled branches of fruit _____ place to cross a river _____
- to be avoided while fastening a horse to a wagon _____
- take flight _____   sketch _____
- musical stroll _____   three _____

Zig-Zag:

This is an interesting challenge. Interlock tap terms from top toward bottom of this 36x36 grid per the following rules.
1. Select or create a terminology category list (turns, steps with flaps, body positions, side travel steps, etc.).
2. Letter each term along a single downward diagonal in the grid, linking terms through a shared letter.
3. Letter contiguously (no spaces or hyphens).
4. No more than 2 shared letters (linked terms) per term.

Sound easy? OK, try this:

5. Include letters on all rows, top to bottom.
6. 2 or more categories per grid, side by side. Different categories words may intersect without sharing letters.

See example: **DISCUSSION ASSISTANCE**, **FINALÉ**, page 93.

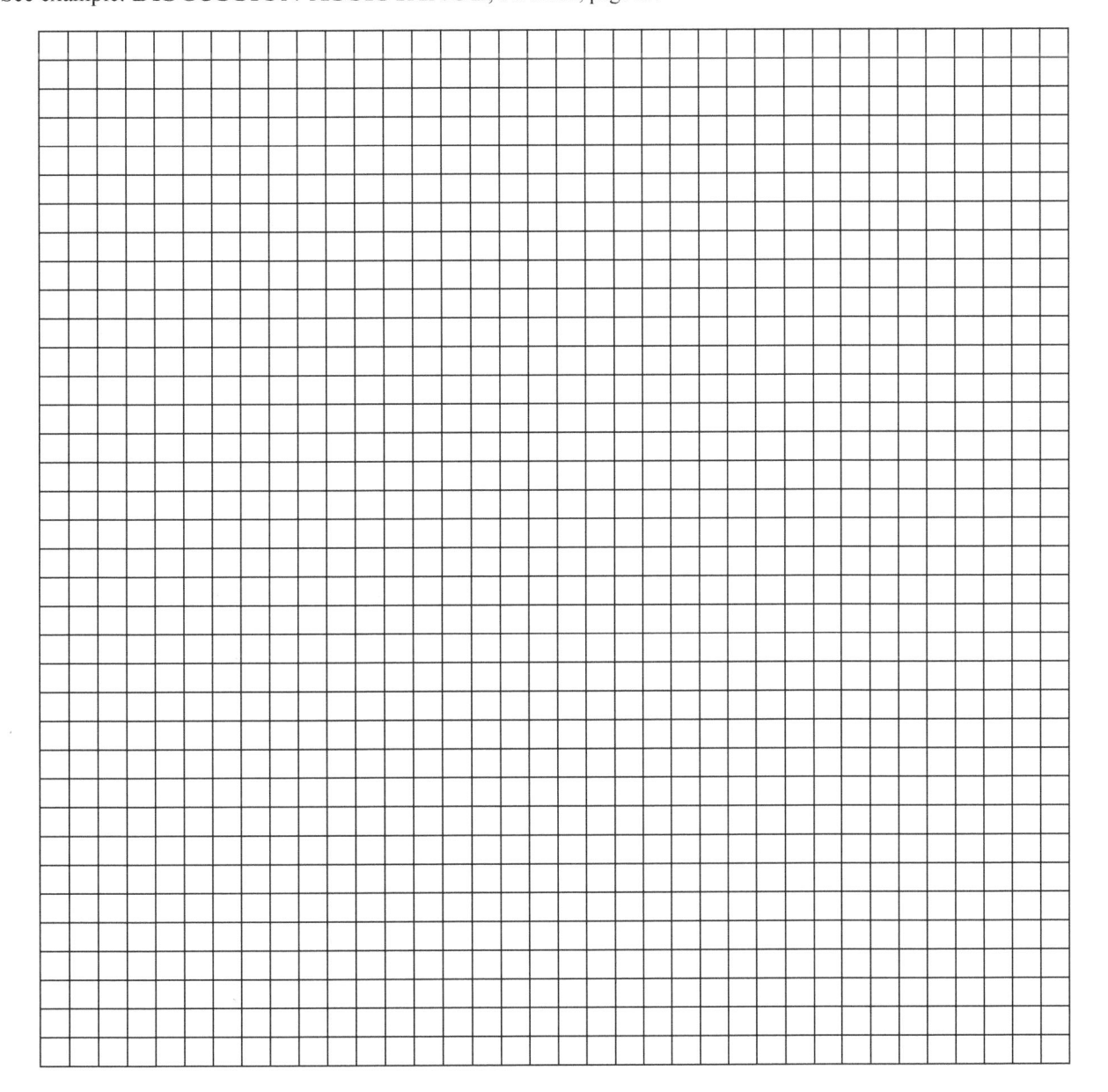

Hidden in the midst:

A single essence: "flap R right, flap L to R, step" &5&a6. An uncredited, undated, hand notated soft shoe, probably from the 1930s, includes this combination, ending "(rolling wing change)" – and it is.

It is impossible to identify when, where, or by whom any tap term, much less step, was created or may have metamorphized. Yet, routine notes and early tappers' quotes must be considered reasonably authentic term sources, if not written origins. Seek earliest and repeated references. If currently not in popular use, consider why.

Page 82

From where to eternity?

Tap terms have been required by frequent and common use, but have many, sometimes multiple, sources of inspiration. Following are a few. Add more examples; for starters: hitch, ess, paddle, cramp, cross-bar, cubanola, legomania, p-u, tiller, brk.

Inspiration:	Terms
sound:	chug,
feet/legs:	tt,
action:	dig,
use:	t-s,
dance form/style:	irish,
person:	eddie leonard,
shape:	jazz triangle,
object:	compass tr,
similarity:	riffle,
appearance:	toe stand,
expression:	shave and a haircut
visual:	vibrate
historic:	trench,
place:	buff,

Consider the possibilities. There are frequently several, and terms often have questionable origins. After all, history (his story) is often numerously reinterpreted hearsay.

Termstring:

From each specified category(ies), fill in the terms that overlap with the specified last and starting letters.

```
DANCE STRUCTURE   _ _ _ _ _ e _ _ t _ _ _ s _ _ _ _ _ _ _ e _ _ _ _ _ _ _ _
MUSIC & RHYTHM    _ _ _ _ t _ _ _ t _ _ _ _ _ t _ _ e _ _ n _ _ _
TURNS             _ _ _ _ _ _ s _ _ _ f _ _ p _ _ _ t _ _ _ _ - _ _ _ p _ _ _ _ _
WINGS             _ _ _ _ _ _ _ t _ _ _ _ _ t _ _  _ _ _ _ d _ _ _ _ _  _ _ _ _ e _ _ _ _
```

Anagrams:

Rearrange the letters into tap terms (may be multi-word).

a pet pinto =	charm =	copy a nest =	deal =
lot of use =	hoe for =	graven pie =	in route =
laid a rose riser =	made or fix =	mish mash =	most pies tempt =
pale =	palm =	past =	puck pi =
ruins a swing =	shrub =	tight rages =	top legion role =

Speaka da language:

Verbally specify a combination. Do precisely what you said. Did the description accurately indicate your intent?

Verbally exchange combinations with another tapper, who then dances them. If not performed correctly, was the description, understanding, or both in error?

Try again to achieve accuracy talking tap.

And write it:

Using different combinations, repeat the above exercise as exchanged notes. Try a different comb.

And see it:

Notate then perform a combination while someone analyzes and notates it. How similar are the notes? Reverse roles.

Husked corn:

"In essence, we must break-out in time-step to flea hop the chorus of pendulum minded who buck the natural slide into the accelerando tempo of rock'n roll. To pull-back now would slap into focus and further accent the steps taken to cramp our style. Never back paddle turn. We must wing forward, meeting the challenge face on, always ready to pickup our shuffles, dig new trenches, measure our entrance, and stamp this flap to an early exit. This twist is no demi feet."

The officious, albeit meaningless (maybe), expounding of double talk was a comedy specialty act from vaudeville through the 1950s. How many indexed terms are included in this monologue? _____

Final Challenge - Every which one-way:

The following Hidden-Words Puzzle includes **TERMINOLOGY INDEX** terms lying in either direction along any of the four major axes (horizontal, vertical, either 45° diagonal).

These rules apply: 1. minimum 5-letter terms
2. compound or hyphenated terms are contiguously lettered
3. French terms are without accent marks
4. no unrequired plurals or tenses

There are 40 terms, find what you can. When stumped, don't give up, return later. Do not abandon hope. When ready, there are two levels of **DISCUSSION ASSISTANCE**. Level I (page 85) is a terms list, Level II (page 88) lists lettering directions. Level III is the solution with starting references.

How about making a couple copies of this puzzle, then after a year or two trying it again to see how much your terminology recognition has increased.

```
S  K  C  I  T  S  E  L  G  G  I  W  W  A  L  T  Z
C  P  A  T  E  O  T  R  S  O  P  R  C  A  Y  B  H
U  H  L  A  S  P  A  X  E  T  M  H  R  N  R  C  R
F  Q  A  C  S  P  O  Y  G  I  O  U  R  U  T  E  E
F  T  U  I  E  T  G  L  U  R  T  O  S  A  F  P  L
T  R  E  V  N  I  N  E  E  A  S  H  C  O  S  L  G
I  E  I  U  C  E  I  O  N  V  H  P  O  S  O  E  A
M  N  O  P  E  X  G  L  I  D  E  H  C  R  A  D  E
E  C  K  L  A  R  A  T  T  L  E  D  N  I  R  P  E
S  H  J  M  A  S  T  F  U  F  L  K  E  E  I  U  L
T  R  I  P  L  E  S  U  O  R  C  A  L  C  Q  I  B
E  A  H  N  E  R  V  E  R  O  L  L  K  R  N  J  U
P  Y  F  L  A  P  T  U  R  N  I  U  A  D  I  A  O
R  O  T  C  A  F  E  M  I  T  P  M  Y  R  L  Z  D
```

Onward:

If this discussion has sparked your interest in the sources of tap steps and terminology, continue with a copy of Marshall and Jean Stearns *Jazz Dance*.

DISCUSSION ASSISTANCE
for **DISCUSSION** challenges (red), plus a few added comments (blue).

TAPS AND STANCE

Fill in using the following (each insert is used only once):
back   ball   does   doesn't   heel   one   one   plié-relevé   raised   stamp   stomp   stood on   tip   toe   two

Each tap shoe includes _two_ taps, the _toe_ or _ball_ tap under the toes and the _heel_ tap. Most tapping is done while supported on _one_ foot. The free foot is _raised_ near the supporting leg. Usually, in order to have a foot free to move, when one foot is _stood on_, the other foot is lifted. Most tap sounds are made by striking _one_ tap at a time. Different parts of the taps may be used. For example, a toe-tap is a striking of the _tip_ of the toe, and a dig strikes the _back_ edge of the heel. Some tap movements are different because they do or don't accept weight. A step _does_ take the weight, while a ball tap _doesn't_. A few tap sounds, such as _stamp_ and _stomp_, are made using two taps at the same time. The proper supporting stance is with the supporting leg heel raised and knee slightly bent, a _plié-relevé_, which permits nearly continuous bouncing on one or between feet.

BASIC SOUNDS and COORDINATION

It takes two:
All listed **BASIC SOUNDS** are single, except one. Which requires 2 different sounds? _chug_

Word-link puzzle:
The terms needed can be found in **BASIC SOUNDS** and **MOVEMENTS** in the **TAP TERMINOLOGY**.

```
            c  h  u  g
               o
         s  t  e  p          j
            c                u
      b  r  u  s  h          m
         s  f  e     s  n  a  p
   s  l  u  f  f  e  t
      i     g     l  e  a  p
      d  i  g     m
      e        s  t  o  m  p
               a
               p
```
(snap/step are interchangeable)

Select landing relationships (2 each line):

	same foot / change feet / both feet	ball tap(s) / both taps
hop	X / /	X /
leap	/ X /	X /
hamp	X / /	/ X
lamp	/ X /	/ X
catch	/ X /	X /
jump	/ / X	X /
fall	/ X /	X /

From the bottom up:
Match the best associations:
- fall — _drop_
- catch — _replace_
- hitch — _replace and kick_
- leap — _airborne_

Tappin':
Just as there are three different definitions of "step" (see **BASIC STEPS** introduction), this manual includes the basic pas plus what three other uses of "tap"?

- _tap dancing_ — the activity (theater dance form)
- _tap sound_ — audio rhythm
- _metal tap_ — attached to shoe

BASIC STEPS

Some assembly required:
Match the best relationships between first and second column lists.

basic sounds	foundation coordinations
basic steps	1M or less
complex steps	2M or more
combination	sequence of steps
phrase	2M, 4M
Step	8M, 16M
routine	64M, 96M

Page 85

Name the steps described as:	
shfl, shfl	__double shuffle__
brush bk, hop, step bk	__draw-back__
shfl, hop, step	__irish__
br-scuff fwd	__riff__
scuff fwd, br bk	__scuffle__
brush bk R, hop L, tpl bk R.	__cincinnati__

Unscramble:	
f i f r	__riff__
l p m a	__lamp__
t l e s e h i w t	__heel twist__
t a r l e t	__rattle__
p h t s e c c t a	__catch-step__
a u p q d e u r l	__quadruple__

Too many, too few:
Read: "Small brush bk. R-step R-small brush bk. L-step L-shuffle step R-heel drop R-heel touch L in front-small brush bk. L-step L-heel touch R in front-brush bk. R-heel step R-step L-brush step bk. R-heel touch L in front-small brush bk. step L-scuff R" a&a1&2&3&4&5&a6&a7&a8. From Eva Varady "Begin the Beguine" STEP IV, this break is an unnecessarily challenging quick read – too many similar step, brush, heel references, too few discriminating steps. Translate this phrase into clearer language.
__Back flaps R-L, qdl R, dig L, bk flap L, dig R, br bk R, dig R w/w, step L, bk flap R, dig L, bk flap L, scuff R.__

From this list   ball change   cramp   flaps   irish   quadruple   shuffles   triple:
The two most used duple rhythm tap steps are __shuffles__ and __flaps__.
Select 3 more terms that begin with a shfl: __triple__, __quadruple__, __irish__.
Two quick steps are called a __ball change__. A step-heel is a __cramp__.
When a dance notes introduction does not identify the dance form, look for shuffles and flaps to confirm tap.

Regarding flaps:
Although flaps can move in any direction, each flap can go in only __one__. To permit efficient movement, flaps may move in the direction of any part of the foot. Which part of the foot leads forward, backward, outside, inside flaps? __toe__, __heel__, __outside__, __inside__ A leisurely br-step is a walking flap. When done running, what must the step become? __leap__ What action makes a swinging flap unique? __free leg i/s swing from side__ A __slap__ is like a flap without transferring weight.

FINAL CHALLENGE - Level I Assistance
The puzzle words as they appear:

ARCHED	FLAPTURN	NATURAL	SEGUE
BRUSH	FRONT	NERVEROLL	STAGING
CATCH	GLIDE	PASSE	STOMP
CHAINE	GRAPEVINE	PHRASE	TILLER
CHOREOGRAPHY	HEELCLIP	PICKUP	TIMEFACTOR
COUNT	HOOFER	RATTLE	TOETAP
DANCE	INVERT	ROCKNROLL	TRENCH
DEVELOPE	LINDY	ROUTINE	TRIPLE
DOUBLEEAGLE	MARQUE	SCOOT	WALTZ
ESSENCE	MAXIE	SCUFFTIMESTEP	WIGGLESTICKS

Basically most:
How many of the 40 listed **BASIC STEPS** are comprised only of one or more step(s) and/or brush(s)? __11__
How many more if hop(s) and/or leap(s) are included? __13__ more
Now include heel(s) and scuff(s). __7__ more
What **BASIC SOUNDS AND MOVEMENTS** are needed to include the remaining 9 **BASIC STEPS**?
__dig(2)__, __pend(1)__, __sluff(2)__, __snap(1)__, __stamp(2)__, __tap(1)__
Notice the movements yielding the largest quantity. As previously emphasized, tapping is facilitated by bouncing weight changes. (OK, pend is listed as a kick.)

Its time had come:
Elmer Wheatly's 1940s <u>Swing Classic</u> Step VII includes: "Hop L., brush R. fwd., step on R. heel (close riff), step L. in place a&a1". Although not in a soft shoe routine, this is a variation of what step? __v-ess__
<u>Rhythm Dance</u> (1940s) by Billy Moyer begins, "Shuffle riff" "ea1". In a Hanf routine <u>It's All Right With Me</u> (Hanf Record #1015) is explained, RIFF SHUFFLE: "A close shuffle with a heel scuff between the fwd. and back brushes. It is a fwd. brush – a scuff – and a back brush.". What one word basic step is described? __riffle__

Crazy:
According to Hanf in an eccentric routine "Satan Takes A Holiday" (Hanf record #544 side B) (probably 1950s):
Step 8: "KEEP KNEES TIGHT TOGETHER DURING THE FOLLOWING TWO MEAS.- Jump up with R foot Fwd. and L foot Back – Land on both feet (together) – Jump up with R foot B and L foot Fwd. – Land on both feet (together)". Name the step.
__knee split jump__

Auld tap syne (old tap since):
Many now less used tap terms repeatedly appear in notes from the 1920s onward. Translate these to **TERMINOLOGY** terms.

paddle wheel turn	paddle tr	shuffle riff	riffle
change kick	hitch	step flat	stamp
double wings	eagle	twist step	sgr
heel jab	dig	toeback	tt
cross steps	gpvn	click	clip

They are all listed in **ALTERNATE TERMINOLOGY**.

BUFFALOS and BOMBERSHAYS

State based tap term:	Country based:	People inspired terms:
virginia essence	cubanola, irish,	Fred Astaire, Jim Bandy, Maxie Ford, Eddie Leonard,
	russian wing and eagle	Charles Lindberg (pilot), Bill Robinson, George Snowden

KICKS

Just for kicks:
For each kick, select the best beginning and end leg and foot or 2 feet/position relationships. (4 per line)

	Begins				Ends			
	Open	/ Close	On Floor	/Off Floor	Open	/ Close	On Floor	/ Off Floor
battment		/ X	X	/		/ X	X	/
swing kick	X	/	X	/	X	/	X	/
balancoire	X	/		/ X	X	/		/ X
developpé		/ X		/ X	X	/		/ X
snap kick		/ X		/ X		/ X		/ X

The eagle has landed:
More simply, the 1916 *Dances Drills and Story Plays* by Nina Lambkin describes under "Sailor's Hornpipe" "Fifth Figure: Scissors Step." "Jump in half stride. Jump and cross feet. Repeat." A side side scissor without kick. Also, "Fourth Figure: Twisting Step." "Heels and toes close together, move sideward left four counts by moving toes to left, then heels." Name that step. ___suzie-q___

TURNS & TWISTS

That's right?
Along with tr dir's, what other 2 types of mvmt's may be specified i/s or o/s? ___Ft lead___, ___r-d-j's___

Where did that come from?
Vaudevillian Jack Wiggins (early 1900s) is credited with popularizing the Bantam Twist (like the rooster), possibly the forerunner of the bandy twist which is credited to Jim Bandy, another vaudeville dancer.

Try a buff R ending hitch x frt (leap, shfl, catch), hitches bk then frt while tr'g rt.   or

Do a buff R. Do a bandy R. Now do a buff into a b-t. Rpt ending the buff w/ st R x frt L, then the two b-t steps x frt. What step preceded the shfl-b/c? ___falling off a log___

A confusing Willie Covan turning hitch kick version: (trav lt) "Step back R L step L, step R and scissors cross R F over L F double turn." Can you figure out this log var? ___Perhaps: (2 c-w tr's) hitch R – L frt S-R, pvt c-w into hitch L (face S-L) – R bk, hitch R – L frt S-R, hitch L (face S-L) – R x frt L___ (Covan's "R" and "L" indicate body and stg dir's.)

ROLLS & CLIPS

Zapped:
Spanish folk dance, especially from the northern Basque region adjacent to France, is characterized in ballet. Which term is listed in this **INDEX**? ___saut de basque___ Which (not in this **INDEX**) is associated with a yellow brick road? ___pas de basque___

Clipped:
From Johnny Boyle's The American Clog Dance Step 4:

" 1   2 &   a   3   4   & 5   &
ball L – ball change R L – heel drop L – ball R – click heels together center – land R L – brush L heel with R toe in crossing –
    6   &   7   &   8   &
hop L – brush L heel again with R toe to original position – hop L – ball R – heel scuff L with wgt – heel scuff R with wgt –
     1   & 2   &   3 &
snap toe togrther standing on heels – toe drops L R – heels click standing on toes – drop L R toes in place –
     4   &   5   &

click L toe to R heel in crossing back – hop R – click L toe again to R heel into original position – hop R –
        6 &   7   & a   8
heel stands L R toes turned up – snap toes together – toe drops L R – heels click wgt on toes".
"Heel scuff" is dig, the pair a d/c, later notated "heel stands". "Ball" avoids flat foot.
What 3 terms are used for clip? __brush__, __click__, __snap__
Which heel clip is elevated? __"click heels together center"__

PICKUPS & WINGS

Pick a pickup:

Which type of actual pickup?		Types
d-p-u	d	**s**ingle
pull-back	s	**s**ingle **c**hange
shfl-d-p-u	sc	**d**ouble
p-u-c-t-t	sc	**d**ouble **c**hange
d-p-u-r	d	
p-u-irish	s	
p-u-c-trench	sc	
d-p-u-c	dc	

Once a young fellow who tapped
Sluffed sideways into a flap
That's an interesting thing
I'll call it a wing
With both feet, an __eagle__, perhaps.

Self defining:
Eva Varady's "Broadway Rhythm" includes "brush R-up to R-side in seconde pos., hop L-step R-in front of L" - - - - " (For more advanced students a wing may be substituted for the hop)". And from Ann Dansetts <u>Advanced Soft Shoe</u> Step Five break: "Hop back L, picking up extra sound on hop."
Described are what wing and p-u steps? __batt wing__, __s-p-u__

What's the flap about?
A pickup, like a flap, can be executed in any one direction leading with any side of the foot. Functionally, a pickup is an airborn flap, as specified in a Billy Clower 1956 routine "I Know That You Know" distributed for Russell Record #5: "shuffle L, flap bk. R (grab-off)" repeated three times. The quote describes what step? __pull-back__

RHYTHM PATTERNS

Name these rhythm patterns:

1a2a3 4a5a6	w-c-t-s	8&1 2&3 4&5&6&7	shim sham comb
1&2 3 4 5&6 7 8	lindy	8&1 2&3& 4&5 6&7&	s-t-s
8&1&2 3&4&5 6 (7)	maxie	1 2&3 4(5) 67 (8)	shave and a haircut
&1&a2 &3&a4 &5&a6&a7&a8	ess comb	a1&a2 a3 a4 a5&a6 a7 a8	drum flap cadence

TAP DANCE STYLES

Stick it:
In dance parlance sticks are legs. What step includes this association? __wiggle sticks__
What other 2 listed terms stem from "leg"? __leg spin__, __legomania__

Toot, toot:
What term suggests a steam locomotive starting to move? __chug, chug, chug, - - -__ (Seems the likely source of the term.)
The term probably came into use when vaudeville railroad numbers were popular, 1920s through 1940s.

POSITIONS

What you see is:
Which positions/movements mimic:
log rolling	__falling off a log__
railroad signal	__r-r-A's__
shaky hand	__vibrate__
struggling captive	__'tack annie__
pushing	__press__
leg tremor (1 leg)	__nerve roll__
(2 legs)	__patter steps__

Match the opposites:
Matched:	arched	flexed
	t/o	t/i
	rel	plié
	i/s	o/s
	o-p	c-p

Last stand:
Each following comb is lead R. Which is the final suporting Ft?
Shfl, heel, step, shfl-b/c.   __R__
Flap, heel, irish x frt, f-r-c, cinc.   __L__
Log, stamp fwd into c-w shfl-b/c ½-tr.   __R__
Shfl, wing chg, hip wing, tt.   __R__

The buck* starts here:
For most tapping the free foot moves from a position near the supporting leg ankle. When introducing some steps, presetting a starting position is helpful (buffalos, back flaps, back essences). Many steps require a starting position. Describe them for:

chug	ball of Ft on flr	snap	heel on flr
snap kick	passé	sluff	Ft on flr
scoot	standing on Ft	heel	ball on flr
swinging flap	Ft raised to sd	heel twist	heel on flr
suzie-q	both Ft on flr		there are several more.

(*Buck is an outdated term for chug.)

Viva la French: The total depends on term selection; e.g., demi plié may count as 1 to 3 terms.
All right ballet students, how many different French ballet terms appear in the **TERMINOLOGY INDEX**? __minimum 21__

FINAL CHALLENGE - Level II Assistance
The puzzle words directions:

ARCHED ⇐	FLAPTURN ⇒	NATURAL ⇗	SEGUE ⇓
BRUSH ⇙	FRONT ⇓	NERVEROLL ⇒	STAGING ⇑
CATCH ⇗	GLIDE ⇒	PASSE ⇘	STOMP ⇑
CHAINE ⇘	GRAPEVINE ⇙	PHRASE ⇘	TILLER ⇗
CHOREOGRAPHY ⇙	HEELCLIP ⇓	PICKUP ⇙	TIMEFACTOR ⇐
COUNT ⇗	HOOFER ⇗	RATTLE ⇒	TOETAP ⇐
DANCE ⇘	INVERT ⇐	ROCKNROLL ⇗	TRENCH ⇓
DEVELOPE ⇘	LINDY ⇙	ROUTINE ⇑	TRIPLE ⇒
DOUBLEEAGLE ⇑	MARQUE ⇗	SCOOT ⇘	WALTZ ⇒
ESSENCE ⇓	MAXIE ⇗	SCUFFTIMESTEP ⇓	WIGGLESTICKS ⇐

GENERAL TERMS

Make it personal: Number an item in each column best associated with the dancer.
The Guys: Unscrambled associated answers are on the same line.

Dancer	Style	Personal Association	Appeared With	Motion Picture
1. Bill Robinson	1_ easy & ambling	1_ Bojangles	1_ Shirley Temple	1_ *The Little Colonel*
2. Fred Astaire	2_ smooth & wide ranging	2_ ballroom popularizer	2_ Ginger Rogers	2_ *Daddy Long Legs*
3. Gene Kelly	3_ athletic & jazzy	3_ umbrella dance	3_ Jerry Mouse	3_ *Singin' In The Rain*
4. Ray Bolger	4_ eccentric & comedic	4_ rubberlegs	4_ Judy Garland	4_ *The Harvey Girls*
5. Gregory Hines	5_ percussive	5_ H--, H--, and Dad	5_ Mikhail Baryshnikov	5_ *White Nights*

Holding a pair of spoons or bones in one hand while moving them up and down against or between thigh and/or the other hand permits rapid, complex rhythms. Even when the "bones" were wood, users were commonly called "bone janglers". Bill Robinson, a wood soled clog dancer of syncopated rhythms purportedly was bestowed Bojangles from the folk musicians' term.

Fred Astaire film featured ballroom dances included Continental, Carioca, (not-so-ballroom) Yam, Piccolino, Wedding Cakewalk, Shorty George, Sluefoot, Martini, Ritz Rock & Roll, plus several reprised styles in *Barkleys of Broadway*.

The young Hines brothers' (Gregory and Maurice) tap duet act toured accompanied by their father as Hines, Hines, and Dad.

The Gals:

1. Eleanor Powell	1_ rapid turn sequences	1_ top hat & tails	1_ Buddy Ebsen	1_ *Lady Be Good*
2. Ann Miller	2_ athletic	2_ million dollar legs	2_ Mickey Rooney	2_ *Easter Parade*
3. Ginger Rogers	3_ "favorite dance partner"	3_ Best Actress Oscar	3_ Lucille Ball	3_ *Shall We Dance*
4. Ruby Keeler	4_ "world's fastest tapper"	4_ Busby Berkeley	4_ James Cagney	4_ *Footlight Parade*
5. Vera-Ellen	5_ lithe and energetic	5_ Rockette	5_ Donald O'Connor	5_ *On the Town*

As a child, Ann Miller received dance lessons to aid recovery from rickets. At age 13 (a forged birth certificate claimed 18) she received an RKO contract. The studio publicity department claimed her capable of 500 taps per minute and, after her sexy 1953 "Too Darn Hot" redition (including a bongo challenge) in *Kiss Me Kate*, had Lloyds of London insure her legs for $1,000,000.

1979 Ann Miller and Mickey Rooney (Broadway debut) opened *Sugar Babies*. After 3 years followed two tours through 1986.

Ginger Rogers received Best Actress Oscar for her non-dancing portrayal of Kitty in the 1940 *Kitty Foyle*.

Reportedly, Ruby Keeler was the first to be slow motion filmed then her taps counted. According to Rusty Franklin in *Tap*, in 1942 Ripley's *Believe It or Not* recorded Ann Miller at 598 taps per minute and proclaimed her "Worlds Fastest Tap Dancer". Speed typist Ruth Myers vied with Miller in 1946 producing 584/627 keystrikes/taps, declared a new record.

Vera-Ellen, another child enrolled in dance to improve physical and psychological health, was a young Rockette in the late 1930s before her age 18 *Very Warm For May* 1939 Broadway debut.

Buddy Ebsen, Lucille Ball, James Cagney, and many other early film stars were tappers before their later non-dance fame.
Which guy tap danced 4 of these gals across the screen?   *Fred Astaire*
(Eleanor Powell, *Broadway Melody of 1940*; Ann Miller, *Easter Parade*; Ginger Rogers, 10 films; Vera-Ellen, *Three Little Words* & *The Belle of New York*)

THE MOVIES

How did I get here?
What other holiday film featured Fred Astaire?   *Holiday Inn*

ARRANGEMENT TERMS

Give me a break:
It's not difficult to determine the function of a phrase that begins with a style standard, but ends differently styled. From Micheal Dominico's Soft Shoe (1950s) Step III: "Flap R, flap L, (across R), step R, shuffle L, hop R, shuffle L, step L, shuffle R, hop L, step R, (behind L) flap L, flap R, B.C. LR. &1&a2&a3&a4&a5&6&7&8". This is a rhythm var of what step?   *soft-shoe-t-s-brk*

Dance vs. Music:
Match the most closely related notation/term from each pair of columns.

Dance	Music	Dance	Music
Step	8M	rout	2 choruses
( )	tacit	hold	vamp
ent	intro	flash step	stop time
exit	tag	song & dance	verse & chorus

Four little words/abbreviations:
Hyphenated notation may be similarly used, but more thoughtfully. Do these notation pairs specify the same comb?

shfl-b/c 2X's	*no*	shfl-b/c-b/c	2 step-heels	*no*	step, step, heel, heel
flap-b/c's L-R	*yes*	flap-b/c L, flap-b/c R	riff-heel-step-heel-step	*yes*	riff, heel, cramp, step
dbl-shfl-p-u-c	*yes*	dbl-shfl, p-u-c	flap, hop 2 X's, scfl 2 X's	*no*	flap-hop, flap-hop, dbl-scfl

If in doubt, rhythm notation or following weight placement usually clarifies intent.

Doubled:
A double step includes two of the same step (dbl-shfl, d-p-u). A doubled step includes the basic step and a variation of equal length - a double length step variation. Doubled steps frequently are called double but may be otherwise named.

Notate then name (abbreviation) the doubled steps based on:

cinc	*br bk, hop, br frt, hop, cinc*	*tpl-cinc*
frt ess	*flap, flap x frt, step, flap open-bk diag, step, flap x frt, step*	*dbl-ess*
buff	*hop-tpl, buff*	*dbl-buff*
w-c-t-s	*w-c-t-s, hop-c-t-s*	*-d-c-t-s*

RHYTHM NOTATION

----let it be:
Ending a numeric rhythm term "let" or abbreviation "lt" (duplet/dplt) indicaates a cluster of evenly spaced sounds. How many taps does each abbreviation specify?

qdlt *4*   splt *7*   tplt *3*   oclt *8*   qnlt *5*   sxlt *6*

Simply notated:
Fran Scanlan's First Step of Sophisticated Soft Shoe, includes "brush R, scuff R, step R (fwd to heel), toe drop R, heel drop R, (the counts 'a6&a7' make a quintuplet step)". The rhythm of this variation of what step can be more easily clarified how?
step?:   *5-tap riff walk*   notation?   *with braces: {even} or {qnlt} or {a6&a7}*

Buddy, do you have the time?
Put in order from briefest to longest spacing within a ct:
a e 1 i &   *i*   *e*   *a*   *&*   *1*

Which are:
As defined, classify the following as **E**ven, **D**uple, **B**roken, **S**yncopated rhythm.

rolling	*E*	{ }	*E*	dbl ess	*E*	r-r-	*E*
maxie	*B*	irish, flap-b/c	*D*	a1 2 3 a4&a5 6 7 a8&	*BS*	shim sham comb	*B*

Page 89

Page 90

STAGING

The endless frontier:
Most dancers want more space to travel. Eddie Leonard (Lemuel Toney), an early 20th century minstrel soft shoe expert, is noted for his solution. What was it?   **a circle**
This staging sometimes appears without turns, referenced "like an Eddie Leonard".

About Face:
When C-S facing as specified, relate stage dir to indicated body dir:

When facing D-S,   bk   **U-S**   ,   l-d-f   **D-S-L**   .
When facing S-R,   lt   **D-S**   ,   frt   **S-R**   .
When facing S-L,   l-d-b   **U-S-R**   ,   r-d-f   **D-S-L**   .
When facing U-S,   r-d-b   **D-S-L**   ,   rt   **S-L**   .

You danced where?
Fred Astaire tapped on a rocking boat deck, a good preparation for up and down walls and across the ceiling of a room in *Royal Wedding*. Figure out how.   The "deck" was a tiltable platform, the "room" a vertically rotating set, difficult to move in.

NOTATION SAFARI

Recognize anything?
As an example of vertical column notation format, here is a 1947 description by Jimmy Sutton, <u>Fast Flash</u> Step Three.

```
              "STEP THREE
Hop L                                  (8)
Shuffle step R (x'd bk of L –
    raising L foot up in fr of
    R – i.e. Buffalo)                  (and a 1)
Flap L                                 (and 2)
Flap R                                 (and 3)
Drop L heel                            (and)
Drop R heel                            (4)
Brush L (back)                         (and)
Hop R                                  (5)
Step L                                 (and)
Stamp R flat (x'd fr of L, toe
    Of R twisted to L or "turned in")  (6)
Step L to L (twisting R toe to R)      (and)
Brush R (in)                           (7)
Repeat cts "6 and"                     (and 8)       2 meas
Brush R back                           (and)
Buck L fwd                             (1)
Double shuffle R                       (and a 2 and)
Pickup change L to R                   (a 3)
Reverse cts "and a 2 and a 3"          (and a 4 and a 5)
Shuffle R                              (and 6)
Pickup change L to R                   (and a)
Tap L toe (x'd back of R)              (7)           2 meas

Repeat all (starting "jump to flap L") (and 8)       4 meas
                                                     8 meas"
```

(There are various column notation formats.)
Rewrite this Step, simplifying by notating as steps you can identify. "Buck" is a chug.
Various interpretations may be notated differently. This is one example.

STEP THREE

Hop-tpl L into buff starting pos, flap L, f-r-c R, d-b L, baby bmb R, i/s br R into rpt bmb.
2M   8   &a1   &2   &3&4 &5&   6&   7   &8
Br bk R, chug L, R dbl-shfl-p-u-c, rev after chug, R shfl-p-u-c-tt L x bk, leaped flap L into
2M   &   1   &a2&   a 3   &a4&a5   &6 & a 7   &8
8M   Rpt 4M.

Page 91

Call to order:
Dance notes tend to build from the general to the specific. As indicated at the beginning of **TAP TERMINOLOGY**, the recommended syntax sequence is:
    (prep, trav) quantity over 1 step lead dir placement (body, finish)
However, the arrangement is flexible, the objective being clarity.
Write the following steps information (found between commas), seeking clarity.
    R irish frt x   __irish R x frt__
    L-R fwd c/s   __c/s L-R fwd__
    into f-r-c U-S face L ½-pvt ( )   __f-r-c L into ½-pvt (face U-S)__
    R-L-R tr p-d-b c-w   __c-w p-d-b tr R-L-R__

In cases of complex (often hyphenated) steps it may prove clarifying to begin by specifying a lead and conclude by indicating the final action foot; e.g., R shfl-hop-tpl-tt x frt L. Always keep in mind that unlike you, those reading your notes have no prior understanding of your intent. Avoid confusion.

There has to be an easier way: (quotes from notes)
Examples, from various 1936-1995 tap routine notes, include pre-term glimpses and/or indication of notation variety and often unnecessarily confusing complexity. Simplify and clarify these descriptions:

    "jump to R foot (FLAT FOOT)" __lamp__
    "quickly leap R in place" __catch__
    "jump to flap" __leaped flap__
    "dig R – dig L – dig R – dig L" __2 d/c's__
    "heel of L hand pushing" __press__
    "hands to chest frt" __n-Sh-p__
    "fingers spread wide – palms toward audience" __jazz Hn's__
    "R ft. front of L calf" __buff starting pos__
    "drop R heel eight times sliding fwd on R" __chugs__
    "keeping knee st. brush R to L" __pend frt__
    "brush L forward, wing R" __pend wing__
    "slide back with seven running steps" __trenches__
    "step back R ft crossed behind L, step L to side, step R front of L, travel to L on this movement" __p-d-b__
    "extend L diag fwd L (no sound)" __tendu__
    "leap R in place, raising L off floor fwd" __hitch__
    "shuffle jump, drop heel" __qdl__
    "brush toe in, heel rest" __close riff__
    "brush R (b)-brush L (b) land on R step L" __d-p-u__
    "step → on R (fall)" __fall R rt__
    "shove fwd both toes simultaneously knees bent" __scoot fwd__
    "stub R heel against L toe" __heel to toe clip__
    "travel R by turning both toes inward then outward" __pigeon toe rt__
    "move to the R – drop RL heels – drop RL toes" __pigeon toe roll__
    "wing L (bringing R through passe x frt)" __hip wing__
    "jump to heel roll a&a1" __c-r__
    "slide R across in front – land on L __running glide__
    "leap R to R – close L in front of R (like a glissade)" __b/c x-over__
    "step R x frt of L, step L bk, step R to R, step L fwd" __diamond__
    "lift R ft behind L knee. twist R ft to Rt. R knee turned in touching L knee. twist R ft to L knee. R knee out AST."
        __legomania__
    "off the ground outside barrel" __hopped barrel tr__
    "click AST hop on L and lift R" __bell__
    "step R – step L – step R – step L. do these last 4 steps as a twist" __sgr__
    "arms in opposition across body" __x-o-A-s__
    "(flap R) cramp roll RLRL &1&a2" __flapped c-r__
    "raise L knee to L as you slide on R to S-L" __flea hop__
    "bring both together with dragging motion on floor" __scoot c-p__
    "step on flat of L ft. – step on flat of R ft. &8" __s/c__
    "brush step back on R ft. across in front of L" __bk flap x frt__
    "step L (fwd over R)" __step-over__
    "Arms stretched out shoulder high – hands dangling" __scarecrow A's__
    "fast steps high on toes" __patter steps__
    "arms out to low 2nd" __scissor open__
    "arms in 2nd, hands down, elbows up" __scarecrow A's__
    "touch R toe (&), scuff R (a), drop L heel (1), step on R heel (&), drop R toe (2)" __5-tap riff walk__

"step L to side, step R across front, glissade LR closing R in back, step L to side, step R across front,
   glissade LR closing R in back"   __gpvn__
"opposite ft. and direction"   __rev__

More complex statements:
"Scuff R fwd in a semi-circle to R"   __scuff into o/s r-d-j rt__
"scuff R, step (B) R (x F of L)"   __scuff, step close x frt__
"step fwd on R ft, kick L leg fwd & circle it ard in frt of R, jump up in air & land on L ft"   __saut de basque__
"raise front part of foot off floor, heel resting on floor, then turn foot to right and drop front part of foot" __h-t into snap__
"shuff R step pull bk L behind R"   __shfl-d-p-u x bk__
"drop R L heels (rocking body first back then fwd)"   __rock R-L w/ heels, rock fwd__
"drag R up to L (making a definite scraping sound on the floor), transfer weight to R foot"   __sluff R c-p into rock__
"do two essence steps back, to L then to R side"   __bk ess's__
"continue turning left as you shuffle R, pickup L, land on R, touch L toe across behind R" __maxie section tr w/o lead flap__
"lunge R to R, spin in place on R, AST drag L toe as in figure skating"   __lunge into compass tr__
"buck for'd on both feet, pull knees back"   __chug both, scoot__
"slap L into cramp roll dropping R heel first 5&a6"   __s-r-c__
"jump to L clicking heels together, coming down in cramp-roll"   __trav'g c-r__

Consider the efficiency of terminology.

FINALÉ

Categories:
Specify the category of terms referred to by each set of associations.

sgl, dbl, tpl, qdl	__time factors__	
soft shoe, r-r, eccentric	__tap styles__	
buck, shim sham, and waltz styles	__clogging styles__	
bgn'g + sgl, dbl, etc. + end	__basic buck t-s's__	
U-S, D-S-L, S-R	__stage directions__	(Yes, there is $5/4$ meter.
rt, bk, x frt, l-d-b	__body dir's__	Listen to Paul Desmond's "Take Five".
$4/4$, $6/8$, $3/4$, $5/4$	__meter__	Dave Brubeck's "Unsquare Dance" is $7/4$.)

Riddles:
What tap expressions may be implied from:

table light	__lamp__	draws a circle	__compass turn__
shakey dowels	__wiggle sticks__	quiet footwear	__soft shoe__
chainé of wild bovines	__buffalo tr's__	sweet feet	__sugar foot__
barber shop	__shave and a haircut six bits__	reptile pelvis	__snake hips__
he plows	__tiller__	ding dong	__bell__
S N's	__essence__	bouncing insect	__flea hop__
tangled branches of fruit	__grapevine__	place to cross a river	__maxie ford__
to be avoided while fastening a horse to a wagon	__hitch kick__		
take flight	__wing, or eagle__	sketch	__draw__
musical stroll	__riff walk__	three	__triple or triplet__

Termstring:
From the specified category(ies), fill in the terms that overlap with the specified starting letters.

DANCE STRUCTURE   __p h r a s e x i t i m e s e q u e n c e n t r a n c e__
MUSIC & RHYTHM   __c o u n t a c i t r i p l e t i m e v e n o t e__
TURNS   __c o m p a s s l u f f l a p i v o t h r e e - s t e p a d d l e__
WINGS   __b a t t e m e n t r i p l e t o e s t a n d o u b l e e a g l e a g l e__

Anagrams:
Rearrange the letters into tap terms (may be multi-word).

a pet pinto = __pointe tap__	charm = __march__	copy a nest = __syncopate__	deal = __lead__
lot of use = __sluefoot__	hoe for = __hoofer__	graven pie = __grapevine__	in route = __routine__
laid a rose riser = __railroad series__	made or fix = __maxie ford__	mish mash = __shim sham__	most pies tempt = __stomp time-step__
pale = __leap__	palm = __lamp__	past = __taps__	puck pi = __pickup__
ruins a swing = __russian wing__	shrub = __brush__	tight rages = __stage right__	top legion role = __pigeon-toe roll__

Zig-Zag:

This is an interesting challenge. Interlock tap terms from top toward bottom of this 36x36 grid per the following rules.
1. Select or create a terminology category list (turns, steps with flaps, body positions, side travel steps, etc.).
2. Letter each term along a single downward diagonal in the grid, linking terms through a shared letter.
3. Letter contiguously (no spaces or hyphens).
4. No more than 2 shared letters (linked terms) per term.

Sound easy? OK, try this:
5. Include letters on all rows, top to bottom.
6. 2 or more categories per grid, side by side. Different categories words may intersect without sharing letters.

How about trying to squeeze in a third category?

Page 94

Husked corn:

"In essence, we must break-out in time-step to flea hop the chorus of pendulum minded who buck the natural slide into the accelerando tempo of rock'n roll. To pull-back now would slap into focus and further accent the steps taken to cramp our style. Never back paddle turn. We must wing forward, meeting the challenge face on, always ready to pickup our shuffles, dig new trenches, measure our entrance, and stamp this flap to an early exit. This twist is no demi feet."

The officious, albeit meaningless (maybe), expounding of double talk was a comedy specialty act from vaudeville through the 1950s. How many indexed terms are included in this monologue? __minimum 35__

FINAL CHALLENGE - Level III Assistance

The puzzle words, directions, and starting reference numbers:

The following Hidden-Words Puzzle includes **TERMINOLOGY INDEX** terms lying in either direction along any of the four major axes (horizontal, vertical, either 45° diagonal).

These rules apply:
1. minimum 5-letter terms
2. compound or hyphenated terms are contiguously lettered
3. French terms are without accent marks
4. no unrequired plurals or tenses

```
 ¹S  K  C  I  T  S  E  L ²G  G  I ³W ⁴W  A  L  T  Z
 ⁵C  P  A  T ⁶E  O ⁷T  R ⁸S     ⁹P ¹⁰C  A    ¹¹B  H
  U  H        S  P  A     E  T  M  H  R     R  C  R
  F     A        S  P  O     G     O  R  U  T  E  E
  F ¹²T     I  E  T  G  L  U  R  T  O  S  A  F     L
  T  R  E  V  N ¹³I  N  E  E     ¹⁴S  H ¹⁵C  O  S  L  G
  I  E  I  U  C  E  I  O ¹⁶N  V ¹⁷H     O ¹⁸S  O  E  A
  M  N  O ¹⁹P  E  X ²⁰G  L  I  D  E ²¹H  C  R ²²A     E
  E ²³C        A ²⁴R  A  T  T  L  E ²⁵D  N     R ²⁶P  E
  S  H    ²⁷M  A  S  T     U ²⁸F  L  K  E  E  I  U ²⁹L
³⁰T  R  I  P  L  E ³¹S     O  R  C     L  C  Q  I  B
  E     H ³²N  E  R  V  E ³³R  O  L  L  K  R  N     U
  P  Y ³⁴F  L  A  P  T  U ³⁵R  N  I  U  A  D     A  O
  R  O  T  C  A  F  E  M  I ³⁶T  P ³⁷M  Y        ³⁸D
```

²²ARCHED ⇐	³⁴FLAPTURN ⇒	¹⁶NATURAL ↗	⁸SEGUE ⇓
¹¹BRUSH ↙	²⁸FRONT ⇓	³²NERVEROLL ⇒	³¹STAGING ⇧
¹⁵CATCH ↗	²⁰GLIDE ⇒	¹⁹PASSE ↘	¹⁴STOMP ⇧
⁵CHAINE ↘	²GRAPEVINE ↙	⁹PHRASE ↘	³⁶TILLER ↗
¹⁰CHOREOGRAPHY ↙	¹⁷HEELCLIP ⇓	²⁶PICKUP ↙	³⁶TIMEFACTOR ⇐
²³COUNT ↗	²¹HOOFER ↗	²⁴RATTLE ⇒	⁷TOETAP ⇐
³⁸DANCE ↖	¹³INVERT ⇐	³⁵ROCKNROLL ↗	¹²TRENCH ⇓
²⁵DEVELOPE ↖	²⁹LINDY ↙	³³ROUTINE ⇧	³⁰TRIPLE ⇒
³⁸DOUBLEEAGLE ⇧	³⁷MARQUE ↗	¹⁸SCOOT ↘	⁴WALTZ ⇒
⁶ESSENCE ⇓	²⁷MAXIE ↗	¹SCUFFTIMESTEP ⇓	³WIGGLESTICKS ⇐

Locations 36 and 38 are both 2 term origins.

ALTERNATE TERMINOLOGY

There are many regional and historical tap terminology variations ranging from self-explanatory through obliqely indirect to confusing, even obscure. Following are a few tap terms, abbreviations, notation formats, and/or definitions or descriptions different than those applied in this reference manual. They are interesting and may prove helpful when interpreting routine notes that don't make sense. Most examples are reproduced as they appeared where found - usually routine notes.

ALTERNATE TERMINOLOGY format is:
unlisted = applied herein
Similar term variations or multiple definitions per term are separated by semi-colons:
"Vernacular phrases" are in quotes:
("translations") of terms/abbreviations are in quotes in parentheses:
(explanation or supplemental information) is in parentheses:
{specific kind} of information is italicized with braces:
Examples are { } nonitalicized braces:
Similar listings with different meanings are separated by 2 vertical bars ||:

2-ways = alt'g fwd\bkwd patt's; invert
"airplane" =
apt ("apart") =
7 = (even rhythm) tpl, shfl-b/c
"*{staging}*" (between quotes) =
    = stg'g {"R" = rt}
∴ || ÷ = rev || rpt; rev

FORMATTING SYMBOLS
Patt's indicated by using geometric figures, sometimes with a center dot: circle, triangle, diamond, square.
(circled ct) = ( ) (silent)
@ = at
{space(s) missing ct's} (rhythm) = ( ) (silent) {3&a4 6}
{2 spaces}; - (space hyphen space) = comma
    (step separator) {irish R flap L irish R}
"*{staging}*" (between quotes) = stg'g {"R" = rt}
{##}/{##} (order/length) = phrase number
    {3/8 = 3rd 2M's}
(, (between parenthesis and comma) = supplemental
    Information {(travel S-L,}
( ) || (*{rpt'd ct}*) = no wt chg; supplemental information
    {step (flat)}; a-s-t || a-s-t {step 5, clap (5)}
(*{Ft}*) || (*{dir}*) = n/w {stamp (R) = stomp} || dir {(B); (x F)}
(RL); (R and L); r,l = R-L {BC (RL); flaps r,l}
(rxl); *{Ft}*-*{dir}* (Ft, hyphen, dir) = lead Ft and dir
    {(R x bk L); R-L = R lt; L-SR = L S-R,
    L-OUT = L o/s tr}
((*{A's}*)) (dbl parenthises); [*{A's}*] (brackets) = port de bras
[ ] (italisized brackets) = trav information
{{ct}} (braces) = hold
*; * to *; "*{identifier}*" = (reference marked comb) {"A" ;see Theme (below)}
* || ** = e || ie {a1*a&a**2}
& = a (when a = &) {&1a&2}
&& = &e; e& {a&&a1}; a& {&&a2}
+ = & (3+a4); additional time, space, etc. {pose, slowly raise arms 1+}
∴; ÷ in rev || ÷ = rev || rpt; rev
. (period) = Ft (not dir) {step L. L}
, (comma) = rock (change wt); rhythm separator {1,a2};
    preceding hold {&7,8}; stg'g separator {step L, to L};
    placement and Ft {, rt R}
{ct}, (ct before comma) = (*{ct}*) (silent ct) {1&2, = 1&(2)}
; (semicolon); _ (underline); – (hyphen); –*{##}* (hyphen ct);
    (circ'd ct) = (*{silent ct}*) {1 2 &3&4}
.. (2 periods); _ (underline) = (space, hyphen, space) -
    (continuation of step) {b/c R rt .. L x bk}
{#}/ (slash after number) = end of phrase {&78/}
/; /TIMES || / = X's {2/} || x {R/L}; a-s-t {scuff/clap}
/; |; - (hyphen) = , (step separator) {hop tpl / tpl t-s}; a-s-t

{#}-{#}-{#} (hyphenated ct's) = cluster ct's to rpt
    {1-&-a-2 2X's}
-{ct} (hyphenated ct) = ( ) (silent) {567-8}
- (hyphen) = tense {B.C.-ed}; step separator
- (hyphen); – (dash); *{#}* (underlined ct's) = hold;
    sustain action; rhythm gap {1a-a2}; n/w
-- (2 hyphens); ( ) (single and/or pair of parentheses)
    = supplemental information
– (dash) = , (comma) (information separator) {feet 2nd –
    arms up}
– (before steps) || – (after steps) = (stg'g before steps)
    {To S-R – step R} || (precedes body mvmt's)
    {step R rt – A's 2nd}
{ct}_{ct} (underline between ct's) = - - - - - (span of ct's)
= (equal sign) = stg'g before steps {move U-S = 4 flap hops}
^ (caret); *{ct}* (underlined) = ct (dynamic accent) {3& ^4}
→ = rt {← = lt}
♩ (quarter note) = met

NUMERICAL
¼ {½, ¾}; 1-FULL || ¼ note= (degree of tr) || ¼ M
½ cramproll = cramp
½ riff = close riff
½ toe = rel; tt
½ wing = wing
1 = step or tap
1+1 = b/c
1's = 1's (designated grp)
1TR = 1 c-w tr {2TL}
1½ chainné = 3-step tr
2 = shfl
2-4; 2/4 tempo = dbl-X
2-ct dbl wings = eagle
2 cts. of 8; 2 sets of 8 = 4M
2 heeldrops = heel roll
2 heels fwd = d/c
2nd time reverse = rev
2-ways = alt'g fwd\bkwd patt's; invert
3 || 3-3-3 = tpl || 3 tpl's
3-beat = 3-tap {5-beat riff walk}
3 STEP CHAINE TURN; 3 step walking turn = 3-step tr
3-tap cramproll = cramp, heel

Page 95

3-tap riff; 3-tap riff walk || 3 pt riff; 3 SND RIFF; three-count riff = riff, heel; riff, step; close riff, snap || riff, heel
3-tap wing = triplet wing
4 = shfl-b/c
4-4 = $^4/_4$
4-6-6 = r-r patt
4-Ct Cramp Roll; 4 Tap Cramproll = c-r
4-ct dbl wings = dbl eagle
4 flaps = flapped diamond
4 Point Graboff = shfl-p-u-c
4 point riff = riff, heel, step
5 = s-w-c-t-s
5-ct side cramproll; 5 pt cramp roll || Five-Sound Cramproll = trav'g c-r || flapped c-r
5-pt graboff; 5 tap graboff = shfl-d-p-u; shfl-p-u-c, heel
5 pt standing cramp roll; 5 sound Cramproll; 5 Tap Cr. Roll = standing c-r; flapped c-r
5 SND CINCINNATI = br bk, heel (hop), flap-heel
5-tap riff; 5 point riff = 5-tap riff walk; riff, heel, cramp
5 tap riff walk = riff, dig, snap, heel
6 = (even rhythm) 2 tpl's; shfl-b/c-b/c
6 point Graboff = d-p-u, 2-heel roll; shfl-p-u-c, heel, tt
7 = (even rhythm) tpl, shfl-b/c
8s; eights = 2M phrases; $^4/_4$ meter

ALPHABETICAL

{upper case} = (stg'g) {HALF CIRCLE US}
a = & (when & = a) {2&a&3}
aa; a-a = ea
a; eh = ¼-ct before ct
A; uh || A = ¼-ct after ct || a; ¼-ct before & {a5A a6}
Ã; ã = at; wt {ã Rt}
a&3 = &a3 (tplt)
abreast = horz line
abv = above
Acknowledge audience = salute
acr || across = x; x frt || x frt
action = start
active foot = free Ft
Advanced Waltz Clog Time Step = d-w-c-t-s
agn ("again") = rpt
ah = a (¼-ct) {&ah1 = &a1}
air flap || air steps = p-u || elevated (airborne) steps
"airplane" = st A's 2nd; st A's 2nd, tilt sd; A's 2^{nd,} bend fwd
AL = A's length
Alongside = c-p
alt = rev 2 X's; other Ft {legspin alt hop}
alt arms = o-A-s
ALTERNATING; alternating to = rev
alternating pick-up = p-u-c
ALTOG. ("altogether") = total X's {4 ALTOG.}
And-er = &a
ANGLE FRT R = r-d-f {ANGLE BK L}
anklerock = sailor rock
ankle turn = piq tr
apart sideways (Ft) = 2nd
apt ("apart") = o-p
arch || arched; arch foot; arching = tap c-p p-r || p-r pose
ard || ARDSELF; around self; around (stg'g) = around; r-d-j || personal circ (stg'g, not formed by grp)
Arm || arm high; arms ballet front = Hn {L arm to hat} || 1st

Arm across body = tr prep
arm flat || arm fold down = reach || A dn
arm in arm = link elbows
Arm Out || arms at chest (or ribs); arms pulled in; pull arms to ribs = 2nd; sd || n-Sh-p
arms following movement; arms swing dn-up = d-A-s
arms lift at elbows = r-r-A's Hn's up
arms overlap || ARMS ROCKETTE STYLE = tiller A's 2nd || tiller A's
arm stiff = press
arms swing frt-bk; Arms Swing Opp. = o-A-s
arms swing par. = d-A-s
arms to 2nd & bent into ribs = jazz 2nd
around = r-d-j into x bk or frt; turn {½ around}
"around the world cramp roll" = c-r-c
ast.; AST; A.S.T. || ast; AST = a-s-t || All (stg'g)
Astride = 2nd (Ft)
at = pos; face
at arch; at side of; back in = c-p
aud ("audience") = D-S
b || b/ || B || b; B; BCK = both; brush || ball (Ft) || ball{H = heel}; U-S; both || bk {f; LB = l-d-b}
back = step bk; br bk; bk flap; bkwd; x bk; U-S; recover; c-p
back{any step}; {any step}bk = bkwd {backflap; frtbr}
BACK BRUSH || back by = bk flap || c-p
back essence = bk flap, b/c; frt ess x bk (may trav sdwd)
back flap = bk flap-heel
back-front = b/c
back in frt of L = bk br R x frt L
back irish = 3 tpl's x bk {frt irish}; close or any irish x frt
back shuffle = shfl x bk {front shuffle}
back slides; Back Trenches = trenches
BACKSTAGE; bk stage = U-S
"back to the woods" = cinc
back tap = ankle coordinated br bk
back toward = i/s; c-p
Backwards Cramp Roll = d/c, 2 alt'g snaps
bal || Balance = balance; balancé || rock
balcr = balancoire
Ball || balls = step; snap || snap both
Ball Beat; ball drop; ball tap; ball = snap
Ballch ;BALL CH; ballchg; b change; BC, B.C., Bch; B.Ch.; B Chg; b-chg.; b-c ;Bc chg; bl.ch.; ball L ch R; ball L, change R; ball ball; ball step; step ball = b/c; 2 successive steps; c/s; step, stamp in less than 2 ct's
ball changing = multiple b/c's; c/s's (gallops)
ballet tap = pointe tap (style)
Ball Tap = tap; (ball on flr, then) tap
ball heel, ball-heel = cramp; step, heel
ball-touch = tap
ball X = step x frt; b/c x frt - i-p
Bandi-twist; Banti Twist = b-t
bamtam twist = {see page 48, **Where did that - -** }
bar = M; 2M
barrel arms; barrel arm style = {see barrel turn}
barrel pirouette = barrel tr
Batma = battement
bb = bmb
B.C. = b/c; step, tap
B-C; B.ch; B.Chs || B/c = b/c's || 2 steps ending both w/w
BCK CHG = b/c bk - i-p
BCLR || B.C.R.L. (flat) = b/c L-R || s/c R-L

BD = bend
b-d-rt = r-d-b
Bear(ing) = trav; tr
beat; bt = ct; tap sound; meter
BEG = bgn
BEH; behind = x bk
Bell Kick = {see page 48, Kick that bell}
bells = bell
bend down – up = demi plié, st'n knees
bend knee || Bend R at knee = lift knee; passé || passé
bend turn = barrel tr
beside = c-p
bg || BIG || B-G= large || long; high || B and G; couple
Bk || bk tap = br bk || tap bk (not tt); p-u
{any step}bk || bk = bkwd {hopbk} || tt x bk; back (anatomy)
bkbr || bkbr (r,l) = br bk || d-p-u
Bk chaine = step x bk into chainé
Bkd; Bkwds; bwd; BWDS = bkwd
bk-d-lt = l-d-b
Bkflp; Bk-Slap; BK BRUSH CHANGE; Br bk & step; br. st.; br bk, step; brush back = bk flap
bk to front || bk to S-R = face U-S || U-S-R {frt to S-L}
bkup ("backup") = jazz diamond
body rock = rock
bodywork = personal styling
B of F || B to B = ball of Ft || ball to bk
bombershay || bomborshay = step, close riff; rolling wing chg || bk ess; pigeon toe
Bomber Shay; bomborshay, bumbershay; bumbushay = bmb; step sd, i/s flap; step sd, i/s br, dig w/w; close riff, step i-p
boogie; BOOGIE TWIST; boogie style = sgr
Boogie; boogie back || boogie walks; "Boogie Woogie" || boogie steps = shorty(s) || shorty's; alt'g heels || 2-ct's each shorty's bk
bop = sdwd rock'n
bounce = heel; jump
BOUNCE FT TOG KICK = bounce kick
bounce knees = rpt'd nat plié, st'n
box step = diamond
BR ("back right") || Br.; brsh = r-d-b {FL} || brush
Br bk on Heel || brush heel = bk scuff || scuff
break; BREAK = connecting mvmt, step, or comb; interlude {drum break}; end of dance; tag (music)
"Break a Leg" (shaky) = rubber legs
breakdown = challenge
Break Out = end of a buck t-s {flap, step}; t-s transition (flap, step, shfl, hop)
bridge || ½ bridge = brk within Step (not at end); any music transition; lunge flat Ft || lunge p-r
Bring || Bring ft Up || bring back = draw {bring L to R} || passé || c-p
Brk; brkout; break-away = break-out
Broad (Ft) = o-p; 2nd
broken = bent; brk comb
"broken ankle" = o/s of Ft on flr (like shorty or sluff into wing)
broken arm swing = o-a-s w/ bent elbows; x-o-A-s
broken rhythm = rhythm chg within M
broken wrist; brkn wrist = flexed Hn
Brsh; Bru || brush || Brush Bk = br || fwd br; flap; clip || bk flap; p-u

brush & scuff || BRUSH SCUFF HEEL = riff || riff, heel
brush ball heel || brush toe heel = flap, heel || riff; flap-heel
brush change; BRUSH DOWN; brush tap = flap
brush cramproll = flapped c-r; f-r
brush heel = scuff
BRUSH R FRT CHNG L FRT = br R x frt into hop-over
Brush, side trench = swinging flap
brush slide = sluff
brush step = non-duplet flap; bk flap; slap
brush toe = br bk, tt
brush up = br raising Ft
B stage = U-S
b/t ("ball tap") = step, tap
buck = chug; s-p-u; d-p-u; s-t-s; stomp-t-s's; any buck t-s; flea hop; fast
BUCK AND SLIDE FWD. = chug
buck rhythm = even rhythm
buffalo = hop-tpl; tpl, flap; hop, shfl, leap; leap, shfl; dbl-buff; tpl; tpl x bk; flapped buff; flap sd, irish x frt; shfl, fall bk – toe dn x frt ankle
Buffalo Break = s-t-s - brk
Buff-falling off log = log; trav'g ½–log (off to Buffalo)
BUFFALO POSITION = buff strarting pos {see buffalo}
builds (music) = accelerando; increase volume
Burst of taps = fast roll; cluster
BWDS = bkwd
C || C# = center; ct || corner # (stg'g)
"call and answer"; "call-and-respond"; challenge-reply; "shout and reply"; "give and take"; "have a talk"; trade; trade-off = challenge
"call out" = grp encouraging a dancer to break out
Carefree Style = rubberlegs
carry = move; lift; w/w
carryback || carryover= irish x bk; bkwd || irish x frt; fwd
catch = clip; scoot
"catch tap"; "catching pullback" = the br during a p-u; s-p-u
C-clkws || clkwse = c-c-w || c-w
Ch || change = chg || leap; catch
Chain Break = common rpt'd Step brk
Chainé; Chaine tr = piqué tr; i/s ch; 3-step tr
Chainé turn RLR = 3-step tr R
Changeable Five Tap Riff Walk = 5-tap riff walk
change || changeable = step; rev {change arms} || alt'g
CHANGE BACK = rock
change kick = hitch kick
changeover || changeover cramproll = chg {pick up changeover} || flapped c-r-c
change pull-back = p-u-c
"Chaplin" = ½-log 8&a1
Charleston bombershay || Charleston Kick = pigeon toe || snap kick
CHASE STEP = lindy
chassé; Chassee = c/s
chene; chene Tour; cheni = chainé
Chim Cham = shim sham
cho; chos. = chorus
"CHOO CHOO" = chugs; alt'g sluffs
chop = step bk w/ st knee -- lift st leg frt (a bkwd *goosestep*); low frt hitch kick w/ st legs (a running goosestep)
choreo = choreography

Chorus Line (A's) || chorus kicks = tiller A's 2nd || bounce kicks
chst = chest
chug = scoot; heel into flat sluff; step, chug; fwd sluff; chug both
CHUG CHANGE = chug, rev
chug(ged) drop; chug step; CHUG OUT = chug
cincinnati = hop-tpl; br-heel-shfl-heel-step
circle = tr {½-circle}
circle cramproll = c-r-c
Circle S.R. = c-w circ
Circle Step = eddie leonard
Circling leg; circle ft || circle RR = r-d-j || o/s r-d-j R
cirl = circ
clap = slap
click || clip = any clip {clickheels}; jump into any clip || toe to heel or heel to toe clip (not toes or heels); dig close x frt; catch
Click Toes = rock both to heel stand, toe clip
clip = step L lt, close riff, rpt
clogs = clogging shoes
close = step c-p; sluff c-p; merge
closed = c-p
close rhythm = clustered
close riff || closed riff = riff, heel, dig w/w || close riff
close riffles = dbl-shfl
closed-X || closed pos || close X frt = x Ft close || // 1st || 5th
CLOSE TO THE FLOOR = sophisticated; low
clump = a 2 blurred (not distinct heel-toe) taps stamp
cnt = ct; contact
cocked = flexed {cocked knee}
"cold duck" = step 2nd, tt x bk; flap 2nd, heel, tt x bk
com; Combo || COMBINATION = comb || Step
Comp. = complete; 1 (usually tr)
complicated = var
compliment (A) = opp; same A as leg to opp sd
connected (A's) = tiller A's
continuous (rhythm) = even
Contrast = rhythm shading
cor || cor. {#} (stg'g) = diag || Cecchetti corner #1, 2, 3, or 4
"corkscrew"; Cork Screw = twist; h-t; flap x into pigeon-toe roll tr; flap t/i
Chorus Line = tiller line
COUNT = rhythm {DO 2&A3 and COUNT 7&A8}
counterpoint = interlocking var's
coupe = catch
couplet = duple rhythm
Covered Off (stg'g) = vert line
covering = area trav'd thru
CP; C-P || c pos= c-p || C-S
cr || cr.; CR; CR HL = x; across || cramp
CR#{#} = corner # (staging)
cramp = heeldrop; accented heel; step, 2-heel roll
cramped pickups = p-u(s) ending w/ heel(s)
cramp heel || cramp = heeldrop || tap, heel
cramp roll; cramp-roll; cramp = cramp; 2 cramps; cramp, heel; cramp, step; step, 2-heel roll; 2 steps, heel; c-r-c; flapped c-r; leap into flapped c-r; any f-r or c-r
Cramp Roll (RLRL) || cramp roll R L = c-r R || c-r-c R, step L
cramp roll time step = -stomp-cramp-t-s
"crawl" = trav'g rock'n
"crazy legs" = legomania

CrissCross || CRISS-CROSS = dbl riff walk || low d-b triangle
Cross = w-c-t-s x frt or bk
cross || cross bk || cross legged = x frt; step x; step x frt || step x bk || x
cross bar = x-over; any step(s) x; trav'g t-s
cross F || Cross Flap = x frt || flap x frt
CROSS IN FRONT || cross over = bk br x frt || x frt; step x frt; tt x frt
Cross Leg Walk = step-heel gpvn or all x's frt
Crossover || CROSS OVER = irish x frt; x frt || bmb
Cross Step = gpvn
Cross Waltz Time Step = s-w-c-t-s x frt
Cr. Roll; CR. RL. || CR = c-r || C-S-R; c-r; heel roll; cramp
C.S. = C-S
ct; Ct = action or rhythm quantity {5-ct riff}; common rhythm seq {maxie Ct}
ctR = c-w tr R {cctL}
curl = bend {curl A}
cut = x ankles; hitch; catch; catch w/ heel clip; stop
cut; cutting; cutaway; cut under; cutunder; Cut step = (usually from sd or bk) catch
cut/out; Cut-out || cut-out cramproll = break-out; i/s leg swing into heel clip/into catch || trav'g c-r
cuts (A) = port de bras through 1st
cut time = dbl-X; $^{2}/_{4}$
dance-in = substitute dancer (usually during rehearsals)
"dancing against time"; "doubling rhythm" = sync'd
dbl = shfl; both
dbl clip || dbl stomp = 2 heel clips || s/c
dbl heel drop = 2-heel roll
D-C = D-S-C
d-circ = personal circ (stg'g)
decided extension = low st leg
deep || deeply = long {deep x back}; gr plié || long
deep knee bend || deep plié = gr plié; lunge || gr plié
delayed syncopation = a or e after ct
deliver (A) = present
Describe = trav (usually stg'd shape)
Developé in = (recover) passé
d-f-r ("diag frt rt") = r-d-f; D-S-R {d-b-l}
dg = dig
dia. || diag (A's) = diag || sd tilt 2nd
diagonal stage R || diag. bk. Rt.= D-S-R || r-d-b
dig || dig; dug = chug; scuff; any dynamically accented tap || loud step or tap; dig; dig w/w; c-p p-r; tt; any tap n/w
Dig Ball = accented step fwd w/w or n/w
dig dig dig = run
dig heel || DIG ST = dig w/w or n/w || dig w/w
dig no weight = scuff
Dig riff = close riff; riff, step
dig strut = dig frt, step c-p (dig lead tap strut)
dig tap; dig-toe || Dig Toe = tt; forceful step; forceful tap i-p or fwd || dig w/w, snap
dip || dip fashion= plié || lunge
dnbt ("downbeat") = ct (usually ct 1)
dnstg = D-S
Do 2 X's in all || Do 3 Xs= rpt || rpt 2 X's
"doodle" = sluff; slide
DOTR = dbl o/s tr rt {DITL}
double || duo = shfl {double b/c}; both; 2 X's; dbl'd; duet || duet
double arms = d-A-s

double buffalo = flapped buff
double chug = chug both
doubled; double down; double-up = dbl-X
double essence = flap lead sgl ess (uses dbl time factor)
double flap = 2 running flaps within 1 ct
double front essence = d-stomp-t-s (end flap x frt, step i-p)
Double grab-off = d-p-u
double heel || DOUBLE HEEL DROPS || double heel step =
    2 heels w/ same Ft || roll || dig, snap
Double Heel Click = shfl; bell
Double Heel Stand = d/c, b/c
double heel twist = h-t both
double irish || double frt irish = irish, shfl-b/c; shfl, hop, tpl
    || shfl-b/c, irish x frt
double jump = elevation landing on 2 Ft; shfl-leap
double Maxie Ford = flapped maxie
Double Off Beat = flap, b/c, scuff (a1&a2); triplet rhythm
Double Paddle Turn = step, 3 flap-steps (dbl = flap)
Double Pickup || Double Pick-up toe bk = br bk, p-u-c, step
    || d-p-u-c-tt
double pull-back(s); pullbacks = d-p-u; d-p-u-c
Double Rhythm = dbl-X
double roll = dbl shfl; 2 cramps
double shuffle || double stomp = 2 shfl's bk; stomp, br bk,
    step (shim) || stomp, stamp
double time = duple rhythm; rhythm change from broken
    to rolling; rolling qdlt's; running (leap not step)
double toe stand = 4-tap toe stand
Double Toe Tap Time Step = shfl-hop-heel-tt-step-flap-step
double-up; DOUBLE UP RHYTHM = dbl-X; qdlt
double wing; dbl wing, 1 ct each || double wing = eagle
    || wing chg
doubling = dubbing
Down; down back = U-S {see, up}
DOWN = squat; fwd; D-S {jump down; BRUSH DOWN}
down center; D.C.; ctr dn = D-S-C
DOWN INTO FLOOR = land
Down over = x frt
down-right = D-S-R
dp; dr; drp = drop
drag = sluff; draw; slide; sluff into low leg lift
Drag around L to R = o/s r-d-j R
drag turn; Drag Ft Tr = compass tr; any sluffed tr
draw = draw to 5th; sluff into rock; move {draw to knee}
draw back = step bk w/ or w/o opp Ft draw;
    (heel stand) both s-p-u a-s-t (2 simultaneous taps)
drawing = draw
drop; drp || DROP TO FLOOR = loud leap or lamp; fall; heel;
    snap; tt; quick plié or squat || squat
Drop B = tap bk
drop back on = rock; step bk
drop ball || drop ball; drop toe; Drop on Toe = step || snap
DROP HEAD TO FLOOR = F dn
drop heel; drop on heel || drop both heels = heel; dig; chug ||
    chug both
drop on; drop weight = fall
DROP SIT = quick squat
drop toe; drop toe down || drop toe bk = snap; tt; toe stand;
    sophisticated ball tap || tt
drumbreak = drum interlude
drum roll = c-r-c
drum slap = heel, slap (or flap); a fast slap (or flap);
    drum flap
d.s.; DS; d-stg; dwnstg || D.S.C. = D-S {SL, SR, US} || D-S-C
D-S-Ft = D-S Ft
D-shff; D-shfl = dbl-shfl
"duck waddle" = shorty; alt'g sdwd dig-snaps
duple time = dbl-X; $^2/_4$ meter
during = a-s-t
DV ("dovetail") = into
dwn = dn
e; E || E; eh (rhythm) || Er = a before & {e&a1} || e ($^1/_8$-count);
    a ($^1/_4$-count before &); i ($^1/_{16}$-count) || a ($^1/_4$-count)
e-e = ea {2e-e&a3}
ea || Ea = eagle; each || each
easy essence = step sd, dig w/w x frt, step i-p
eccentric = isolate hip up; novelty or comedy styling
Eccentric Rond de jambe = sluefoot
eighth note rhythm = even 2 per ct {&1&2&3}
ELB = elbow
embellish = non-tapping stylistic mvmt; wm
encircling = r-d-j
entire foot = flat
er = e or a {1er&A2}
ESSENCE BACK = bk ess
Exactly = rpt
EXD(S); EXT; extension = extend
exec ("execute") = do
exhibition dance || exhibition steps = performance || flash steps
explode = snap {explode arms}
extend foot up = starting pos
extreme = long {extreme step up stage right}
"eyes right" = F rt
f; fc || F = face || Ft; frt {diag's: LF, RB}; D-S; face
FA ("forced arch") || F.A. ("Ft apart") = p-r || 2nd pos; o-p
Fac; FC || faceback; face back to audience; fUS
    || facing L front = face; facing || face U-S {fDS} || l-d-f
fake kick = flexed batt or swing kick
fake snap kick = low snap dev
FAKED BUFFALO = leap 2nd, step (no shfl)
fall || Fall b change = leap; exaggerated eccentric leap || c/s
fall RLR = trenches
fall(ing) off the log = hop-over; x'g hitches; twisting hitches;
    hitches frt\bk
fall-over = step-over
"Faluffalo" = (buff starting pos) fwd flap sdwd, p-b, flap
fan || fan kick = fan kick; r-d-j; br into r-d-j || elevated r-d-j
fancy = flash
F.A.P. ("forced arch plié") = lunge p-r
Far; far out = long {step far}
fashion = style; appearance {shorty george fashion}
fast; fast as possible || fast irish = dbl-X || qdlt irish
f.b.c. = flap-b/c
f-c-r = flapped c-r
Fd = fwd
feed = trav
feet together = c-p
fermata (music) = hold until cued
FI, FO; F-in, -out || F-fwd, -opp = (stg'g) face in\out of ctr
    (usually ptnr's or circ) || l-o-d\u-l-o-d
Fig ("figure") = comb; staging; body line
figure = step; Step
file = vert line, facing along line

fingershaking = vibrate
Fin. || finish at S.R. = end || face S-R
Finish position = pose
finish L x frt = irish x frt
fisted ("fist") = closed Hn
fist to shoulder; fists to chest; hands to shoulders in fists
    = n-Sh-p
fl; Fl.; flap on toe = flap
flam = very tight rhythm cramp; fast dplt
flamp = br, stamp
flap = fwd flap; slap; fwd br, stamp or stomp
flap ballchange R,L,R; fl. B.Ch = flap-b/c
flap bk L. (X F of R.) = bk flap L x frt R
Flap Cramp Roll; flap drum roll; flap, cramproll (&1&a2)
    = flapped c-r
Flap Double-heel = f-r; f-r-c
"flap down (like a horse)" = slap
flaphldrp = flap-heel
flapped buffalo || flapped paddle turn = flap-tpl || paddle tr
flap roll = f-r ½- pivot
flaps = 2 flaps
Flap-side = o/s flap
flash dnc; flashing = performing flash steps
flat; flat step = stomp; step flat; stamp (usually w/o volume
    accent)
flat brush = stomped br
flat foot tap = stomp; unaccented stomp
flat slap = br, stomp; br, stamp
"flat" tap || flat tap; foot tap || flat foot stand = snap ||
    stomp; stamp || stamp
flavor = styling
Flex || Flexed = raise {Flex L Ft XBk}; ankle controlled tap;
    arched || p-r
flex kick = swing kick, dev, or snap kick w/ flexed ankle
Flex Knee; flex R to L knee; FOOT TO KNEE = passé
flex L next to R = c-p L p-r n/w
FLICK KICK = snap kick
fling || fling kick = Ft x knee (think Scottish) || swing kick
Flip = bk flap; bk br, fwd flap
flomp = br-stomp
floor pattern = stg'g
floor steps = low
floor wing = wing mvmt; (from semi-squat) stand into
    d/c, d-p-u into semi-squat (faked russian wing)
flop = unaccented st leg stamp
flourish = wing mvmt
Flp; flp.; flps.; flp.st. = flap(s)
flxd = flexed
fol. = following
Fold; Folding into line = merge
foot down = step
footing = Ft
FOOT JUMP = hop-over
for'd; forw.; forwd; frd || FNT; fr; Ft; Frnt. = fwd || frt
Formation || foreward = stg'g; Grp stg'g; facing || D-S
forward cramproll; Fwd cramp roll = flapped c-r
forward pull-back = fwd d-p-u
forward tap = ankle coordinated br fwd
four-noted = 4 tap patt; qdlt
Four Point Riff; four tap riff = riff, heel, step
fours = 4M comb's
four to a bar = $^4/_4$

fr || Fr.; ft || frwd = frt; from || frt || fwd
Frap = riff, step
FREE = n/w
freeze = hold
front; FRT; frontstage || frnt = D-S || l-o-d
front-back = b/c frt-i/p
front essence = flap-b/c
Front Jeté = exaggerated running flap fwd
front shuffle = shfl x frt; fwd br, tap (ankle co-ord)
Ft || FT; F.T.; F-t; f-t; Ft. tog; ft come together = frt || c-p
F to Rt = o/s; r-d-f {B to Lt}
Full twist = pvt tr
{any step}fwd = fwd {stampfwd}
Fwd circle = o/s r-d-j
gaining = longer mvmt resulting in slight trav
gallop = c/s; $^2/_4$ meter
Geo. = shorty
Gesture frt (A) = present
gld = glide; sluff
glide = sluff into w/w
glissade = b/c x-over
go = trav
"goin' home" || "Going South" = finish; exit || trav U-S; exit
going down = kneel
"going noplace" = jazz diamond
Goofus = comedy shim sham
GP = grand plié
gr. = Grp
grab = clasp
graboff; grab-off = any p-u; p-u-c; d-p-u; d-p-u-c;
    p-u-c-tt; p-u-c, heel; br bk, p-u-c; shfl-p-u-c;
    shfl-p-u-c, heel; shfl-d-p-u; shfl-p-u-c-tt; any complex
    p-u var; maxie segment; maxie segment, heel
grab roll = shfl-p-u-c; shfl-d-p-u; d-p-u from p-r
    (see pickup roll below)
Grace Beat || grace tap = e or i; unnotated ct fraction ||
    16th or 32nd note rhythm; bk flap
grape-vine steps || grapevine style = stepped gpvn || gpvn
grapevine; half grapevine = b/c x-over; (bgn x bk)
grotesque = eccentric
grows = slowly raises or extends
"gutbucket" = intricate rhythms in p-r
H; h/ || H ("head") || H ("hard") = heel || focus {H frt}
    || dynamic accent
half break; HALFBREAK = s-t-s; any t-s w/o brk comb;
    any 1M brk
half-time = dbl-X
half toe = rel (to ball of Ft); tap
"Halleluiah"; halleluiah style = vibrate Hn's
hand = pass; A {hands 2nd}
handoff = present
hand pushing; hands pushed || hands spread = press
    || jazz Hn's
hands to R = d-A-s
hand under = u-Hn
hard; Hard; H = dynamic accent
h/c || Heel Change = d/c; r-c || roll
hd = H; Hn
h.d. ("heel drop") = heel
heel; heel dig; heeldig; hldg; heel drop; heel out; heelstep;
    heel tap = dig n/w or w/w
heel ball = dig, snap

heel beat = heel; heeldrop or dig leaving heel on flr; chug
heel brush; heel scuff = scuff
heel brush back = bk riff; bk scuff
heel change = d/c; 2-heel roll; dig w/w, step
heel click = heel clip; standing heel clip
Heel Close = dig, step c-p
heel cramp; heel drop; heel dr. = heel n/w or w/w; accented heel; cramp
heeldig; heel-edge = dig w/w or n/w
Heel Down = heel
Heeldrop Moving Fwd; HEEL FWD; heel thump = chug
heel-edge = i/s heel dig (often to sd)
Heel fwd; Heel out || heel rest; heel fwd rest= dig || dig w/w
Heel grind; heel-turn = h-t
Heel Hit = heel clip
heel rest = dig
heel rock = dig w/w, rock bk; dig w/w, step; heel – raise toe
heel roll = c-r; c-r-c; 2 cramps; rock'n roll; hop, shfl, chug
heel scuff || Heelscuff = dig (as in close riff) ; scuff || scuff
heels Hornpipe style = sailor rock
heel skid = chug
heels R.L.R.L. = 4-heel roll
heel step; heel stp || heelstep = dig, snap; dig n/w or w/w, step; dig; d/c || dig w/w
heels to R, toes to R; heels toes = heels lead suzie-q
Heel Stub = chug; chug both
heel tap || heel tap fwd; heel touch = heel; dig; heel n/w || dig
Heel Thump = accented chug
heel-toe; HEELTOE = dig, snap; walk; dig, tt
heeltoe gallop || Heel-Toe scoop = dig w/w, snap, catch close bk || riff
heel to floor = dig
heel twist || heels twist = h-t into snap; pivot || pivot // Ft
Heel Walk = digs w/w; dig, snap
Hes ("hesitation"); hld = hold
hi = high
High kick = gr batt
High on Half-Toe = st leg rel
hinge = i/s slide (usually w/ high passé)
hit || hit; hit toe || hit toe frt = tap; dig w/w or n/w; Hn slap; toe clip; heel – step (a-s-t) || clip; tt || tt x frt
hitch = catch; slide; sluff into catch; slide w/ st leg
HITCH-KICK = 4-ct hitch kick; hitch, tap frt; hitch w/ heel clip; extend st leg frt
Hit ft in air = bell
hit legs = slap frt of thighs
hl; HL; hl beat; Hldrp; heeldrop || Hldig; hl; hit heel fwd = heel || dig
hldrp = cramp
hlst = dig w/w
hn; hnd.; hnds = Hn(s)
hold || Hld = (*silent*) (rhythm); rock || hold (no mvmt)
hold elbows = link elbows
hold arms out || hold shoulders = 2nd || tiller A's 2nd
"holdup" position = dbl A reach over-H
home || "home" = starting location (stg'g) and/or pos (line) || end {"take it home"}
hook = dev or snap kick from passé; link (A's)
hop || hop onto || hop on both feet = step, hop; leap; jump || leap || jump
hop & straighten knee = scoot
hop-3 = hop-tpl

hop back || hop-step = skip bk || hop
hop double hop = hop, shfl, hop (dbl = shfl)
hop kick; Hop Kick Step = bounce kick
hop L to R = flea hop
Hor; Hrz = horz
hot steps = flash steps
HP L X R = hop L, step R x frt L
h-t-snap = h-t into snap
i || I = ¼ ct {iea1} || irish
IB ("in back") = x bk {IF}
IFOR ("in frt of R") = L x frt R {IBOL}
"improvography" = freestyle, adlib
in; in close; in close to = c-p; short {in close rt}
in advance = in frt; before
in line with = //; same height
IP; I.P.; in spot; in same spot; on place = i-p
inside = t/i
inside 3-step tr = i/s p-d-b tr
inside jumped flap = swinging flap
Inside Slide = flea hop
interlace (stg'g) = merge
interlude = bridge
into || into body (A's) = c-p; passé || n-Sh-p
invert(ed) || toe inverted = rev; t/i || t/i
invert comb = seq comb from end to bgn
invert dir = u-l-o-d
inward || inward circle = i/s || c-c-w
irish || Irish Step = hop-tpl || irish
Irish Flap = drum flap
is = i/s
IT || ITL = i/s tr {OT} || i/s tr lt {ITR}
jab; jab heel = dig
jazz kick = snap kick
jazz line (A's) = bent elbows
jazz OAS = x-o-A-s
jazz palm; J.H.; JH = jazz Hn
jazz square; J.S. = jazz diamond
J.H. & shake = vibrate
"jingle step" = patter stps
"jive dancing" = faked
jmp; JMP ("jump") = elevation
jump = leap; lamp
JUMP BK RL = b/c bk
Jump both = chug both
jump cramp roll; jump to heel roll = c-r
JUMP DOWN || jump up = jump D-S {JUMP UP}; jump into squat || jump; jump from squat
jump(ed) flap; jump to flap = leaped flap; running flap
jump flat = lamp
jump hop = elevation from 1 Ft, landing 2 Ft
jump kick = bounce kick; hitch w/ snap kick
jump out; jump leap out; JUMP SPLIT = jump landing 2nd {jump in}
Jump over = fall; glide
jump R ft x back over L en l'air = R bk hop-over
JUMP RIFF = leap, riff, land
JUMP SLIDE TOG = (from o-p) scoot c-p
jump tempo = fast 4/4
Jump to LRL = trenches
JUMP UP HIT HEELS; jump up click heels land; click feet in air = bell
"kazotskys" = polzounoks

Page 101

k-b-chg = kick, b/c
kick = snap kick; dev
kick; klick = clip
kick dance || kick line = tiller || tiller line; tiller A's 2nd
KICK DRAG = flea hop
Kick Jump = bounce kick
Kitch Kick = hitch
knee; knee bent; knee up = passé {step, knee, reverse}
knee hitch; knee-kick = snap kick
knee crossed = t/i
knock; knock toe = tt; 2 tt's
knock kneed = both plié t/i
l; L; LF; L.F.; L ft.; lft = L {r}
L || "L" (A's) = step L; lt {R}; S-L; c-c-w || 3rd
land = a specific step ending an elevation (not tr) {land chug}; cramp landing
land heel = dig w/w
large step = long
layout = tilt {layout right}
"Lazy" shim = stomp, sluff
LB; LBD || L-B = l-d-b {LFD; RF} || U-S-L
L bk R = L x bk R
ld = lead
L.D.D. ("lt diag dn bk") || L.D.U. ("lt diag up frt") = l-d-b || l-d-f
L.D.S. = D-S-L
Lean = rock; tilt
leaning x frt (or x bk) = (bending fwd) step-over fwd (or bk)
leap || leap-back || leap B.ch. = catch; fall; elevate (not land) || p-u-c || c/s
leap cross || LEAP DOWN ON = b/c x-over || catch; trench
leap flap; leap to flap = leaped flap
Leap Flat = lamp
leap in place = catch
leap 4 times; leap R AST extend straight leg L foot bk; leap onto R - L bk = trench; hitch
leap L over R = hop-over
leap riff = leap into riff, land (like leaped flap)
leap toe = leap, tt
left front || left side = D-S-L {right back} || S-L
leg = Ft {flap L leg Lt}
"legability" = high kicker; tiller dancer
leg in circle; Leg Swings Around || leg around back = r-d-j || o/s r-d-j
Legomania; Leg-o-mania || Leg-O'Mania = eccentric "rubber-leg" styling; knee t/i / t/o || legomania (Irish version?)
legs stiff, leap RLRLRL; legs apart, steps RLRL = patter steps
LF DUG TO R = tap L c-p
LH = L heel {RH}
Lift; lift/off = maintain flr contact during elevation; scoot
lift heels || Lift to Knee = heel clip || passé
lighter || lightly = comedic || low-short; quick
Linde || Lindy = lindy || step-b/c
LINDY; Lindy bk = rocking steps x bk - i-p
Line across stage = horz (stg'g)
line number || Line Step = tiller || tiller comb
lines meet = merge
l-i.p. = L i-p
"listen" = hold
L.I.T.; ltrn L = c-c-w tr L {L.O.T.; rtrn L}
L-L-L = X's {tap L-L-L}

LJA ("long jazz arm") = reach
lo = low
lock || lock arms = st (anatomy) || link elbows
L.O.D. = l-o-d; trav dir
Log-over = log glide
long A swing = o-A-s
loose knees = slight plié (usually p-r)
LoR ("L over R"); L to R; L to R diag. = L x frt R {RoL}
Low = dn
low fan kick || Low kick = r-d-j || snap kick
lr.; lwr = lower
L-R = chg (from L to R); rock
LRL turn = 3-step tr
LS; L.S.; L side = S-L
Lt. || LT = lt {Rt.} || L toe {RT}
L to R = c-p
Lunge = sluff or lamp into lunge; sluff w/w; chug; p-r; long step; long step into demi plié
L U.S. corner = U-S-L {R D.S. corner}
L x R; LXR; L X over R || LXBR; Lxbr; LXIBR; LXBOR; back L x R = L x frt R; step L x frt R || L x bk R {RXFL}
M('s) {##}; {##}M = specifies numbered M('s) {M's 13-16; 5-8M}
march || MARK TIME = steps i-p || even (rhythm)
Maxie || maxie ford = maxie segment, step || shfl, leap, tt
maxie ford break; maxine ford (feminine version?) = maxi
maxie ford turn = tr'g maxie segment; saut de basque; saut de basque, step; shfl, b/c
medium = dance form or style
medium slow tempo = soft shoe
MEAS; meas.; Ms = M('s)
Mesh = merge
Met. Bt. = met
Meter = medium tempo $^4/_4$
"Michael Jackson toe jump" = toe stand both
military cramproll = c-r
military t-s = drum flap; drum flap cadence
"Minstrel Hands" = jazz Hn's at sd's of face
Mirror(ed) = rev
module = segment
"Mooch" = scoot both
Motion = stg'g
moderate pos (A's) = nat A's between waist and chest
move = trav
movement = comb; seq (dance); phrase (music); stg'g
move toe only = snap
move toes = // h-t both
move up = trav D-S (especially, in frt of grp)
moving out || MOVING OUT IN = ent || taps 2nd - c-p
musical comedy (style) = song and dance; tiller
MUSIC DOUBLES UP = dbl-X
N.B. ("nota bene") = NOTE
near; next to = c-p; close
Negro time-steps = all -stomp-t-s's
nerve flap || nerve tap = st leg flap || nerve roll
nerve shuffle = quick ankle controlled shfl or taps i-p (no knee swing); rattle; 2-tap nerve roll
NEUT = neutral
n-t-o; NTO ("no t/o") = // t/f
NW; n.w.; nowt = n/w
O = circ
OAS = o-A-s

ob ("oblique") = diag; frt diag
o-d ("opp dir") = rev dir {(after r-d-f) o-d = l-d-f}
off ‖ off L.= lead {cramp roll off R} ‖ S-L
off bt ‖ off-time ‖ "Double Off-Beat" = sync'd; upbeat;
    any non-ct; unaccented; even ct's; flap-b/c ‖
    sync'd ‖ flap-step-scuff
off-beat time-step = d-stomp-t-s; (any) -stomp-t-s
OFF THE LOG STEP = log
o-frt ‖ out back = frt diag ‖ bk diag
O.H.; O-H; O/HEAD; OV/HEAD; OVHD = over-H
on ‖ on; onto = during (a-s-t) ‖ w/w; trav {flaps on S-R}
on spot = i-p
ONE FOOT PICK-UP = s-p-u
on this = a-s-t
on toes = toe stand; rel
OP; O-P ‖ open = o-p ‖ hold; o-p; scissor open (A's)
Open = hold (pos); silent (rhythm)
open ball change = b/c 2nd
Open Formation = staggered
opposition ‖ opposition; opposite arms = alt ‖ o-A-s
os ‖ OS ‖ O.S. ("other side"); opposite feet; other Ft = o/s ‖
    off-stage ‖ rev
OSF ("on same foot") = w/w
OTL = o/s tr lt {OTR}
out (A) ‖ out (Ft) = frt; open {scissor out} ‖ 2nd;
    o-p {out front}
out-back-down ‖ out-in-out; triple kick ‖ in and out = slow tpl
    ‖ snap kicks 2nd - x frt - 2nd ‖ x frt - 2nd; i-p - 2nd
outward = o/s
over; over-crossed ‖ OV/R = x frt; x-over ‖ x frt R
OVER ST = step-over
over the leg; "over the log"; "Over the Top" =
    any hop-over
own circle ‖ own L = circ ‖ lt
P ‖ in P = pir; i-p ‖ i-p
Paddle ‖ paddle-wheel turn = scuffle; shim ‖ paddle tr
paddle roll ‖ paddle & roll; "paradiddle" = shim ‖
    shim sham comb {see page 49, *Merrily we - - -*}
Paddle Step ‖ paddles = paddle tr; step, 3 b/c's ‖ shim
palm flat = flexed wrist
palm out = palm D-S
palms to floor = press dn
palm up = jazz Hn
par; Par.; para.; PARR = //
Parallels; parallel drops = suzie-q
Parallel passé = passé frt
Parallel Travel = suzie-q; trav'g rock'n; horz trav
part = ptnr
Pas de bourreé ‖ pas de bouree change = i/s flap, b/c 2nd
    ‖ p-d-b
Pass'e; POS'E = passé
Pat ‖ pat toe a la Fred Astaire = snap; patter step ‖ snaps vamp
Patn = patt {maxie ford patn}
Patter; "pitter patter"; patter runs; "penquin ball changes" =
    rapid sophisticated unaccented taps; running on
    ball taps; any several taps run; patter steps; taps
patter ‖ PATTER RHYTHM = rhythm ‖ odd number
    of rolling taps during even number of ct's
pattern = stg'g
pau; pause = hold
p-b-chg = passé, b/c

PDB; P.D.B.; PAS DE BOURR'EE; PAH DA BOURREE;
    Pot-te-bor-ay; Pas de Bas = p-d-b {PDBLRL = p-d-b L}
PDBras = port de bras
Pencil turn = compass tr; piqué tr
pendulum ‖ pendulum kick ‖ pendulum swing = pend wing;
    balancoire ‖ balancoire ‖ pend
perch ‖ perch turn = piqué; pose ‖ piqué tr
perpendicular = vert
personality tap = flash steps; shine
Petite Battement = low snap kick
phrase = Step
pick change = p-u-c
pickup = quick br bk before ct 1; hop, shfl, hop; 2M intro
pick up; pick-up = lift; p-u-c; br bk; flex ankle, br bk
PICK UP BK, TIP = p-u-c-tt
pick-up change; pick-up spring = (w/w) flex ankle
    into heel stand, p-u-c or s-p-u
pickup count; Pick-up ct; pickup note = a or & (before ct 1)
pick up heel step = low d-b
pickup roll = d-p-u from flat Ft
pickups = d-p-u
pick-up step ‖ PICK-UP SPRING = (Ft on flr) flex R ankle,
    bk flap R – flex L ankle; (w/w) flex ankle to heel stand,
    s-p-u ‖ br bk, leap
picture = pose
pigeon roll = pigeon-toe roll
pigeon toe ‖ pigeon stamps = both Ft t/i ‖ s/c t/i
piqué; in piqué = tendu
pique plié = p-r piq tr
Piquet = piqué
PIRR; pivot ‖ pirouette = pir ‖ piq tr
pivot; pivot around ‖ pivot tr = tr; pir ‖ paddle tr; slow pir
Pivot Walk = step fwd, ½-pivot
pl ‖ PL = i-p ‖ plié
place ‖ place; in place; to place; place beside ‖
    place R toe to L = preset ‖ c-p ‖ tt R x frt L
Place heel = dig n/w
plant = stamp
plate = metal tap
plea = plié
plié ‖ plié out onto; plié lunge = demi lunge ‖ lunge
point; pt; PT; Pt Tap ‖ point ‖ point toe = tendu; tap;
    tap tendu; tap 2nd; tt; pivot ‖ tip of toe ‖ tt
pointer = forefinger
Pony Line = tiller line
pop = p-r pos
pop in; pop-in ‖ pop kick = A's quickly to jazz 2nd ‖ snap
    kick
pop turn = rel into snap ½-pivot
pound = stomp
PP ("parallel position") = //
P/R = p-r
prelude = danced intro (usually an ent)
PREP. ‖ Prep jump = prep; tr prep ‖ jump c-p into
    bounce kicks
prestage = preset
previous = rpt
production tap = tiller
Prog.; progress; Progressive; progression = trav('g)
propeller turn = barrel turn
psh = push
pstn. = pos

ptd || ptg = pointed || pointing
pt tp = tt
p/u = p-u
pull || pulling = sdwd or bkwd sluff, chug, or scoot (often
    ending w/ st legs); draw; p-u (the br); d-p-u; br bk; d-b;
    into {pull R passé} || draw
Pull Away; short pulling steps = scoot(s)
Pullback = scoot both
pull back || Pull Back; pull-bk, pull-back; PullBack = bk flap;
    d-p-u || any p-u; p-u-c; d-b; br bk; draw; scoot both Ft
    bkwd; shfl-p-u-c-tt; chug bk; (Hn's or A's) n-Sh-p
pull back; pull-back change; pullback leap; pull leap = p-u-c
pull back; pull-back double = d-p-u
pull back knee = snap kick
Pull Bk || pull bk. = bk br || d-b
Pull backs || Pull Bks RL = low d-b's || br bk R, p-u-c L; d-p-u
pullfeet = scoot
pull hop; Pull Up || s-p-u
pull in || "pulling the trenches" = draw || trenches
Pulling = bkwd
pull knees back = scoot
Pull Step = sluff, step; scoot
pull-thru; Pullthru = sluefoot; snake hips; r-d-j
Pull Up = shfl, hop; p-u
pull wing = wing
pulse = chug both; chug
"pump"; "pump wing" = hip wing
"punch tap" = flash step
push; Push hand || push; push off; push-off = press ||
    sluff; impetus into tr or elevation; jump; push tr;
    step into push tr
push and cross = {see page 57, **Give it a shove**}
push beat = accented **&**
Push-heel; Push fwd, Drop heel = chug
pushing = press
push turn = pivot; step into pivot
pvt || PVT; Pvt. = ½-pivot || pvt; pir
qt = ¼ {3 qt turn}
Quad = qdl
quadruple time = quadruplet rhythm
quadruplet = scuffle, heel, step
quarter taps = 1 ct (¼ note) spacing {eighth tap rhythm}
quick bourres = patter steps
quick irish = qdlt irish
quiver; Quiver Fingers = vibrate
R || r = S-R {L}; c-w; e (⅛ ct) {&aR1} || a (¼ ct) {&er1}
RA = R A
railroad = flat sluff (usually several)
raise knee; raise leg at knee = passé
rank = horz line
rattle = duplet shfl; shfl; rolling (rhythm)
R/C; Roll/Change = r-c
R.D.D. ("rt diag dn bk") || R.D.U. ("rt diag up frt") = r-d-b
    || r-d-f
r diag; right diag || RB; RBD = r-d-f || r-d-b {LFD}
RDJ; R de J; Ronde'jambe = r-d-j
R DS; R. Frt. Cor. = D-S-R {R US}
Recede = trav U-S
Receding cramp roll = bkwd f-r or flapped c-r
Reclining = tilt bk
REL ("release") || Release (music) = end pos or pose || bridge;
    interlude

Release = raise {release arm}
relevé to 2nd = b/c 2nd
Rep.; rep; REPT || Repeat above step as is.= rpt || rpt phrase
repartee = banter
Rep. & Alt.; repeat; Repeat Opp; Repeat and Reverse;
    Repeat alternating feet = rev; alt
Repeat exactly = rpt
repeat foot RR – LL = rpt R rt, rev
rest || rest steps = hold; (*silent*); w/w {heel rest = dig w/w} ||
    easy techniques
restrain ("refrain") (music) = rpt'd phrase
resume; return = recover
ret ("return") || RET || retire; retiré ("withdraw; return") =
    st'n; recover || exit || passé; x ankle
RETARD; ritard; decelerando = ritardando
retire (A) = lower
reverse || reverse and repeat || reverse to start R = invert || rev;
    alt 2 X's || rev
reverse wing = eagle
reversing cramp-roll = c-r-c
revolution = tr
rev rep rev = alt 3 X's
Revue = rpt
rf || RF; R.F. = riff || R (Ft)
rf-dg = riff-dig
RH || RH (right-hand) || rh. = R heel || c-w; R Hn {LH}
    || rhythm
rhythm = tempo
Rhythm Break || rhythm time-step = brk comb || s-t-s
riff = riff, heel; close riff; 4-tap riff walk; 5-tap riff walk;
    riff, dig
riff R, riff R = 4-tap riffle
riff #5 = 5-tap riff walk
riff pivot turn = riff tr
riff scuff; riffscuff = riff
riff shuffle = riffle
riff toe heel = riff, cramp
riffle = riff; scuffle; riff, heel, br bk
riff wings = running side riffs
right exit = S-R {left exit}
Right toe extend = tendu
"ring the bell" = bell
RIP = R i-p {LIP}; R i/s pir
"rival dance" = song and dance patter challenge
rng = running
rock(s) || rocking step = sway; tilt; sailor rock(s);
    flap-heel, invert || sailor rock
rock back = rock
rock both heels || rock both heels R…L || Rocking Heels =
    heel roll w/ h-t's || rock-n-roll heels || pigeon toe roll
rocking on heels = h-t both
ROCK STEP = step
R of stage = S-R
roll = cramp; c-r; dbl-shfl (especially bk); rattle;
    nerve roll; any tilted tr; o/s sluff w/ o/s edge of ball of Ft
    (as in w-m)
roll body = rock fwd, bk
Rolling off the log = log
rolling wings = dbl eagle; any multi-wing comb
rond; Ron De Jambe = r-d-j
ronde versé; ronverse = renversé
R.O.T.; R.O.; R.T.; rt; Rt.; RT = rt o/s tr {L.I.T.}

Round Break = s-t-s – brk
round in rear = o/s r-d-j
Round Kick = fan kick
R.S.; R side ‖ R stage; Rt ‖ R side to audience = R; S-R ‖ S-R
  ‖ face S-L
R side, back, L side, front = face S-R, U-S, S-L, D-S
R toes pointed to R = t-o
r to l ‖ R to R (Diagonal) = 2 steps; R c-p
  ‖ r-d-b {L to L (Diagonal)}
rt-pass (stg'g) = shift rt
rubber-legs = sailor rock; hop R – L kick lt, step L x frt into
  3 sailor rocks
run = even rhythm; roll; trench; leap
Run fwd flat = lamp
run kick = hitch
running B.Ch. = c/s
running pull-back = running d-p-u-c
runs = 3 runs; running tpl's
rvs = rev
R with L = c-p
RxfL; R X in F of L = R x frt L
s = (silent) {s2 or 2s = (2)}
S ‖ S# ‖ S-2 = step ‖ "side"# (stg'g) ‖ Step Two
S & D ‖ S & H = song and dance ‖ shave and a haircut
same ‖ same way = rpt ‖ l-o-d
saw wing; scissor wing = hip wing
s.b.c = shfl-b/c
sc ‖ S.C. = scuff ‖ C-S
scf = scuff
scissor out (A's) = scissor open
Scissors; scissor kick ‖ SCISSORS STEP = sd
  kick; eagle rock; hitch; high hitch ‖ eagle rock
scissors kick; scissor-kicks = hitch kick; 4 frt hitches;
  low frt hitches
scoop = step sd, draw into step c-p; scoot
scoot ‖ scoot change = slide; scoot to c-p; fwd scoot;
  fwd scoot into chug ‖ trench
scoot kick; scoot bk = slide – snap kick
scrape = outward rolled-over sd sluff (into wing); wm; sluff
scrape-shuffle; shuffle wing = triplet wing
scratch wing = wing chg
scripple = scuffle-step
scuff ‖ scuff with wgt = fwd flat Ft (stomped) br; br; dig;
  scfl ‖ dig n/w or w/w
scuff cramproll = scuff into c-r
scuff heel = scuff
scuffle = dig, br bk; shim, heel; heel, dig, bk flap, heel; riffle;
  scuffle, step
scuff toe = br
scuff toe and heel; scuff toe heel ‖ scuff toe to heel = riff ‖
  toe to heel clip
s-d ("same dir") ‖ s-d-b ("side diag bk") = l-o-d ‖ l-d-b or
  r-d-b depending on lead
sd trench = catch, tap 2nd
{any step}sd ‖ sdws ("sidewise") = sdwd {tapsd} ‖ sdwd
SEC; seconde = 2nd
Receding Cramproll = bkwd flapped c-r
second time = rpt
"see-saw" = rpt'g fwd\bkwd patt's; invert
semi = demi {semi-lunge}
set ‖ set of 8 = comb ‖ 2M
sh; Sh.; shff; shu; shu.; shuf; SHUFF = shfl

shake; shake hand; shake wrist = vibrate
sham; Shim-Sham Shimmy = shim sham comb
sharp; sharply (tr) ‖ sharper = quick; snap ‖ faster; cleaner
sharp kick ‖ sharply face; sharp turn = snap kick ‖ snap pvt
Sh. B. C.; Sh. B.Ch.; Sh. bl. ch. = shfl-b/c
Shds.; SHL(S); SHLD = Sh(s)
Shff-riff; shuffle riff = rifl
shff-t-step = basic t-s
shfl into dbl p-u-c-t-t = shfl-p-u-c-tt
shift; Shift weight = rock
"shine" pos. = x-o-A-s
shoot ‖ shts ("shoots") ‖ shoot open = quick; snap;
  (A's) scissor open from chest; quick reach ‖ quick reach
  ‖ scissor open
shove = sluff
"showboat"; upstage ‖ showdown = show off; attract attention
  ‖ challenge
SH R HOP L X R OVER; shuffle hop cross = irish x frt
Sh. st. = tpl
Shuf ‖ shu. shu. = shfl ‖ dbl-shfl
shuffle ‖ shu*ful* = duple rhythm shfl; flap; br fwd, step c-p;
  br's fwd-bk in less than 2 ct's; tpl; fwd slap
  ‖ slow (even rhythm) shfl
shuffle around = shfl x frt
shuffle cramproll = shfl, leap, heel
shuffleleap; Shuffle Leaps = running tpl(s)
"Shuffle Off to Buffalo" = flapped buff; any buff
Shuffle PlBk ‖ Shuffle pull back = shfl-p-u-c ‖ p-b
shufflestep; SH CHANGE; shff = tpl
shufflestephldrp; shuffle toe heel = qdl
"shuffle three" ‖ "shuffle and four" = (cueing) tpl ‖ shfl-b/c
shuffling = sluffing (walk style)
shuttle turn = paddle tr
side ‖ side in = lead part of Ft {side flap} ‖ i/s
side angle = bk diag
side brush L bk = o/s br l-d-b
side by side = c-p
Side coupes = snake hips
Side Cramp Roll = trav-c-r
Side dig = dig 2nd, step c-p
sideleap = leap sd
side R = S-R
side riff = fwd riff sdwd
side_together = steps 2nd - c-p
"sidewinding" = suzie-q
"sight seeing" = i/s edge of Hn above eyebrows w/ palm dn
sign = reference mark {see Theme}
silent = hold
single = solo
single essence = step lead ess (using sgl time factor)
Single Off Beat = flap-b/c; duple rhythm
single pull-bk = d-b (w/ hop or heel); br bk, heel
Single Time = at tempo
Single Travel = trav'g rock'n R – sluff L
Singlewing = wing
sink ‖ Sinking (A's) = plié; grand plié; kneel ‖ lower
sit = rock into hold; squat
situation = narrative dance
skate = sluff ending w/w; sluff into lunge, heel – raise
  st leg bk
skid ‖ skids = chug; flea hop; heel sluff; short sluff ‖
  scoots 2nd - c-p

skip || skipping cramp roll = d-b fwd || hop-c-r
s.l. || s-l ("same line") = S-L || l-o-d
sl; sl. || SL; S L = slap; flap || S-L {SR}
Slam = stomp; stomp ending w/ st knee; scoot
Slap || slap steps || slap step = flap; br; accented br bk;
    bk flap; long flap || flaps || flap-step
slap cramp roll = flapped c-r
"sleepy" = slow relaxed even rhythm, esp. w-c or
    soft-shoe
slide = sluff; sluff into w/w or n/w; slide both ft c-p;
    draw o-p; tap into sluff
slide bk; slide both bk || slide tog || slide diag back =
    scoot || scoot c-p || trench
slide chug; slide fwd & drop heel; slide heel = chug
SLIDE STEP = step, sluff c-p
SLIDE SWITCH FT = wiggle sticks
slide to knee recover = draw to passé
slide around to side || slide to side = r-d-j || flea hop
slide ft up = sluff to c-p
slight jump = catch
slip || slip; SLUR = slide || sluff
"slop" leg = sluefoot
Slope arms = A's 2nd w/ sd tilt
slow bc; slow ballchg = 2 steps
slow || slow steps = ½-X || walks
slp = slap
sluff = chug; tap-sluff (2 sounds)
sluff walk = alt'g sluffs bk (think "moonwalk")
"slurp" = close riff, snap
sm {"small"} || sm. Ft. work = low-short || sophisticated
small fan-kick || small lunge = low r-d-j || step flat o-p
small tour jete = saut de basque
"Smurff" = 3 taps sd, step c-p
snake hip style || snake leg = hip isol's up-sd || snake hips
snap = cramp; toe or heel clip; snap kick
snap flap = quick flap {ea(1)}
"Snap Triple" = quick (ankle controlled) tpl w/o leap
snatch || "snatch beat" = p-u || pick up (music)
SND ("sound") = tap (audio)
s-o-d ("same opp dir") = u-l-o-d
soft shoe rhythm || soft shoe turn = tplt's || paddle tr
"song-and-dance man" = vaudeville dancer; soft shoe
    performer
Sou Sou ("sus-sous") = scoot
soutenue = pvt
s-p ("same place" || "same pos") = i-p || unchanged {arms s-p}
sp; spk.; "spank" || spank = bk or i/s br; br; bk br x frt; flap;
    bk flap || flap; bk flap; slap (w/ Hn); snap
spank, heel, step = low d-b
spank, step; spankstep = bk flap
spat = patter steps
specialty = trademark
spike = dig
spin; spin turn = pir; snap tr; piqué tr
spiral tr = pvt tr while chg'g plié level
split time = 2/4; dbl-X
spot; spot step || spot turn = done i-p || piq tr; ch; pvt
spread eagle; spread eagle wings || spread eagle position
    || Spread Eagle = eagle || wide 2nd || shfl, leap, bk flap
spring || spring up = leap; jump; high elevation;
    (elevation) landing 2 Ft || medium to high elevation
s-p-u-c = p-u-c

squatting turn = p-r pir or piq tr
squat wing = russian wing or eagle
ss = soft shoe {ss brk}
St || ST; ST.; St.; St; st; Stp = stg || step; stop (land from tr)
ST (NO WT); l step nowt = tap
stab = tt
stage rear = U-S
stairs = D-S diag(s) (performance stg's commonly include
    audience access near D-S corner(s))
stamp; stamp n/w = stomp
stamp/c || stamp ch; stampch = b/a || s/c; stamp, step
stand = w/w; upright
standing cramproll = qdl, dig
stand tall = rel
start/travel R = (trav rt) R lead
st.b.c.L.R.L. = step L, b/c R-L
std ("stand") = upright; hold
{step} step(s) = named step {shorty geo. steps}
step = comb; Step; stomp; tap; phrase; leap; chug
STEP ANGLE = diag
step bk AST heels twist = twisting shorty bk
step chainé = 3-step tr
step-close = steps sd - c-p
step cross = b/c x-over
step down = land (after tr)
step flat; step on flat; step on flat foot = stamp;
    unaccented stamp
step fwd twist = sgr
step half toe = step
step heel; step upon heel; step toe up || step heel toe =
    dig w/w || dig w/w, snap
stephldrp = cramp
step L and R F = b/c
step n.w. = step, rock
"step on" = dynamic accent
step over = x frt
step, pirouette; step pivoting = piqué tr
step plié = lunge
Step Point = tap strut
step R in place as L shoots out to L = catch R – L lt
step roll = step, 2-heel roll
Step R X L in back = steps R - L x bk R
steps backward (or fwd, st legs) = patter steps
step toe = step
step turn = chainé; piq tr
stiff; str.; strait = st
"stinger" = button
STIP = step i-p
stomp || stomp change = chug; stamp || s/c
Stomp Roll = heel rolls alt'g rt\lt
"STOP" (Hn) = press
stp || stp. tog. || stp trn = step; stop || steps o-p - c-p || land
STR || St.R; stg rt = st || S-R {St.L}
str. taps = tap strut
strad || straddle = jump 2nd || 2nd (Ft)
straight out to side = 2nd
straight tap = ankle coordinated tap, flex ankle
straighten feet = // t/f
strain ("refrain" music) = phrase of lyrics (usually 2M to 8M)
stretch = lunge; extend; reach
strike = clip; toe clip; tap (sound)
strike toe = tt; toe to heel clip

st. RLIP = b/c R-L
strong fingers || strong (A's) = flat Hn || large mvmt(s)
strut; strut step || strut kick = strut; step-heel || low snap dev
Stp. || sts || STR = step || steps || step R {STL}
stub = clip; toe clip; toe to heel clip; loud tap i-p or x bk; kick an object
style comb = flash steps
Sue-z-que; Susie Q; Suzie "Q"; suzy-q; su-z-q; SUSIE Q TWIST = suzie-q
sugar = sgr; shorty george
sugarfoot (sdwd) = o/s flap, close riff
sugar foot; Sugar foot twist = pigeon toes i-p
sugarft; sugars; Sug-Twist; Sugar Walk; steps twisting hips = sgr
Supp. ("support") = w/w
Suspend = hold
Suzi (1 Ft suzie-q) = trav'g rock'n
suzie-q; Susie Q = bmb; baby bmb; dig x frt, step 2nd – h-t t/o, step i-p; sgr; i/s br, stamp t/o x frt
S.W. ("same way") = l-o-d
swap || swap pullback || swap wing = rev || p-u-c || wing chg
swap pick-up = p-u-c; shfl-p-u-c-tt
sway || sway; swing (A's) = rock || d-A-s
swaztika (A's) = r-r-A's
swift = snap {swift turn}
swing = fwd br; swing kick
Swing Arms Alternately = o-A-s
swing body around = pvt
swing leg around || swing around to back = r-d-j || o/s r-d-j
swing leg in circle || swing leg in half circle = leg spin || r-d-j
SWING OPPOSITE; swing in opposition = o-A-s
swirl = ankle coordinated circular sluff; r-d-j
swish = sluff
switch = chg {switching pullback = p-u-c}
swivel = pvt on both ft (usually several i-p); step-pvt; h-t
swivel boogie || swivel steps = twisting shorty || sgr's
"swizzle" || swizzle sticks = rotate torso from waist (not hips) || wiggle sticks
synchronized wing = eagle
t; t-tap || T = tt || tr; tap (ball or heel)
T&H = riff
Tacet = tacit
tacky; tacky annie = 'tack annie
tag = bridge; segue; exit vamp
"tag it on" = a danced tag; final post-chorus interlude
Take = pose; dramatic F
tanglefoot = h-t; {see page 49, **Tanglefoot**}
tap = tt; br; step; chug; n/w {flat tap}; buck & wing (style); step into paddle; p-u
tap back = p-u; p-u-c
tap ball || tap ball of R ft to R; tap toe out; toe drop R to R (or Rt) = tap; snap || h-t R t/o into snap
tap bk; tap in bk || tap toe bk = ball tap bk (not tt) || tt
tap both toes = // snaps
tap flat = stomp
tap heel || tap heel fwd = dig || dig; scuff
tap sautebasque = saut de basque
tap spring = running fwd flap; tap, leap
TAP STEP || tap w/w = tap, step; tap strut || tap, rock
tattoo (rhythm) = roll
tch, Tch; TCH ("touch") = tap; tendu
"tea for two" = frt ess comb; gpvn

tempo = meter; style
TENDUE = tendu
Theme; "Theme Step"; Theme I {A; 1st} = referenced comb {rpt IIa 2 X's}
thesis = ct 1 (down beat, primary accent)
through = passé {step through R}
Throw = high kick
Thump = chug both
TI; T.I.; T-I; toed in = t/i {T.O.}
TIME || Tm = meter || X
tight = close; short; c-p
Time step arms = press A's fwd, open 2nd, Hn's to waist
TIP ("tr i-p") || tip; toe-back; toeback; toe pt tap = pvt; pir || tt; tt bk or x bk
tip-tap = p-r tapping
Tiptoe = en pointe(s)
tn = tr
TO || to || to a = t/o || into; c-p; face; chg || into {jump to a flap}
to aud = D-S
to cross = x
toe = tt; ball of Ft; tap; step {toe heel x bk}; snap
Toe-Back; Toeback; toe hit || toe change = tt x bk {TOE FRONT} || toe stand x bk, step
toe beat = tt or snap leaving toe on flr
toe-click; toe together = toe clip
toe clip step = toe to heel clip into step
toe cramp || Toe Clamp; toe down; TOE FLAT = snap w/w || step p-r; snap
toe dig; toedig = tt; forceful ball tap or step or tt; tap; accented step, rock
toe dig, scuff = riff
toed-in = both Ft t/i
toe drag = sluff
toe drop = snap w/w or n/w; tt; br bk, heel, tt bk, heel &1&2
toe-heel || toe heel (or heeldrop); toe heel cramp || TOE HEEL TWIST; Toe-heel drops = tt, heel; cramp; close riff || step, heel; cramp || trav'g rock'n; pigeon toe roll
toed in; toe pointed in || toe in..out..in = t/i || h-t's w/ snaps t/i - t/o - t/i
toe flat = snap
toe jab = tt
toe jump || toe punch = dbl toe stand || toe stand; tt
Toe Pt || toe point (or pt) tap; toe stab || toe tap; toe tip = tendu || tt || tt; tap; tap tendu
Toe Stand || TOE STAND PIR = toe stand both || toe spin
Toe Tap = tap; pointe tap (style); br
toe-tip || toe-tip cramp-roll = tt || faked toe stands R-L, b/c
Toe Toe = b/c
toe touch; touch toe = tap; tt; p-r c-p
toe twist = h-t; twisting shorty
toe unpointed || toes up, drop toes, toes up = flex ft || rock'n roll
toe up = heel (usually precedes snap)
TOG; tog.; TG ("together") = c-p; step
tog w/ ("together with") = a-s-t; c-p
to L || to place = L; land L || i-p; c-p
TOR ("to rt") || to the = rt || trav
touch || touch; touch-tap; Touch-Toe; Tch || touch-step = tendu; step; dig; br || tap; tap c-p; tap frt; tt; step; clip || step c-p; tap, step
touch to sole = toe clip

tour jeté leap = saut de basque
tp || tpbk = tap || tt x bk
tr || TR ("turn rt") = face {tr D-S} || c-w tr {TL}
"trade eights" = Step-length challenges
trading cramproll = c-r-c
Trailing; TS ("toe scrape") = sluff; draw
Train Style; train step || train time step = stamp fwd, steps i-p - bk - i-p || r-r series
Trans. ("transition") = interlude
Travel Around; turn = circ
Traveling cramp roll = flapped c-r
Traveling Time Step = cubanola
Traveling wing = i/s p-u (no sluff)
Travel Step = step sd, i/s flap
tread-mill pull-backs = running d-p-u-c's or shfl-p-u-c's
trembling; tremer ("tremor") = nerve roll
trench = o/s sluff
Trench Step; trench slide; TRENCH RUNS || trench step with touch bk = trench(es) || trench, tt
trick = complicated step (especially acrobatic), Step, or rhythm
Trip.; trpl || Triple = tpl || qdl
Triple Pull Bk. = cinc
Triple roll = tpl, step, roll (time factor bgn'g c-r)
triple sh = 6-tap rattle
triple step = tpl
triple time = triplet rhythm
triplet || triplet $1/8^{th}$ = running tpl; flap-heel || triplet {&a3}
trn; trns || trn bk.R = tr(s) || c-c-w tr R
trunk = torso
trvl = trav
tSL ("tr S-L")= face S-L {tUS}
t step = t-s
t-t || TT ("torso twist") = tt; snap || twist above waist
TU; turning bk on self = tr
Tuck; tuck knee = passé
Turn; turning || TURN; circTurn around by Brush Step X = circ; face || bk flap x frt into pvt
TURN HEAD; TURN & LOOK; LOOK = F
turn heel out || turning toe out = t/i || h-t t/o
turning ½ to bk = ½-tr (face U-S)
turning back to || Turn to; turning to = face || face; tr
turning R to L = c-w tr (face S-L)
Turn L, Drag R = piq compass tr L
turn L step LRL; TURN TO SR RLR || turn to back on RLR = 3-step tr || p-d-b tr
turn on toes; twist = pivot
turn-over = F {turn-over L shoulder}
turn R = tr R c-w
turn sharply = snap tr
turn toward L shoulder = face L
twist || TWIST FT; twist heels; twisting on heels; twisting toe; toe twist = pvt || h-t (or both)
twist drops = pigeon-toe; suzie-q
twist feet || twist heels = pvt tr || pivot // Ft
twist heels & toes; twist travel = suzie-q
twisting steps = twisting shortys bk; sgr; suzie-q
twist knees = swing // knees
TWISTS; twist forward; Twist Out; twist step; twist walk || TWIST B. CHANGES = sgr || b/c or c/s sgr's
twist-snap = h-t into snap

twist step = sgr; step – t/o h-t
two-riff; two tap riff = riff
Two Step = flap-b/c
TWO STEP CHAINE TURN = ch
two to a bar = $2/4$
u (rhythm) = a {&au = a&a}
UND ("under") = c-p bk of p-r Ft
Unwind(ing) = (from Ft x'd) pivot; Ft x, pivot; rev tr; cont or rev dir of r-d-j to start pos
unxing; UN-X-ING = o-p
up || up; up frt = passé; U-S; br || D-S
UP; Upst; upstg || upper rt = U-S {CHAINNE UP} || U-S-R
Upbt ("upbeat") || up beat = & (before ct); increase tempo || even ct
up-down stage lines = vert (stg'g)
uprt = upright
up to = close
U.S. || U-S, S-R = U-S || U-S-R
U.S.C.S. = U-S-C
"Vaudeville Time Step" = shim sham comb
veer = arc; gradually trav
Vrt = vert
vert-V = V-A's
Virginia Essence = ess comb
vision to = F
w/a ("with a") || w/r = w/ || w/ R
"Wag heels" = // pvt (usually alt'g sd's)
waggle toes = h-t
Wait = hold
walk || Walking Riff = quick steps || 5-tap riff walk
walk turn || walking turn; 3 step walking tr = walk in circ || 3-step tr
wall {#}; {dir} Wall = Cecchetti #5, 6, 7, 8 {L Wall}
Waltz Balance = bal fwd, invert
waltz clog || W. clog = shfl-b/c; d-w-c-t-s || w-c
way; way to || way back = long {step way rt} || x bk
wd; wide = long
weave = pigeon-toe roll {(from 2nd) weave inward to c-p}
western flyer = {see page 58, top}
WGT = wt
"Whap" = sluff c-p into raise Ft behind knee
Whip = fouetté
whole of the foot = flat Ft
Wide b-c = b/c 2nd
"wiggle" = twist; multiple 4-tap pigeon toe rolls alt'g lead (i-p)
wiggle ankles = roll onto instep(s) or o/s of Ft; sailor rock
wiggle legs = wiggle sticks
windmill || windmill; propeller (A's) || windmill turn = leg spin; d-A-s; r-r A's || barrel tr A's || barrel turn
wing = wm; eagle; "flapping" A's; sd riff
wing-back = shfl bk, wing
wings; wing set; double wing = eagle
wing time step = wm t-s
wk; work = comb
WLK = walk; step
Wobble = rubber legs
Work high = non-sophisticated (pick up Ft)
working = trav'g twd; facing
WORKING SIDE = lead
wrist thrown back || wrist broken = press; flexed Hn || flexed Hn

w-w = w/w
W/W ("w/o wt") = n/w
X || x; X; xs; XS; Xs = rpt || X's
X || X'g; x'ing; X-ING || X heel = x frt || x'g || step-heel x frt
xB; Xbk; XIB || X, b of L; X b L; xRbk; XRBL = x bk {XIF} || R x bk L
X f = bkwd mvmt x frt {flap l X f r = bk flap L x frt R}

x over; Xover || XOL; XROL; X R OVER L; X-R OV/L; XIFL; R.X.frt.L. = x frt; step close x frt || R x frt L; step or step-heel R x frt
XR || X R behind L = br R x bk || shfl x bk
X-R over L turn = step x frt into pvt
x step = time step
XT ("cross tr") = step into pvt

TALKING RHYTHMS

This discussion is designed for tap instructors, offering suggestions encouraging the inclusion of rhythmically spoken terminology as an integral part of class presentation. The suggested verbal examples are *italicized*.

INTRODUCTION

The most effective dance training technique is demonstrated instruction – literally, show and tell. Movement flow is most easily understood by copying, and most easily remembered by verbal reference – terminology.

When tapping, the essential third element is sound – rhythm. Talking rhythms, the combination of simultaneous demonstration and term sequence (like speaking sentences) with directly associated rhythm, yields faster and more accurate assimilation (two secondary objectives of tap training) with improved recall.

How is this done? With practice. Whether presenting new steps or variations, warm ups or training combinations, or staging and routines, instruction is necessary, so verbalize the rhythm as part of the presentation and, when needed, as a practice reminder or cue. Most dance instructors do this in some way, so consider whether a more comprehensive approach would be useful.

As is common in ballet, introduce material as complete thoughts (sentences, phrases) of consistent language. This may initially require some thought but soon becomes as natural as other verbal communication. This technique is equally successful for instructors, students, tap notation reading or writing, memorization (mental review without tapping), and rehearsal. Resultantly, tap sequences are more rapidly learned by mind and body (ya cain't have tap without both).

TIMING

Not every tap need always be verbalized, but if desired it is doable.

Verbalization may be as simple as *shuffle ball change* spoken rhythmically a1a2 *shuf fle ball change*, but frequently requires creatively modified syllables to either extend or accelerate (compress) speech.

Examples:

triple	&a1	*tr ri ple*
flap ball change	a1a2	*fl lap ball change*
irish	a1a2	*i ir ri ish*
buffalo	1&a2	*bu u fa lo*

and:

inside flap	a1	*inside flap*	(spoken <u>rushed</u>)
shuffle across front	a1	*shuffle cross-front*	(compound-word)
back flapped shorty georges	a1 a2	*back flapped <u>shorty</u> <u>georges</u>*	(for 2 shorty georges)
or:		*shor ty shor ty*	

Sometimes greater creativity is helpful.

steps x bk - 2nd, b/c x frt - 2nd	12a3	*pas de boo change*
r-r-4, r-r-4, shfl-flap-step-b/c-b/c		*rail road 34, rail road 34, rail road fl lap step &7&8*
		& 1 &2 & 3 &4 & 5 & a 6 &7&8

While each person will develop a personal set of mental/verbal rhythmic restructures, terminology clarity and consistency should be maintained. For students, the simultaneous and repeated association of term, coordination, and rhythm quickly yield familiarity and an understanding response.

STUDENT INTERPRETATION

When repeating demonstrated patterns, gradually reduce verbalization allowing each student's mind to select its unique pattern of references and better hear the shading of the actual taps.

Try this:

Flap, 2 heels, irish x frt, hop, rolling wing change.
   a1   2 3   a4a5   6   a7&a8
Fl ap, heel heel, i rish cross front, hop, a rol ling wing change.

then: *Fl ap, two heels, i rish* (a5 no speech), *hop, five ev en taps* (8).
    a1, 2 3, a 4a5, hop, 12345.
    a1, (2 3 4 5), hop, a7&a8.

The references may include any relavent information. For example, if the above 2M was lead R:
Fl ap, heel heel, i rish cross front, hop, right rol ling wing change.

With each repetition, select information likely to next be most useful to the students – steps, rhythm, directions, weight shifts, arm/body movements, staging, etc.

CUEING

As students accustom themselves to verbal/movement associations, pre-action prompting (cueing) becomes a useful next application.

Consider the following variations:

    A. Stomp frt R, snaps t/o - frt - t/o - frt w/w, shfl-b/c L, step L.
          1   2 3 4 5   a6 a7   8
        Stomp, <u>snaps-out</u> front out <u>with-weight</u>, shuffle ball change, step.

    B. Rpt 1st 6 ct's of A., (trav rt) b/c L x bk R - R rt, step L x frt R.
        Stomp, out front out front, grape vine, back right, <u>cross-front</u>.   (*grapevine* is spoken during the shfl)

    C. Rpt 1st 5 ct's of A., shfl L (face S-L), b/c L bk (S-R) - R i-p, c-w ½-tr into step L S-R.
        Stomp, snaps 3 4 5, face left, next right, twist.   (*next right* during b/c)

    D. Rpt 1st 5 ct's of A., shfl-b/c c-c-w tr, step L (face D-S).
        Stomp, 2 3 4 turn ing left ball change, <u>face-front</u>.   (*turn* spoken during last snap)

        Rpt A. thru D.   (note the pre-action cues)
        Stomp, out front out front, shuffle ball change step.
        <u>Again</u>, 2 3 4 5, <u>travel</u> right, pas de <u>bourré</u>.
        <u>Ending-twists</u>, 2 3 4 5, left (6) then right, (8).   (notice *left* is the a before (6))
        <u>With-turn</u> 2 3 4 5, left turn end front (8).

Verbal rhythms are a useful tool but should not be continuous. Other instructions, associations, and dancer corrections are necessary. When setting a routine, reduce cueing as possible. During rehearsals use sparingly. Not only is cueing handy as a class and rehearsal reminder, but, with an experienced, alert class, permits spontaneous variations of warm ups, progressions, etc.

Beginning in the 1940s several dance training aids music companies included in their lines Spoken Lesson versions of their routine and technique class recordings. Most prominent was Al Gilbert who produced Stepping Tones Records routine and class "flippy" records (later, tapes and CDs). The A side featured verbal instructions with the accompaniment, the B side instrumental only. Each came with printed notes. Part of the appeal was that most routine arrangements were available as inexpensive "singles" (1 routine per 45 rpm or compact 33) intended for student personal practice at home. Al's notes included the recorded verbal cues following the steps.

Several "Teaching Systems" include specific terminology lists with lesson plans (such as *TAP the Spoken Class* by Jules Stone) encouraging "Teachers: Have the students repeat the names of the above terms. Understanding the terms, will help the students to master the exercises and dances very quickly."

Speaking and hearing cueing leads to its opposite, identifying the footwork. Language paints pictures. You see the brown fox jumping over the fence or cramproll, 2 back flaps. The mental conversion is reciprocal. Seeing the bounding fox or roll and flaps combination easily evokes a description. As you think it, you see it; as you see it, you think it, including the rhythm. When you watch a dance performance, identify to remember, the parts you like.

When verbal rhythmics are regularly applied, the habit tends to become a natural flow of spontaneous helpful, guiding information. See the <u>SHOWOFF</u> routine as an example.

Give it a try.

ROUTINES

The following tap routines are offered as examples of different styles and applications of the dance form. While all are designed for foundation training, they gradually progress in difficulty. Different choreographic approaches provide opportunities to apply different steps, staging techniques, and characterizations to foster new incites. Most phrases are R lead to ease rearrangement. Originally selected acompaniment may not be available. Suitable alternative music can be found, with specific arrangements possibly encouraging adjustments to the routines. Enjoy!

WALTZ CLOG

The first, a simple Dutch clog, is presented as a compositional project. A Step format is suggested, along with Step and break phrases which can be sequenced, intermixed, supplemented, and replaced as desired. The project can yield many different results plus a better understanding of the relationships of steps, phrases, Steps, characters, and the resultant finished piece.

GOING DUTCH

Select simplest variations for a first routine for youngsters (ages 6 to 8), or any to build a simple character couples dance for older beginners. As with any characterization, exaggeration with allusion to character, not folk dance authenticity, is the objective; e.g., "hands on hips" styling is back of wrists on top of pelvis sides with elbows forward, and forward bends are with a straight (flat) back. To perform, perhaps apron with bonnet and vest with cap costuming, even including wood shoes.

Routine structure:

Commonly, six 16M Steps (96M, 3 choruses). The simplest Step structure is *AAAB* of four 4M phrases (3 the same then a break) equalling 16M per Step. Most simply performed, all phrases begin the same (*C*) and are in two 2M parts (being *A=CD* or *B=CE*), all Steps ending with the same break. *C* is 2 waltz clog time-steps, *D* is a Step variation, and *E* is a break combination. For example:

```
        S-w-c-t-s's R-L,    dig R r-d-f, step R c-p, (clap), rev dig-step-clap.
4M      1&2&3 4&5&6(C) 1         2        3       4      5      6 (D)
8M      Rpt above 4M 2 X's. (CDCD)
        Brk: S-w-c-t-s's R-L, (tr'g c-w) run i-p R-L-R (lifting free Ft bk), (face D-S) stamp L near R, (slap both thighs), (clap).
4M      1&2&3 4&5&6 (C)              1 2 3                               4                     5                  6 (E)
16M
```

Thus the *AAAB* Step structure may be notated *CDCDCDCE*. The following "names" are for easy cueing identificaion, or create your own.

Step variations: (*D*)

NOTE: Many instructors use "vernacular names" (see **ALTERNATE TERMINOLOGY**) to reference frequently presented comb's.

"Brush hop"	Step R, brush L x frt R, hop R – L l-d-f, rev.	1 2 3 4 5 6
"Kicking dust"	(Face D-S-R) step R, scuff L, leap into b/c i-p, (face D-S-L) rev.	1&(2)&3 4&(5)&6
"Dust the shoes"	Step R r-d-b – flex L w/ heel on flr (R Hn on hip), (bend l-d-f twd L, L Hn "brushes" rt then lt above L toe), rev 3 ct's. 1 (2 3) 4 (5 6)	
"Slapenzee"	Steps R-L, lift R x bk L near L hip (L Hn slap i/s of R Ft), rev step-slap, step L.	1 2 3 4 5 6
"Slap-n-clap"	(Bend slightly fwd, R slap frt of R thigh), rev, (upright, 2 claps), (slap both thighs), (clap).	1 - - - - - 6
"Dig-snap walk"	(Trav r-d-f) dig-snap R, step L c-p bk R, rpt.	1 2 3 4 5 6
"Scuff walk"	Scuff R x frt L into low o/s r-d-j, hop L, step R, rev.	1 - - - 6
"Turn & stamp"	3-step tr R rt, stamp L, stomp R, (clap) raise R.	1 - - - 6
"Drum flap pvt"	Drum flap R, step L fwd into c-w ½-pvt, rpt.	&1&a2 3 &4&a5 6
"Balancé"	(F up-rt, bend lt, R A up-rt) balancé R rt, rev bal (F dn-rt, bend rt, R A dn-rt).	1 - - - 6
"Scissor arms"	Leap R r-d-f (scissor A's open) – st L l-d-b, b/c L-R (nat A's), rev.	1(2)&3 4(5)&6
"Sugar foot circle"	(Trav in c-w circ) 6 sugar Ft's lead R (jazz Hn's in frt of Sh's: sd bend wrists to tilt Hn's rt-lt-etc.).	
"Strolling boy"	(Clasp wrist behind back) flap R, shfl x frt L, flap L, rpt 1M.	a1 a2 a3 a4 a5 a6
"Stumble"	Dig R w/w, tt L x bk R, snap R, step L frt, rpt.	12a3 45a6
"Dig change"	D/c fwd R-L, step bk R-L, rpt.	&1 2 3 &4 5 6
"Heel stand"	Scuff R, dig w/w R, rev c-p, snaps R-L, rpt 1M.	a1 - - - - a6
"Clipenzee"	Toe clip, b/c rt, (clap), heel clip, b/c rt, (clap).	1 a2 3 4 a5 6
"Skating"	(Trav D-S-R) flap R – st L bk, 2 chugs R, rev.	a1 a2a3 a4 a5a6
"Bandy twist"	Stomp R, br bk R, hop L, b-t R (or c-w tr).	1a2 34a5a6
"Irishes"	Irish R x frt L, steps L lt - R rt, irish L x frt R.	a1a2 3 4 a5a6
"Sliding irish"	Step R, sliding irish L, rpt.	1&2&3 4&5&6
"Slides"	Step R x frt L, slide R l-d-b, step L, step R r-d-b, step L x frt R, slide L r-d-b.	1 2 3 4 5 6
"Pas de bourrée"	Scuff R, hop L, p-d-b R, step L, (clap).	1& 234 5 6
"Turning hops"	Flap R rt, (c-w tr) shfl-hop 2 X's, rev.	&1&a2&a3 &4&a5&a6

"Greeting"　　　　Tt R, step R (Boy: tt x frt w/ brief bow -- Girl: tt x bk w/ brief curtsy), rev, 2 steps (hold Hn's or link elbows).
　　　　　　　　　　1　　2　　　　　　　　　　　　　　　　　　　　　　　　　　　　　　　　　　　　　34　56
"Partners clap"　　(Face ptnr, clap R Hn's-L Hn's-both Hn's-own-both), (clap own 2 X's).　　1 2 3 4 5 &6
"Shoulder to shoulder"　　(Face P) step R, dig L w/w x frt (twist rt bend twd P, L Sh's close or touch), step R, tt L x bk
　　　　　　　　　　(upright, face ptnr), jump, hold (or clap).　　12345(6) – 6
"Wring the dishrag"　　(Facing ptnr's hold both Hn's, opp leads trav'g same stg dir) Steps sd - x bk into o/s tr (back to back,
　　　　　　　　　　arch both A's) - step l-o-d finishing tr (A's 2nd), both step l-o-d x frt into ¼-tr (face l-o-d, i/s A's frt,
　　　　　　　　　　arch o/s A's), step i-p, step u-l-o-d (starting pos).　　1 2 3 4 5 6
NOTE: Bottom "Chiming" partner pliés into each lift, supporting top ptnr's hips slightly above his.
"Chiming"　　　　(P's back to back, both elbows linked, B tilts fwd) G tips bkwd onto his back kicking lower legs),
　　　　　　　　　　rev support (B tucking knees to chest, st legs vert – F D-S "surprised", tuck), both upright. (12)3 (4&5)6
NOTE: Bgn these Tyrolean comb's w/ 2 tt-c-t-s's.
"Tyrol"　　　　　　(Maxie segment saut de basque) step R rt into c-w tr, shfl L, leap L, tt R x bk R, rpt. 1&2&3 4&5&6
"Tyrolean slaps"　　Lift R Ft frt of L thigh (L Hn slap i/s R Ft), swing R Ft bk-rt (R slap o/s R Ft), rpt frt slap,
　　　　　　　　　　leap R (lift L knee frt) into rev frt - sd slaps, step L.　　1 2 3 4 5 6
"Bells"　　　　　　Step R x frt L, bell L, rev.　　1(2)&3 4(5)&6
"Ptnr'd bell"　　　　(P's close, G rt) B: step R x frt into bell L away from G, step L x frt R,
　　　　　　　　　　(B: R A around G's waist) step R rt into hip lift – G: rev bell.　　1&23 4&56

Break combinations: (*E*)
"Brushes"　　　　Step R, br's L frt - bk x frt R - frt - bk, step L c-p.　　1 2 3 4 5 6
"Brush & toe"　　Steps R-L, br's R frt - bk x frt L, tt R x frt L.　　12 34 5 (6)
"Pas de bourrée, nod"　(Hn's on hips) P-d-b R lt (or o/s p-d-b tr R), dig L lt, (nod H dn), step L (H up). 1 2 3 4 (5) 6
"Pout"　　　　　　B/c R-L, stamps R-L-R, (fold A's, scowl).　　a1 234 (56)
"Scold"　　　　　(L Hn on hip) toes lead 3 suzie-q's rt (R extended forefinger shake w/ taps), t/f both heels a-s-t 2 X's. 12345 (6)
"Shrug"　　　　　4 d-b's R-L-R-L, rel (shrug Sh's, side-tilt H), lower heels to flr (relax Sh's, ctr H).　　&a1&a2&a3&a4 (56)
"Showoff"　　　　Jumps 2nd – x, pivot tr, bow.　　12(3456)
"Suzie-q"　　　　(Fingertips on knees) toes lead 4 suzie-q's rt, dig R, (shrug w/ jazz Hn's by Sh's). 1 - - - 5 (6)
"Happy"　　　　　3 b/c's R-L trav'g rt, 2 jumps i-p, (2 claps).　　a1a2a3 4 5 &6
"Well?"　　　　　Hop R, tt L x bk R, hop R, tt L x frt R, (2 claps), (bent A's open frt w/ palms up, tilt H).　&1&2 3 4 (56)
"Dbl tt"　　　　　Flap R, shfl L, hop R, 2 tt's L x bk R, leap L, shfl R, hop L, tt R x bk L.　　&1&2&3a (&) 4&5&6
"Toe-tap turn"　　(C-w tr) step R, tt L x bk R, rev step-tt (end tr), steps R-L.　　1 - - - - 6
"Irish-tt turn"　　(C-w tr) step R x bk L, irish L, tt R bk, hop L, step R. 1&2&3456
"Leap toe-taps"　　Step R rt, tt L x bk R, leap L, tt R x bk L, rev leap-tt, step L c-p, both heels a-s-t.　　12 a3a4 5 6
"Clip & clap"　　　Jump 2nd, scoot c-p into 2 heel clips, (slap frt of thighs), (clap).　　1 &23 4 5 (6)

Other w-c-t-s's: (*C*)
"Heel-toe-heel t-s"　　Step R, br bk L, heel R, tt L x bk R, heel R.　　1&2&3
"Dig time-step"　　Step R, shfl L, dig L w/w x frt R, step R.　　1&2&3
"Buffalo t-s"　　　Buff R rt, flap R rt – raise flexed L t/o x frt R ankle (bend lt).　　1&a2&3
"Walking clog"　　Dig-snap R, heel R, shfl L fwd, b/c L fwd - R c-p bk L.　　&1 & {2&a3 }
"Double shfl t-s"　　Step R, dbl-shfl L ending x frt R (face r-d-f), b/c L x frt R - R i-p.　　{1&a2&a3}

Staging:
　Consider modifying by changing facing directions or using twists, turns, and/or traveling. Partners can have opposing leads, perform facing, clap partner's hands, swing arms with joined hands or linked elbows when traveling. Make it real clog with wood shoes. Select an idea, an approach. How about a narrative dance? Several of the Steps suggest a cleaning, flirtation, argument, or comedy theme; redesign them into a beginning, middle, and end visual plot. How about classical music? Although the techniques are simple, their arrangement can yield interesting results. Explore. You are the arranger.

PREPARING A ROUTINE

Although introduced in READING NOTES, here are a few more suggestions which may prove helpful.
　　Marque the routine:
　　　　1. Sequence the steps by phrase, then by Step.
　　　　2. Resequence seeking *comfortable* staging and overall coordination.
　　　　3. Check the rhythm and ease toward performance tempo.
　　　　4. Transition into the next Step.
　　　　5. After about 3 Steps, take the time to get a *feel* for the accompaniment and associated performance style. If a group number, what is your involvement with the other performers; if a solo, your most effective presentation, possibly even routine modifications.
　　　　6. Progressing through the routine, memorization and presentation should naturally mature. If not restricted, allow personal styling to emerge.
　　　　7. Eventually, "thinking about the routine" should become "thinking about the audience". A studio mirror is useful for identifying visual adjustments which yield a more entertaining performance.

TECH-TAP

Demonstration routines are intended to display students' current training techniques. Skills are emphasized using simple Step formats, transitions, and staging. This is a useful learning tool, adaptable to any age, techniques, training level, or style and, with some forethought, can be performable. Because of the immediate familiarity with the material, these routines serve as an excellent student introduction to interpreting tap notes. Give each student a copy, possibly accompanied by a short suitable terms/abbreviations list.

TOTS' TAP

A simple coordination $^4/_4$ technique review routine for 6 to 10 year old beginners. Simplify or repeat Steps for younger students. Rhythms are notated even (&1&2&3&4). If possible, duple rhythm (a1 a2 a3 a4) is preferable where appropriate.

Music: 2 choruses, tempo comfortable for students.

Routine by Terry Dill

STEP ONE - ENTRANCE

Enter from S-R twd C-S. For large stg, trav from U-S to C-S or D-S-C.

Flap R (both A's reach dn-rt), heel R, rev (reach up-lt), rpt 1M.
2M   &1   2   &3 4   &5 6 &7 8

S-w-c-t-s R, step L, rpt 1M.
2M   1&2&3   4   5&6&7 8

Rpt 1st 2M. Brk: 4 flap-b/c's (d-A-s, forming horz line facing D-S).
4M   1 - - - 8   &1 &2 &3&4 &5&6 &7&8
8M

STEP TWO

(L Hn on hip – flat R Hn low frt w/ palm dn, fingers rt) stomp R frt t/o, h-t's into snaps t/i - t/o - t/i w/w (twist R wrist lt - rt - lt).
1M   1   2   3   4

Rev 1M. (Hn's on hips) 4 irishes x bk R-L-R-L.
3M   5 - - 8   &1&2 &3&4 &5&6 &7&8

Rpt 1st 2M. Circ brk: (Trav in c-w circ, d-A-s) 4 flap-b/c's R-L-R-L.
4M   1 - - - 8   &1&2 - - - - &7&8
8M

STEP THREE

Flap R rt (d-A-s rt), tap L c-p, rev flap-tap, step R rt, low kick* L x frt R (o-A-s), rev step-kick.
2M   &1   2   &3 4   5   (6)   7 (8)

3-step tr R, (clap), rev 1M   (*Demonstrate as low snap kick. Let class duplicate as able.)
2M   1 2 3   4   567 8

4M   Rpt above 4M.
8M

STEP FOUR

P-d-b R lt, (2 claps), rev.
2M   1 2 3   &4   567 &8

(P-d-b) hop L, tpl R x bk L, step L lt, step R x frt L, rev.
2M   1   &a2   3   4   5&a6 7 8

(x-o-A-s) 6 hop-tpl's x bk L-R-L-R-L-R, 4 running tpl's i-p R-L-R-L.
4M   1 &a2 3&a4 5 - - 8 1 - - 4   &a5 &a6 &a7 &a8
8M

STEP FIVE

Leap fwd into b/c R-L, dig R, step R c-p, rev.
2M   & 1 2   3 (4) &5 6 7 (8)

4 irishes x bk R-L-R-L.
2M   &1&2 - - - - - - &7&8

NOTE: Where port de bras is not specified, demonstrate nat A's, allowing students to interpret as personally comfortable.

(Var of 1st 2M) leap R rt into b/c (reach frt R-L), dig R r-d-f (Hn's near waist), step R c-p, rev.
2M   &1 -- & 1 2   3 (4) &5 6 7 (8)

2M   Circ brk: See STEP TWO.
8M

STEP SIX

        (Face D-S-R, trav bkwd U-S-L) step R, low snap kick L frt, b/c L-R, rpt kick-b/c 2 X's, b/c L-R.
2M   1   (2)   &3   (4)&5 (6)&7   & 8

        (Face D-S-L, trav bkwd U-S-R) rev above ct's 1 - 5, 3 b/c's R-L.
2M   1 - - - 5   &6 &7&8

        (Face and trav D-S, Hn's on hips) step R, low snap kick L x frt R, rev step-kick 5 X's, stamps R-L (A's reach up R-L).
4M   1   (2)   3 - - - (8) 1 - - - (4)   **5**(6)**7**(8) --   5 7
<u>8M</u>

STEP SEVEN

        (Buff starting pos: R t/o x frt L ankle) buff R rt (scissor A's), irish R x bk L, flap L, step R, flap L, b/c R-L.
2M   1&a2   &3&4 &5   6   &7 & 8

        3 buff's R rt (scissor A's), irish R x bk L.
2M   1&a2 3&a4 5&a6 &7&8
4M   Rev above 4M.
<u>8M</u>

STEP EIGHT

        2 baby bmb's R (trav S-L), (face and trav D-S-L) fwd flap R, step L c-p, fwd flap R, b/c L-R.
2M   1 2   3 4   &5   6   &7   & 8

2M   Rev above 2M.

        Irish R x frt L, long step L lt U-S-L – extend R D-S-R (bend rt over R, A's 2nd), draw R twd L, rev step-draw, step L c-p.
2M   &1&2   3   (4 5)   6 (7)   8

        C-w irish tr R, b/c R rt x-over L frt, br's R r-d-f - bk x frt L, tt R x frt L (pose: present both A's frt), (say "Done!").
2M   &1&2 &3&4 &   5   6   7   8   (1)
<u>8M</u>

FINIS

SUE'S BUCK AND WING

A training routine emphasizing pickups, wings, glides, clips, and non-standard time-steps with a few standard rhythm combinations and a touch of flash. Intended to be developed as a performance solo for a comfortably skilled dancer.

Music: Any up beat $^4/_4$, intro, 2 choruses, minimum 130 met.   Choreography: Terry Dill

At higher tempos some elvations may revert to heels and steps.

STEP ONE – ENTRANCE

        (→ C-S, steps x and sdwd l-o-d as needed) 3 cubanolas sgl L - dbl R - tpl L.
6M   8&1&2&3&4 56 &7&   8&1&2&3&4 5&6 &7&   8&1&2&3&4 5&a6 &7&

        Leap R (not hop) into cross bar.
2M   8   &a1 2&3 &a4&a5 &6&a7
<u>8M</u>

STEP TWO

        Hold, stamp R, 2 chugs R, b/c L-R, L shfl-p-u-c-tt, L hip wing, tt R x bk L, chug L.
2M+1 ct (8)   **1**   a2 a3   & 4   &5&a 6   a&a   7   a8

4M-1 ct Rpt from stamp 2 X's excluding last chug.

        Brk: p-u-c-maxie R,   lamp L.
2M   &8&1&a2 &3&4&a5 &6 (7) **&**
<u>8M</u>

STEP THREE

6M   3 d-f-a-t-s's R (1st 2 w/ full tr's, 3rd w/ dbl tr).   81&2&3&4 (56) &7&   4M

        Brk: hold, low balancoire R x frt L into c-c-w ½-tr (face U-S), step R, b/c L lt x-over R bk into c-w ½-pvt, tt L x bk R, stamp L.
2M   (8)   1   2)   3 (4)   &   5   6   7
<u>8M</u>

STEP FOUR

        3 d-b's R-L-R, stamp L, 5-tap riff walks R-L, d-p-u R.
2M   {8&a1&a2&a **3**   &a4&a   5}{a&a6 a&a7}

2M   Rpt 2M.

        (This phrase is a fred astaire rhythm brk var:) Hop L, tpl R, tt L x bk R, chug R – st L l-d-b, step bk L, tt R x frt L, glide L,
                                                                               8   &a1 & (2)   a&   3   &   4

        chug L, dig R, step-tt-glide R, rev from last chug.
2M+1 ct a&   5   & a (6){&   a7a &a} (8) &

        Leap R rt – tendu L lt, sluff i/s r-d-j L into glide R, rev, runs fwd R-L-R-L, br bk R, tt R x bk L, heel L, dig R, heel L.
2M   1   &   2   3&4   {5 & a 6 a}(&){7   &   a   8}
<u>8M+1 ct</u>

STEP FIVE

2M Bk flap R, irish L x frt R, flap R rt, irish L x frt R, flap R rt, step L x bk R (face S-L).
{&1 &2&3 &4 &5&6 &7 &}

4M Q-s-t-s R ending bk flap L-step R S-R (face D-S), log glide L (face D-S-L), (twist c-w to S-R into) rev (end facing D-S).
8&1a&a2 &3 & 4&a5(6)7 2M

2M D-s-wm-t-s R, stomp L, br bk L, hop R, flap L, step R, stomp L l-d-f (lean slightly bk), rock L.
8&1&2&3a&a 4 & 5 (&) a6 & 7 (&8)

8M

STEP SIX

C-r R, toe clip, snaps R-L, R toe lt to L heel clip, heel L, R toe rt to L heel clip, heel L, tap R rt, R heel to L toe clip, snap L,
a&a1 {& 2 & 3 & 4 & 5 & 6

2M step R x frt L, L toe to R heel clip, heel R, step L lt.
& 7 & 8

2M Tap R c-p, chug R r-d-f, step L close x bk R, rpt 4 X's, stomp R frt.
&} a1 & 2a&3 &a4& 5a&6 &a7& 8

4M Rpt 4M.
8M

STEP SEVEN

S-r's R rt – c-p, hold, eagle, dbl-eagle chg L into tt R x bk L, hop L into c-w tr, bk flap-b/c R (face D-S).
2M {1&a2 &a3&} (4) &a5 a&a6 a (&) {a 7& a 8}

4M Rev 2M 2 X's.

Brk: S-r L lt, i/s f-r-c L, shfl R, wing chg L, rev shfl-wing chg.
2M 1&a2 &3&4 &5 &a6 &7 &a8
8M

STEP EIGHT

Br R r-d-f, hop L, step R x frt L (A's 2nd, bend rt-frt D-S), (trav S-R) c-c-w hopped barrel tr L, (face D-S) shfl-p-u-c-tt's R-L.
2M 1 & 2 &(3)&4 &5 & a 6 &7&a8

4M Rpt 2M 2 X's.

Brk: rpt ct's 1 - - - (3) (upright, no tr), br L l-d-f, hop R, step L x frt R (slight lt bend), hold, tt R x bk L into c-w tr, hop L
1&2&(3) & 4 & (5) & 6

2M step R x frt L (face D-S-L), rock L – t/o p-r R x frt L pose (V-A's, torso and F D-S).
7 (8) -- (8)
8M

FINIS

Did you notice?
    Rolling tplt into qdlt rhythm shading. Step Four, phrase 1
    Irish maxie variation. Step Five, phrase 1.

SOFT SHOE

This style offers an easy introduction to "adding something personal" to the tapping or by providing time to expand the presentation with prop handling, characterization, or partnering. Two examples, a romantic partnered duet for teens or older and a basic soft shoe with some rhythm shading, suitable for any age as solo, group, or duet. Seek a relaxed demeanor and extended body line, allowing the torso, arms, and head to gently sway or slightly twist. Exude ease.

STILL IN LOVE WITH AMY

A fluid (almost balletic) partnered romantic soft shoe, ideal as a duet but easily arranged for any number of couples. A young couple characterization, the G slightly coquettish, the B cautiously dominating.
"Once In Love With Amy" (Hoctor #1703), 4M intro, 2 choruses separated by 4M bridge, 4M fading tag, 115 met. Chor: Terry Dill

INTRO

4M Wait off S-L, G S-R and frt of B.

STEP ONE - ENTRANCE

(Face and trav C-S, d-A-s) flap-b/c R, (gpvn, face D-S, A's: B waist high, nat; G press low sd's, slight twist) flap L x bk R,
a1 a2 a3

2M b/c R x-over frt, (B: A's relaxed 2nd behind G) steps R rt - L x bk R, 2 R b/c x-overs frt - bk.
a4 5 6 a7 a8

2M (St A's 2nd, bend twd lead Ft) step lead paddle tr's R - L.
{1&a2&a3&a4} {5 - - - -8}

2M Rpt 1st 2M.

Brk: flap lead bk paddle tr R, (trav U-S) d-b's L-R-L, bk flap R, stamp fwd L.
2M {a1&a2&a3&a4 &a5 &a6 &a7 &a 8}
8M

Page 117

STEP TWO

|2M| Soft shoe ess comb R (relaxed A's 3rd frt, G ends tap R).
    &1&a2 &3&a4 &5&a6&a7&a8

|2M| B: ess's L - R, c-w bk paddle tr L (A's 2nd, bend lt) – G: rev.
    &1&a2 &3&a4 &5&a6&a7&a8 – 2M

NOTE: Next 4M, from rt-frt G moves lt-frt of B (M1-2), returns to rt-frt (M3), then slightly S-R (M4).
B: R shfl-hop-tpl x bk, rev as c-c-w tr (shift S-R) – G: rev &a1&a2&a3 shfl R x frt into R i/s piq tr shifting S-L to frt of B,
    &a 1 &a2 &a3&a4 -- &a 4

(scissor open A's) B: (→ D-S-R,) flap R – G: tt L x bk R, (→ D-S-L) step L, Both: 2 chugs, c/s fwd, rev comb from flap a5,
    a5 – a 5 a6 a7 a8 a1 a2 a3 a4

|4M| (p-d-b, P's rev shift, B → S-L behind G) steps x bk - sd, hop, step x frt, (scissor A's) B: lamp L l-d-f – G: stomp R r-d-f.
    5 6 a 7 **8** – **8**

|8M|

STEP THREE

|2M| (Face D-S, A's extended 3nd frt) bk ess's R - L, flap R x bk L (face D-S-R), low pend's L w/ hops bk-frt-bk (low o-A-s).
    a1a2 a3a4 a5 a6 a7 a8

|2M| Rev 2M.

|2M| (Face D-S, G L o-Hn on B R Hn, F twd raised leg during b/c's) bk ess comb R,
    a1a2 a3a4 a5a6a7a8

(G bk's under D-S arched A's – R n-Sh-p) shfl-hop-tpl L lt (B tpl x frt, shift rt ending G's bk-rt, joined Hn's at G's rt-frt waist),
    {&a 1 &a2

|2M| (→ D-S-R, pass G c-w tr) flap-heels R - L, hop L, jazz triangle R (G ends rt of B), buff starting pos L (link elbows, F P, smile).
    &a 3 &a4} (&)a 5 6 7 (8)

|8M|

STEP FOUR

|2M| (Face and → D-S-L) flap L, step R close-bk, small b/c L x-overs frt - bk, o/s flap L lt, br's R x bk - r-d-f - x frt ankle.
    a1 2 a3 a4 a5 6 7 8

|2M| Rev 2M.

(Face D-S-L, tap struts) Tap st L long x frt R (tilt bk), step L c-p (upright), rev tap, leap R into long tap L x frt R, rev leap-tap,
    1 2 3(&)a 4 5 &

|2M| rock into heel R (upright), scuff st L D-S-L (face D-S), bk flap L x frt R.
    6 (&) a (7) a8

|2M| Buff R, irish R x bk L, hop R, dig w/w L l-d-f, snap L, step R close-bk L, catch L (face D-S-R), rev dig-snap-step.
    1&a2 a3a4 {& 5 & 6 & 7 & 8}

|8M|

INTERLUDE

(Release elbows, G rt, strolling in personal c-w circ's) 6-tap riff walk R, 5-tap riff walk L (face U-S), ch R S-L,
    {&a1&a2 &a3}*(&)a4 5 6

(cont circ D-S) eccentric riff walk R, p-d-b L, b/c R x-overs bk - frt (face D-S, G frt of B),
    a7&a8 &1&a2 3 4 5 a6 a7

|4M| G: med swing kick R rt (slap R thigh) – B: rock R, rev kick-slap.
    & (8) -- (&) 8 (*note rhythm shading)

STEP FIVE

|2M| (G rev – B:) bk ess L, qdl R x bk L, 3-step tr L S-L (shift from behind G, catch G's L Hn in R), hold.
    &1&2 3&a4 5 6 7 (8)

(B: tendu R rt, pull\release G – G: step L into c-c-w tr, scuff R, hop L, step R D-S of B,
    & 1 a 2

G: step into Both: demi lunge L S-L (A's 2nd sloping dn-rt), hold, b/c R x bk - L c-p (face D-S-R, demi plié prep for lift),
    3 (4) & 5

|2M| G: high frt passé R (A's 3rd R) – B: close behind G (waist support), into frt lift, lower into demi lunge R S-R.
    (&) -- (5 6) 7 (8)

B: draw L c-p w/w, step R fwd D-S-R (fists on hips), pose, rock L a-s-t G: (→ D-S-R) i/s piq tr L, 2 ch's,
    (12) 3 (4 - 7) (8) – 1 (2) 34 56

|2M| step R into demi lunge S-R – tendu L lt (both jazz Hn's frt of R Sh), hold.
    7 (8)

G: pose – (B: → D-S-R) saut de basque R, step R, scuff st L low x frt R, R hop-over L,
    1&a 2 3 4

|2M| step L l-d-b (face D-S-L) – draw tendu R (A's slope dn-rt), rpt saut de basque-step ending frt of G.
    5 (6) 7&a 8

|8M|

STEP SIX

(Both: A's 2nd) G: side scissor kick L – B: (var) skip L x frt R, leap R S-R – st L lt (catch G's R Hn),
                         &1 2   –   &1   2

B: (pull\release G's Hn) draw L c-p (face S-R) – G: ch R twd B, flap-b/c R behind B (waist support, Both face S-R),
           (3 - - - 6)   –   34   &5 &6

(G: pulls B bkwd c-c-w circ) Both: 18 small runs (or patter steps) L lead, (face S-R, bend fwd, → bkwd S-L) 12 runs (end c-p).

4M   {&a7&a8 - - - - &a4   triplets   &a5&a6 - - - &a8}

(→ S-R) B: b/c L fwd, hold, G rpt, B: 2 b/c's, G rpt, Both: L d/c-b/c-d/c-b/c, 3 fwd low d-b's, br bk R, heel L, tt bk R.

4M   a1   (2)   a3(4)   a5a6 a7a8   a1 a2 a3 a4 {&a5&a6&a7 &   a   8}

8M

STEP SEVEN

(G close behind facing B, tilt bk strut style, G's o-Hn B's fore-A's, o-A-s w/ slight torso twist each tap) tap struts R-L-R-L,

2M   12 34 56 78

(G o-Hn's B, A's 2nd, bend twd each walk, c-w circ) 6 walks*, 2 walks* G (face D-S) – B (face U-S) into c-w tr (end behind G).

2M   (*exaggerated Castle Walk)   a1 a2 - - - a6   a7 a8   –   a7a8

(G frt, o-Hn's B, A's 2nd) fwd paddle tr R, bk paddle tr L. (NOTE: Retain ptnr's relative Ft pvt'g pos's

2M   &1&a2&a3&a4   &5 - - - - - 8   by making steps slightly diag frt or bk as needed.)

Brk: (release Hn's, during comb G shifts rt) ess R, bk flaps L-R x bk L into c-w tr, (→ S-L) i/s p-d-b tr (face D-S), b/a R-L lt.

2M   &1&a2   &3 &4   5 6 7   **& 8**

8M   (*NOTE: A step from the 1915 Castle Walk exhibition ballroom style created by Vernon and Irene Castle.)

STEP EIGHT

S-soft-shoe-t-s R, bk ess brk L, rev t-s.

4M   {1&a2&a3&a4} {a5 - - - &a4} {5&a6&a7&a8}

Soft-shoe-t-s-brk's R-L.

4M   {a1&a2&a3&a4}a&a5a6a7**&8** 2M

8M

TAG - EXIT

Flap R D-S-R, step L close-bk R, sluff o/s r-d-j R, b/c R-L (face U-S-L), (→ U-S-L) 5-tap riff walk R, flap L, b/c c-w tr.

2M   a1   2   &-3-&   a4   a5&a6   &7   &8

(G shifting rt x frt) c-w buff tr R, ch R, (G rt, B: bent R A frt, L Hn on G's L – G: L link B's R fore-A, R Hn on upper-A,

        1&a2   34

H tilts against B's upper-A or Sh), liesurely brush-step R, low frt leg swings into slow walks off stg (music fades).

2M   5   6   (- - - - -)

4M   (Try to feel romantic.)

FINIS

NEW SOFT SHOE

An upbeat soft shoe with expanded styling and a double time insert. A chance to "play with the audience". For small group or solo.
Music: 8M intro, 2 choruses, about 120 met. An example of Measures listed referencing music score.   Choreography: Terry Dill

Intro (arrange as desired)   **ENTRANCE**

4M   Wait off S-L. (For increased ent distance, wait 2M then rpt the following 2M.)

        (Facing and trav'g C-S w/ relaxed o-A-s) step fwd R, brush fwd L, skip L fwd, rpt comb, flap-b/c's R-L (d-A-s).

2M   (note even to duple rhythm shift)   &   1   &   2   &3 &4   a5 a6   a7a8

        Rpt ct's &1-6, (face D-S) stamp L.

2M   &1 - - - 6   **&** (78)

8M

Chorus (first)   **STEP ONE**

        Flap R r-d-f (sway rt), b/c L-R, rev, bk flaps R-L (Hn's near thighs), shfl R, hop L, 3 steps fwd R-L-R

        a1   a 2 a3a4   {a5&a   even rhythm   6&   a   7 & a

        (palms up, raise extended A's frt to waist height), scuff L frt (A's open).

M1-2   8}

M3-6   Rev above 2M 2 X's.

        Brk: Rev ct's a5 - - 8 of 1st 2M, hop L, sgr fwd R-L-R-L-R (alt opp'g slight press dn and Sh's isol frt).

M7-8   a1&a2&a3&a4   a   5 6 7 a 8

8M

STEP TWO

   Dbl-shfl L into irish L x frt R, 3 flap-b/c's R-L-R.
M9-10 {&a1& a2}   a3a4 a5a6 a7a8
   Paddle tr L (st A's 2nd, tilt lt), bk flaps R-L, o/s flap R rt, i/s flap L c-p, qdlt irish R x frt L.
M11-12 &1&a2&a3&a4 (note faster R flap)(&)ea{5& a6 &a 7&a8}
M13-16 Rpt above 4M making small c-w circ during 3 flap-b/c's.
 8M

STEP THREE

   Heel R, (p-d-b) steps L x bk R - R rt, t/o flap L x frt R, flap-heel R rt, flap L x bk R, br R rt into low o/s r-d-j, heel L,
    a   1 2 {a3 &a 4} &5 a (&)   6
   step R x bk L, rev br-heel-step.
M17-18 &   a(7)& 8 (or w/o sync'n: {&5&6&7&8})
M19-22 Rev above 2M 2 X's.
M23-24 Brk: Rev (lead R) STEP ONE brk.
 8M

STEP FOUR

   (Lead v-ess's w/ step) v-ess's R-L, (flap leads) dbl ess R, frt ess's L-R, trav ess L lt.
M25-28   1&a2 3&a4 &5&a6&a7&a8 a1&a2 a3&a4 a5&a6&a7&a8
   Flapped jazz triangles R-L, swinging flaps R-L.
M29-30 a1a2a3 a4a5a6   a7 a8
   S-soft-shoe-t-s R, qdlt irish L, flaps R-L, s/c R-L. (The last 2M is a soft-shoe-t-s-brk comb.)
M31-32 1&a2&a3&a4 a&a5 a6 a7 **& a** (note rhythm **&a** into STEP FIVE)
 8M

Chorus (repeat)   ## STEP FIVE

   (The 1st 6M of this Step are done dbl-X featuring buck t-s's.)
   S-t-s's R-L-R, fall L, trenches R-L-R, leap L.
M1-2 8&1-2&3& 4 - - - 3& 4   5 6 7 & (rhythm ct'd 4M at sgl-X.)
M3-6 Rpt above sustituting d-t-s's. Rpt t-s's substituting q-t-s's, sync-d-b-brk L ending stamp R, (clap). 4&5&a6&7&8
   Brk (normal tempo, face and → D-S-R): Flap-heel's L-R-L, (face D-S) b/c R x-over frt, br R into high balancoire rt,
           {&a 1 &a2 &a3}   a4 &
   (slap R thigh w/ R Hn), flap R x bk L, qdlt irish L x bk R.
M7-8 5   a6   {7&a8 (note cont'g even rhythm into STEP SIX)
 8M

STEP SIX

   (→ D-S-R) 3 flap-step's R to c-p, heel L, dig R, br bk R, heel L, shfl R, heel L, tt R x bk L, heel L, flap-b/c R.
M9-10   &a 1 &a2 &a3} a 4 & {5 &a 6 & a 7& a8
M11-12 Cont even rhythm into} Rev above 2M.
   Bk flap-b/c's R-L, bk paddle tr R (c-c-w).
M13-14 a1 a2 a3a4 &5&a6&a7&a8
M15-16 Rpt 2nd 2M of STEP TWO.
 8M

STEP SEVEN

   (Face D-S-L, gpvn → U-S-L) steps L lt - R x bk L, 2 b/c L x-overs lt frt - bk, sgl ess L,
            1 2   a3 a4 a5&a6
   step R rt, scuff fwd L into low o/s r-d-j, skip L x bk (face D-S-R).
M17-18 a 7   a8
M19-22 Rev 2M. Rpt 2M thru ct 6a, scuff fwd L into c-w pir, (face D-S) step L x frt R. 7 (8) &
   Brk: (maxie ford) Flap R rt, heel R, shfl L, leap L, tt R x bk L, rpt maxie segment, flap R rt, chug R, (clap).
M23-24   a1 {a 2& a 3} a4a5&a6 a7 **&a** **8** (2 accents)
 8M

STEP EIGHT

M25-30 Rev 1st 6M of STEP ONE.
   Brk: (Similar to STEP ONE) flaps bk R-L, shfl R, hop L, steps fwd R-L-R, scuff L x frt R into c-w tr, skip L (face D-S),
           {a1&a 2& a 3 & a 4} (&) a5
   step R rt, tt L x frt R (A's: L up – R fwd), nod H (F dn) – pose, (hold 3-5 seconds, F audience and smile).
M31-32 6 7   (8)
 8M

FINIS

SHIM SHAM

Next is a freestyle structured narrative "argument" version of a challenge routine, requiring a minimum of two sources of taps. A soloist can prerecord his "challenger" with his accompaniment and modify the ending (perhaps a dbl-X challenge); otherwise, any combination of soloists and/or Group(s) can be arranged. The following is staged for a Boy soloist and 2 Grp's of Girls.

SHIM IT UP

A comedy shim sham challenge for a Boy soloist and 2 Grp's of Girls initially divided and [hidden] U-S-R and U-S-L, off-stage, behind U-S drape, or in blackout with soloist in follow spot. Notes include characterization pantomime and staging.
2M intro, 2 choruses, 140-155 met.   Choreography: Terry Dill
NOTE: For STEP ONE and 2M of TWO use tpl's for shims and shams; i.e.; t-shim = tpl; t-sham = tpl, step, tpl.

ENTRANCE

+2M   Start before music: From off D-S-R B briskly walks twd D-S-C, as music bgn's B abruptly stops, looks S-L then S-R.

STEP ONE

2M   B: T-shim sham comb R (t-shim R, t-shim L, t-sham R).   8&1 2&3 4&5&6&7
        (Cock H rt then lt "listening"), t-shim R, 2 heels R, ("listen"), rev t-shim - 2 heels, (shrug), bgn walking S-L.
6M   (8 - - - 7)   8&1   2 3   (4 - -7)   8&1   2 3   (4 5)   (6 7)
 8M

STEP TWO

        [(1 G U-S-R) t-sham] – soloist (S-L of D-S-C) abruptly stops "startled", [G: t-shim, 2 heels].
2M   8&1&2&3   4&5   6 7
        B: (facing D-S-L, backing S-R, "listening" to locate challenge, bgn'g w/ digs) shims R-L, [(G U-S-R) 2 shims done quietly].
2M   8&1 2&3   4&5 6&7

        B: (more emphatically) shims R-L, [(G U-S-L) sham] – B "startled" quickly tr's and "looks" U-S-L seeing no one.
2M   8&1 2&3   4&5&6&7
        [U-S-R G: shim, 2 heels] – B (faces D-S, Hn at chin "brewing an idea", → D-S-C) 2 slow walks R-L.
2M   8&1   2 3   (4 - -   - - 7)
 8M

STEP THREE

        B: (→ S-R) stamp R rt (low scissor open A's), step L c-p (A's scissor x), rpt, step R rt, irish R x frt L, step R rt.
1 ct+2M   (8)   1   2   3 4 5   a6a7   8
2M   [U-S-R G: rpt above 2M (stamp step shim sham)].
4M   B: rev 2M, [U-S-L G: rpt B's 2M].
 8M+1 ct

STEP FOUR

        B: Irish maxie R
2M(-1ct)   8&1&2 3&4&5 6 (7) (Same ct 8 as above)
        [1 G U-S-R and U-S-L: irish maxie ending All G's: loud stamp] – B grins "satisfied" then "shaken" by stamp.
2M   8&1&2 3&4&5   6 (7)

        [U-S-R G: shim, 2 heels], [U-S-L G: shim, 2 heels] – *B backs twd U-S-C "looking" rt then lt.
2M   8&1   2 3   4&5   6 7   (See NOTE in STEP FIVE.)
        (G's appear U-S) B: c-r R, (c-w ½-circ to face U-S) o/s flap R, dig c-p L w/w, rpt flap-dig 2 X's,
            (8)   1&a2   {&a   3   &a   4 &a5
        ("discovers" G's) o/s flap R, abruptly stops and rock L – a-s-t – G's: (trav twd B) flap-b/c's R-L (d-A-s).
1 ct+2M   &a}   (6 - - - 8)   a5 a6   a7a8
 8M

STEP FIVE

        B: (still facing U-S, bk'g D-S) bk ess's R - L - R, bk ess L into c-c-w ½-tr a-s-t G's: (A's press dn sd's, trav S-R and S-L of B
                                a1a2 a3a4 a5a6   a7a8   –
        forming sgl horz line) 8 running flaps lead R (G nearest S-L of B ending about 4´ lt of B).
2M   a1 - - - a8
        (All face D-S, B looks confused) G's: flapped 3-step tr R, (G S-L of B taps his L Sh, beckons him to follow S-L) chug R S-R,
                                            a1 a2 a3   a4
        All rev flapped tr (consolidate line), catch R (face D-S-R).
2M-1 ct   a5 a6 a7   &

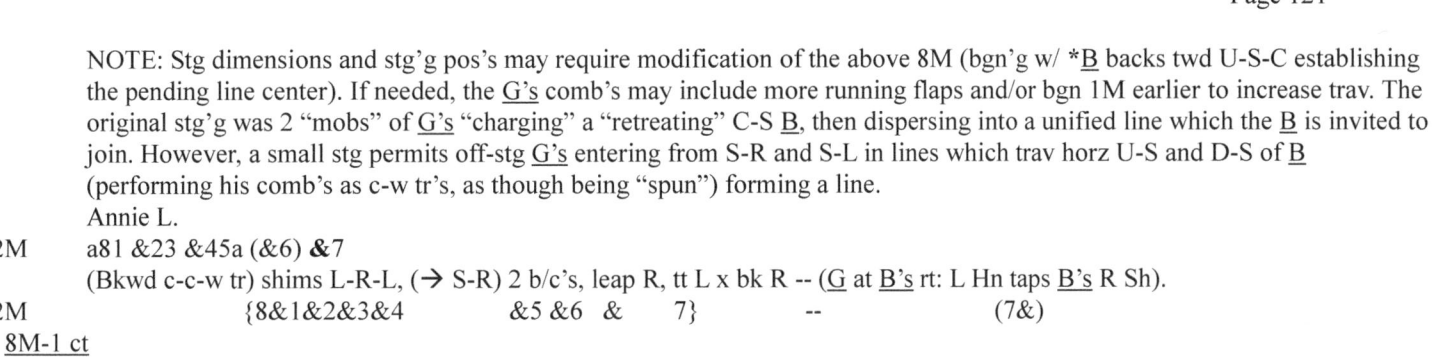

NOTE: Stg dimensions and stg'g pos's may require modification of the above 8M (bgn'g w/ *B backs twd U-S-C establishing the pending line center). If needed, the G's comb's may include more running flaps and/or bgn 1M earlier to increase trav. The original stg'g was 2 "mobs" of G's "charging" a "retreating" C-S B, then dispersing into a unified line which the B is invited to join. However, a small stg permits off-stg G's entering from S-R and S-L in lines which trav horz U-S and D-S of B (performing his comb's as c-w tr's, as though being "spun") forming a line.
Annie L.

2M   a81 &23 &45a (&6) **&7**
      (Bkwd c-c-w tr) shims L-R-L, (→ S-R) 2 b/c's, leap R, tt L x bk R -- (G at B's rt: L Hn taps B's R Sh).
2M   {8&1&2&3&4   &5 &6 &   7}   --   (7&)
8M-1 ct

STEP SIX

    (Challenge: B watches rt) S-R G's: L shfl-p-u-c-tt R x bk (present L A low twd B), B: rpt 1M (B ends F and A lt).
2M   a8 &a 1   (2 3)   a4&a5   (67)
    S-L G's: L shfl-d-p-u R x frt, L shfl-p-u-c-tt R x frt (present R A rt), B: R shfl-p-u-c-tt L x bk, hip wing R,
         a8 &&a1   a2 &a 3   a4 &a 5   a&a
    tt L x frt, rpt wing w/ step x bk (face S-L), hold.
2M   6   a&a   7   (8)
    (Counting G's from S-R Grp I are odd numbers Grp II are evens. Grp I lead L shift behind Grp II, Grp II and B lead R, Grp II shift x frt, B trav's D-S\U-S) 2 cubanolas (opp shifts alt'g dir's).
4M   8&1&2&3&4 5 6&7&   8 - - - 7&
8M

STEP SEVEN

    (Still opp'g leads, bkwd tr) br x bk into t-t-s, (G's close as pairs – B D-S or merge as ptnr if short a G) t-stomp-wm-t-s - brk,
                8   1&a2&3&   **4**&5&a6&7a&a 8&1&2&3
    (Face D-S) Grp I clap, All (Grp I shift x frt, Grp II behind, F twd ptnr): side scissor kick, eagle rock (low scissor A's last 1M,
4M+1 ct   4   &5   6 &7 &8
    merge B, into tiller line, tiller A's 2nd).
    NOTE: The above 8M stg'g requires practice. If dancers are widely spaced on a wide stage, oscillate pairs twd\away (no shift), gradually closing spacing, during last 4M of STEP SIX. Last 4M STEP SEVEN can bgn w/ Hn's on adjacent wrists, then, during triangles, move up A's to Sh's consolidating line.
    (All tiller:) heel (or rock snap) L into strut R x frt L, rev 2 X's (on last step bend fwd), (st'n to upright during jazz traingle)
                   1 -- 1   2   34 56
    steps L l-d-b - R r-d-b.
2M   7   8
2M   Rev 2M substituting low snap kicks for passés.
8M

STEP EIGHT

    High frt batt into step c-p R-L-R-L (last step // slight plié), 4 bounce kicks R-L-R-L.
4M   (1)   2   (3)4(5)6(7)   8   12 34 56 78
    (S-R G's R lead, S-L G's L, G's step x bk and trav bk, B steps c-p and remains i-p:) bounce kick x frt into o/s high r-d-j to
                                                                                            1
    open frt diag (almost 2nd) into jump, rev 3 X's.
2M   2   34 56 78
    (G's trav horz twd nearest exit as D-S drape and lighting lower) Rpt above 2M stepping 2nd then x bk (S-R G nearest B
2M   1 - - - 8
8M   notices B still kicking C-S, runs to him, grabs his R A, yanks and hauls him running twd off S-R as music fades and drape closes w/ blackout).

FINIS

RHYTHM

Of the five basic tap styles (including waltz clog, buck, soft shoe, and shim sham) rhythm is the most diverse, permitting a broad range of creative interpretation. The following are an example; the first routine being a more flamboyant styling, the second a sophisticated rhythm project. Although up-tempo, the primary objective is interesting rhythm sequences. Begin at a moderate tempo. Increases must include accurate rhythmics.

SHOWOFF

Suitable for solo or small group, a moderate tempo mix of buck (even and duple rhythm) and syncopated Steps with rhythm shading, flash inserts, and a few surprises. For those interested, a detailed example of *verbal combinations* is included. If used, adjust to your needs.

Intermediate rhythm-buck staged for a small group (6-10) beginning in a single horz line. Rhythm clarity is essential, especially during interlocking phrases. To improve music/count recognition, try rehearsing Groups sequenced separately then interlocked.
Music: Intro, 2 choruses, 130-140 met.   Choreography: Terry Dill
(The ent and 1st phrase STEP TWO taken from GONE TAPPING by Louis A. Crescenta.)

INTRO

?M   Wait off S-L or preset U-S-C.

STEP ONE - ENTRANCE

(Enter or trav D-S to C-S.)
Flap R, b/c L-R (d-A-s rt), rev, flap R, tt L x bk R (Hn's n-Sh-p), step L (F and reach dn-lt), b/c R bk-L i-p (F and reach up-rt).
2M   a1   a 2   a3a4 a5   a   (&6)   a   (&7&)   a   8
Fl ap ball change, fl ap ball change, fl ap toe, step, ball change.
4M   Rpt above 2M 2 X's.
Re peat a2, fl ap a4 a5 a wait, a wait, a8.
Last time ball change, a left ball change, flap toe step, face down.
Brk: (Face D-S) leap R. riff L x frt R, heel R, step L x frt R, heel L, step R rt, rev 1M.
2M   {a   1&   a} (2&)   a (3&)   a   4 {a5&a}(6&)a(7&)a8
<u>8M</u>   *Leap r iff heel, step, heel step, <u>reverse</u> r iff heel, right, heel left.*

STEP TWO

Bk flap R, heel R, shfl L, heel R, step L x frt R, heel L, step R rt, heel R, steps L lt - R x frt L, heel R, step L lt, s/c o-p R-L
           a1   {a   2&   a   3}   a   4   a   5   &   6   &   (7)   **a 8**
2M   (A's scissor open fwd R then L).
Fl ap, heel shuf fle, heel step, heel step, heel step step, heel step, right left.
(During the following 6M alt'g dancers trav into 2 staggered lines, shift 1 dancer, then merge into 1 line.
Counting from S-R, <u>Even</u> numbered performers trav bkwd ct's &1 --5, <u>Odd</u> numbered fwd ct's a3 --5)
(Trav as needed) cinc R, flap-b/c L, flap R, L shfl-p-u-c-tt R x bk L, b/c R-L.
2M   &1&a2   a3 a 4   a5   a6 &a 7   a 8
Right cin cin na ti, two lines ball change, fl ap, shuf fle pick up toe, ball change.
2M   (<u>Odd</u> trav S-L, <u>Even</u> S-R opposing shift staggered lines) rpt 1st 2M changing stepping dir's as needed.
Fl ap, heel shuffle, move side, heel step, heel stag ger, heel step, stamp change
2M   (Original <u>Odd</u> bkwd, <u>Even</u> fwd merging line) rpt 2nd 2 M.
<u>8M</u>   *Cin cin na a ti, re merge ball change, fl ap, shuf fle pick up toe, ball change.*

STEP THREE

Buff R, irish R x bk L, flap L, leap R – st L lt, step L x bk R, stamp R.
2M   1&a2   a3a4   a5 & (6)   & (7)   **& (8)**
Buf fa lo right, i rish cross back, fl ap, leap, step, stamp.
2M   Rev 2M.   *Left buf fa lo, i rish cross back, fl ap, & (6) & (7) stamp.*
(→ S-L) trav'g bandy twist R, (face and trav S-R) flap R, fwd d-b's L-R.
2M   12a3a4   {&5   &6& 7&8}
Bandy twist shuf fle ball change, fl ap, left for ward, right for ward.
(→ bkwd in c-w circ, end facing D-S) 7 d-b's lead L, b/a R - L lt.
2M   {&a1 - - - &a7}   **a 8**
<u>8M</u>   *Draw-back left, six more two, and a three, and a four, (etc.), break left.*

STEP FOUR

Hop L, step R, flap L, step R, s-t-s L,   R t-t-s - brk.
4M-1 ct   1   2   &3   &   4&56&7&   8&1&a2&3& - 4&5&6&7
Hop step, fl ap step, sin gle time left fl ap step, tri ple time one-two-three fl ap break, shuf fle hop fl ap ball change.

(Interlocking t-s's next 4M: <u>Even</u> begin ct 8, <u>Odd</u> ct 1)
S-stomp-t-s R, t-t-s L, fwd scuff R into o/s r-d-j into c-w tr, hop L, cramp R x bk L, step L c-p, (clap). stamp fwd R D-S-R,
   8 & 12&3&   4&5&a6&7&   8   1   2&   3   &   **4**
Stomp right hop <u>single</u> flap step, triple time on the left and end it, scuff, hop, cramp step clap, stamp,
step L i-p, qdlt irish R x bk L, step L D-S – (<u>Odd</u> end:) shfl R, hop L (All face S-R).
4M   5   {a6&a   7}   –   &7   &

<u>8M-1 ct</u> *step, quick irish, step, <u>face right</u> (&).*

STEP FIVE

(<u>All</u>: → U-S) s-t-s R w/ i/s slide "hop", s-t-s L, 2 bmb's R, 4 trenches R-L-R-L (o-A-s).
4M   8&12&3&   4&56&7&   a81 &23   4 5 6 7
Single slide step the-first/one, single left six and seven and, travel up, and again, trench two three four.
D-t-s R, (→ D-S) d-t-s w/ slide L, 2 baby bmb's R, (slow ¼-tr c-c-w to D-S) 4 trenches R-L-R-L (2 o-A-s's, 2 d-A-s's), (clap).
4M+1ct 8&1&2&3&   4&5&6&7&   81 23   4 5 6 7   8
<u>8M+1ct</u> *Right and one double a time step, left and slide down stage (&7&), stamp step, one more, trench turn down stage.*

STEP SIX

(Volume and mvmt shade the 1st 4M. Bgn w/ soft taps and minimized mvmt's, building to widening swings-tr-clap-stamp.)
(R forefinger near lips = "shshshsh" thru ct 4) f-r-c R rt, br bk L, heel R, tt L x bk R, heel R, rev comb,   step R.
2M   (Note rhythm shift.){&1&2   &   3   &   4} {a5&a6} a7(&)a 8
Soft flap roll change, brush heel toe heel, reverse syncopate, heel toe, heel step.
Hop R into rolling wing change L lt, swinging flap R x bk L, rev flap, swinging flap R x bk L into c-w tr,
      &   a1&a2   a3   a4   a5
Hop a rolling wing change, swing flap, two more, turn right,   (For an effective contrast, the amplitude increase
L shfl-d-p-u R x bk L (face D-S), (loud clap), stamp L lt.   requires some experimentation.)
2M   a6 &a7 (&)   **a**   **8**
shuffle pick up back, clap stamp.
Br bk R, heel L, riff R x frt L, heel L, step R x frt L, heel R, step L lt, leap R rt, rev riff-heel-step-heel-step.
2M   {a   1   &a   2}   3   (&)   a   4   {5   &a 6} 7(&) a   8
Brush heel, riff heel, step, heel step, leap riff reverse, step, heel step.
(During the next 2M each dancer trav's and twists "randomly" then returns to original stg pos)
L lead 16 patter steps (vibrate Hn's, A's jazz 2nd), (clap), step L, scuff R[*].
2M   1&a - - - &a6   &(7)   &   8
<u>8M</u> *Patter roll 2&a (etc.) 5&a done, clap, step scuff.*
[*]NOTE: This phrase can become a brief comedic interlude of dancer personalities; e.g., robot, losing balance fwd\bkwd, "mechanical" rev'g tr's, circ'g finger-tip-gripped ptnr's, bumping butts (especially coy <u>G</u> to surprised <u>B</u>), etc. Have some fun.

STEP SEVEN

(→ S-R, c-w tr's) piq tr R w/ tt L x bk, b/c tr R-L c-p (face D-S-R), chug both 2 X's, scuff L, skip L x bk R, rev skip.
2M   1   & 2   a3   a4   a5   a(6)   a7   a8
Turn toe land, ball change, two chugs, scuff, skip back, again.
(→ S-L) step L lt, tt R x bk L (st A's 2nd, bend lt, spot dnwd D-S) into 3 c-w trav'g barrel turns, (upright) c-w dbl o/s pir
            1   &   2 & 3&4 &5&   (67)
to face S-L) b/c R-L.
2M   a 8
Step toe barrel, two barrel, third turn, <u>double pirouette</u>, ball change.
(→ bkwd S-R) dbl-shfl-p-u-c's R-L, 8 shfl-p-u-c's R-L-R-L-R-L-R-L, (trav D-S) R flap-shfl-p-u-c-tt c-w tr, step R rt D-S.
4M   {&a1&a2 &a3&a4}   {a&a5 - - a&a4}   &5 a6 & a 7   & (8)
<u>8M</u> *Double shuffle pick change, second time (&a4), shuffle a change, and two, three, four, (speak thru seven), down stage,*
flap shuffle pick up toe, step.

STEP EIGHT

2M   (Face S-L, → U-S) rev 1ST 2M of STEP SEVEN (remember to change facing diag to U-S-L).
Up stage turn ball change, chug chug, scuff hop step, skip back.
(Face S-L, → bkwd S-R) lead L 7 running d-p-u-c's, fwd br R, s-p-u L.
2M   {&a1 - - - &a7}   &   a8
Running double changes, travel back, and a four, (etc.), and seven, brush pick up.
Fall R D-S (face D-S) – st L l-d-b, steps L x bk R - R rt - L lt, tt R x bk L into c-w tr, hop L, steps R-L (face D-S).
2M   1   (2)   3   4   5   &   (6)   a   7 8
Fall, hold, back side side, turn hop step step.

8 shfl-p-u-c's lead R (d-A-s).
2M   {a&a1 - - - a&a8}
Shuffle and change, a&a2, and three, and four, (thru seven), now break.
Brk (shave and a haircut var): lamp R r-d-f, L shfl-d-p-u R x bk L, step L, scuff R, heel L, tt R x frt L (A's low jazz 2nd
                1   {a2 &a3}   4 (5)   a   6   7
Shave a and a hair cut, scuff heel done.
w/ palms up), (shrug – tilt H rt – smile) pose.
2M   (8)
8M

FINIS

RHYTHM FILL

This is a rhythm study in a sophisticated style requiring low, close ankle control when up-tempo. Carefully interpret the rhythm. Many sequences are tricky, but may encourage soloist experimentation. Many phrases are not notated. Complete {_____} them. Don't just "plug in" steps. Dance the phrases, seeking comfortable, interesting combinations. The objective is not to duplicate the presented combinations, rhythms, or staging; but to use these as a foundation concept from which to build a routine you would enjoy performing or watching. Especially, experiment with the rhythms, mixing rhythm types, vary sound qualities and accents, and/or shifting clusters. Change the notes as you see fit. Begin at a medium tempo, then increase as desired. Listen to the results. Enjoy the exploration. Music: 2 chords, 16M intro, 2 choruses, exit of desired length, 120-160 met.   Choreography: You and Me

EXTENDED INTRO - ENT

(Ent U-S-L, R Hn on hip, a relaxed Coles stroll c-c-w spiral arcing C-S-R to D-S-C then C-S-L to U-S-C then vert to D-S-C. First 10M: each 2 ct R lead walking comb is alt'd 4 X's = 2M.)
   Dig-snap (walk), scuff-walk   , scuff R, heel L, walk R, (free R Hn) 5-tap riff walk, (→ C-S) 6-tap riff walk (last a 5-tap).
10M 1   2 3 - - - 8 &   12 - - - 8 &   a   12 - - 8   {1&a2}& - - 8&   {a1&a2& - - - - - - a7&a8
(Face and trav D-S-C) dbl riff walks R-L.
2M   &a1&a2&a3&a4 - - - 8}
(→ rt S-R) step-heel R, alt x frt - rt - x frt, cont stg'g w/ flap-heel R-L, o/s flap R, tap L c-p, (clap).
2M   1(&) a   2(&)a 3(&)a 4(&){a   5& a 6&a   7& a   8}
(→ lt S-L) br L lt, heel R, step L lt, scuff R x frt L, heel L, step R x frt L, f-r-c L lt, rpt scuff-heel-step, f-r-c L lt, bk br R, heel L,
      {1   &   a   2   &   a   3&a4   &   a 5} a&a6   {&   a
step R x bk L, scuff L lt, heel R, step L lt.
2M   7   &   a   8
16M

STEP ONE

Qdl R x bk L, (face S-R) stomp L frt S-R, bk flap L, (irish w/o hop:) shfl R x frt L, heel L, step R x frt L, stamp L D-S-L
   &a1}a   (&)   **2**   3a   &4   &   5   **6**
(scissor open L A, face D-S-R), steps R x bk L - (face D-S) L lt.
2M   7   8
I/s flap R, scfl L lt, heel R, tt L x frt R, heel R, _____.
2M &a   1&   2 &   3
S/c fwd L-R, b/c bkwd L-R, scfl-step L, scfl-cramp R, scuff L, heel R, (→ r-d-b) bk flap L x frt R, cramp R,
   a 1   a 2 &a 3   &a 4a   &   a   5&   a6
bk flap-heel L x frt R, scuff R frt, heel L, bk flap-heel R x frt L.
2M a& a   7   &   a8 &
2M _____.
8M

STEP TWO

(Face D-S, → S-L) shfl R x bk L, b/c R-L, step-heel R x frt L, f-r-c L lt into c-w tr, br R x bk L, skip R x bk, scuff L D-S
2M   a1   a2   3 4   a5&a   6 (&)   a7 (&) a (8)
2M into o/s r-d-j. Rev above 2M w/o r-d-j.
Stomp R frt, 2 heels L – draw R c-p, heel L, dig R, _____.
2M **1**   2 3   a   4
B/c R-L, (clap), _____, s/c (or stamp, stomp).
2M a 1   2
8M

STEP THREE

2M　　Heel L, (→ S-R) <u>any bmb R</u>,_____.
　　　　　&

2M　　Lamp L, step R c-p, step L x frt, scuff R r-d-f, (face D-S-R) c-r R, scuff R, heel L, t/i stamp R fwd, 6-tap bmb L, (clap),
　　　　　　1　2　　&　　3　　　　　　&a4a　　　&　　a　　　5　　　　　　&a6&a 7　&
　　　　fall into stamp L lt.　**8**

4M　　Rev 4M.
<u>8M</u>

STEP FOUR

2M　　C-r R, h-t's into snaps R-L rt,_____.
　　　　　1&a2　　　　　　3　4

2M　　_____.

2M　　Flap-heel L, tt R x bk L, heel L, flap-heel R, tt L x bk R, chug R, step L close-bk R, scuff R.
　　　　　a1　2　a　(&)　3　　a4　5　　6　　　　　&7　(&) a　　　　　　　　8

2M　　(C-w tr) bk flap R, 2 b/c's, (→ S-L or c-c-w small circ) fall L, close riff R, step L lt, rpt riff-step 3 X's,
　　　　　　　　&1　　a2 a3　　(4)　　　　　　　　　&　　　　{5a　　&　　a6a &a7 a&a} (8)
<u>8M</u>

STEP FIVE

2M　　T/o snaps R-L into 10-tap pigeon-toe roll to 2nd, scoot both c-p into standing heel clip, both chug, R d-p-u-tt R, (clap).
　　　　　　　　1 &　　　a2&a3&a　　　　　　4-&　　　　　　　　a　　e5　a6&a 7　　&　(8)

2M　　F-r-c R rt, step L c-p, s-r R rt, (→ S-L) bk flap-heel R x bk L, step L lt, low d-b (w/ heel, not hop) R x bk L, fwd low d-b L l-d-f.
　　　　　{a1&a　　2}　　&3&4　　　　　　&5　&　　　　6　　　　　　　　{&a7　　　　　　　　　　　&a8}

2M　　Flap-heel R x frt L, step L D-S-L, chug L,_____.

2M　　(Your rhythm.)

2M　　Brk:__(Visually different styling.)_____.
<u>8M</u>

STEP SIX

　　　　Shfl L x frt R, heel R, flap L D-S-L (into c-c-w paddle tr var:) R shfl-b/c o-p, scuff R, heel L, step R o-p, step L,
　　　　　{1&　　　　　a　　2&}　　　　　　　　　　　　　　　　3& a 4　　　&　　5　　&　　{a

　　　　rpt scuff-heel-step, heel R, step L, R shfl-b/c o-p (face D-S).
2M　　　　6　a　　&　a　　7　　a& a 8}

2M　　Hold, stomp R D-S, draw R c-p, heel L, dig R, bk flap R, rev heel-dig-flap, dig R w/w, (→ S-L) o/s flap L, step R c-p, stamp L.
　　　　　(1)　　**&**　　　(2)　　&　　3　　&a　　4　&　5&　a (6)　　　　　　&a　　7　　**&** (8)

2M　　_____.

2M　　_____.

2M
<u>8M</u>

STEP SEVEN

2M　　_____.

2M　　_____.

　　　　(Trav lt U-S-L) i/s flap R, step L lt, rpt flap-step 2 X's, (trav c-c-w small circ) close riff R, step L, rpt riff-step (face U-S),
　　　　　　　　　{&a　　1　　　&a　2　&a3　　　　　　　　　　　　　　&a　　4　　　&a 5

　　　　br bk R, heel L, step R x bk L (face S-R), stamp L lt D-S, step R x bk L (face D-S).
2M　　　　&　　a　　6}　　　　　　　　　　　　　**&**　　　(7)　　　&　(8)

　　　　(→ S-L) o/s flap L, step R x bk L, b/c R x-over bk, 5 runs L lt - R x bk L - cont L-R-L, scuff R into o/s r-d-j
　　　　　　　　&a　　1(&)　　　　2&　　　　　　　{3　&　　　　a 4 &　　a}

　　　　and slow o/s pir L – R frt to 2nd, (face D-S-L) chug L, cramp R close-bk L, scuff L.
2M　　　　　　　(5　6)　　　　　　　　　　　　　　a7　　　&a　　　　　8
<u>8M</u>

Page 125

STEP EIGHT

(→ bkwd U-S-C) skip L bk, scuff R, hop L, cramp bk R, fall L x frt into b-t c-c-w tr, step L 2nd S-L, scoot both Ft into
                                  &1   a   &   2&   3   4 {&a5a   &} (6)   &

heel clip, (clap).

2M   7   & (8)   (From here it's all yours.)

2M _____.

2M _____.

2M _____.

2M _____.

8M

EXIT

(Perhaps a Coles stroll, exiting U-S-R. Including hop, c/s, fwd\bkwd rocks will vary the visual quality from the ent. Perhaps end with a wave to the audience.)

FINI

IRISH CLOG

There are many traditional national clog styles which have been interpreted as tapping. Irish Step Dancing includes distinctive steps - there's a reason it's called an irish - rhythms, and combinations which evolved into tap steps. The following composition offers a glimpse into that evolution and subsequent variations. Although not authentic, STEPS ONE - THREE reasonably depict how folk dance can be the possible source of tap steps. Each first occurrence is noted in braces {}, the term thereafter being used.

WILD-n-IRISH

Irish Step Dance clog style (a jig) transitions to syncopated swing, a contrast of rigid-torso precision with freestyling.
NOTE: Most jigs are $^6/_8$ meter. The following dance notation is $^4/_4$, notated 1 ct (&a1) per musical 3 ct's, 2 notation ct's = 1 M of $^6/_8$, 1 dance M = 2M of $^6/_8$. A $^6/_8$ music phrase is 4M (notated 2M, a Step phrase) requiring 4 phrases (16M of $^6/_8$) per Step. 8 Steps require 128M (2 choruses of 64M) of jig. Be forewarned, there will be many triplets.

Music: 2-4M intro, 2 64M choruses of any traditional Irish jig, about 120-130 met.   Choreography: Terry Dill

If a custom music arrangement is possible, it may be more interesting with a swing style bridge beginning the last 2 ct's of STEP THREE, then returning to traditional jig the last 2M of STEP EIGHT.

INTRO

2-4M   (Preset horz line facing U-S) Pose (Irish stance): upright, Ft // 1st (A's st, dn along sd's, flat Hn's palms in, horz F usually frt). This traditional stiff upright body, t/f // legs, arched Ft lifted low bk or frt (not x'g), sharply separated pos's, and most steps performed w/o trav is generally maintained thru STEP THREE.

STEP ONE

Hop L – lift R 90° bent knee hip high frt, steps R bk - L i-p, br's fwd-bk R {shfl}, hop L, step bk R {irish} into
    &   1   2   &   a   3   4

c-w ½-pivot (face D-S), step-heel {cramp} L, irish w/ high knee R, step L, stamp R c-p.
2M   5   &   6&a7 {qdlt irish}   &   8

Heel R, tap L frt, heel R, step L c-p {tap strut}, rev comb, heel R, shfl-steps {tpl} L-R, stamp L, step R rt {b/a}, rpt stamp-step.
2M   &   1   &   2   &3 {&a   4   &a5   &a6} **&**   7   **&**   8

Leap L, steps R-L {b/c}, heels R-L {c-r}, scuff R (knee 90°), step bk R, hop R, step bk L, scuff R, hop L, tt bk R, hop L, step R c-p.
2M   1   &2   &a   3   4   &   5   6   &   7   &   8

Dig L, br bk L, hop R, step bk L {d-b}, rev br-hop-step, dig w/w L, step R, heel R, tt bk L, heel R, step L, heel L, R t/o tt x frt.
2M   1   &   2   &   3 & a   4   5   &   6   &   7   &   8

8M

STEP TWO

2M Scuff R rt into leap ending b/c R-L (face S-R), scuff R, bk br-step {flap} R, scuff L, br bk L {scuffle}, shfl L, heel R, stamp L.
    1   & 2   3   & 4   5   &   6& 7   8

2M Shfl R, hop L – high knee R, heel L, step R, qdlt irish L, br frt R, hop L, tt R bk, hop L, step R (face D-S), rev br-hop.
    1&   a   2   &   3&a4   5   &   6   &   7   & 8

2M Step L, tpl R, qdlt-irish-heel L, tpl R, tpl-heel {qdl} L, 2 flap-heel R - L.
    {1 &a2 &a3& a   4&a 5&a 6   &a 7   &a8}

Stomp frt R, br bk R into leap {catch} – lift L Ft bk (knee bent), br frt L i-p into catch – st R low-frt, dig R, bk flap-heel {shim} R,
    1   2   &   3   &   4   &5 {&

rev dig-flap-heel, shfl-b/c R.
2M   a 6&   a   7&a8}
8M

STEP THREE

2M Leap R, t/i tt L lt, hop R, t/o dig L lt, hop R – high t/f knee L, step // L x frt R, b/c i-p R-L, hop L into rev 1M (ending // 1st).
    &   1   &   2   &   3   &4 &   5 - - - 8

2M Shfl L, hop R, tt bk L, heel R, scuff frt L, hop R, tpl L, rev 1M.
    1&   a   2   &   3   &   4&a 5 - - - 8&a

2M Shims L - R, qdlt irish L, flap R, shfl L, hop R, (→ and F lt) 2 b/c x-overs frt.
    {1&a 2&a 3&a4} &5 &a 6   &7 &8

2M Jumps 2nd - c-p, hop L, br-scuff {riff} R, hop L, tt bk R, (→ and F rt) 2 b/c x-overs frt, (clap, F D-S), legomania R (r-r A's).
    1   2   &   a 3   &   4   &5 &6   &   (7&8&)
8M

STEP FOUR

2M (Freestyle, → lt) p-u-irish R x bk L, L shfl-d-p-u R x frt, L shfl-p-u-c-tt R x bk, hop L into leg spin R (A's 2nd), rpt &7.
    1a&a2   a3 &a 4   a5 &a 6   &   7   &8

2M (Nat A's, → rt) hop L, rolling wing chg R, trav'g rock'n R heel-toe-heel, (2 claps), b/c 2nd L-R, i/s d-p-u R ending c-p.
    &   a1&a2   3   4   5   &6   & 7   a&a8

Scuff R, heel L, (c-w p-d-b tr) 2 step-heels R-L - step R x frt, 2 sliding irishes L-R, scuff L x frt R into slow i/s pir, step L,
    & (1)   2   3   &   4& 5   a6a7   a8a1   &   (2-3)   &

f-r R x bk L into c-w tr, bk flap R (finishing 2nd tr), step L 4th frt (prep A's) into dbl o/s pir (4 accelerating tr's total).
4M   4&a5   &6   &   (7-8)
8M

STEP FIVE

2M Leap R, dig L lt, hop R, t/i tt L lt, leap L, t/i tt R rt, hop L, dig t/o R rt, d-b R, d-b w/ p-u L, d-b R, catch L.
    1   &   2   &   3   &   4   &   5&a   6&a   7&a   8

B/c 2nd R-L, trav-c-r R i-p, (→ rt) R snap lead 8-ct pigeon-toe roll, d-p-u R - L x bk, hip wing L into tt R x bk L,
    & 1   ea&a2   {&a3&a4&a   5&a   6   &a7}   a

hip wing L, step R x frt L.
2M   &a8   a

(C-c-w eddie leonard to U-S) scuff L lt, b/c L x-over bk, (→ l-o-d) leap L into c-c-w tr, riff R,
    1   a2   3   &a

dig R w/w into ½ heel spin, piq tr L l-o-d, heel L, i/s p-d-b R. Rpt 2M completing U-S ½-circ (face U-S).
4M   4   (5) 6 (&)   a   7&8   2M
8M

STEP SIX

(→ D-S portion of eddie leonard w/ c-w tr's) leap L l-o-d into tr, tpl R (finishing tr), rpt leap-tpl tr's 2 X's, step L l-o-d,
    1   &a2   3 &a4 5&a6   &

br bk R into c-w tr, high hop L, step R.
2M   a   (7)   &   8

2M Rpt above 1st M, rpt 2 X's ct's &a(7)&8 (finishing eddie leonard, face S-L). 1&a2 3&a4 &a(5)&6 &a(7)&8

2M (Irish stance) qdlt irish L, chug both 2 X's, qdlt irish R (½-tr c-w, face S-R), scoot both 2 X's w/ separated heels L-R.
    1&a2   a3   a4   5&a6   &a7   &a8

(Nat stance, twisting gpvn → S-R) irish L x frt R (face D-S-R, → U-S-R), step R rt, qdlt irish L x bk R (face D-S-L),
    &1&2   &   3&a4

(cont alt'g twists, → D-S-R) 2 b/c x-overs, d-p-u R - L x frt, R d-p-u-c-tt L x bk.
2M   a5   a6   a&a   7   a&a   8
8M

STEP SEVEN

(→ lt) 3 c-r's L, scuff L lt into c-r, hop R, dig w/w L x frt R, step R rt – t/o h-t L, shortys bk L-R (A's jazz 2nd, vibrate).
2M   e&a1 e&a2 e&a3   &   4a&a(5) &   6   &   7 8

Flapped shorty bk L, saut de basque R, tt R x bk L, step R S-R, tpl L x bk R, cinc R x bk L (face D-S-L),
          &1   2 & 3   &   4   &a5   &6&a7

(→ D-S-L) 2 runs into R toe slide – L high knee frt (A's over-H).
2M+1 ct   8&   1

Fall frt L into c-w tr, p-d-b snap finish tr R, lamp L l-o-d, (→ u-l-o-d) step bk R, d-b L, d-b R w/ p-u, rpt 2 d-b's,
        2   3   a4   & (5)   &   6&a 7   a&a 8&1 a&a2

(Face D-S) pend L bk into wing R, fwd pend wing, bk pend L into wing chg, br R S-R into slide S-R, fall R, fwd flap L x frt R.
4M-1 ct   3   a&a   4a&a   5   a&a   6   7   &   a8
8M

STEP EIGHT

Step R, shfl L, catch L – dev R x frt, log glide R into c-w tr, shfl-b/c R (finishing tr).
2M   1   &2   &   3&a4(5)6   &7 &8

(→ bkwd U-S) 2 slow bkwd sluefoot R-L, 2 sluefoot into heel R-L, o/s r-d-j R – heel L, flap R x bk L rev &a7.
2M   1-2 3-4   &5 &6   (&) --   &   a7   &a8

P-u-irishes R-L x bk, flap fwd R, step L c-p bk, rpt flap-step 3 X's ending // 1st (A's moving to sides, torso stiffening).
2M   a1&a2 a3&a4 {&a   5   &a 6   &a7 &a8}   (style transition)

("Irish stance" and style) hop L, qdlt irish R bk, skip bk L, step fwd R, step fwd L into c-w ½-pivot (face U-S-L),
                                 1   &2&a (3)   &a   4   5

step R c-p (INTRO pose, F twd audience over R Sh), (knee pop: quick t/o p-r R), (informal salute L Hn twd S-L -- wink R eye).
2M   6   (7)   (8)   (1)
8M

FINI

IT'S AN ORIGINAL

A probably 1940s example of routine notes which include tap step names with descriptions. Most notes include no notated definitions, sometimes one or two. These notes offer a unique insight into an effort to create and clarify terminology.

"SCALAN SYNCOPATIONS
A fast buck
created by
Fran Scanlan

      Scanlan Traveling Time Step,
Shuffle R, hop L, shuffle R, ball-change R-L
 8   &   1   &   2   &   3
Shuffle R, Hop L, step R (cross behind), shuffle L, step L.
 4   &   5   6   &   7   &
Repeat all two more times on the same foot. Follow with the Break.

      The Irish Buck Break.
Shuffle R, hop L, step back R, shuffle L, hop R, step back L,
 8   &   1   &   2   &   3   &
Shuffle R, hop L, shuffle R, step R, shuffle L, step L.
 4   &   5   &   a   6   &   a   7

      Scanlan's Slide Combination.
Hop L, shuffle R, hop L, tap R toe in back
 8   a   &   a   1
Repeat to the counts 2a&a3
Turn a quarter turn to the right and drop L heel to the floor, flap R
                                     4   & 5
fwd, drop R heel, flap L fwd., drop R heel, flap L back,
       6   &7   8   &1
drop L heel, cross right foot in front of left, slide back on
    2   3   4
right foot, leap fwd. onto left, shuffle R back, tap left back,
             5   & 6   &

land on right foot, tap left toe back.
 a   7
Repeat all on the same foot.

    Scanlan's Syncopated Jette.
Shuffle L, hop R, shuffle L, step L, flap fwd. R, flap fwd. L,
 8 &   1   & a   2   & 3   & 4
ball-change R-L, shuffle L, leap to right foot, tap left toe back.
 &   5   & 6   &   7
Tap left foot fwd. while making a quarter turn to the left, hop R,
 8   &
step fwd. L, tap R fwd., hop L, step R fwd., tap L fwd.
 1   2   &   3   4
leap fwd. onto left foot, cross right behind left, pause, do a full
 &   5   6
turn to the right.
 7
Repeat the same step on the same foot.

                                                                      page 1

    Sam's Syncopated Toe Back Strut.
Hop L, shuffleR, hop L, tap R toe back, pause, shuffle R,
 8 & a   1   &   2   & 3
tap R toe crossed in front of left, flap fwd. R, tap L toe back,
 4   & 5   &
pause, flap L fwd.
 6   & 7

    Scanlan's Toe Clog Break.
Shuffle R, hop L, shuffle R, step R, shuffle L, hop R, tap L
 8 &   1   & a   2   & 3   & 4
toe back, * hop R, tap L fwd., leap to left foot, tap R toe
          &   5   &   6
back, drop L heel, tap R heel fwd.
      &   7
    * All taps after this sign are done while making one complete
turn to the right.
    Repeat this step and break to take up 8 bars of music.

    Scanlan's Syncopated Toe Heel Turns
Hop L, shuffle R, hop L, tap R toe back, pause, hop and make a
 8 &   a   1   &   2   &
half turn to the right, tap R heel to floor in front.
                        3
Repeat to the counts 4 & a 5 & 6 & 7. End facing audience.
Hop L, shuffle R, hop L, tap R toe back, leap fwd. onto R foot,
tap L toe back, hop on R making a half turn to left at same time,
tap L heel to floor in front, hop on R making a quarter turn to the
left, cross L foot in front of R, step over L foot with
the right and face audience.
    Because of the syncopation the last part of the step is much
easier to do than it is to count. 8 & a 1 & (2) & 3 4 & (5) & 6 7 rest
on 2 & 5. The entire step is repeated to take up bars of music.

    Bill Robinson Roll and Break
Hop L, shuffle R, hop L, shuffle R, shuffle R, hop L shuffle R
 8 &   a   1   & 2   & a   3   & 4
shuffle R, hop L, shuffle R, shuffle R, hop L,
 &   a   5   &   6   & a   7

The Break.
Shuffle R, shuffle R, hop L, flap R, shuffle L, shuffle L, hop R,
 & 8   & a   1   &2   & 3   & a   4
flap L, shuffle R, hop L, flap R.
 & 5   & a   6   & 7

The entire step and break are repeated on the other foot.

                                                                                                              page 2

Throw-out Step.
Step L, shuffle R, step R, (raise the Left foot behind the right).
   8   & a   1
tap L toe to floor in back, leap to left foot and throw right leg out
   2   3
to right, leap to right and raise left behind, tap left toe back,
           4   &
leap to left foot and throw out right, leap to right foot and
  5   &
raise left behind, tap L toe back, leap to left foot and throw
                  6   &
out right, leap to right foot and raise left behind.
     7
Repeat on same foot 2 more times then do a standard chain break, starting with the left foot.

The standard chain break starting with the left foot.
Shuffle L, hop R, step L, shuffle R, step R, shuffle L, step L,
  8 &   1   2   & 3   &   4 &   5
shuffle R, step R, step L.
  & 6   &   7

Scanlan's Leg Spin Step
Hop L, step R, brush L fwd, hop R, shuffle L, step L back, hop L and
  8   &   1   2   & a   3   4
start right leg spinning in back, right toe touches floor, hop L,
                                                           5
right toe touches floor, hop L, right toe touches floor, hop L.
      &   6   &   7
This step is repeated on the same foot. After doing it the second time continue the leg spins for eight counts more.

The Final Break
Hop L, shuffle R back, tap L back, land on R, tap L toe back.
  1   & 2   &   a   3
Step fwd. L, step right with right, bring left foot to right foot,
  4   5   6
nod head.
  7

                                                                                            page 3"

These notes are generally quite clear but occasional interpretation is required. Find the p-u-c in the Slide Comb and again in the Final Break. The Throw-out Step begins on a supporting foot and there are 2 typographical oversights.

NOTE TO INSTRUCTORS:
The above routine notes may be copied and provided free to students as learning aids.

AFTERTHOUGHTS

The frequency range of human hearing is approximately 20-20,000 Hertz (vibration cycles per second). People are also sensitive to infrasonic (lower) and hypersonic (higher) vibrations outside personal audible limits. Different parts of the human body physically resonate to different, mostly lower, sound frequencies. Your torso (50-100 Hz) and legs (a very low 2-20 Hz) literally feel the amplified bass rhythms of a marching band or rock combo. Yes, the music really does move you.

Infants respond to music, instinctively moving with audio, as well as visual rhythms. Speech recognition tests with toddlers indicate words with distinctive syllabic and tonal rhythms are more quickly copied, especially when rhythmically emphasized. Nursery rhymes are not merely an entertainment. Language development is learning development.

I have been asked by publishers whether **TALKING TAP** is a dictionary, technique manual, text, workbook, film reference, or history review. Hopefully, it is a useful, enjoyable enlightenment which you will continue to find informative. There is much more to add. I encourage your maintaining a printed copy, annotating additional vocabulary, thoughts, and ideas; personalizing its ongoing value.

This book is more than a reference, even the **TERMINOLOGY** is not simply a glossary. Sequential perusal offers an improved structural and historic understanding of tapping, terminology, and notation. Encountering and using progressively more complex notation builds functional familiarity.

If you have not previously used dance notes, try it. Having encountered an enjoyable pattern, combination, or routine, it's a shame not to preserve it for future revival and the benefit of others.

TALKING TAP emphasizes tapping and language. When ready, watch for the next publication, which explores tap dance coordination, use of props, 1920-1940s fad and Latin styles, a multitude of additional steps, and a **DISCUSSION** including early stage and Broadway tap.

Arguably, all tap technique terms are basic or the term would not be used. Dance is functional, as must be its description. Dance terminology needs to accurately describe the action. Evaluate your statements, seeking clarity. Ultimately, the language of tapping is rhythm. Enjoy keeping your feet interesting.

By the way, what's the dance step photographed on the cover?

Terry

NOTES

NOTES

NOTES